MARC GOLD:
"DID I SAY THAT?"

Articles and Commentary on the
Try Another Way System

Marc W. Gold

RESEARCH PRESS COMPANY
2612 North Mattis Avenue   Champaign, Illinois 61820

7007581

||

In memory of Morey and Fanny Gold

Contents

CHAPTER 1

The Try Another Way System
in Perspective

The Try Another Way System is a philosophy and technology focused on people who find it difficult to learn—those individuals who have been seen by society as different from most other people. It includes (a) an organizational structure for all the decisions that have to be made in designing powerful procedures and (b) a large number of instructional procedures, some of which have been developed in other systems. I view the system as one of many approaches to provide efficient and effective services to people who find it difficult to learn. It is complementary to other systems rather than something to be used in place of them. The particular form of task analysis utilized in the Try Another Way System was initially designed for teaching manual tasks to people labeled "moderately, severely, and profoundly retarded." The system presently includes strategies for teaching a wide variety of tasks to a wide variety of people. It is still, however, not a catch-all or an end-all, and it should not be viewed as "all you need" to do a good job. All other available systems, techniques, and philosophies should be investigated thoroughly, for each can provide additional assistance to those people with a strong commitment to training.

ROOTS AND CONTRIBUTORS

Writing this section presented several problems. First, I wanted to avoid something that looked like I was paying homage to a bunch of friends. Second, I was concerned about how to approach this section, and third, I had some trouble deciding if this should be included in the book at all. Obviously the third decision was yes. Regarding the issue of approach, I have found people curious and interested to know how this system came into existence and also wanting to know details going back into my early history. Thus, I decided to include a bit of that. Finally, the people mentioned in this section, in my mind, provided significant knowledge, motivation, and feedback toward the development of the Try Another Way System, so including them here is something that I am perfectly comfortable doing.

Perhaps the most basic value found embedded throughout the Try Another Way System is the deep respect evidenced for all people, especially

1

those with various handicapped labels. I must attribute the roots of this to my father, Morey Gold, who operated a bicycle and key shop on the main street of the Mexican ghetto of East Los Angeles from 1930 until 1966 when he passed away. My earliest memories include spending time there with him talking to people of many different income levels, backgrounds, capabilities, and stations in life. Watching him befriend people with alcoholism, drug addiction, severe psychiatric problems, and various other difficult life circumstances provided me, I am sure, with the basic set of values reflected in the Try Another Way System. In addition, his respect for manual skills and for tools and machinery certainly has had its impact on me and on this system.

My first professional exposure to the field of service delivery to handicapped children came at Los Angeles State College from Francis Lord, Caro Hatcher, Frieda Mayers, and Max Katler, all people who held very high standards of performance in work with handicapped children and who provided me with an understanding of the accepted practices of the day in Special Education. Francis Lord, especially, was uncompromising in insisting on the development of a set of professional ethics for people working with handicapped children.

When I began my work as a student at the University of Illinois in 1966 and then when I became a member of the faculty in 1969, Keith Scott, Bob Henderson, and Bob Sprague provided support, a knowledge base, and guidance. Their influence on my work has been significant. Without their contributions the system could not possibly have evolved.

During my employment at the University of Illinois I was involved in the supervision of six persons (Pat Wood, Mary Merwin, Craig Barclay, Sid Levy, David Pomerantz, and Steve Zider) obtaining their PhDs. Their work, their perceptions, and their criticisms did a great deal to set the basic structure of the system and to carry it through its first period of development.

Having completed his PhD, Steve Zider became a member of Marc Gold & Associates, Inc., and he has continued to be my major source of feedback on the system itself and on its use in our various projects. He and the rest of the staff of the corporation are obviously the current contributors to and movers of the present work.

Ronna Gold, my wife, has been one of the most helpful critics of the system throughout its development. As someone not involved in the human services field, her input has been invaluable, supplying a viewpoint different from that of any of the others who have provided feedback. This has been especially true in regard to the development of the philosophical parts of the system.

The Try Another Way System is alive. It keeps growing and changing. The people who are using it correctly do not take any of it at its face value and are always questioning it, suggesting changes, and using it flexibly. One of the disappointments I occasionally am confronted with is hearing people say, "The Try Another Way System says to do it this way." The system really offers options. It's the interaction between all of those options and the capabilities and sensitivities and experiences of the people using the system that results in the successes to which the system has contributed.

PHILOSOPHICAL PRINCIPLES AND CONCEPTS

It is not true to say that we began with a well-defined philosophy and developed the system from it. In fact, the philosophy and technology have developed together in an interactionary process. The philosophy and the technology are of equal importance. The following are some of the philosophical principles that characterize the system:

1. One can best serve handicapped persons by training them to do marketable tasks.

2. Persons labeled retarded respond best to a learning situation based on respect of their human worth and capabilities.

3. Those labeled handicapped have the breadth and depth of capabilities to demonstrate competence, given training appropriate to their needs.

4. A lack of learning in any particular situation should first be interpreted as a result of inappropriate or insufficient use of teaching strategy, rather than inability on the part of the learner.

5. To this point in its development, testing is at best limiting to the person labeled mentally retarded.

6. Labeling is both unfair and counterproductive.

These principles will become evident in the remaining chapters.

Many concepts follow from these principles. A few examples of key concepts are balanced relationship, chameleon phenomenon, competence, competence/deviance hypothesis, deviance, expectancy, mental retardation, power, private deviance, public elected deviance, public nonelected deviance, and zero order tasks. Some are discussed in this book, and all are included in the *Try Another Way Training Manual.**

Although it is not appropriate to discuss all the concepts at this point, elaborating on a balanced relationship will perhaps help put the articles in the book into perspective..

Establishing and maintaining a balanced relationship between the learner and trainer is, in some respects, the essence of the system. *A balanced relationship* is based on mutual respect of (a) personhood, (b) abilities, (c) rights, (d) time commitment, and (e) personal preferences and feelings. If mutual respect in these areas exists, benevolence, patronization, and artificial concern are excluded. This kind of mutual respect leads to the recognition that both parties have a responsibility to adapt. They must adapt to each other in terms of the learning process and the content, and they must adjust to each other in respect to their human relationship. Quite simply, the relationship between any learner and trainer should rest on the same basis as that for any sound relationship between two persons working together toward a common goal. This basis of respect and recognition allows each

---

*Marc W. Gold, *Try Another Way Training Manual.* Champaign, Ill.: Research Press, 1980.

to be free to be himself or herself, adapting only for the sake of the relationship or the common goal. This concept is difficult to understand and observe when the learner is a person with profound learning problems, but, to me, the concept is every bit as applicable.

ELEMENTS OF THE BOOK

The following chapters are articles roughly sequenced in chronological order. This sequencing provides a glimpse into the evolution of the system. A glance at the coauthors for the articles indicates people who have had an influence on the system.

Because most of the articles are reprints, there is some redundancy between chapters. The reprints are from a wide variety of journals in several disciplines. Publishing under those circumstances, I needed to explain key concepts to each particular readership. I hope this small amount of repetition will not be offensive.

The format includes a prestatement and poststatement for each article. These are personal comments. The prestatement gives some background on the article, often explaining how I happened to write it. The poststatement comments on various aspects of it. Sometimes the poststatement provides an update on issues discussed; sometimes it notes a change in the use of terminology. Often it signals the beginning of a stage in the system's evolution.

As a service to the reader, we have updated the references which were in press when the articles were originally published. Thus in a few cases you may see a date on a reference that is later than the publication date of the article in which it appears.

CHAPTER 2

Preworkshop Skills for the Trainable: A Sequential Technique

Marc W. Gold

PRESTATEMENT

This article was written while I was a doctoral student at the University of Illinois at Urbana-Champaign. It describes a program that I conducted as a teacher of adolescent individuals labeled trainable mentally retarded in the Los Angeles city schools. The article was written and published at the suggestion and with the support of Dr. Laura Jordan, professor of special education at the University of Illinois.

There is a difference between intelligence and trained ability. Some tasks require a high degree of intelligence but little formal training. Others require trained ability, but a minimum of intelligence. And some require both. This article is concerned with the second group of tasks, those that require a minimum of intelligence, but some specific training. The article will describe an approach to teaching to trainable mentally retarded children the skills required by this group of tasks. It includes examples of such factors as social development and the development of discrimination and eye-hand coordination.

The techniques described herein, while applicable to trainables in many situations, were developed in a public school prevocational training program for adolescent trainable children. The techniques have also been used with eight to ten year old trainables.

The reader is reminded that the specific skills described here are meant as examples of the sequential technique. They are provided for illustration, and can be generalized to other areas of training.

The sequential technique and the following examples are based on these tenets:

This article originally appeared in *Education and Training of the Mentally Retarded,* 1968, *3* (1), 31–37. Reprinted by permission of the publisher.

1. The pupil is given only one new item to learn at a time.

2. A new step is not added until the old one has been thoroughly learned.

3. Any task to be taught is carefully analyzed and reduced to a series of the smallest possible steps.

The entering behavior of each child must be evaluated. Entering behavior is simply the child's existing skills and attitudes, as specifically related to what is being taught. For example, recognition of numbers is not an entering behavior to be considered for a lesson in tying shoelaces, but level of finger dexterity is.

A statement of anticipated terminal behavior must be included in the planning of a sequence. Terminal behavior is the performance (social, emotional, vocational, etc.) to be achieved by the end of the sequence, the degree of learning to be accomplished. Failure is not hard to recognize, but it is necessary for the teacher to state in advance what the goal of the sequence is in order to recognize and evaluate success.

Each child begins a sequence with a different composite of entering behavior. Consequently, some children move smoothly from step to step in a sequence, while others may run into difficulty along the way. When this happens, the teacher must reexamine the task where the child failed, and teach whatever behavior may be missing, whether it be understanding of the commands, ability to manipulate objects, or any other factor. This is not a digression from the sequence, but a normal part of it.

Review is also a normal part of a sequence. A review should not be a quick verbalization of previous steps, but should be a re-creation of earlier steps, taking only as much time as is necessary to again reach terminal behavior (successful accomplishment) for each step.

When planning, the teacher should prepare for a hypothetical child with minimum entering behavior in all areas. Then, as the children go through the sequence, they will indicate by their performance which steps are necessary and which are not. The teacher should be prepared when smaller steps are needed. Illustrations of this will be given in the examples.

The examples are of tasks broken down into their component parts as they might be taught in preparation for many of the activities of a sheltered workshop.

Because there is such a variance of ability and age, the examples will be presented in the form of steps rather than lessons. Mastering each may be simple, or may require days or weeks of practice. The first part of Examples 1 and 2 will be a thorough breakdown of the sequence to give the reader an idea of the many factors to be taken into consideration. The teacher must be prepared to fill in the gaps all the way through the sequence, it being the function of the teacher to create an environment in which the student can develop at his own rate.

Single words in capital letters will be found throughout the examples. These are words that are used with the children for the first time in the sequence. The teacher must be aware of new vocabulary and be prepared to teach it. Children learn proper terminology as quickly as they do watered down terminology. There is good reason for using normal instructional language—it is much easier for the teacher to teach comprehension of natural language than to be limited to a trainable vocabulary. If the difficult instruction is paired several times with demonstration by the teacher, the children soon learn it, and can generalize it to other similar instructions. For example, if the children learn the instruction, "Remove the bolts from the pile and sort them according to shapes," the learning will generalize to the instruction, "Remove the transistors from the pile and sort them according to value."

EXAMPLE 1: SORTING

It will be assumed for this example that the students can hear, sit in their seats, and attend for short periods, and that they are motivated by the materials used. If they cannot do these things when the sequence is begun, then teaching these behaviors must be included as part of the sequence.

Task 1. Poker Chips. (The children—and the principal—may be told that these are counting discs!)

1. Each child is given a pile of 20 to 30 red and white chips. The class is told not to touch them until they are told to do so. On these first activities it is most important to develop the concepts of "begin" and "stop." A compromise at this point will cause problems later.

2. The teacher says, "Pick up one red chip." For the child who does this correctly, one of the following assumptions can be made: (a) he understands the entire instruction and is able to carry it out; or (b) he is able to copy someone who did it correctly. For the child who does not succeed, the following assumptions *might* be made: (a) he does not hear or is not attending; (b) he does not want to do it (for many possible reasons); or (c) he does not know the meaning of one or more of the words in the command (*red, one, chip, pick up*).

   These possibilities apply to success or failure at all subsequent steps, but as the teacher learns more about the student, she should better understand the reasons for his performance.

3. The pupils learn to pick up one red chip on demand, to REMOVE all the red ones from the pile, to do the same with white, to SEPARATE the two colors, and then do the same with additional blue chips, once they can handle red and white.

   When they perform consistently well on the above tasks, the children begin working in pairs, two children making use of one pile of chips. Working cooperatively is an important ability and must be included as part of the sequence. This step should be made only with a task that the students perform successfully. This is so that the teacher can be reasonably certain, should difficulties arise, that the problem is a function of the pairing of the children rather than of manipulating the chips or dealing with the colors, since cooperative work is the only new part of the situation. The next few steps might involve moving to progressively larger working groups. This makes for much easier teacher preparation and distribution of materials, but must not be done at the expense of individual learning needs. As the class begins to spread out, in terms of level of function, they should be grouped accordingly.

Task 2. Plastic Beads.

1. Each group is given a large pile of several hundred beads. There are three different shapes—cylinders, balls, and cubes—and six different colors—red, blue, yellow, green, purple, and orange. The class is given a familiar command such as, "Remove the red ones from the pile." Except for the addition of more colors and different shapes, the children are not doing anything new. Had they been asked to remove the *green* ones and not succeeded, it would have been impossible to tell without further investigation whether the problem was the new set of materials or the introduction of the color green.

2. The children become familiar with all of the colors in the same way as they did with the chips. Depending on the class, this might be the appropriate time to begin compound directions. With appropriate practice at each step, the sequence of teacher commands might be as follows:

   a. "Remove the green ones and the yellow ones (or other color pairs) from the pile." After this is done *well,* say,

   b. "Boys, remove the green ones and the yellow ones. Girls, remove the orange ones and the purple ones," then the following commands in order:

   c. "Boys, orange and red; girls, blue and yellow."

   d. "The people on this side of the table: red and orange. The people on that side of the table: yellow and purple."

3. The attention of the pupils is next drawn to the three shapes, one at a time. When first told to remove all of the *balls* from the pile, some children will remove all of the balls while some will remove balls of only one color. If a child does the latter, he may not yet have generalized the concept of *ball* to all colors of balls.

4. When the three shapes are familiar, the pupils are told: "Remove all of the *red cubes* from the pile." Some children will remove all red beads, some will remove all cubes, and some will perform as instructed. Removing "red ones and yellow ones" is easier than removing "red cubes." The former involves removing anything that *either* word applies to; the latter involves removing only those beads that fit *both* parts of the command.

There are similarities between Tasks 2 and 3. Both tasks involve sorting, with similar directions, the same cooperative social situation, and the form dimension. The combination of these similarities and the general factors (attention span, coordination, listening skills, etc.) which carry over from the progression help facilitate the next. In proceeding from Task 2 to Task 3, it is not possible to limit the number of new variables as much as was done with the change from Task 1 to Task 2.

Task 3. Bolts, Nuts, Washers.

1. Each group is given a pile of bolts, nuts, and washers, two shapes and sizes of each, as:

   Nuts—hexagonal and square, two sizes of each
   Bolts—hexagonal and square, two lengths of each
   Washers—flat washers and lock washers, two sizes of each

   It is probably best to start with size difference of 1/4 inch or more, but it should also be pointed out that after the children are thoroughly familiar with the tasks they should be given experiences with 1/8 inch and then 1/16 inch differences. A question might be raised regarding immediately giving the children more than one type and size of each item. In most cases, the child whose entering behavior is such that he has to learn the difference between nuts, bolts, and washers is not at such a level of differentiation that size differences will cause him confusion.

2. The class is told, "Remove all of the BOLTS from the pile." There are several ways to familiarize the children with the word *bolt*. The teacher can show the class a bolt, give one to any child who needs the actual object in front of him, or have each child remove a bolt from the pile to show that he knows what to look for.

3. The same procedure is followed with NUTS and with WASHERS. While the children were removing the bolts they were already becoming familiar, indirectly, with nuts and washers; consequently these steps should be learned quickly.

4. The class is told that there is more than one *shape* of nut in the pile. They are told to find one of each shape. Some will make the distinction according to size, some to shape, and some will do both and remove four different nuts from the pile. At this point the distinction between shape and size is made.

5. The class is told, "Remove the nuts from the pile and SORT them ACCORDING to shape."

6. The same procedure is followed individually with the bolts and with the washers.

7. The children are then directed to sort bolts, nuts, and washers according to size.

   The skills necessary to successfully complete steps 6 and 7, especially if discriminations of differences of 1/8 inch or 1/16 inch are incorporated into the sequence, will be considered as terminal behavior for the sequence.

   Lesson planning at this point may move in many possible directions using all of the preceding example as entering behavior. Some of the possibilities are: the addition of screws, nails, etc.; the addition of more sizes and shapes; the grouping of all items according to size for use with Example 2 of this paper; and the assembling of combinations of nuts, bolts, and washers (also Example 2).

EXAMPLE 2: SIMPLE ASSEMBLY TASK

Task 1. Nuts, Bolts, Washers (all of the same size).

1. The class is given a pile of objects all of the same size, including hexagonal bolts, hexagonal nuts, flat washers, and lock washers; the washers are the correct size for the bolt and the nut screws onto the bolt. The length of the bolt is not significant.

2. The class is told, "Remove one nut and one bolt from the pile."

3. Then, "SCREW the nut onto the bolt." For many children the ability to screw a nut onto a bolt will be part of their entering behavior and need not be taught except in terms of attaching a verbal instruction to an already known behavior. In the case of Down's Syndrome children (mongoloids), however, this is usually a very necessary step. It is sometimes appropriate to put children with particularly poor fine motor functions and eye-hand coordination through a sequence of learning to thread one object onto another. This might begin with a very large nut and bolt, requiring more wrist than finger action, and progress to smaller nuts and bolts, requiring finer coordination.

4. The teacher says, "ASSEMBLE a bolt, a FLAT WASHER, a LOCK WASHER and a nut." (Teacher demonstrates each step as she gives the instruction.) The emphasis should be on the order of the assembly. The order in which parts are assembled is the most difficult aspect to learn. Step 4 can also be done using a piece of masonite with holes of the correct size bored in it. If this is done, the order of assembly is bolt, flat washer, board (masonite), lock washer, nut.

5. The class is told, "Make as many ASSEMBLIES as you can until you are told to stop." This actually represents three new variables—speed, accuracy, and the phrase "as many as you can." Up to this time there has been constant correction and assistance. Therefore accuracy is, in a productive sense, nonexistent. But with the introduction of speed, accuracy becomes an important factor. When speed is first introduced, the quantity goes up and the quality goes down. The teacher must attempt to hold the quality (standards of performance) up while increasing the rate of the children's performance.

   It is important for children to realize that they are learning how to do something and not really making something that will be used. If this point is not made clear, it will show up as a motivational problem when the teacher asks the class to disassemble all of the assemblies so that the parts may be reused.

6. The class continues as above, but two or more sizes of each part are added to the pile. Some children will put large washers on small bolts, but this problem is usually resolved quickly. For purposes of illustration, the ability to perform the assembly task with speed and accuracy will be considered terminal behavior for this sequence. As with Example 1, the lesson planning may move in many possible directions, using all of the preceding example(s) as entering behavior. Some possibilities are assembling simple toy models, envelope stuffing, collating, and more complex nut and bolt assemblies.

EXAMPLE 3: SELF DIRECTION

The setting for this example is an on-campus work experience program. The tasks are raking leaves, watering, working in the school lunch room, sweeping, etc. Since this example is concerned with the overall concept of self direction, the skills needed for the specific tasks will not be discussed.

Entering behavior for this example is not based on previous examples, but includes an attention span of several minutes (in this situation) and the absence of hostile or aggressive behavior. It can be used to develop behaviors which are necessary for most other tasks.

This sequence is presented in much abbreviated form. The teacher should be able to fill in the sequence by applying the approach illustrated in Examples 1 and 2. Example 3 is given to illustrate the following steps in planning a sequence:

1. Identification of a needed behavior (self direction).

2. Establishment of a reasonable goal for terminal behavior (working independently).

3. Establishment of a beginning step that requires a minimum of entering behavior.

4. Planning of specific steps (the lessons by which they are taught to be ingeniously devised by the reader).

The terms "frequent supervision," "infrequent supervision," and "unobservable supervision" (see below) refer to the visibility of the supervision to the child. In keeping with board policy in most school districts, the teacher will inconspicuously maintain some level of supervision over the children at all times. The reason for its being unobservable to the child is that children cannot learn self direction, and in this case independence, unless they are given an opportunity and the responsibility to try.

The framework of this sequence is as follows:

Task 1. Work individually, in a restricted area, with direct and constant supervision.

Task 2. Work alone in a restricted area with infrequent supervision.

Task 3. Work alone in a less restricted area with unobservable supervision.

Task 4. Work with others in one particular unrestricted area with infrequent supervision.

Task 5. Work independently, moving from place to place, as necessary to perform the task, with unobservable supervision.

Task 6. Work in small groups, moving from place to place, as necessary to perform the task, with unobservable supervision.

The ability to function successfully on Task 6 will be considered terminal behavior for this example. As with the other examples, this terminal behavior can serve as entering behavior for many different learning experiences. Some of the most relevant sequences are increased independence in the home, the use of public transportation, use of community recreational facilities, and limited employment.

CONCLUSION

The examples presented in this paper are not intended as recipes for sorting tasks, assembly tasks, or a limited form of self direction. They are presented to illustrate an approach and to point out the kinds of variables to be taken into consideration when planning a curriculum for trainable children. It is the author's opinion that a comprehensive program for such children does not have time for long rest periods and extensive lessons on the effective utilization of egg cartons. But there *is* time for training these children to function in such a way as to be participating members of our society. To exist in society, trainable individuals must feel that they have a place. What better way is there to make a person feel that he is worthwhile than to make him able to do something useful?

POSTSTATEMENT

It is interesting to note that some of the seeds of what later became the task analysis part of the system were present this early in my writing. Preparing a plan for a hypothetical child later became the concept of a composite learner. The entire issue of breaking tasks into component parts was the root of content task analysis. The clear specification of anticipated terminal behavior led to the concepts of Criterion I and Criterion II.

It is surprising to find myself using the dehumanizing term *trainables.* This article also shows a fairly strong emphasis on verbal commands. For the students who were involved in the program that focus was probably quite appropriate. Speaking of students, notice that I insisted on calling the 14- to 18-year-old adolescent individuals in this program children throughout the entire article. This is technically correct since it is a public school, but it connotes something I try not to convey. The comment that disturbs me is the one implying that children with Down's syndrome necessarily

have "particularly poor fine motor functions and eye-hand coordination."
In the past 10 years my associates and I have never found any systematic
differences along these lines for those individuals with Down's syndrome who
have participated in our studies. I am aware of the literature showing such
differences, but our data did not. I am inclined to follow our data. Near the
end of the article I suggest the possibility of "limited" employment for the
people discussed in the article. It seems incredible that I had such a restricted
expectation then, but I really did.

CHAPTER 3

The Interdisciplinary Approach:
A Nominal Fallacy

Marc W. Gold

PRESTATEMENT

This paper, which has not been previously published, was presented at the annual meeting of The Great Lakes Regional American Association on Mental Deficiency, at Michigan State University on September 25, 1969. This was the first presentation I made after receiving my PhD degree and taking a position at the Children's Research Center, University of Illinois at Urbana-Champaign. It is obvious from the title that I was impressed with new credentials and wanted to show that I had a fancy vocabulary. The title happens to say exactly what I wanted it to say but in a way that also ended up saying some things (about me) that I had not intended to express. I remember feeling somewhat intimidated by presenting along with Bill Cruickshank, someone I deeply respected at the time, and still do. He had just opened the Institute for the Scientific Study of Mental Deficiency in Michigan, which adhered to the interdisciplinary approach, a concept that I disagreed with and felt the need to react to. My dilemma, expressed in the opening paragraph of the paper, was to separate criticisms of him from criticisms of the concept.

In the process of preparing this paper, I found myself torn between two realities. One was a knowledge of programs throughout the country which are considered interdisciplinary; the other was a general awareness of the quality of Dr. Cruickshank's work, coupled with the fact that prior to my presentation he would be describing an interdisciplinary approach he developed. I decided that the only way out was to preface my remarks with a statement

This paper was originally presented at the annual meeting of The Great Lakes Region American Association on Mental Deficiency, Michigan State University, September 25, 1969.

ascribing my comments to interdisciplinary programs in general so that they would not be related specifically to the program described by Dr. Cruickshank.

At one level the interdisciplinary approach is seen in virtually all programs concerned with the mentally retarded. In school settings, for example, teachers, psychologists, social workers, speech therapists, public health nurses, and representatives of other disciplines are all involved in one way or another with decisions regarding retarded children. In institutions there are people from medicine, psychology, social work, and other disciplines involved in decisions regarding patients. At a second level there are university campuses, clinics, and diagnostic centers which are involved with the mentally retarded and are also involved in the training of university students. Again, representatives from a number of disciplines contribute in one way or another to the diagnosis, prescription, and remediation of clients. At a third level there are programs such as that described by Dr. Cruickshank and the Child Development Clinic directed by Richard Koch at Children's Hospital in Los Angeles, which have been organized for the express purpose of approaching retardation from an interdisciplinary standpoint. Inherent at all three levels is the false assumption that to have various disciplines involved when working with children is to, in fact, have an interdisciplinary approach. Communication requires much more than access or exposure. Communication requires conscious effort not only to exchange information but also to understand information being received.

In discussing communication within an interdisciplinary setting, I begin by enumerating some of the functions of such a setting. Included are diagnosis, prescription, remediation, dissemination of information, consultation, community resource development, and data collection. Considering that all or some of these functions are performed by all or some of the disciplines involved, one can clearly see the complexity of communication.

The situation is further complicated when one brings up the whole area of semantics. Many of the terms and concepts frequently used have different meanings to different people. Different people within and between disciplines use the same words to mean different things, and people within and between disciplines, when hearing terms, conceive them as meaning different things. For example, when an educator sitting in an interdisciplinary conference uses the word educable, the social worker, the pediatrician, the public health nurse, and the psychiatrist may all have different interpretations or no interpretations at all of what is meant. And worse than that is the probability that they will lose a piece of information that could be relevant to their functions. When a doctor uses the label mongoloid, what does it mean to the teacher? Unfortunately, because the labels commonly used are so frequently from the field of medicine, teachers and others have come to feel that those labels tell them something. If, in fact, knowing that a child is mongoloid or brain damaged or phenylketonuric will help the teacher or the ward employee in working with the child, then that information should be specifically expressed. But it should not be assumed that the teacher is aware of all available information about the unique learning characteristics of mongoloid children or the particular characteristic of other groups given labels. When labels are used, the implications of those labels should also be given to the teacher or other worker.

This discussion of labels brings up an interesting point. I mentioned that one of the functions of an interdisciplinary team is diagnosis. In many instances that is the sole function of an interdisciplinary team. All too often, the net effort is a diagnostic evaluation, usually written by the head of the team, which reflects that person's orientation and fails to include information contributed by the various team members. If the head of the team is a psychologist, there is little other than psychological information made available to those people with whom the child will be placed. When the head of the team is a medical doctor, the report is frequently in the form of a diagnosis, medical in orientation, with little relevance to those people working directly with the child. When diagnosis is the sole function of the team, their efforts generally result in a report which is filed and is not used to benefit the child.

It is also interesting to note that the diagnostic label which a child receives is generally a function of the heaviest emphasis on the interdisciplinary team. For example, if a child is taken because of school performance to a clinic that has all the various disciplines just discussed and is run by a special educator with a heavy emphasis on learning disabilities, then the child will probably be diagnosed as a learning disabled child with some emotional overlay. If the same child is brought to a different setting, say an experimental program for emotionally disturbed children, she will be diagnosed as emotionally disturbed with academic deficits. This is not uncommon at all and occurs even though both teams may have representation from the same disciplines. The fact that there are so few clear-cut, single-factor situations does not help. In most situations, then, a child's label is a function of where she got it.

Moving from diagnosis to prescription and remediation, one sees another problem, or to be more positive, another opportunity for real interdisciplinary communication to take place. If the lines of communication are open and if people are attempting to understand and to integrate ideas, there is the opportunity for one discipline to suggest courses of action based on information from all of the other disciplines. If the social worker, in describing a family, speaks in terms that indicate general lack of interest in the child or conditions that are less than appropriate, there are implications for other people that the parents are not likely to administer medication according to prescription, that it would be foolish to rely on medication, and that perhaps another approach should be used. Or, in planning her program, the public health nurse should take the two pieces of information—that the parents are not responsible and that the doctor wants the child on medication—and then set about to either straighten out the parents or find some other way to work around the problem. In other words, the social worker's report can be significant to other people on the team. The same reasoning, of course, applies to the contribution of every team member.

Another problem of communication within an interdisciplinary setting is the ignorance of each discipline regarding the most basic principles in each of the other disciplines. In most areas there exists a handful of publications, articles, or books which get at the essence of the discipline and which are the guidelines for the team member from that discipline. It seems to me that an efficient and effective facilitator of communication within an interdisciplinary team would make such publications available to fellow members. It would not hurt anyone to spend some time each week reading this kind of information, especially if he is integrally involved with people from other disciplines who are working together to benefit children. This seems so much more efficient than the present system where many, many hours are wasted because information is not transferred or utilized.

I have discussed diagnosis, prescription, and remediation in terms of communication problems and opportunities. So far as the functions of the dissemination of information, consultation, community resource development, and data collection are concerned, the problems and opportunities of communication that I have been discussing apply. The one additional point that I might make concerning these areas is related to research. The creative interdisciplinary team could be involved with research in a variety of ways. It could conduct research, translate and implement research, and communicate findings to people in the field who do not have direct access.

In conclusion, may I suggest that each member of the interdisciplinary team evaluate his performance not in terms of what he contributes to the team, but what he is able to get from the team that will allow him to more appropriately meet the needs of our children.

POSTSTATEMENT

In preparing for this book, I read this paper for the first time in about 6 years. I realized it was full of grammatical and punctuation problems and quite redundant, but it did contain some ideas that I still believe in. (Fortunately the worst of the original grammatical offenses have been corrected for this book.)

Some categorizations and assumptions are offensive now; for example, "straighten out the parents." That expression should have been elaborated upon or eliminated. As it stands, it tends to support the notion that professionals are right and parents are wrong or that professionals should be in control. I don't believe either assumption. At this point I also disagree with the inference that individuals with Down's syndrome (called mongoloid in the paper) have "unique learning characteristics." There are individuals in this field who believe that is true. I did, but do not now, as mentioned in the poststatement of the previous paper. In our research my colleagues and I have, at various times, separated out and analyzed the performance of persons with Down's syndrome and never found it to be categorically different from other individuals.

The basic notion presented in this paper is still valid. There still are multidisciplinary teams in which individuals of different disciplines operate parallel to one another without interacting in such a way as to make use of one another's data to make maximally effective decisions about the people being evaluated. The majority of multidisciplinary teams, in my estimation, are still a long way from genuinely being interdisciplinary, but there are obvious exceptions to this assessment.

A point that might have been made in this paper, but wasn't, is the poor connection the field has always made between description and prescription. For those individuals labeled retarded, and all of the labels that go along with it, the field has yet to identify clear relationships between diagnostic categories and specific instructional strategies. There are certainly those in the field who would disagree; however, I feel the data stand by themselves. Powerful instructional technology cuts across diagnostic categories, eliminating the value of such categories for those individuals teaching or training persons. Until we no longer need categories for political and economic reasons, they will be used, but they should be employed only by people making political and economic decisions.

CHAPTER 4

The Preparation of Secondary Teachers of the Mentally Retarded

Marc W. Gold

PRESTATEMENT

Donn Brolin, who was at Stout State University in Menomonie, Wisconsin, at the time, brought together at Stout State eight persons who were considered to be leaders in the field of secondary vocational education programs for the retarded, along with approximately 350 participants. Each of the eight was asked to address certain issues, to present to the audience, and to help generate some guidelines for developing programs. In 1970 special education and vocational and technical education had not yet developed many cooperative relationships. The conference probably helped to stimulate what has become an increasingly active relationship between two branches of education. Among those who attended the meeting were Gary Clark from the University of Kansas and Chuck Kokaska from California State University at Long Beach. Another person who attended was the late Richard Hungerford, who had been actively involved in vocational education of the retarded since the close of World War I.

Mr. Hungerford was a professor at Harvard before doctorates meant anything, even there. This was my first opportunity to meet him and to listen to him. He was a most interesting individual, and I cherish having had the opportunity to talk with him.

At the time this conference took place my general strategy was not very much different from the proverbial bull in a china shop. As you will see from this paper, I was extremely critical, not particularly diplomatic, and quite sarcastic. During the conference I was asked, in front of the audience, to critique some things about the conference. My reaction was so negative and insensitive that Gary Clark and Chuck Kokaska, who were and still are my friends, took me aside and basically said that I was a total jerk and that I had blown it completely. After reflecting on their comments and the way I had handled myself, I made appropriate apologies and privately resolved

This paper originally appeared in D. Brolin and B. Thomas (Chm.), *Preparing teachers of secondary level educable mentally retarded: Proposal for a new model.* Project Report No. 1, Department of Rehabilitation and Manpower Services, School of Education, Stout State University, Menomonie, Wisconsin, April 1971. Reprinted by permission of the publisher.

not to act that way again. To the best of my knowledge, I have kept that commitment to myself and have tried to retain the ability to be critical in a way that preserves people's dignity, including my own. The reason I choose to share that experience here is that it was a clear-cut, identifiable turning point in my strategies as a professional in the field.

In writing this paper I found myself beginning with some degree of confusion. The material we received requested that a paper be prepared focusing, in part, on the competencies that secondary teachers must have in order to meet the needs of the retarded. On page four of the materials a rather comprehensive list of competencies for teachers of mentally retarded students was presented. Perhaps it would be simple and expedient to say that I agree with everything on page four, and then sit down. However, I do find something missing from the material, and that is how to convert the terms used into a meaningful program.

In looking over the literature review I noticed an interesting phenomenon. There were many comments made regarding programs for the retarded that seemed to provide equally meaningful guidelines for the preparation of teachers of the retarded. For example, on page two of the proposal, the last paragraph begins as follows: "The combined work-study program in which students spend part of the day or week acquiring work experience and specific job skills in the community is one of the most significant recent developments in the programs of rehabilitating the mentally retarded." This seems to be just as appropriate a method of preparing teachers of the same people. That is, whatever program is eventually decided upon should consist of experience concurrent with classroom work at the University. The specific experiences should parallel the objectives of the proposed training program.

There are, however, two kinds of experiences not inferred from the proposal. One is the world of work. It seems as if most teachers who are in positions to prepare the mentally retarded for successful existence in the world of work have never been there themselves. They go from high school into college, out of college into teaching positions, never having experienced what it is to work in anything more than a candy shop or their uncle's delicatessen. Perhaps one of the requisite experiences for someone in a program designed to prepare one to train the mentally retarded is to spend time on the kind of job one might expect the retarded to have, such as that of a dishwasher, a factory worker or some other position which would provide a real taste of what manual labor is all about.

The other missing experience is the world of our retarded students. Since a teacher assumes the responsibility of helping an individual prepare to exist successfully in the world, it makes sense that the teacher have some idea of what the student's world is. In most instances, especially in urban areas, the world of the student and the world of the teacher have little in common. And yet many teachers go about the business of preparing students to exist in the teacher's kind of world, which just does not make sense at all. The teacher must develop an awareness, understanding and sensitivity about the world in which his students live. This can be done in part by reading about the environment in which his students exist. For example, if the teacher is going to be working in urban areas with black students, he should, as part of his academic responsibility, read books by Eldridge Cleaver, James Baldwin, Malcolm X and others who espouse the philosophies of at least a portion of the black culture. But the experience cannot stop there. If the teacher is really going to understand the world in which his students live, he has to get out into that world. He has to know, for instance, what it means to be a brain-damaged child existing in a family where the father is a lawyer, the mother is a teacher, and the other children are on their way to college. Just having dinner with such a family might teach him plenty. If his students live in a ghetto, he would know what it means to walk at night through tenements, past dead rats, or be prepared to run, fight, etc., etc. Only when the teacher has a clear understanding of what successful existence in the students' world is can he help prepare students to be successful in that world. And only after he has experienced some of that world will he come to realize that the ideals and values which govern his behavior are only one set and not *the* set of ideals and values.

Prospective teachers who are not willing to find out what life in a ghetto is all about should not be licensed to impose their ideas from another world on ghetto students. The same goes for us.

Other experiences which should run concurrently with course work include DVR staffings, classroom activities, placement interviews, employer-employee mediation, job station location, parent counselling and service club presentations.

It is quite amazing how the preparation of teachers of the retarded should parallel the preparation of the retarded themselves. The experience a prospective teacher obtains should be coordinated with discussions in class. This is the same for the pupil with whom the teacher will eventually work. For example, if the prospective teacher is studying behavior modification or other behavioral management approaches, he should be working with kids somewhere, experimenting and trying out what is being discussed in class. The professor teaching the course should, as part of his responsibility, observe the student attempting to apply the techniques, and provide feedback. This is the same with the mentally retarded students for whom the job situation should be coordinated with classroom work.

An important decision related to the development of an effective program relates to the generalist-specialist controversy. It has been my experience that successful public school programs are usually staffed by persons with a very strong specialization in one particular area. Areas relevant to the program being described here would include such specializations as public relations skills for finding job stations, classroom skills related to the academic aspects of a secondary program, and skills related to pupil-teacher or group interaction. The point I am making is that, in addition to a comprehensive general program which encompasses the various areas described in the proposal, one facet of the program be to identify possible areas of concentration. In the second or third year of the program a student, after getting a good overview of the program, could begin preparing himself, in depth, for that particular facet which interests him most. Having the good general background in all aspects of secondary work education programs for the retarded and also having in-depth knowledge and skills in one particular area would put students in the strongest possible position for obtaining employment of their choice and really doing a good job.

There is another area of teacher competency that is mentioned in the proposal but is not described in depth, and that is specific techniques of training, instruction and evaluation. Within the last few years a technology for training the mentally retarded for vocational skills has begun to emerge. Research on behavior modification, such as that of Zimmerman and Crosson, on work sample tasks, such as that produced here at Stout State University, on stimulus control procedures, such as that done at the University of Illinois, and other useful techniques are now available for application. It would seem most appropriate that included in your program would be specific courses, and concurrent experiences for acquiring such techniques. These techniques are not learned merely by reading and discussing them in class. They are learned through reading, discussion and concurrent experience in which the student is using the techniques and getting feedback. Unless specific techniques are taught and definite criteria are established by which to decide if students are able to utilize them, then most of the terms used to describe the proposed training program are nothing more than words to fill an outline. Terms such as remedial academics, learning classroom setting, personal guidance, skill development experiences and community work experience do not explain anything at all. They merely fill gaps and allow one to think he has said something. Until these terms are defined as specific training procedures, specific experiences with specific goals, there is no program at all.

In summary, I suggest that the method used to train prospective teachers and the methods they learn for teaching retarded adolescents should be very similar and should have, as a focus, experience concurrent with and related to classroom learning, resulting in a set of specific, definable, measurable skills.

POSTSTATEMENT

The comments made in the paper are still relevant. In fact, they now apply to individuals labeled moderately and severely retarded, whereas when the paper was written, programs for those individuals were *permitted* in most states instead of being *mandatory*; they were few and far between. The comments are also still relevant for teacher preparation.

The major shift in my thinking, relative to this paper, is a change in commitment toward inservice rather than preservice training. There is still a place for preservice training programs for teachers of people labeled handi-capped; however, my own efforts at this time and my preference on where the majority of our energies and major emphasis should go are in favor of further development of teachers already working as regular classroom and special education instructors.

The one particular issue in this paper that has still been overlooked is the importance of teachers gaining a thorough understanding of the world that the student lives in. We are still preparing students to exist in our world rather than theirs. This remains a significant shortcoming in present programs.

CHAPTER 5

Discrimination Learning

Marc W. Gold and Keith G. Scott

PRESTATEMENT

This chapter appeared in *Training the Developmentally Young,* edited by
Will Beth Stephens. It was written in 1970 and published in 1971. At the
time, I was seeking funding for my research, conducting the 1-year retention
study on the original research with the bicycle brakes, and trying to establish
a line of research. Although there was no intentional activity to develop the
task analysis system, it will be obvious that this chapter and the discussion
of task analysis reflect the beginnings of the system.

Keith Scott had been my advisor for the thesis. Having been trained by
David Zeaman and Betty House, he had a focus at that time on attention
theory and discrimination learning. Our intention with this chapter was to
provide practitioners in the field with an understanding of this perspective
without their needing a number of courses in psychology and learning.
Keith's emphasis had been on basic research, while my thesis activity had
been the application of the findings from that basic research. This chapter,
then, was an attempt to provide useful descriptions of some of the concepts
and techniques that were used in the thesis and that were developed from
attention theory.

The retarded child is surrounded with a variable environment and from it he
must select those features that are relevant to the activities in which he is
engaged. This means some events must be attended to while others are
ignored. One of the characteristics of the retarded is a reduced ability to
independently select the relevant aspects of a task. Their teachers must
arrange the educational environment first to attract the child's attention to
the relevant aspects of tasks and second to help him learn to do this for
himself. This chapter is concerned with ways to accomplish these goals.

GENERAL PRINCIPLES OF ATTENTION

Before we turn to specific training procedures it is necessary to define terms and principles relevant to discrimination learning. The theory behind these ideas is the extensively researched Attention Theory of Zeaman and House (Zeaman, 1965). Attention refers to the process by which a child focuses on some aspects of the stimuli to which he is exposed (Zeaman and House, 1963). *Attention in this context, and in this chapter, is concerned with what the child looks at rather than the length of time a child spends doing something.*

Discrimination and Generalization

All learning requires that the child detect some differences in the events he hears, sees, or touches. Thus, in learning to recognize letters the child must discriminate differences in position of the vertical stroke to discriminate a *d* from a *b*. Similarly, some aspects of the letters must be ignored such as the slope of *b* and *d*. In a social setting the child learns to attend to certain physical characteristics such as body shape and facial features to discriminate men from women. With current fashions and styles some features such as length of hair must be ignored. Learning to detect the relevant dimensions of variation is necessary before the child can respond to differences. In our examples this would involve saying *b* or *d* or responding in the socially appropriate way to a man or a woman.

Once a child has acquired a discrimination he must learn to transfer the training. The discrimination must be generalizable to new situations. Thus, having learned to discriminate between one male and one female, the child must *generalize* his learning to apply to other individuals as well. However, the generalization may be too great. Behavior that is the appropriate social response to a young woman teacher might not be appropriate with an older woman or grandmother. If the child gave the same response to all people regardless of age or sex we would say that he had *overgeneralized* and was not discriminating. At first the young child commonly calls all men "Daddy." He has learned to discriminate men from women but overgeneralizes in attaching the label to all men. Later he will learn that some men are daddies and others are not, and that one particular daddy is his. Further, "My Daddy" is a particular person who may wear different clothes and sometimes be pleased and sometimes angry. Despite these variations in mood and appearance he is still "My Daddy." Generalization needs to be sufficiently broad to permit acceptance of unimportant or irrelevant details about Daddy while other critical aspects can be sharply discriminated so that he is not confused with other men. *We need to engineer the pupil's attention so that he learns to attend to those aspects of the situation that are relevant to his learning and to ignore those that are irrelevant* (Scott, 1966).

There are two important kinds of stimulus variation to consider in engineering a pupil's attention and discrimination. First, there is simple discrimination. Here a child who learns to discriminate red from green may at first overgeneralize and confuse red and orange. With repeated training where only red is reinforced this confusion will be removed. However, in other ways his learning one color discrimination will also aid in learning other color discriminations. The child learns that there are also systematic dimensions of variation in the world. This second kind of stimulus variation is called *mediated generalization.* Not only does the child distinguish between the particular colors red and green, he also learns that color is a dimension on which things in the world vary. As he plays with his blocks the child learns that one way to sort them is in terms of their color. Another way to sort the blocks is in terms of their form or shape. The child, in making a discrimination, must learn to attend to the dimensions on which things differ as well as, and perhaps before, he can see differences between particular stimuli within those dimensions. He must learn the dimensions of difference that are relevant to discriminations among people, among blocks, or among letters and words.

Attention Theory

A major postulate of attention theories of discrimination learning has been that solving a discrimination consists of learning a chain of two responses (Zeaman and House, 1963). *First the child must learn to attend to the relevant dimension of difference between the stimuli and then choose the particular stimulus that is correct.* An apparatus, called the Wisconsin General Test Apparatus, shown in Figure 1, has been used in the laboratory to investigate this result. With this apparatus the tester sits behind a one-way vision screen and arranges two stimuli, *e.g.,* a red square and a green square, so that they cover two holes in the sliding tray. Under one of the colored squares is hidden a small reward object such as a candy. The tester slides the tray forward and the child now tries to find the candy by moving one of the squares to uncover the hole. The child, to be scored correct, must find the candy on his first try.

The traditional view of learning was that the child acquired the discrimination between the red and green stimuli slowly by building up little increments of habit. In this view, retarded children's slowness in acquiring habits is due to their acquiring smaller than normal increments each time they make a correct choice and are reinforced (Scott, 1978). This view of normal-retardate differences is illustrated by the hypothetical curves, shown in Figure 2, which show learning of a habit as gradual and incremental. Research in discrimination learning has shown that learning is not a matter of building up little bits of habit, and that these curves, commonly seen in some older writings, are created by inappropriate methods of grouping data which mask the shape of the individual curves (Zeaman and House, 1963).

A more accurate view of the course of learning and of the difference between normal and retardate learning is shown in Figure 3. Here we see that *learning consists of an initial period of responding at chance followed by a sudden onset of learning, or a point* (labeled A and B in Figure 3) *where the child makes an insightful solution to the problem.* An important point can be seen in Figure 3. *The difference between normal and retarded children*

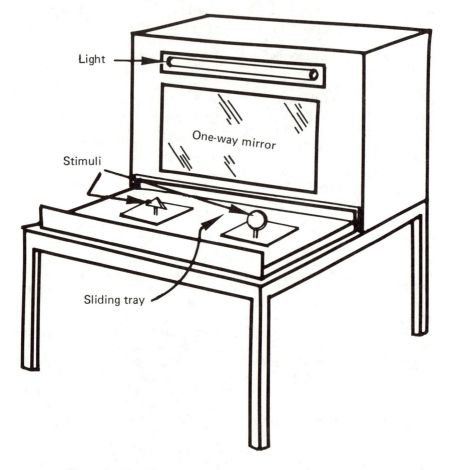

Light

One-way mirror

Stimuli

Sliding tray

Figure 1. The Wisconsin General Test Apparatus or WGTA.

lies not in the rate at which performance increases but rather in the length of time it takes the retarded child to reach the point where he begins to learn. More detailed analyses of data show very clearly that the retarded child takes longer to attend to the relevant dimension, and thus begin learning, than does a normal child (Zeaman, 1965).

Once the retarded child attends to the relevant dimension he learns very rapidly and essentially at the same rate as his normal peer. It follows that a large part of the teacher's job in facilitating the learning of retarded children consists of arranging the teaching material so as to direct the child's attention to the relevant dimensions of the problem.

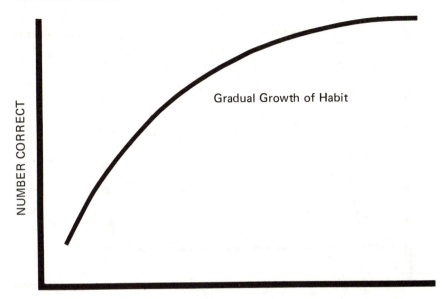

NUMBER CORRECT

Gradual Growth of Habit

TRAINING

Figure 2. Schematic diagram of the course of learning when the growth of a habit is seen as gradual. The curve should be compared with those in Figure 3 which are more representative of the performance of an individual subject.

Dimensions and Shifts

A useful way to conceive of a dimension is as a meaningfully related group of items. Thus, the various colors—red, green, blue, orange, and so on—make up the color dimension. As learning theorists study learning about groups such as animals (*e.g.,* bird, bear, dog, and so on), they have often called the groups or dimensions "clusters." The general point is that to make learning about things efficient the adult or child must achieve some organization of the material into effective groupings. This has at least two major effects. First, it allows the child to focus on the critical features by directing his attention to what is relevant. Second, in remembering the material later it provides for direction of his memory search.

When a child learns one color discrimination and subsequently is taught another but different color discrimination, his learning of the second problem is much faster than of the first. That is, in learning the first discrimination he learns both that color is a relevant dimension and which particular color is correct. In learning the second problem, since he is already attending to the color dimension, the child has only to learn to pick which of the new colors is correct. The second problem is then said to involve a shift of attention within a dimension and is called an *intradimensional shift.* If the second

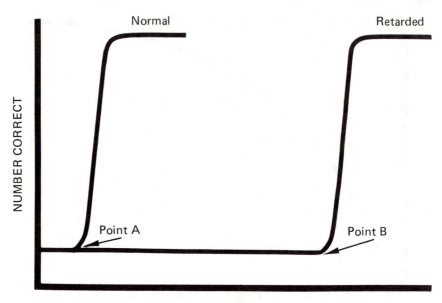

Figure 3. The course of learning for normals and retarded children as training progresses. As can be seen the children learn at the same rate once they reach a critical point (A for the normals and B for the retarded) where they attend to the relevant stimuli. The diagrams are schematic.

problem involves a shift of attention to a new dimension, such as form, it would be described as an *extradimensional shift* (Wolff, 1967). In Figure 4 schematic learning curves are shown for children who, having learned one discrimination, are now learning a second discrimination. The solid line would represent the curve for a child who, having learned one color problem, is now learning another color problem (intradimensional shift). The dotted curve is for a child who, having learned one color problem, is now learning a form problem (extradimensional shift). As can be seen, when the second problem is solved using the same dimension as the first, learning is much faster.

SOME SPECIFIC CONCEPTS ABOUT ATTENTION

Redundancy

Sometimes a problem can be learned in more than one way. Such problems are said to be *redundant*. An example would be the discrimination between a red square (the correct choice) and a green triangle. A perfect solution could be achieved by selecting the red object without looking at its shape. Alternatively, a perfect solution could be made by selecting the square while

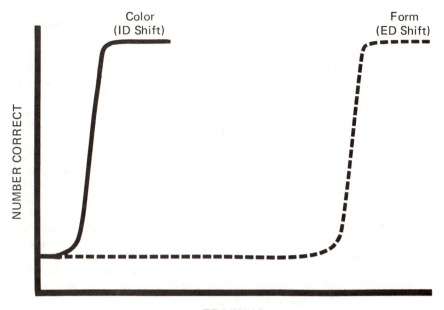

Figure 4. Schematic diagrams showing the effect of introducing new problems on a previously trained dimension (color) and a new dimension. Such problems are known of as intradimensional (ID) and extra-dimensional (ED) shifts.

ignoring the color. When two dimensions or stimuli are always together they are thus said to be *redundant*.

Different effects of redundancy have been investigated (Zeaman, 1968). One important finding is that learning occurs more rapidly as the number of redundant relevant dimensions increases. The more cues a pupil has to help solve a problem (within reason) the faster he will solve it. A child will learn to pick the large, yellow triangle more quickly than to pick the triangle. Having three relevant and redundant dimensions makes the task easier.

Irrelevant Cues

Related to redundancy is the finding that when variable irrelevant dimensions are fewer, the child will learn more quickly (Zeaman, 1965). Irrelevant dimensions may be variable or constant. If a child is learning a problem where form only is relevant, then all other dimensions are irrelevant. If all of the forms (stimuli) are the same color and size, then color and size are *constant* and *irrelevant*. If the forms are different colors and sizes and change for each form from trial to trial, then color and size are *variable* and *irrelevant*. If the child is learning to discriminate triangle from square, then having different colors and sizes of triangles and squares would impede learning. Having all triangles and squares the same color and size would not get rid of the color and size dimensions. However, holding them constant does not impede learning. *In summary, retarded children can take advantage of more than one relevant and redundant cue at a time to help solve a problem. They also learn faster when irrelevant information is kept to a minimum.*

Fading

One other use of cue redundancy occurs in a technique called *fading* (Terrace, 1966; Moore and Goldiamond, 1964). Here an already established discrimination is used as a crutch to aid in the acquisition of a new and more difficult discrimination. For example, let us suppose that a child can already distinguish between a red and a yellow stimulus but cannot do this for a circle and an ellipse. At the start of training both colors and forms are made redundant. That is, the circle is always yellow and the ellipse always red. This problem could be solved by the use of either color or form. At first, knowing the color discrimination, the child will use it to solve the problem. Gradually, through the course of training, the difference between red and yellow is decreased until both are orange while the forms remain constant. If the rate at which the crutch cues (colors) are faded is not too great, then the child will proceed through the course of learning with few or no errors. This procedure is thought to minimize frustration and is one method of facilitating the acquisition of difficult tasks. When using fading, one should also avoid fading so slowly that time is wasted and the child is put through many unnecessary and boring trials.

Clustering

The way in which stimuli are grouped can affect the ease with which they are learned and remembered. Thus in learning lists of words, items that belong to a category or *cluster* are more readily recalled (Bousfield, 1953). For example, a list of words that consists only of animals, vehicles, or people's names would be recalled better than a list of unrelated words. Children or adults tend to remember by grouping words from the same category. In order for this powerful facilitator of remembering to operate the child must, of course, possess the concept that the items do belong to a class or group. It can be seen that this process, called *clustering,* has much in common with the concept of a dimension. To cluster is much like attending to the relevant dimension.

Criterion

Learning is generally said to have occurred when the child has achieved some criterion of performance. For example, an experimenter might decide that *criterion performance* (learning) for a particular experiment is six consecutive correct responses. This is an arbitrary decision. But when the child makes six consecutive correct responses, the experimenter assumes that the child has learned the task. Whether or not the criterion is appropriate is determined by observing the child's performance following criterion. If there are many errors after criterion, it is an indication that the experimenter's criterion was not appropriate and that learning, or the elimination of errors, has not taken place. In such a case, the criterion would be changed and reevaluated.

Overlearning

A concept closely related to criterion is overlearning. *Overlearning* is defined as trials beyond criterion. This does not mean correct trials only. However, frequent errors in overlearning usually indicate that a too weak criterion has been selected. Overlearning is important in two ways. First, retention is greatly influenced by the degree of original learning (Belmont, 1966). That is, if a child is brought to a strong criterion and/or is given some degree of overlearning, this will increase his retention of the material. Second, over-learning facilitates transfer on an intradimensional shift. This means that the child who gets overlearning on a problem where the form dimension is relevant will rapidly learn subsequent form problems even though the specific forms change.

Easy-to-hard Sequences

Another finding from research on discrimination learning involves the use of easy-to-hard sequences. *A sequence of easy-to-hard problems is learned more quickly than hard problems alone* (House and Zeaman, 1960; Zeaman and House, 1963). If, for example, you wanted a child to learn to sort a pile of two different-length bolts where the difference was one-eighth inch, he would learn best by starting with a pile of bolts where the difference in length was one-half inch, then moving to a one-fourth inch difference, then one-eighth. This procedure helps the child identify the relevant dimension, length, because he starts out with large differences on that dimension. When the differences get smaller he will be attending to the relevant dimension, greatly increasing his chances of solving the problem. The child who must learn to attend to a dimension where the differences are small to begin with has a much more difficult problem to solve (Shepp and Zeaman, 1966).

Failure Sets

Still another important finding is the powerful detrimental effect of failure sets. Retarded children who experience prolonged failure on difficult problems often will fail to solve even very simple problems (Zeaman, 1965).

This formation of a *failure set* is the result of the child's ceasing to attend to any of the relevant cues in the learning situation. Thus when the teacher or experimenter makes some change in the problem to bring it within the child's ability, it makes no difference. The child is not oriented to the task and does not observe the change. Materials and procedures should be programmed so as to minimize the child's experience of failure. The technique described in the lesson plans that follow illustrate some methods of attack. Also, when the child makes the wrong choice from two or more possibilities, he should be told to try another way instead of being told he is wrong (Gold, 1969). This method emphasizes where he can go to succeed instead of where he has failed.

Novelty

Most teachers are well aware of the attention-attracting features of a novel event. *Novelty* is a powerful controlling variable in directing attention and can be defined as some discrepant occurrence in a pattern or sequence of events or stimuli. Children who have formed deep failure sets will sometimes start to attend to a novel stimulus suddenly introduced in the series of learning trials. In general, unless an adequate level of stimulus variability is maintained during a training session, children will cease to attend. Often they are said to be "daydreaming" or "bored."

The question then can be asked, What is the optimal level of variability that will maintain attention? (Berlyne, 1960). One clear answer is that the task should differ from what the child has been doing by a margin just wide enough to hold the child's attention. In practice this may be difficult to judge. However, the two extremes—for a task to be either totally repetitive or so difficult that the child cannot solve it—lead to the extinction of attention and can be readily detected. Unfortunately these extremes frequently are rampant in the workshop and classroom.

SPECIAL TRAINING PROCEDURES

Some training techniques which are related to discrimination learning are useful in training the retarded.

Match-to-sample

One such technique is called *match-to-sample* and is sometimes used in discrimination learning experiments (Heal and Bransky, 1966). This technique consists of presenting an object (stimulus) and having the child select from a group of objects (response choices) the one that matches. This technique is not unfamiliar to the classroom teacher. Using some of the concepts described, this procedure can be used to program many kinds and levels of learning. By controlling the number of relevant and variable irrelevant dimensions a series of easy-to-hard problems is not difficult to achieve.

Oddity

A similar procedure involves *oddity* (Brown, 1970). That is, three or four objects are displayed before the child. All but one of them are alike. He has to tell which one is different. The ways in which the stimuli are alike and different can vary greatly. For instance, if you are teaching the concept of male-female, a child might start out with problems where there are two identical pictures of a boy and a picture of a girl. After he chooses the odd picture, with sets like these, six consecutive times, say, give him cards on which there are still two boys and a girl, or vice versa, but where the two alike pictures are not identical. Following successful solution, or criterion, on that set, you could change to pictures of adults or pictures where the sex differences are more subtle. The same idea, of course, can be used with the match-to-sample technique. The important thing is to know how to control the relevant and irrelevant dimensions, which in turn do much to control the level of difficulty of the task.

Task Analysis and Sequencing

The lessons to be described utilize lesson planning rules and concepts such as task analysis and sequencing. *Task analysis* refers to breaking a task down into its component parts. The steps listed in sample Lesson 1 are an example. The concept of task analysis is very important for teaching retarded children. Using task analysis, we find that tasks that are usually seen as consisting of two or three difficult steps are really twenty or thirty simple steps. Examples of this are folding a piece of paper in half, tying shoelaces, walking to the store, and calling the telephone operator in an emergency. *Sequencing* merely refers to putting the steps into a logical order.

A NOTE ON PERCEPTUAL-MOTOR LEARNING

Tasks such as tying shoelaces are frequently called perceptual-motor. This has been thought to describe the supposed reliance on visual perception of the task details and the use of particular dexterous motor movements. When a child cannot learn such tasks, we usually attribute his failure to one or both of two causes. The first is the inability to perceive rather than to discriminate. The second is the failure to make certain movements instead of learn a sequence of movements. *It should be emphasized that most of the moderately retarded have difficulty in learning where to put the lace and when to move the fingers rather than being unable to see the lace holes or to make the component specific movements.* Observation of a child eating will often allow simple confirmation of his development. Discrimination between foods of different color and texture can be observed as the child systematically eats one food rather than another. His skill in manipulating utensils is also apparent. If the child did not possess the necessary perceptual-motor abilities, he could not make the discriminations involved. If such a task is seen as a discrimination learning problem, then we begin to see the task as a sequence of discriminations to be taught rather than relying on some perceptual or motor ability that requires large-scale general training. That is, conceived of in terms of discrimination, the teaching program is one of training a specific task sequence.

THE APPLICATION OF SOME PRINCIPLES
IN THE SHELTERED WORKSHOP

The potential of Zeaman and House's Attention Theory was demonstrated recently in a study on the acquisition of a complex assembly task by retarded adolescents by Gold (1969). This was the first reported study utilizing the Zeaman theory in an applied setting. Procedures developed from Attention Theory were used to train sixty-four moderately and severely retarded adolescents with an average IQ of 47, who were enrolled in four sheltered workshops, to assemble a 15-piece and a 24-piece bicycle brake. One-half of the subjects worked with the parts of the 15-piece brake as they came from the factory. That is, in order to decide which way a part went on, the subjects had to attend to the form dimension (the shape of the part). The other subjects worked with parts that were color coded. Coding consisted of painting red that surface of each part that is facing the subject when it is placed in the proper position for assembling. This constituted a cue redundancy, making form and color relevant and redundant. All subjects also worked with the parts of the 24-piece brake as they came from the factory (form only). Sixty-three of the sixty-four subjects reached a criterion of six correct out of eight consecutive trials on both brakes. The one subject who failed reached criterion on the training brake only. The results of the experimental procedures were dramatic. First, the subjects who had cue redundancy on the 15-piece brake learned it in half the trials needed by the group that had only the form dimension relevant. The average number of trials needed to reach criterion on the 15-piece brake was thirty-three for the form-only group and seventeen for the color-form group. On the 24-piece brake the average for all groups was twenty-two. Second, the use of very systematic programming of the task meant that virtually all subjects learned to assemble the brakes. None of the directors of the sheltered workshops expected any of the clients to be able to learn the tasks at all.

SAMPLE LESSONS

To illustrate the principles involved in discrimination learning two sample lesson plans for the moderately retarded are presented. One involves the techniques that are used in teaching a child to tie his shoes, the other demonstrates the sequence of activities encountered in sorting bolts. Reminder is made that these are illustrations and are not to be followed rigidly. Varying situations and individuals may necessitate additions to or rearrangement of the sequence.

Lesson 1

Purpose: To promote opportunity for the child to learn to tie shoelaces.
Materials: The child's shoes, long laces, or a lacing board.
Techniques and concepts to be illustrated: Criterion, cue redundancy, task analysis, overlearning, fading.

Procedure:

A. List the steps in tying shoes. The descriptions used here are for you and, in most instances, should not be used with the child. Follow these steps with a shoe in front of you.

   1. Get shoes.
   2. Put on shoes (correctly? maybe not yet) which already have laces in them.
   3. Pull tongue up and straight.
   4. Hold a lace end in each hand.
   5. Pull them tight. (More steps might be needed here if lower part of lace is loose.)
   6. Release laces.
   7. With palms facing up, pincer grasp one lace in each hand, approximately one-third the distance from the shoe to the end of the lace.
   8. Cross the laces so that the lace on top moves into the other pincer grasp.
   9. Let go of that lace.
   10. Grasp the other lace, which is the one behind.
   11. Bring it toward you, then, with the thumb, push it through the hole.
   12. With the same hand, let go.
   13. Grasp the same lace behind the hole.
   14. Pull it so that you now have one lace in each grasp.
   15. Pull both laces tight.
   16. Let go.
   17. With a pincer grasp (always the same hand, but let the child choose which hand) lift up the lace opposite the hand used, one-third of the distance from the shoe to the end.
   18. With the other hand grasp the two parts of the lace together, at the shoe, so that the two parts of the lace that are between the two grasps are equal and taut. This leaves one-third of the lace free.
   19. Release the grasp that is away from the shoe (Step 10).
   20. With the free hand grasp the other lace one-third of the distance from the shoe.
   21. Bring the lace all the way around your side of the loop extending above the other grasp.
   22. Release the grasp on that lace.
   23. Grasp the two parts of that lace and push the longer part so that it shows between the shorter part and the loop being held in the other grasp.
   24. With the forefinger of the hand holding the loop, push the part showing, through the hole, letting go with the other grasp.
   25. Grasp the end of the long loop.
   26. Let go of the grasp that has been close to the shoe since Step 11.
   27. Grasp the part of the lace which was pushed through the hole in Step 17.
   28. Pull both loops tight.
   29. Let go. (Note: Many of our friends who know how to tie shoes suggest alternatives to our procedures. May we suggest that you use your own method, but task analyze and teach it using the techniques presented here.)

B. Establish criterion: When the child has tied his shoes correctly ten times without help we will assume he has learned the task.

C. Decide on ways to direct child's attention to the relevant dimensions of the problem. Make the two halves of the lace different colors. This will be a cue redundancy because the actual relevant dimension for this task is position—position of the laces and of the fingers. The addition of a color should help. You might also put a black spot on each lace one-third the distance from the shoe to the end of the lace.

D. Decide on a training procedure. The training procedure tells how to teach the task and should not be confused with the steps of the task itself.

  1. Teach the child to respond to the command "pinch here," so that before he actually begins tying shoes he knows how to make a pincer grasp where you tell him.
  2. Teach him to respond to the commands "pull tight" and "let go here." For the other movements use as little talking as possible.
  3. With his shoe on and the laces fairly loose (or with the lacing board) say out loud to yourself, "pinch here," pointing to a point on one of the laces. Then you make a pincer grasp at that point.
  4. Point to the same place, give the same command, and ask the child to do it.
  5. When is able to make a pincer grasp at the right point for approximately five consecutive correct times, continue the same procedure for the other commands.
  6. In the classroom you would probably begin with Step 4 (grasp a lace end in each hand). Pointing to both laces say, "pull tight (5). Then, "let go" (6). These two steps are probably best learned together until the child can do them correctly five consecutive times. Then with your commands, tell him to "do it by yourself" and have him do Steps 5 and 6 to a criterion of five consecutive correct times without verbal assistance.
  7. On the next trial, when he finishes Step 6, say, "hold your hands like this (palms up), pinch here (wait for him), and pinch here" (7).
  8. Without saying "let go," say "good, let's try that much again." Take his hands away from the laces.
  9. Tell the child to go ahead (Step 4). Bring him to a criterion of five consecutive correct trials where you give him verbal assistance only on Step 7. Five consecutive trials without any help should follow.
  10. On the next trial, with the child grasping the laces, you mimic Step 8 and say, "go like this." The purpose of this is to determine which lace the child naturally places in front. Once you know this you can show him how to do it and watch to see that he is consistent. By moving his hands, show him how to do Step 8. Then, pointing to the top lace, say, "let go here" (9).
  11. Again, take his hands away from the laces without saying "let go" and use the procedures described in Step 9. Bring him to criterion on Steps 4 through 9.

12. Use the same procedures for the rest of the steps.
13. When the child has reached criterion on the entire task, give him several days or weeks of overlearning.
14. Then remove the color cue. If the child's performance drops, try using the original procedures, but without the color cue, bringing the child again to criterion.
15. It might be necessary to reinstate the color cue. If so, either give the child more overlearning trials with the color before removing it again, or try using a fading procedure. This might consist of making the two colors more and more alike, or making just the very ends of the laces different colors.

Evaluation: By having a predetermined criterion, you will know if the lessons are successful. The teacher must be prepared to make changes in the procedures in order to meet the individual needs of the children. The lesson described is not seen as *the* way to teach children to tie shoes. It is seen as one way. You will have to modify it. The reason the lesson is included in this chapter is to demonstrate how to use some of the techniques and concepts described.

Lesson 2

Purpose: To assist the child in learning to sort bolts into categories of size, length, and head shape.
Materials: Several hundred bolts with the following characteristics:

1. Hexagon head, 1 inch × 3/8 inch (all bolts standard thread)
2. Hexagon head, 1 inch × 1/4 inch
3. Hexagon head, 3/4 inch × 3/8 inch
4. Hexagon head, 3/4 inch × 1/4 inch
5. Hexagon head, 1/2 inch × 3/8 inch
6. Hexagon head, 1/2 inch × 1/4 inch
7. Round head, 1 inch × 3/8 inch
8. Round head, 1 inch × 1/4 inch
9. Round head, 3/4 inch × 3/8 inch
10. Round head, 3/4 inch × 1/4 inch
11. Round head, 1/2 inch × 3/8 inch
12. Round head, 1/2 inch × 1/4 inch

The bolts described have differences on three dimensions—head shape, length, and width.
Techniques and concepts to be illustrated: Criterion, cue redundancy, easy-to-hard sequence.

Procedure:

A. To teach the vocabulary for the bolts and for the directions, refer to the article by Gold (1968).

B. Establish criterion: When the child sorts the pile twice without errors it will be assumed he has learned the task that is represented by that pile.

C. Present the child (or children) with a pile containing the hexagonal, 1 inch X 1/4 inch bolts and the round, 1/2 inch X 3/8 bolts. In doing this you have provided a task on which there are three relevant and redundant dimensions.

D. Either use labels and commands the child knows or, nonverbally, remove one kind of bolt and put it in one place (container) and put the other bolt in another container.

E. Ask the child to start. If he has difficulty, you start slowly sorting the pile and encourage him to do the same.

F. Following criterion, change the task to each of the following, establishing criterion each time.

1. Make all dimensions relevant and redundant. That is, sort hexagonal 1 inch X 3/8 inch from round 1/2 inch X 1/4 inch bolts.
2. Keep one dimension constant and irrelevant and sort for the other two. That is, use one head shape and sort 1 inch X 3/8 inch from 1/2 inch X 1/4 inch bolts. Or use one length and sort hexagonal 1 inch X 1/4 inch from round 1 inch X 3/8 inch bolts.
3. Keep two dimensions constant and irrelevant and sort for the third. That is, sort hexagonal 1 inch X 3/8 inch from hexagonal 1 inch X 1/4 inch bolts, and so on.
4. Do Steps 1 and 2 above using the 3/4 inch with the 1 inch and/or the 3/8 inch bolts. This will constitute a move toward a finer discrimination.
5. Use all bolts and sort on all relevent dimensions (twelve piles). You might need to start without 3/4 inch bolts. In this case there would be eight piles.
6. Use all the bolts and have variable irrelevant dimensions. That is, sort all of the hexagonal bolts from all of the round bolts. In this case length and width would vary but would not be relevant.
7. Use other combinations, remembering the rules about cue redundancy, relevant and variable irrelevant dimensions, and easy-to-hard sequences.

Evaluation: If the child is able to perform at criterion given any combination of categories, he has not only learned to sort bolts but has developed a sorting skill that will transfer to many other tasks.

SUMMARY

Retarded children learn rapidly once they attend to the relevant stimuli and dimensions in a learning situation. A major task of the teacher of the developmentally young is to program the instructional materials in a manner which will direct and maintain attention and thus facilitate learning.

Research on discrimination learning provides a number of key concepts, *e.g.,* the dimensional organization of stimuli, that have led to theories about attention. This theoretical framework in turn provides the teacher with the language, behavioral rules, and techniques to plan carefully sequenced training. Not only is learning made easier for children, but in addition, the teacher is able to avoid unfortunate side effects, *e.g.,* the formation of failure sets.

The procedure is illustrated by a report of research demonstrating the assembly of complex mechanical equipment by retarded adolescents. Also two model lesson plans, and the procedure by which they are developed, are outlined. The chapter thus provides a systematic plan for programming the acquisition of relevant tasks in terms of specific training as an alternative to planning a broad and vague program aimed at "perceptual-motor abilities."*

POSTSTATEMENT

I cringe every time I see the word *retardate* in something I wrote. You might find it for the next several articles, but then it should be gone. If you ever see it again in something I write after this book, please call immediately. The word *child* is used appropriately in the chapter because the book was primarily about children. The term is sometimes erroneously interpreted to mean anyone labeled retarded. The word should be used selectively to mean those people who, chronologically, are adolescents or younger. The chapter also uses all male pronouns, something that has changed for many of us since that time.

Strange coincidence: while I was reviewing this chapter for the book, my royalty check for the original chapter came in from Harper & Row. It was for 4 cents. Universities say to faculty members, "Publish or perish."

In reviewing this chapter almost 10 years after it was written, I find most of the concepts still to be helpful for people who train. The vocabulary is a compromise between the technical jargon of the researcher and the language of classroom teachers. We did not go quite far enough in describing the concepts in terms that people without a prior knowledge of psychology would need for a thorough understanding.

I found some interesting things in this chapter related to our current technology. For example, the definition of criterion is what later came to be Criterion I in the Try Another Way System. Several years later we added a second definition of criterion (II) which was that the criterion for any piece of learning must be repeated demonstration of the behavior under the circumstances where it is ultimately expected to occur. Also, what we referred to as training techniques in the chapter, specifically match-to-sample and oddity, became two of the subheadings under the term *format* in the system, referring to the organization of content presentation.

One of the most interesting points in the chapter is one that I had since overlooked. The point is that tasks that are too easy or too difficult tend to turn off the learner. The implication, obviously, is that the level of

*Preparation of this chapter was supported by Grant MH07346 and by a career award K4HD46370 to Keith G. Scott.

difficulty should be kept in the middle range. The way we approach that in the system now is dividing the task into teachable components and matching to the learner the particular level of power and amount of delay in providing correction for errors. The perspective presented in this chapter, controlling level of difficulty, is a useful addition to what we have been teaching.

In looking at the sample task analyses, I find them to be incomplete but all right for starters. The term *procedure* was used in the sample lesson for tying shoelaces. The part listed as *A* under Procedure now is referred to as the content task analysis. Section D, "Decide on a training procedure," would now be the process task analysis and would be included alongside the corresponding content steps. The format used for the sample lesson is forward chaining and would be described in a section termed *Format* in our revised system.

Section C discusses the use of a color cue. In research that we did subsequently, that will be described in this book, we found that color coding was not a particularly useful technique because the time for removing the color cues was as much as that saved in the first place. We did not use the color coding with shoelaces, but we achieved the effect with some other tasks that we used. At this point we are hesitant to suggest color coding unless the procedure includes some ways for fading out the cues fairly early in training.

Perhaps the most significant change in my thinking since this chapter is a general move away from a reliance on Zeaman and House attention theory as a basis for the Try Another Way System. There is no question that the attention theory perspective is very useful for understanding how individuals make discriminations and learn many things. Over the years, however, we have expanded the range of theoretical positions that we turn to for assistance so that at this time the attention theory and discrimination learning perspective is one of a variety that can be found embedded within the Try Another Way System. This chapter, then, provides a fairly clear picture of which parts of the current system have their roots in our early research and in our particular application of this theory.

CHAPTER 6

Stimulus Factors in Skill Training of Retarded Adolescents on a Complex Assembly Task: Acquisition, Transfer, and Retention

Marc W. Gold

PRESTATEMENT

The acquisition and transfer parts of this study constituted the research for my PhD thesis. That work was done in the fall and winter of 1967. It was a product of many of my past experiences: I was raised in a bicycle shop and taught adolescent individuals labeled trainable mentally retarded in the Los Angeles city schools. At the University of Illinois I became very interested in learning theory, especially the attention theory of Dave Zeaman and Betty House, and I became interested in research that would translate all of that into useful knowledge for the field.

The original proposal for this experiment did not specify the two tasks. The tasks were described as consisting of a number of different parts to be assembled, with the first task being mostly two-choice problems (a part could go on either one way or another) and the second task being a multi-choice problem (any particular part could go on one of several different ways). The two tasks for the study needed to have considerable face validity, which means people would look at them and be able to easily recognize that they were complex, real tasks, ones which would not normally be considered within the capabilities of people labeled moderately and severely retarded. I was also seeking tasks for which data collection would not be a problem. In other words, the person judging correctness would have a clear decision to make as to whether or not a part was correct or incorrect rather than having to judge the learner's response along some scale from correct to incorrect. Having described the task in such detail, I then spent approximately 1 week doing nothing but trying to create or discover appropriate tasks. When I finally came upon the idea of the bicycle brake, I felt extremely stupid. I had assembled thousands of them as a youngster, but it had taken me a long time to realize that they would be ideal tasks for my project.

This article originally appeared in the *American Journal of Mental Deficiency*, 1972, *76*, 517–526. Reprinted by permission of the publisher.

45

Once the tasks had been selected and task analyzed, I did two pilot studies prior to doing the thesis itself. During the pilot studies many bugs were worked out of the procedures, data collection techniques were refined, and decisions were made about how to prepare trainers. Performance by the individuals involved in the pilot study also was extremely important in providing motivation to continue with the study, which at the time was pretty far in left field. The other purpose of the pilot studies was to arrive at a set of procedures which would produce results that could not be explained through conventional reinforcement explanations. With the assistance of Warren Steinman and Herbert Quay I developed procedures through which the results could be clearly described in terms of stimulus variables rather than reinforcement variables. The two reasons for wanting this were, first, to show the value of attention theory, and, second, to provide some alternatives to what was then, and still is, the overwhelming reliance on reinforcement strategies in programs for people labeled retarded.

In the study of vocational skill training with the retarded, the manipulation of stimulus variables to achieve rapid and effective training has not been experimentally investigated. Virtually all of the experimental research related to training and performance in a vocational setting is operant, uses as its primary focus the utilization of reinforcement contingencies, and is concerned almost exclusively with production as opposed to the acquisition of skills. These studies suggest the value of such procedures in maintaining and increasing production levels in sheltered workshops (Brown & Pearce, 1970; Evans & Spradlin, 1966; Huddle, 1967; Hunt & Zimmerman, 1969; Zimmerman, Overpeck, Eisenberg, & Garlick, 1969; Zimmerman, Stuckey, Garlick, & Miller, 1969).

Nonexperimental research on the vocational training of the retarded is voluminous. It deals primarily with predictive assessment and evaluation rather than training (Burdett, 1963; Ladas, 1961; Meadow & Greenspan, 1961; Tobias, 1960; Wagner & Hawver, 1965). Most studies which are not operant and deal with training concern themselves with social skills and abilities and work adjustment (Acker & Thompson, 1960; Cowan & Goldman, 1959; Kolstoe, 1960; White & Redkey, 1956).

The large volume of research, with the exception of operant work, lacks theoretical foundation and falls short of providing a strong basis for developing an effective technology for increasing the skill functioning of the mentally retarded.

Basic research in discrimination learning with the mentally retarded appears to provide such a foundation. It has resulted in a body of information describing some learning characteristics of this population in controlled situations. From this research, a number of effects have emerged that are both replicated and produced by clearly defined manipulations. Consistent behaviors have been obtained in different situations and with a variety of retarded populations.

One model which has generated much empirical information about stimulus and training procedures in the area of discrimination learning of the retarded is the attention theory of Zeaman and House (1963). The Zeamans postulate that the relevant cues are not attended to on every trial, but that the subject must learn a chain of two responses: (*a*) attending to the relevant dimension and (*b*) approaching the correct cue on that dimension.

The effects of dimensional learning are not usually observed directly on the first problem or set of problems. It is in the solution of subsequent problems that the effects are observed. Consequently, the paradigm generally used in discrimination learning experiments usually includes training and transfer. Using this paradigm, the present study extends investigation of two effects, number of relevant dimensions on original learning and effects of overlearning on transfer, as applied in a complex assembly task.

The term dimension, as used in discrimination learning, refers to properties of the classes of stimuli, that is, color, form, etc. When a child learns to respond to red instead of green he is attending to the color dimension. In putting a bicycle brake together one must attend to the form dimension in order to solve the problem of which way the part goes on. When the child learns to respond to red and then transfers, or shifts, to a new set of problems where orange and blue are used and blue is correct, he has made an intradimensional shift, that is, he has shifted to a new set of problems where the relevant dimension is the same, but the instrumental response differs.

In one kind of intradimensional shift, red and green might be used both for training and for transfer, but if red is correct for training, then green becomes correct for transfer. This is a reversal shift. Reversal shifts and other intradimensional shifts are generally compared with extradimensional shifts. If, after learning a color relevant problem, like those just described, the child is transferred to a problem where triangle is correct, this constitutes a shift from the color dimension to the form dimension, and is called an extradimensional shift.

When two stimuli such as red and triangle, from different dimensions, are continually paired, the stimuli are said to be redundant. Painting one side of each part of a bicycle brake provides the subject with a cue redundancy (color-form). Both cues and dimensions (or either) can be redundant.

Experimenters interested in the role of attention in learning have studied the effects of varying shift manipulations, cue redundancies, and overlearning. Overlearning is administered when a subject is given training beyond some predetermined criterion point at which a high level of performance has been reached, and where it is assumed learning has taken place.

Numerous studies suggest that the facilitating effect of overlearning on intradimensional shifts is perhaps a general phenomenon (Blank, 1966; Campione, Hyman, & Zeaman, 1965; Furth & Youniss, 1964; Heal, 1966; Marsh, 1964; Ohlrich & Ross, 1966; Tighe & Tighe, 1965; Uhl, 1966; Youniss & Furth, 1965). Most of them show the effects of overlearning by comparing its effects on intradimensional and extradimensional shifts. Overlearning has been shown to impair extradimensional shifts with the retarded (Shepp & Turrisi, 1969).

Another consistent finding is that learning rate increases as a function of the number of relevant dimensions. In a discussion of discrimination learning Zeaman and House (1963) describe a hierarchy of stimulus dimensions and combinations based on experiments with retarded subjects.

House and Zeaman (1960), manipulating the number of relevant dimensions, found that training on a simple task will facilitate more rapid learning on a more difficult task. Discrimination was established between stimuli differing in color and form, presented in either of two ways: as flat patterns on gray backgrounds; or as cut-out three dimensional objects. Easy-to-hard sequences were more efficient than hard discrimination trials only, even though subjects given the easy-to-hard sequence were required to solve more problems than those given only the hard discriminations. The total number of trials required for the former group (summed over all the problems) was less than the number required for those subjects given the task originally.

While training and transfer have been studied extensively, little has been done to investigate the effects of training and transfer procedures on long-term retention. The literature on long-term memory in mental retardation was recently and comprehensively reviewed by Belmont (1966). He concluded that the basic research to date has been plagued with methodological problems. However, one clear result was apparent. The studies did indicate that retention is related to the degree of original learning. Similar conclusions were made in a more recent review by Hermelin (1967).

Crosson (1969) trained seven severely retarded males (mean IQ = 27) to perform two tasks, including the operation of a drill press and the use of a hammer in the assembly of flower boxes. Two-month and twelve-month follow-up studies were conducted with highly significant retention effects obtained.

A general purpose of the present study was to develop a structure and methodology for studying the application of stimulus control procedures to the acquisition of complex work tasks. The author contends that the literature abounds with examples of the futility of correlational approaches to the problem of vocational training. The specific purpose of the present study was to examine the effects of cue redundancy and overlearning on the acquisition and transfer of a complex assembly task skill, and to study their effect on long-term retention. The retention study is reported separately.

ACQUISITION AND TRANSFER STUDY

The independent variables were the Number of Relevant Dimensions (form-only or color-form) and Amount of Learning (criterion or overlearning). Learning was defined as reaching a performance criterion of six correct out of eight consecutive trials. Overlearning consisted of 20 trials beyond criterion.

The dependent variables were (a) trials to criterion, (b) manipulation errors to criterion, and (c) discrimination errors to criterion. Of the 25 steps involved in assembling the training task, 15 were manipulative, that is, were solved by appropriately moving parts into place, and 10 were discriminative, that is, were solved by determining which way a part was to be placed. Of the 33 steps involved in assembling the transfer task, 23 were manipulative and 10 were discriminative.

The following hypotheses were formulated to test the assumptions of the study: the use of a cue redundancy facilitates learning of a complex assembly task; the use of a cue redundancy on the training task does not impede transfer to a single relevant dimension task; and overlearning facilitates intradimensional transfer on a complex workshop assembly task.

Method

Subjects

Subjects were 64 retarded adolescents enrolled in four sheltered workshops. Descriptive data for the population are presented in Table 1. Workshop directors were asked to select the 18 to 20 lowest performing clients, excluding from selection clients with severe sensorial or physical handicaps, and clients with full scale or performance IQs above 60. Use of minimal selection criteria was in keeping with the applied nature of the study. Following selection, 16 subjects from each workshop were randomly assigned to groups with the restriction that 4 subjects from each workshop were in each group. Information concerning age, sex, IQ, clinical type, and length of time in the workshop was obtained for descriptive purposes only.

Three subjects were dropped, all during the first week of the experiment. One was dropped because of job placement resulting in termination as a workshop client, a second because of complete refusal to participate. The third subject was dropped because the project director, upon observing the thickness of his hands and the shortness of his fingers, believed the subject incapable of handling the small pieces of the transfer task. To test this, he was given three parts from the transfer task and told to pick them up and to turn them over. He could not do so, necessitating his removal from the study. As a point of interest, this subject was brought to criterion on the training task. His performance was within the range of the subjects in the group to which he had previously been assigned. Having reached criterion on the training task, the experimenter started him on the transfer task. As had been

Table 1
Descriptive Characteristics of Subjects

Group	IQ		CA (in years)		Workshop Experience (in months)	
	Mean	SD	Mean	SD	Mean	SD
Form-only-Criterion	47.75	5.89	21.81	5.05	33.25	26.59
Form-only-Overlearning	46.31	4.11	21.31	3.94	33.06	28.27
Color-Form-Criterion	48.06	4.99	22.06	6.63	31.69	29.81
Color-Form-Overlearning	46.62	5.90	22.06	5.18	26.00	28.60

predicted, he was unable to perform even the simplest manipulations on the caliper brake.

Replacements for subjects dropped from the experiment were drawn at random from the original pool of subjects in the workshop where the replacement was necessary.

Materials

The apparatus consisted of a 1.14 m x 38.10 cm tray containing 15 compartments, one for each part of the training task. Each compartment can be divided so that the tray then contains enough compartments for the transfer task. Each of the compartments is 38.10 cm long. The dividers are 2.54 cm high. A 1.27 cm divider runs parallel to the front of the tray, 7.62 cm back. The purpose of this divider is to separate the parts that are being used for a trial from the parts to be used in subsequent trials.

The training task was a Bendix, RB-2, coaster brake, consisting of 15 parts. Two groups of subjects worked with the parts as they came from the factory (Form-only Groups). Coding consisted of painting that surface of each part that is facing the subject when it is placed in the proper position for assembly. All but four of the parts can be put on one of two ways, only one of the ways being correct. The transfer task was an Oxford, No. 584, rear, men's lightweight, caliper brake, consisting of 24 parts. The parts of the caliper brake are much smaller than the coaster brake and can be put on up to eight different ways, only one of which is correct. All groups worked with the parts of the transfer assembly as they came from the factory (Form-only). There was a quantity of each part in its respective compartment so as to further approximate workshop conditions and so that there was no interruption within trial blocks, for disassembly.

Experimenters

Four experimenters were used in the experiment, one at each workshop. Four subjects from each workshop were in each group, making the effects of workshops and experimenters constant across groups. Although these variables were confounded, this was the only practical arrangement due to the distance separating the workshops. Further, statistical checks were made to identify any workshop-experimenter effects by including this as a variable in the analysis.

The experimenters were recruited from among volunteers in the workshops and acquaintances of the workshop directors. Previous experience and training included some business schooling for all experimenters, and some volunteer work with retarded children for two of them. None of the experimenters had had specific training for work with the retarded.

The experimenter training period consisted of six half-day sessions. Training included assembly and disassembly of the brakes, demonstration procedures, recording and correction procedures. To test inter-experimenter reliability, the experimenters judged five trials on the training task brake performed by a retarded person not being used in the study. Of a total of

500 judgments (trials x steps x experimenters) there were 12 disagreements. A judgment was considered in disagreement if it contrasted with the judgments of the other experimenters. It should be noted that errors had to be corrected as the subject proceeded, making this test less than conclusive.

Some time was spent discussing the many incidental problems which might arise. Examples of such problems are: what to do when a subject continues to ask if he did something right; what to do if a subject needs assistance on a manipulation step and how to score such steps. Much of this part of the training procedure was based on anecdotal records kept during the pilot studies. To maintain control and maintenance of experimenter consistency, the project director spent an average of half a day on alternate days with each experimenter throughout the experiment.

Procedure

The subject was seated at a table on which the tray was placed, with four disassembled brakes in the compartments. The experimenter was seated beside him. Before the subject's first trial on the training task, and before the subject's first trial on the transfer task, the entire procedure was demonstrated once by the experimenter. The demonstration consisted of the experimenter bringing one of each part forward, in front of the compartment divider, so that one set of parts was in position, then assembling the unit. Errors were made, according to a standardized demonstration format, and verbal cues that would be given when the subject made an error were used. The most frequently used cue was "Try another way," followed by "Good," when the correction was made. Other verbal cues included "Stop," and "Turn it over." The purpose of the demonstration was to show the subject how to respond to the few verbal cues used, and not to teach the task. Both tasks used essentially the same verbal cues.

The first day of the experiment for each subject consisted of one trial performed by the experimenter (demonstration) and three trials by the subject. On all subsequent days, the subject had four trials. Each subject began the transfer task on the day following criterion, or overlearning, on the training task.

Subjects failing to reach criterion by 55 trials were stopped and given a score of 55. This happened with one subject and only on the transfer task.

Data collection consisted of placing a plus (+) or a minus (-) in cells corresponding to steps of the task. The form used was a matrix on which the columns represented steps of the task, and the rows represented trials. A minus was given when the experimenter had to intervene. A self-correction procedure was not used due to the nature of the experiment. That is, if a part did not fit, the subject would have self-corrected and would have been given a plus where a discriminative error was made, resulting in inaccurate data. Instead, the experimenter corrected before the part was placed wrong on the assembly.

Several levels of reinforcement were used. Overall reinforcement consisted of paying each subject the same amount which he was paid for doing his regular work. This varied between workshops and between clients in the same workshop. Immediate reinforcement was given after the subject had corrected an error. When an error was made, the experimenter said, "Try another way." After the correction the experimenter said, "Good." The reinforcer *good* was also given at the end of each trial. A completed assembly constituted a trial.

To correct manipulation problems, it was sometimes necessary to give more than verbal assistance. These assists were recorded both as errors and assists, but because of the nature of the assistance, were not corrected and reinforced as was the case with other errors.

Results

A 2 x 2 x 2 x 4 (Stage X Number of Relevant Dimensions X Amount of Learning X Experimenters) factorial analysis of variance was performed on each of the following dependent variables: trials to criterion; manipulation errors to criterion; and discrimination errors to criterion. Subjects, the replication factor, was a random factor. All other factors were fixed. The confounded effects of Experimenter and Workshop were included as a variable in the analyses to check the effectiveness of the controls. No significant main effects of, or interactions with this variable were found and are not further discussed.

Reliable effects for the trials to criterion dependent variable included main effects due to Number of Relevant Dimensions ($F = 9.84$, 1/48 *df*,

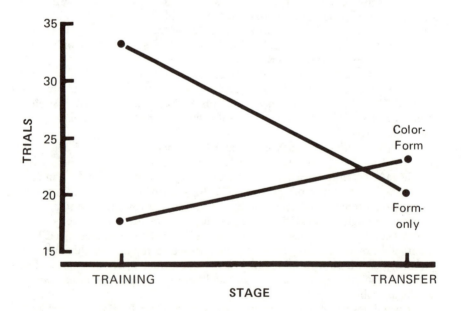

Figure 1. Trials to criterion on training and transfer for the Form-only and Color-Form Groups.

$p < .01$), Stage ($F = 8.56$, 1/48 df, $p < .01$), and Number of Relevant Dimensions by Stage interaction ($F = 54.48$, 1/48 df, $p < .01$). The interaction is shown in Figure 1. The Form-only Group required significantly more trials on the training task than on the transfer task. They also required significantly more trials on the training task than the Color-Form Group on either task.

The only reliable effects for the manipulation errors to criterion dependent variable was due to Stage ($F = 65.52$, 1/48 df, $p < .01$), indicating that the mean number of manipulation errors was greater on training (32.17) than on transfer (10.78).

Reliable effects for discrimination errors to criterion were obtained for Number of Relevant Dimensions ($F = 8.74$, 1/48 df, $p < .01$), Number of Relevant Dimensions by Stage ($F = 51.96$, 1/48 df, $p < .01$), and Number of Relevant Dimensions by Stage by Amount of Learning ($F = 7.21$, 1/48 df, $p < .01$). The means comprising the triple interaction are shown in Figure 2. The interaction reflects the fact that overlearning affected only the number of discrimination errors made by the Color-Form Group on the transfer task ($t = 4.88$, 1/48 df, $p < .01$).

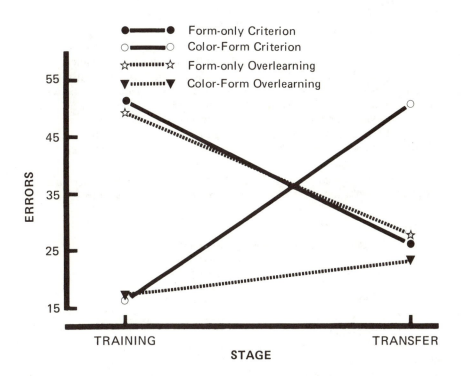

Figure 2. Discrimination errors to criterion for training and transfer with groups as a parameter.

RETENTION STUDY

The retention interval was 1 year. The same independent and dependent variables were used. In addition Order of Presentation was included as an independent variable. That is, half of the subjects started with the caliper brake (transfer task in the acquisition and transfer study) so that an unconfounded retention measure could be obtained for both tasks.

Method

Subjects

Subjects were 53 (83 percent) of the 64 transfer subjects used in the acquisition and transfer study. The other 11 subjects had left the workshops for various reasons.

Materials, Experimenters, and Procedure

The same apparatus, tasks, and experimenters were used. The procedure was the same except that no demonstration and no overlearning trials were given and half of the subjects started on the caliper brake.

Results

A 2 x 2 x 2 x 2 (Number of Relevant Dimensions X Amount of Learning X Order of Presentation X Learning/Retention) analysis of variance, incorporating original learning and retention data was performed. Highly significant main effects on retention were found for all dependent measures. In addition, a number of significant interactions were found. Because all of these interactions were functions of the large between-group differences in original learning, it was decided to report the overall retention effects, but analyze the retention data separately. Table 2 shows the main effects for the six dependent measures.

A 2 x 2 x 2 (Number of Relevant Dimensions X Amount of Learning X Order of Presentation) factorial analysis of variance was performed on the

Table 2
Means and F Ratios for Original Learning and Retention
Using the Combined Data

Measure	Original Learning	Retention	F
Trials to Criterion – Coaster brake	26.09	14.31	66.55
Trials to Criterion – Caliper brake	21.75	16.88	14.71
Manipulation Errors – Coaster brake	33.47	6.18	66.16
Manipulation Errors – Caliper brake	10.98	4.48	90.14
Discrimination – Coaster brake	35.05	9.21	95.53
Discrimination – Caliper brake	32.67	17.74	40.18

retention data, with the same dependent measures as were used for the acquisition data. Reliable effects for the trials to criterion dependent variable included main effects due to Number of Relevant Dimensions on the coaster brake ($F = 6.26$, $1/42$ df, $p < .05$), Order of Presentation on the coaster brake ($F = 8.54$, $1/42$ df, $p < .01$), and Number of Relevant Dimensions by Amount of Learning interaction ($F = 5.95$, $1/42$ df, $p < .05$). The interaction is shown in Figure 3.

Using Scheffe's procedure the interaction is shown to be a result of the superior performance of the Color-Form Overlearning Group over the Form Overlearning Group on the coaster brake ($Ss = 13.32$, $3/42$ df, $p < .05$).

The only other reliable retention effect was for the discrimination errors to criterion dependent measure on the coaster brake. The Color-Form Group had significantly fewer discrimination errors (mean = 5.20) than the Form-only Group (mean = 13.23), ($F = 18.75$, $1/42$ df, $p < .01$).

DISCUSSION FOR BOTH STUDIES

That the manipulation of stimulus variables could achieve rapid and effective training was demonstrated. The addition of a color cue to a task that did not already have one made the task much easier to learn. This supports findings from basic research in discrimination learning with the retarded and suggests a powerful tool for training procedures in sheltered workshops. For example, complex tasks such as electronic circuit board assemblies use color coded parts and are assembled by putting the parts in a particular place on the board. The relevant dimensions for solving the problem are position

	FORM ONLY	COLOR & FORM
CRITERION GROUP	14.38	14.26
OVERLEARNING GROUP	18.80	9.79

Figure 3. Trials to criterion on the coaster brake on retention.

and color, and are usually redundant. The present study suggests that tasks which utilize more than a single relevant dimension might be within the capabilities of the retarded, at least so far as the discriminations are concerned. Such tasks have been thought to be too difficult because of the fine discriminations involved.

Another possible use of cue redundancy is to color code for training purposes, and remove the redundancy when criterion is reached. Using the training task of the present study as an example, clients could be trained with a color-coded brake, and then moved into production of the same assembly without the color coding. How to facilitate the removal of a color cue is the subject of a study in progress. If an efficient procedure is found, the result could be to significantly reduce training time on those contracts that lend themselves to color coding.

That the use of a cue redundancy does not impede transfer to a single relevant dimension task was not supported. The theoretical foundation for this hypothesis was based on interpretation of several studies and not on the studies themselves. The rationale was that the shift from Color-Form to Form-only was an intradimensional (ID) shift and that the shift from a compound to a single relevant dimension represented an easy-to-hard sequence. The nonsignificant findings regarding this hypothesis are not surprising in view of the ambiguous nature of the rationale.

The data, while not supporting the hypothesis, do present an interesting comparison. The performance of the Color-Form Overlearning Group on the transfer task was virtually the same as the two Form-only Groups. This might be interpreted to mean that the use of color, as a cue redundancy with form, does not inhibit transfer to a form-only task when overlearning is given. Failure to find a significant effect might have been due to attenuation of the overlearning effect and should be clarified in subsequent studies.

An overlearning effect had been expected. It was not found. This may be due to the use of a rigid criterion of six correct out of eight consecutive trials. Overlearning has been defined in the present study as 20 trials beyond criterion. Many of the steps, for both tasks, were learned during the early trials and were overlearned by the time criterion was achieved. Thus the overlearning operation was perhaps not effective and a significant Amount of Learning main effect or interaction was not found. Operationally, overlearning may have occurred on many steps of the training task before criterion was reached. In subsequent studies criterion will be lowered to minimize this effect and to clarify the effects of overlearning. In addition, two parts (shoes) will be left out of the training task brake. This results in the elimination of nine manipulation steps and should further clarify the effects of overlearning on the transfer task.

The 1-year retention study produced dramatic retention effects. During the retention interval subjects had no access to the brakes and worked on the same kinds of simple tasks as were performed before the study. The highly significant retention effects support the use of rigid criteria for original learning. Since a portion of sheltered workshop subcontract work is seasonal, these findings have implication for training on such contracts.

The superior performance of the Color-Form Overlearning Group over the Form Overlearning Group on the coaster brake is interpreted as a combination of the effect of color during relearning and the nonsignificant, unexplainable difference between the Form-only and the Form Overlearning Groups.

An important outcome of this study is the discrepancy demonstrated between the capabilities of moderately and severely retarded individuals and what is presently expected of them in sheltered workshops. While certain manipulations produced an increase in learning rate, even the lowest performing groups and individuals did far better than was expected of them by the workshop personnel.

Expectancies held by workshop personnel are a result of their training and experience. Workshops are staffed primarily by professionals from the field of vocational rehabilitation. As a function of their training, these professionals direct the large part of their activity toward the social aspects of the work environment. By admission, they do little in the way of cognitive and skill development, not because they negate the importance of such emphasis, but because they do not have the necessary training to do so. The level of functioning of sheltered workshop clients, then, remains essentially unchanged, apart from the improvement gained through the alleviation of maladaptive social behavior. Workshops presently accept subcontracts that require little in terms of ability or training. A result is a low level of habilitative training and a low level of remuneration. This restriction in selecting contracts is one cause of the unprofitable operation of most sheltered workshops. Increasing income, both for the clients and the workshop, would allow for improved services and programs and a better life for those served.

The discrepancy between the retarded persons' capabilities and the workshop personnel expectancy is further illustrated by describing the initial contacts made for the present study. When contact was first made with the workshops to be involved in the study, the directors were shown the training task brake and asked if they felt their clients were capable of assembling it. All four directors said their most able clients would be incapable of learning the task, even on an assembly line. Assembly of the transfer task brake was regarded as even more difficult. The most limited clients, with the one exception, learned the task.

Subjects were not timed in the present study, but some general information regarding time was obtained both from the pilot studies and the present study. A typical training session of four assemblies lasted less than one-half hour. This tended, after the first session, to be less than 20 minutes. Using 20 minutes as the trial block time and the grand mean for all subjects for each task, 23 trials, the average time taken to reach criterion on each of the two tasks was less than 2 hours.

Workshop personnel, for the most part, balk at the idea of working on a one-to-one basis, training clients for a new contract. Lack of sufficient staff, and success with group methods are given as reasons. However, the kinds of contracts presently found are of a simple nature, easily learned, and consequently do not require much individual training. To implement more habilitative and intensive training programs, profitable and complex contracts are necessary. Such contracts would require more one-to-one training but would also provide funds for sufficient personnel to support a sophisticated training program, making the process circular.

In the present study, even the lowest performing group exceeded the expectancies of the workshop personnel. In addition to this significant performance, it should be noted that manipulation of stimulus variables produced even better performance. It is not good enough to merely elevate expectancies for the persons who are retarded. Procedures must be developed and implemented to realize and challenge these new expectancies. The present experiment represents one step in such a program.*

POSTSTATEMENT

This experiment was supposed to "prove" the value of stimulus control procedures and the capabilities of people labeled moderately and severely retarded. The results exceeded our expectancies. I thought that the field would look at this study, do a 180-degree turnaround, and be cured. I cannot believe how naive I was. The actual results of the study were:

1. It did stimulate change in people's expectancies for what people labeled moderately and severely retarded could do in terms of assembly tasks.

2. It provided the start for a line of research to pursue the development of sheltered workshop and work activity center training programs.

3. It pointed out the value of training on production tasks in sheltered workshops.

4. It added to the demonstration of the usefulness of basic research findings to applied settings.

5. It launched me into an exciting and fun career, and with a bang.

The amount of literature on vocational training of the retarded has rapidly increased since this study was published. I doubt that much, if any, of that can be directly attributed to this study. It is also my impression that the proportion of studies on training to correlational approaches has changed dramatically and that training studies are in the majority.

There are several interesting technical aspects to this study. A distinction is made, for example, between discrimination errors and manipulation errors. Explanations of these terms may be found in the manuscript. For the most part we no longer separate those two kinds of errors. Several members of the

---

*This work was supported in part by Small Grant No. OEG-0-9-232021-0769 (032) from the Bureau of Education for the Handicapped, United States Office of Education, Department of Health, Education and Welfare, and by PHS Grant MH-07346 from the National Institute of Mental Health.

staff of Marc Gold & Associates, Inc., however, still find this to be a meaning-ful distinction. As with most of the parts of our system we are content to leave such issues to the discretion of the person using the system.

Another issue relates to the recruitment of experimenters. In the film *Try Another Way** the statement is made that the initial training time for a trainer is just a few days. That is a very misleading statement. It resulted from the training that we did for this study. What the statement should say is that it takes a few days to train someone to follow a particular set of directions for teaching one particular task to a group of people. The experimenters had no training for doing task analysis or specific preparation for teaching any tasks other than the two in the study. On the other side of the coin, the sys-tem has developed in such a way that while it takes considerable time to teach someone to fully use it, we are able to teach it to individuals with little or no prior formal knowledge or background in the field. The Try Another Way System has been demonstrated effective through five generations of trainers, that is, people who were trained by people who were trained, etc., etc., by our corporate staff have used it successfully. This first study with the bicycle brakes really provided the basis from which all of that grew.

The procedure section of this study states that the purpose of the dem-onstration is to show the subject how to respond to the few verbal cues used, rather than to teach the task. At present we consider demonstration to be a strategy which has little power but which may be very helpful to somebody who is fairly capable and yet not very helpful for someone who finds learning to be difficult. Whether or not to do a demonstration is a trainer decision that is based on the nature of the people being trained and the complexity of the task.

It is important for the reader to recognize the difference between re-search and practice. In a research situation it is often necessary to base deci-sions on considerations for data reliability and accuracy. This study reflects that point in regard to self-correction, an important part of correction pro-cedures. Self-correction represents the point where the trainer assumes that the learner has most of the knowledge needed to be correct but is still making an error. It is hoped that if the trainer does nothing after the error is made, the learner will recognize the error and correct it, and possibly make no errors on that particular step thereafter. In a research situation this would cause some problems in data collection in some cases. Thus, in this study self-correction was not used.

This study gave us the feeling that color coding was going to be very helpful. Our current thinking about that will be described in the poststate-ment for the study on the removal of a color cue (Chapter 12). Incidentally, we do feel that tasks which intrinsically use color coding, such as printed circuit board assembly, should be carefully considered for training situations since they do provide strong discriminative assistance for the learners.

---

*Glenn Roberts (Producer). *Try Another Way*. Indianapolis: Film Productions of Indian-apolis, 1975.

In the third paragraph of the discussion section, one will find the following sentence: "The nonsignificant findings regarding this hypothesis are not surprising in view of the ambiguous nature of the rationale." What this would have said if I had expressed it in English is that for this particular hypothesis, we were full of baloney all along and reaching for the stars, and it's no wonder we got those results. This section also mentions two effects that need to be looked at in future studies, both of them having to do with overlearning effects. As our research program developed, we changed our minds about needing to study this more and never did follow up on these two points. Further in the article the discussion of retention effects suggests the value of learning to a strong criterion if sheltered workshops are going to have seasonal contracts. Two years after this study was done, Steve Zider, who is currently operations analyst for Marc Gold & Associates, Inc., was employed in a work activity center where a particular group producing spring loaded hinges at 100% of the industrial norm lost the contract for a 6-month period because of a general slowdown in the economy. Six months later the contract was returned to the shop. During the first week of production after 6 months of being away from the contract the productivity of the group was 92% of the industrial norm. This seems to be an interesting empirical validation of the value of training to a strong criterion.

Near the end of the manuscript there is a discussion of one-to-one training. This was published 7 years ago, and still rehabilitation programs and educational programs strongly reject the notion that individualized instruction is efficient and possible within existing circumstances.

Finally, the point is made that elevating expectancies is simply a first step. Frequently our work will be described as showing the potential of the mentally retarded. Our position is that potential can never be shown. We have merely shown persons to be capable of doing something that they did not do before. If we then go on and teach them something far more complex, we have done that again. There would seem, however, to be no end to how far we might carry this, never arriving at a place that showed potential, because there would always still be somewhere else to go. The other point at the end of the article is that if we are really to change the life circumstances of people labeled retarded, we must effect changes in more than people's expectancies. Changing expectancies, however, is where any hope to make major changes must begin.

CHAPTER 7

Research on the Vocational Habilitation of the Retarded: The Present, The Future

Marc W. Gold

PRESTATEMENT

Thank goodness I wrote this chapter. It is really the only academic writing I have done. When Norman Ellis invited me to write the chapter, I was very excited. The *International Review* is held in high regard by researchers in the field of mental retardation. Ellis' editorial strategy is to invite people to write chapters but reserve the right to accept or reject them depending on their quality. I never worked so hard writing something. I spent the entire summer of 1972 doing literature reviews and putting the chapter together.

The way the invitation came about is worth noting. Norm started a series of conferences that were, and still are, held once a year in Gatlinburg, Tennessee. They are called The Gatlinburg Conferences. From 100 to 150 researchers gather each year for a few days to present, argue, and share. In 1970 I was invited to present a paper on middle-road research and on vocational training of the retarded. To the best of my knowledge, this panel (Rex Forehand, Charlie Galloway, and I) was the first to present applied research at The Gatlinburg Conferences. The panel was well received, which provided a real high for all of us. Sometime after that presentation Keith Scott and Norm talked, and from that came an invitation for this chapter.

In addition to applied research being a fairly new thing for the *International Review*, it was also the first time there had been a chapter on the vocational aspects of mental retardation in the research literature, with the very notable exception of the excellent chapter by Wolf Wolfensberger in the book *Mental Retardation*, edited by Al Baumeister, which came out in 1967. Few of Wolfensberger's present followers are aware of this chapter or of his prior interest in the vocational aspects of mental retardation. The reference for that chapter (Wolfensberger, 1967) may be found in the chapter presented here. For those of you who have not read Wolfensberger's chapter, I strongly suggest that you do. You will find it still full of valuable information 13 years after its publication. One last note on that chapter. It was very helpful to me in writing this chapter, both in terms of content and style.

This chapter originally appeared in N. R. Ellis (Ed.), *International review of research in mental retardation*, Vol. 6 (New York: Academic Press, 1973). Reprinted by permission of the publisher.

Most of the writing in the present chapter was done, as I mentioned, during the summer of 1972. The large section on vocational evaluation actually started out as a term paper for one of the first courses for my PhD program at the University of Illinois. I expanded it somewhat, brought it up to date, cleaned up most of the problems that it had, and built it into this chapter. Incidentally, I got a *B* on the original paper, from my good friend Robert Henderson.

I. INTRODUCTION

The intention of this review is to describe the present status of research on the vocational habilitation of the retarded and to propose directions for future efforts. This is not intended as a review of the literature. References are used only to support statements made and to provide the reader with resources for more in-depth study. The vocational training of mentally retarded individuals presently utilizes the resources of three primary disciplines: rehabilitation, psychology, and education. Research from these disciplines is discussed. Research from two other sources not normally associated with rehabilitation is also discussed in terms of its potential contribution to the field. These are industrial management and industrial engineering. Throughout this paper the term *field* will be used where reference is to disciplines, activities, individuals, and organizations whose primary function is the habilitation of the mentally retarded.

An attempt is made in this article to emphasize the importance of the relationship between principles developed in laboratory settings and the application of these principles to vocational training. For the reader who is content with existing levels of expectancy presently held by society and by professionals in the field, or who believes that we have succeeded so long as the retarded are kept busy in workshops or placed on any job, this review has little value. For those who believe that there is a substantial gap between how the retarded function vocationally, at present, and how they could function, this paper contains descriptions of what is being done and what could be done to achieve the goal of maximum opportunity for growth.

Before exploring the possibilities for change, it is necessary to provide a perspective. While this volume is international in scope, the context to which this article refers is the United States, where the economic system is capitalistic, and where a surplus labor force (the unemployed) is almost always present.

A. A Social Perspective

Historically, people have organized themselves to accommodate, change, or eliminate other people who are sufficiently different to call unfavorable attention to themselves (Heiny, 1971). Farber (1968) perceives such people as constituting a surplus population. In terms of work, they are either not specifically trained for existing jobs in the labor market, or they are incapable of, unwilling to, or prevented from filling such positions. He further points out that society could easily function without them. Because of the considerable energy spent on their maintenance however, they play an important organizational role by (1) requiring the generation of special institutions such as special education and vocational rehabilitation, (2) by providing an excess labor pool, and (3) by aiding in the perpetuation of social classes.

The implications of Farber's perceptions to the vocational training of the retarded are clear: some of the energies presently used for *maintenance* of this unproductive portion of the population should be directed toward *training* the retarded to somehow effectively compete in the labor market with other members of the surplus population who are not additionally stigmatized by the label "retarded." This, of course, is the goal of research on the vocational habilitation of the retarded.

Farber suggests four kinds of programming which could be used to facilitate the assimilation of the retarded into the mainstream of society: (1) better use of techniques for training the mentally retarded to adapt; (2) changes in family structure and environment; (3) restructuring of societal institutions and their interactions; and (4) changes in the values by which society functions. Farber (1968, and personal communication) is pessimistic about the vocational and social prognosis of the retarded in the absence of a revised modern society. The position is taken here that certain changes would greatly enhance the chances for vocational viability of the retarded, and that the nation is fast developing a technology that will allow achieving this goal within the existing value structure of contemporary society. The larger goal of complete assimilation, including independent or semi-independent living and full participation in society, is another matter. There is a great deal of activity in this country attempting to revise institutional arrangements in the direction of community residential units (e.g., Kirk, Karnes, & Kirk, 1955; Kugel & Wolfensberger, 1969). The interaction between this activity and the development of a technology of instruction will certainly have an impact on society. The ultimate success of fully assimilating the retarded into society, as Farber points out, will still be dependent on the degree to which contemporary values are modified toward personal growth of all people rather than institutional efficiency.

Related to the influence of the values of society there is the basic issue of societal expectancies for the retarded. The interaction of economic and industrial growth with the development of increased societal awareness has resulted in the set of perceptions which society and the social sciences presently hold regarding the retarded. The amount of national resources committed to the retarded, the kinds of programs developed and funded, and even the specific kinds of skills taught are reflections of these perceptions and interact to perpetuate existing practices and expectancies and to resist change. The large discrepancy between the kinds of lives led by the retarded in the United States and in European countries such as Sweden (Kylen, Sommarstrom, & Akesson, 1971), Holland (Dybwad, 1961), Denmark (Dolnick, 1971), and England (Williams, 1967) must be, in the main, attributed to our societal expectancies.

How this country developed to its present level regarding expectancies for the retarded is not appropriate for discussion here. However, a few comments about the vocational training literature will serve to complete the perspective into which Sections II and III are intended to be placed.

B. A Pedagogical Perspective

The vocational habilitation of the retarded has a long history, in terms of both service and research programs. One major criticism of virtually all of the literature, experimental and programmatic, is that it has described behavior of the retarded in the context of simple, menial tasks which require little training, skill, or attention, even for the retarded. No distinction has been made between performance on the simple tasks used and more complex tasks. The literature is consistent in its finding that the retarded, who are unsuccessful in competitive employment, fail because of their inability to handle the social interactions necessary to function in a work setting. Although a positive relationship has been shown between production rate and employers' judgment of job success (Chaffin, 1969), no identified studies report failure to perform on the actual task as the reason for dismissal. The author contends that this consistent finding is an artifact of the jobs on which the retarded are placed. That is, they are placed only on those jobs where little or no training is required to learn the necessary skills. This relates back to the inappropriate expectancies held by both professionals and the public, handed down since early work with the retarded (e.g., Delp, 1957; Tredgold, 1908), which preclude placing them on jobs that require more than minimal skill training. If expectancies are to be revised, all research findings and activities to date must be considered only within the context of performance on simple tasks. Data on production, deviant behavior, perceptual-motor behavior, attention span, and social interaction might well be influenced by the level of difficulty of the task. With very little data available where complex tasks were used, an incomplete picture of the retarded is all that is available.

A second major criticism of the literature is the lack of definable training techniques. The lack of training purported here may seem surprising because of the frequency with which the term appears. When *training* appears throughout our literature, it almost without exception refers to exposure rather than treatment, or, it refers to placing clients on a job station where it is hoped training occurs. Training, as used in this review, refers to controlled, systematic manipulations of the environment, administered in such a way that its effect can be measured and recorded. The rigidity of this definition is, in part, a reaction to the osmotic nature of what is usually called training. Perusal of the literature reveals hundreds of descriptions of training programs which yield no evidence of specific techniques for developing vocational behavior (e.g., Affleck, 1967; Etienne & Morlock, 1971; Greenstein & Fangman, 1969; Kolstoe, 1960). Organizational structures in which development is supposed to occur, descriptions of content to be covered, and resources involved are usually reported and not the actual mechanisms which directly effect development. There is an emerging trend away from exposure and toward training. Changes are occurring across the entire range of activities embodied in the field (e.g., Burke, 1971; Prehm, 1970). The rest of this chapter explores such changes in terms of existing knowledge and new directions.

II. THE PRESENT

This section attempts to describe the existing state of the field. The age of many of the references attests to the paucity of activity, making the past and present synonymous in some areas. Hopefully, an accurate perspective of conditions present through 1971 is given.

A. Service Programs

Service programs are defined here as programs designed primarily to prepare the students or clients in their charge for successful adult living.

Schools and workshops are the two major sources of vocational training service programs for the retarded. Included in these categories are institutional and noninstitutional settings and public and private agencies. While patterns of service are changing, in the direction of community-based residential facilities and independent living, existing service programs can still be classified as school or workshop programs.

1. Schools

School programs for the retarded have existed in one form or another for many years (e.g., Cegelka, 1970; Kokaska, 1968; Mathews, 1919; Patterson & Rundquist, 1933; Thomas, 1928). The literature on school programs has the following characteristics: (1) Most of the literature is descriptive (e.g., Muller & Lewis, 1966; Sengstock, 1964; Etienne & Morlock, 1971). (2) Research on school programs is primarily concerned with the effects of *in situ* variables such as socioeconomic level, employment status, and IQ, and uses follow-up data as the primary measure of success (e.g., Doleshal & Jackson, 1970; Kennedy, 1966; McIntosch, 1949; Miller, 1954). (3) Almost none of the research is experimental in terms of manipulating training procedures (see Section II, B, 2). (4) The emphasis is on organization structure (e.g., Budde, 1969).

The current trend, which originated with the work of Eskridge (1964), is toward programs operated jointly by school systems and state departments of vocational rehabilitation (e.g., Ayers, 1969; Brolin & Thomas, 1971; Clark, 1967; Henze & Meissner, 1970; Younie, 1966). With the emphasis still on organization, little evidence of the training process appears. Direct observation of programs across the country leads the author to the following conclusions: (1) Little connection exists between classroom activities and work activities. (2) Where work experience is part of the program, training is left to the students' job supervisors. (3) Criteria for success are poorly defined. (4) Subjective evaluation of student performance by the job supervisor is often the only measure by which the student is judged. (5) There is a reliance on the creativity and enthusiasm of staff in the absence of a technology of systematic training.

As university programs specifically designed to train personnel for secondary programs develop (e.g., Brolin & Thomas, 1971; Hamerlynck & Espeseth, 1969; Redkey, 1971; Younie & Clark, 1969), attention should shift away from organizational matters and toward the technology of instruction.

2. Sheltered Workshops

The history of the sheltered workshop movement for the retarded is well documented elsewhere (e.g., DiMichael, 1960; Nelson, 1971; Wolfensberger, 1967). This movement has resulted in the establishment of three main types of workshops for the retarded: the transitional shop, where clients coming from school programs, homes, or institutions prepare for placement into competitive employment; the extended-care or terminal shop, where clients believed to be incapable of achieving competitive employment work for indefinite periods; and the comprehensive shop which attempts to service both types of clients. The comprehensive shop, which often provides services for persons with a variety of handicaps, is the most common, probably because of the diverse needs and limited resources of most communities. Some workshops are beginning to accept only clients sponsored by divisions of vocational rehabilitation (transitional shops). Other shops, influenced by parent groups and departments of mental health, are moving more toward extended care services. With the tremendous proliferation of many types of sheltered workshops, meaningful quantitative documentation of trends is difficult.

In addition to the population being served, workshops differ from one another in their philosophy regarding the function of work in the shop. For those agencies with a heavy emphasis on counseling and placement the shop is often perceived (but not described) as a holding place between counseling sessions or before placement. Shop staff are viewed as having to do more with goods and production than with clients and often are not included as an integral part of the habilitation program. The position taken here is that this perception usually results in major staff problems, a caste system, and a significant amount of client time spent in nonhabilitative activities. Where counseling and placement are heavily emphasized, work is not usually seen as the medium for change and growth.

In agencies where the emphasis is more on extended care than on placement, work is again perceived as a holding device, but in this case, a permanent one. Work is what is required to keep clients busy, to help support the shop, and to maintain an image of productivity. In the extended-care shop, one seldom finds a systematic attempt to increase productivity on existing contracts or to obtain increasingly complex and remunerative contracts. As far back as 1958, Dubrow (1958) expressed the feeling that extended care workshops should be largely self-supporting. However, few, if any, such shops exist today, 13 years later.

In comprehensive shops, where there are varying degrees of emphasis on counseling and placement and varying ratios of transitional clients to extended-care clients, all of the criticisms given for extended care and transitional shops are applicable. Little real training is carried out in the shop. Contracts and production remain at menial, low-remuneration levels, and little attempt is made to change. Excuses for the status quo typically include staff having little time to seek more habilitative and remunerative contracts, or to work on new programs; the lack of good contracts even when sought; and general labor conditions. Although the value of a full-time procurement person is well documented (e.g., Dolnick, 1963, 1964; Wolfensberger, 1967), few such positions exist. It is not easy to demonstrate the availability of good contracts. There are several possible reasons for the difficulty: (1) Workshop personnel have no confidence in their clients' ability to perform accurately and consistently on anything more than very simple, repetitive tasks. (2) Clients are perceived by the working community, and the professional community, as being capable of only the most menial, nuisance-type work. (3) Procurement officers do not have contacts established for more complex contracts, except where a limiting bias has already been firmly established. (4) Most shops are not presently equipped, in terms of staff, attitude, machinery, or industrial know-how to handle effectively the increased training, quality-control, and production demands of such contracts. Highly sophisticated techniques of production efficiency and client training (see Section II, B, 2) are just beginning to evidence themselves in workshops.

Regardless of the type of shop, one issue stands out above all others as the key to successful shop operation—contracts. The kind and amount of work found in the shop is of paramount importance.

The main difference between sheltered workshops and other service facilities (e.g., schools, institutions, hospitals) is that workshops utilize work as the primary medium for client development. At least, philosophically this is true. In most cases the work found in sheltered workshops does not provide this medium. Instead, nonwork activities are instituted to effect change, or the shop merely provides a milieu and hopes change occurs.

If the full potential of sheltered workshops is to be realized, major emphasis must be on contracts or subcontracts. They must be selected on the basis of habilitative value. The ideal work contract has the following characteristics: (1) It requires skills that must be taught rather than skills which the clients already have. This includes some skills learned and transferred from other contracts. (2) There must be sufficient lead time to set up production and training to allow for client considerations and not just production considerations. (3) The contract should be heavy on labor. That is, the amount of shop space taken up by the contract should be in proportion to the number of clients employed on the job. If a contract takes up 40% of the shop floor, it should provide full-time work for at least 40% of the clients. This emphasis is the opposite for industry where labor is kept at a minimum. (4) The contract should have enough different operations to allow for a variety of job stations. A simple contract has only simple operations. A complex contract has the potential for a range of different operations. (5) The contract should be profitable for both the shop and the clients. Bidding should take into consideration the same factors that are considered by any subcontractor. This would exclude nonwork programs, counseling, and some, but not all, of the time needed to train clients. If clients are producing with at least the same quality as nonhandicapped workers, and are paid a wage commensurate with nonhandicapped workers, labor rate should *not* be the factor reduced to allow for competitive bidding. Production efficiency, client training, material handling, and service to the customer should be the main parameters manipulated to effect competitive bidding.

The points mentioned above represent only an initial attempt to clarify the importance of contracts. But, it seems clear that a truly habilitative milieu, for both transitional and extended-care clients, depends heavily on the effective use of contracts. For a highly relevant industrial perspective the reader is referred to Brewser (1969) and Levine (1967).

The issue of automation is directly related to both school and workshop programs in terms of its effects on contracts and placement. An excellent discussion on automation and the mentally retarded is found in the work of Kokaska (1968). His review provides a perspective from outside and within the field. He concludes that the retarded have evidenced the ability to maintain themselves in competitive employment despite the advent of automation. DiMichael (1969), who has periodically and accurately described the rehabilitation field, evidences optimism regarding the effects of automation on the handicapped. He points out the qualitative rather than quantitative changes in the labor force, and also gives examples of how the handicapped have been able to adapt. In a review of current literature, Nixon (1970) identifies further support for an optimistic outlook for unskilled and semi-skilled labor in the next decade. He also discusses the need for more research on job analysis for adequate matching of retardates' full potential with specific job opportunities. Research related to this and other issues in the field is discussed below.

B. Research

Research is defined here as activities which have, as their primary focus, obtaining information leading to the development of a technology for the field. Because it is current practice to separate evaluation and training, they are discussed separately. However, an attempt will be made later in the article to justify merging evaluation and training into a single and far more efficacious endeavor than is the case at present.

1. Prediction and Evaluation

The extensive literature on vocational evaluation and prediction is full of *statistical* significance but devoid of *practical* significance. Dependent measures of performance on the tests developed and utilized are correlated with measures on instruments for which validity and reliability have not been established with the populations, and under the conditions in which they are used. Where prediction is the goal, concurrent validity is often used

as an index of predictive validity. In addition, criteria for vocational success are often established retrospectively, and are not easily generalized
across work situations. Despite the boredom likely to be generated, the
author felt an extensive review was necessary in order to substantiate the
criticisms given above and at the end of this section. Consequently, the
literature on prediction and evaluation is euphemistically reviewed here in
some detail.

a. **Intelligence Tests.** Most studies indicate that intelligence tests correlate with work potential, but have limited utility as predictive measures.
In a study comparing a group of retardates employed outside the workshop
with a group of "terminal" workshop subjects, a statistically significant
difference was found between groups on the Performance sections of the
WAIS and the Wechsler-Bellvue, but not on the Full Scale (Appell, Williams,
& Fishell, 1962). In another study Kolstoe (1961) found no statistically
significant differences between the IQ scores of employed and unemployed
retardates. Verbal and Performance scores were not discussed. Meadow and
Greenspan (1961), using the WISC as part of a battery of tests, found that
information obtained from this battery was not sufficient for predictive
use. Fry (1956) found a performance efficiency quotient derived from the
WAIS Performance IQ to be the best predictive measure of work success.
This study was done using 38 institutionalized girls to determine the qualifications necessary for successful performance both inside and outside an
institution. The quotient was correlated with a job rating from a laundry
foreman, with assistance from a psychologist.

Bae (1968) found that once the subjects in her study were screened and
accepted into training programs, good and fair trainees were not differen-
tiated by WISC and WAIS Verbal, Performance, or Full Scale IQ scores.

The Binet has been shown to correlate with other tests used for vocational assessment. Wagner and Hawver (1965), working with a population
of trainable adults, found a correlation of .64 between the Binet and the
O'Conner Finger Dexterity Test ($p < .001$). Significant correlations were
also found between the Binet and several other manual dexterity tests.

The Porteus Maze Test was studied to determine its value in differen-
tiating employed from unemployed retardates. Tobias and Gorelick (1962)
describe a study done at the Association for the Help of Retarded Children
(AHRC) in New York City. The subjects consisted of 32 ex-trainees of a
workshop. Sixteen had held jobs in competitive industry for at least 6 months.
The other 16 had not found employment. All subjects had at least 1 year of
training. The groups were matched on IQ. Results from the Maze Test yielded
a difference between groups significant at the .01 level. With a dividing point
of 8.5 (raw score), the Porteus Maze Test would have correctly assessed 24
of the 33 subjects in the study. According to Porteus (1959), the test measures "planfullness." Tobias and Gorelick suggest that the reason the Maze
Test predicted success in competitive employment but not in the sheltered
workshop is that, because of the extensive control of the environment in the
workshop setting, the value of "planfullness" is eliminated. In competitive
employment such control is usually not found. It has been the author's

experience to observe just the opposite. That is, industrial production is characterized by organization, efficiency, and constancy of movement, and other controls, while sheltered workshops are usually inefficient, in comparison, and lack control of all but the most deviant, nonproductive behavior. A correlation of .35 ($p < .01$) was found between the Maze Test and a work efficiency rating based on the average hourly earnings for a 4-week period, using 65 trainees.

In an earlier study, Tobias and Gorelick (1960c) found that the Goodenough Scale could predict work efficiency as well as the WAIS Full Scale IQ does, but not as well as the WAIS Performance IQ. The Evaluation Tests (Tobias, 1960), a battery used at AHRC, was used for the correlation. The Goodenough Scale and the WAIS Full Scale correlated .40 and .43, respectively, with the Evaluation Tests. The WAIS Performance IQ correlated .50 with the Evaluation Tests. All three correlations are significant at the .01 level.

b. Manual Dexterity Tests. Many manual dexterity tests have been used with the retarded (e.g., Ferguson, 1958; C. H. Patterson, 1964; Mocek, Lerner, Rothstein, & Umbenhaur, 1965), although the retarded have not been included in the normative sample. The Wagner and Hawver study (1965) previously described ran multiple correlations between the following manual dexterity tests: O'Conner Finger Dexterity Test; O'Conner Tweezer Dexterity Test; Minnesota Rate of Manipulation Placing Test; and Minnesota Rate of Manipulation Turning Test. Correlations of each of the four tests with each of the other three ran from .66 to .82, and were all significant at the .001 level. This would indicate that they are all, to some degree, measuring the same thing. Each of these tests was correlated with the criterion ranking of the chief instructor which was based on the following criteria: (1) respects authority and is willing to take directions; (2) generally completes assignments; (3) work is usually of good quality; (4) seems to get along reasonably well with co-workers; and (5) learns new workshop skills without too much difficulty. Correlations with the ranking were: O'Conner Tweezer Dexterity Test—.50 ($p < .01$); Minnesota Rate of Manipulation Turning Test—.53 (p < .01); O'Conner Finger Dexterity Test—.66 ($p < .001$); and Minnesota Rate of Manipulation Placing Test—.64 ($p < .001$). A Kendall Coefficient, which is a measure of interrelationship between rankings of all variables, was significant at the .001 level, indicating that some general factor is involved.

In the correlational study done by Wagner and Hawver (1965), the Goodenough-Harris Test correlated .48 with the O'Conner Finger Dexterity ($p < .05$); .38 with the O'Conner Tweezer Dexterity Test (not significant); .54 with the Minnesota Rate of Manipulation Placing Test ($p < .01$); .48 with the Minnesota Rate of Manipulation Turning Test ($p < .05$); .82 with the Bender-Gestalt Test ($p < .001$); .55 with the Stanford-Binet (L, M, L-M) ($p < .01$); and .71 with a criterion ranking based on workshop performance as evaluated by the chief instructor of the workshop ($p < .001$). Twenty-seven subjects, 11 females and 16 males, were used. The ages ranged from 21 to 34 years (mean = 23.7, SD = 3.1). IQs ranged from 13 to 49 (mean = 34.4, SD = 8.8).

Distefano, Ellis, and Sloan (1958) measured the proficiency of mental defectives on a variety of motor tests and examined the interrelationships among the tests, MA and CA. The subjects consisted of 40 males ranging in MA from 5.33 to 11.50 years (mean = 9.90, SD = 2.19). The range for CA was from 9.66 to 29.00 years (mean = 19.73, SD = 5.10). There were 36 females. The CA range for the females was from 11.48 to 32.41 years (mean = 22.25, SD = 7.07). MA range was from 5.50 to 10.83 years (mean = 9.14, SD = 2.01). The tests used were the Lincoln-Oseretsky Motor Development Scale, the Rail Walking Test, the Minnesota Rate of Manipulation Turning Test, the Hand-Steadiness Test, and the Strength of Grip Test. Except for performance on the Minnesota Rate of Manipulation Turning Test, the males were more proficient than the females, although this difference was significant only on the Rail Walking Test ($p < .05$). The Lincoln-Oseretsky turning and placing performances were found to be the most highly related to MA in both the male and female groups. Correlations between the Lincoln-Oseretsky and MA were .40 for males and .58 for females. It was inferred that intelligence and motor proficiency, as measured by the tests used, are positively related in mental deficients whose CA is beyond that time during which rapid development in motor and intellectual ability usually occurs.

Elkin (1967), in a correlational study of work sample tasks, intelligence tests and dexterity tests, found significant correlations between his four work sample tasks, between age and total work performance, between length of institutionalization and task performance by males, and between male total work scores and 17 of the 19 predictive variables used in the study.

Tobias and Gorelick (1960a) studied the effectiveness of the Purdue Pegboard in evaluating work potential of retarded adults. They found that, as the Purdue Pegboard increases in complexity, so does its linear relationship with intelligence. Using 73 retardates with IQs ranging from 35 to 78 (mean = 63, SD = 10.6), they found that the WAIS Full Scale IQ correlated .56 ($p < .01$) with the Right- Left- Both scores of the Purdue, and .67 ($p < .01$) with the Assembly score. The WAIS Verbal IQ correlated only .34 ($p < .01$) and .43 ($p < .01$) respectively, with the Purdue tests. But the WAIS Performance IQ correlated .57 ($p < .01$) with the Right- Left- Both score and .73 ($p < .01$) with the Assembly score. A correlation of .44 was found between the WAIS Full Scale IQ and the wire clamp assembling. The correlation between the Purdue and the wire clamp assembling was .75. No correlation was reported between the WAIS Performance IQ and the assembly task. A correlation of .54 ($p < .01$) was found between the Purdue and hourly average of disassembled screws. This was found using a group of 25 retardates ranging in IQ from 30 to 50. In another analysis, a correlation of .64 ($p < .01$) was found between the Purdue and hourly earnings. This was with a group of 68 retardates. No other information was given for this group. Tobias and Gorelick concluded that the Purdue Pegboard appeared to be a superior instrument in predicting productivity on the type of work available at the workshop where their research took place. For a nonfield perspective on dexterity tests, the reader is referred to Fleishman and Hempel (1954).

c. **Work Sample Tasks.** The work sample technique, also known by several other names (Bailey, 1958; Cohen & Williams, 1961; Overs, 1964; Sinick, 1962; Rehabilitation Institute for the Crippled and Disabled, 1967; Usdane, 1953), has become quite popular. It involves standardizing and obtaining normative data on typical work tasks. It is used extensively throughout the country (Speiser & Cohen, 1966), although the rationale on which it is based currently has only face validity. DiMichael (1960) noted that the mentally retarded perform below norms on standardized tests of manual ability, and that actual job samples have a face validity lacking in standardized tests. He also points out that the client can be compared with other employees who are producing in the same workshop. Sinick (1962) pointed out that factors such as recency of schooling, educational deprivation, insufficient motivation, excessive anxiety, cultural deficiencies, cultural atypicality, and bilingualism are less likely to influence work task performance than conventional tests. The resemblance of work tasks to actual jobs, causing the client to believe that he is truly being trained for such a job, is given as a possible advantage. Bailey (1958) describes a number of benefits derived from the use of the work sample approach. Among these are the following: (1) They provide prevocational experience. (2) The client learns to see, feel, smell, and become fatigued by work. (3) The client is motivated. (4) The client gains a realistic concept of work. (5) The client readjusts goals or gains confidence and seeks higher attainment. (6) The work trial method helps those who cannot succeed find out before there is too much frustration. These questionable benefits seem more relevant to other than the retarded, if at all.

Several approaches in the development of work sample instruments are found in the literature. DiMichael (1960) advocates a standardized battery of work samples to assess different abilities. However, there obviously needs to be evidence that differential performance on work tasks is related to differential performance on jobs (Sinick, 1962).

Overs, Koechert, and Bergman (1964) discuss the compromise between reliability and validity. Those instruments that are highly reliable, such as many of the manual dexterity tests, lack predictive validity because of the narrow range of behavior they sample. Instruments such as behavior rating scales or ratings of performance on subcontract work in a workshop may be highly meaningful, but lack reliability because of the absence of standardized methods of reporting, measuring, and describing behavior. The potential value of the work sample approach, then, is to develop standardized methods of reporting behavior in a situation that is commensurate with the kind of work the client is likely to be doing. Overs and his colleagues describe an attempt to do this. Although the project was not designed specifically to meet the needs of the mentally retarded, all of the principles discussed apply. Typical psychometric test development procedures were used. This would seem a superfluous note but for the absence of such procedures in the development of many work sample batteries.

The Evaluation Tests (Tobias, 1960) is a work sample battery designed for use with the mentally retarded. The tasks consist of folding table cloths, sorting buttons, lacing display cards, assembling pistol key chains, assembling puzzles, packaging poker chips, and racking for electroplating. Skills tested include manual dexterity, visual-motor coordination, ability to follow directions, the ability to follow a sequence of multiple, ordered operations, degrees of depth perception and spatial relationships, and the ability to count incidental to completing tasks.

The test is administered under natural workshop conditions. A trial consists of the completion of a given number of units. The time taken for completion comprises the raw score which is converted to a percentile score. Before the first trial the client learns the task to be done. Upon demonstration of the ability to execute the task the test begins. Three trials are given for each test, and are administered 2 days apart. Trials are also separated by other kinds of work, or by trials on other tests in the battery. Administration of the battery takes up to 3 weeks. The third trial is considered most important. It still only represents nonreinforced performance, but after practice. Normative data were obtained using a population of 60 retardates, some with accompanying handicaps, ranging in age from 17 to 25 years. The IQ range was from 42 to 83 (mean = 66.5, SD = 8.18). Intercorrelations between the tests show that most of the tests seem related. That is, clients who do well on one test tend to do relatively well on the other tests. The pistol-assembly task, which correlated the highest with the other tests, was used for comparisons with other criteria. The percent decrease in time taken to complete 50 assemblies over trials correlated -.07 (not significant) with IQ. This suggests that intelligence is not related to the rate of improvement. The correlation between IQ and hourly wage was .14 (not significant). The correlation between the Evaluation Tests and hourly wage over a 1-month period was .52 ($p < .01$). This suggests that the tests might have some predictive value in similar situations, especially with the development of local norms. It should be noted that the group from which normative data were collected had a mean IQ in the higher range of retardation. Further analysis, or more data, is needed before this instrument could be used confidently with lower level retardates.

Ladas (1961), using a standardized battery almost identical with the one developed at AHRC (Tobias, 1960), studied the relationship between work sample learning rates and workshop productivity. He found that learning rate was not independent of other factors and was not effective, in this study, as a predictor.

Katz (1959) found that the mean of a battery of work samples (Ladas, 1961) correlated .72 with the Purdue Pegboard, .68 with the Bennet Hand Tool Dexterity Test, and .69 with the O'Conner Tweezer Dexterity Test. Although information was not reported for particular subjects used for the study, the workshop report shows a mean IQ for the workshop clients of approximately 52.

The TOWER System (Rehabilitation Institute for the Crippled and Disabled, 1967) is a work sample battery developed for use with the handicapped. It utilizes over 100 work samples covering the following 14 broad occupational families: clerical, drafting, drawing, electronics assembly, jewelry manufacturing, leather goods, lettering, machine shop, mail clerk, optical mechanics, pantograph engraving, sewing machine operation, welding, and workshop assembly. The nature of many of the work samples, the amount of receptive and expressive language required, in addition to the general criticism of work samples included in this section, suggests that the TOWER System has limited value for all but the most capable retardates found in vocational training programs.

Criticisms of work sample batteries include the following: (1) Work samples are more a training exercise than an instrument of evaluation as traditionally conceived. (2) They are time consuming, in need of continual revision, and devoid of pressures that characterize the competitive work situation (Blackman & Siperstein, 1968). (3) Scores obtained during the initial practice periods in an activity do not predict terminal efficiency (Parker & Fleishman, 1961). (4) Existing batteries are very expensive.

These criticisms are appropriate because of the way in which such tests are presently administered. Problems inferred from these criticisms can be eliminated. If measures of acquisition rate and performance rate are made separately and under standardized conditions, and if norms are developed, then the instrument may legitimately be considered evaluative, even in the traditional sense. The difference is the kind of information obtained. With most skill tests rate of performance is the measure taken, with little effort made either to consider the effects of acquisition on this measure, or to look at acquisition rate as equally important information. It is not surprising that Parker and Fleishman (1961), and others, find scores obtained during the initial practice periods to be less than representative of terminal efficiency. For the retarded it is even less surprising to find acquisition and performance confounded during early trials, which is usually the only condition under which test data are obtained.

The criticism by Blackman and Siperstein (1968) that work samples are time consuming may be correct, but must be considered in light of the quantity and quality of information obtained per unit of time spent. In addition, if the client is learning the kinds of skills he can use later, while he is being evaluated, this would make much more efficient use of such time.

Work samples need not be devoid of pressures that characterize the competitive work situation. Pressure could be one of the parameters added to present test batteries. For example, having learned and then produced a particular work sample task, a client could work on that task next to other workers, or be instructed to produce a given number of units in a specified period of time. In addition to subjective evaluation, the comparison of his performance under one of these conditions with his performance under the no-pressure conditions following acquisition would yield quantifiable, objective information relevant to his functioning under pressure. The general procedure inferred from this example could be used to evaluate many aspects of work-oriented behaviors.

d. **Other Relevant Research.** In a study that has some implication for the evaluation procedure, Tobias and Gorelick (1960b) studied the tendency of

retardates to arrange and organize their completed work far beyond requirements of the job. The term used to describe this phenomenon was "orderliness." They used the entire population in a workshop (AHRC) which consisted
of 60 retardates with a mean age of just below 22 years and ranging in IQ
from 26 to 75. The procedure was to test one retardate at a time. Each subject worked on a simple assembly task. Two trials of 1 hour each were given.
On one of the trials the subject was told to put the finished products on the
table. On the second trial he was told to drop the finished products into a
box on the floor. Half of the group started one way, half the other. Three
groups were identified: (1) Rigid Ordering—arranged finished products in
some geometric arrangement such as straight lines, or all placed in the same
direction; (2) Vague Ordering—started a pattern at the beginning of the hour
but did not maintain it for the full hour (It was postulated that this was due
to short attention span and distractability); and (3) Haphazard Arrangements—
no patterns. When Groups 1 and 3 were compared, a difference of 6 was
found between mean IQs ($p < .05$). This suggests that, although there is overlap between groups, there is a tendency for the more intelligent retardates
to use a haphazard arrangement. When "orderliness" was compared with
productivity for Group 1, the trial that allowed the Rigid Ordering Group to
"order" showed a lessening in production that was significant at the .01
level. The same comparison done with the Haphazard Group showed no
significant difference in production rate. As might be expected, the Vague
Ordering Group showed a smaller difference in production under the "order"
condition than the Rigid Ordering Group, but was more affected by the condition than the Haphazard Arrangements Group. From these data it might be
inferred that, with those retardates that fall into the Rigid Ordering Group,
productivity rises as external conditions prevent "orderliness" from occurring. Acceptance of the results of this study would have implications
for work organization, especially where the workers are lower-level retardates.

Franks and Franks (1962) compared conditionability to work adjustment. A classical conditioning paradigm was used. The subjects were conditioned to elicit an eyeblink response to a tone. Three groups of retarded girls
were used. Group 1 consisted of 18 girls working effectively in the community. The IQ range for this group was 32 to 74 (mean = 58). Group 2 consisted of 36 girls who were working fairly effectively, but only within the
hospital setting. This group ranged in IQ from 38 to 86 (mean = 70). Group 3
was composed of 12 girls who were considered occupationally inadequate and
did not carry a regular work assignment. The IQ range for this group was
from 40 to 82 (mean = 64). Data indicated that Group 1 conditioned most
readily and was most resistant to extinction. This group was followed closely
by Group 2. There was some overlap during acquisition by Group 2. Group 3
was considerably worse than the other two groups at acquiring the conditioned
response and was the most susceptible to extinction. Group 3 differed significantly ($p < .01$) from Groups 1 and 2 combined, on both acquisition and
extinction. According to the authors, these data are consistent with the
theory that poor conditioners may profit less from life's experiences and

be less likely to build up good work habits. They also infer from the data that factors other than brain damage are related to the presence of poor conditionability and hence to poor work adjustment. Those subjects whose vocational adjustment was poor were also those who were relatively poor at forming conditioned eyeblink responses in the laboratory.

In an effort to study self-concept development, O'Neil (1968) measured the ability of mentally retarded adolescents to rate relative work potential. He used a pictorial comparison method with staff members providing a standard for evaluation. He found that the trainees were able to use work standards to evaluate their own potential for community placement for themselves and their peers. Trainees who were later employed were more consistent raters. Their results did not establish that self-concept development and level of work adjustment were clearly related.

e. **Summary on Prediction and Evaluation.** In summary, no attempt has been made to distinguish between acquisition and performance, i.e., between learning ability and production ability. Equally important, no attempt has been made to make the evaluation period fruitful to the client in terms of the development of the skills which are being evaluated. If anything is gained from the evaluation period, it is usually adjustive in nature with the clients often spending many hours or days being nonproductive and not learning new skills. It is also possible that many retarded clients, who are in a work setting for the first time, develop inappropriate concepts regarding work, which are based on nonproductivity and low-level tasks and which are reflected in future performance. Current prediction and evaluation procedures and tests as they are presently conducted are not very successful.

2. Training

In the introduction to this article, training is defined as controlled, systematic manipulations of the environment, administered in such a way that their effects can be measured and recorded. This definition is equally applicable to both research and service. If training is not administered as defined, clients spend most of their time in nonhabilitative activities, what growth takes place is inferred or goes by unnoticed, and programs remain static in the absence of feedback regarding their effectiveness. In order for programs to facilitate growth "by the hour" rather than "by the week" or "month," training, as defined, must take place.

Research on training may be dichotomized as the development of procedures to either modify existing rates of behavior or facilitate the acquisition of new behaviors. Not much training research has been done, much less implemented. While the rest of the review draws selectively from the literature, the section on training is, hopefully, comprehensive.

a. **Modifying Rates of Existing Behaviors.** Most sheltered workshop clients do not understand the relationship between the money they receive on Friday and their performance during the week. Many do not understand "money" at all. While it is true that reinforcement should occur immediately following the desired behavior, it is impractical to do so in most work situations, even sheltered ones. Common practice is to pay workers, or clients, on a weekly basis. Parenthetically, the money many sheltered workshop clients make often goes either to their home or into a savings account, neither of which is particularly reinforcing (Campbell, 1971). Most of the studies reported here address this problem.

Evans and Spradlin (1966) investigated the effects of incentives and instructions as controlling variables of productivity of institutionalized, mildly retarded males (mean IQ = 66.67, SD = 7.22). The incentive schedules used involved a piece-rate plan in which a unit of pay was provided per unit of work produced, and a salary plan in which a unit of pay was provided at the end of a specified unit of time, with no production contingency. The task was to pull a knob. Number of responses per session was the dependent variable. All subjects received all conditions. Although there was a statistically significant ($p < .05$) difference in production, in favor of the piece-rate condition, the authors point out the real difference was only about 10% in terms of absolute productivity. This difference is surprisingly small when viewed from the position of reinforcement theory. Two no-salary conditions were subsequently tried. In one, subjects were told to pull the knob. In the other they were told not to pull the knob. The authors concluded that (1) money, even when it is noncontingent on responding, does lead to higher response rates than when no money is involved; (2) verbal instructions are a potent antecedent variable with high-level retarded subjects; and (3) a high response rate can be reestablished by instructions, as well as decreased or maintained. The tendency to underestimate the control of antecedent variables in situations where they are very powerful was also discussed.

Huddle (1967), working with institutionalized retardates, utilized a 16-piece television rectifier assembly to study the effects of competition, cooperation, and monetary reward on work performance. Paid subjects received 1 cent per unit, paid daily. He found that payment of monetary rewards had a significant effect on performance. Reward, however, was confounded with experimenter and institution, making this data difficult to interpret. No other significant main effects or interactions were obtained.

In a study of the effects of immediate monetary reward on performance Steinman (1971) gave pennies for task completion time which was faster than mean base rate performance to eight mentally retarded adults on a simulated production line packaging task, which consisted of packaging checkers. All subjects improved their performance on the task under reinforcement. Steinman suggests that a training program might begin with the use of continuous reinforcement or low variable-ratio reinforcement and move gradually toward the once-a-week pay period which is commonly found in workshop programs, and competitive work situations.

In a similar study by Hunt and Zimmerman (1969), productivity in exit ward patients participating in a simulated workshop setting was examined as a function of introducing a bonus pay procedure. The primary difference between this study and the one by Steinman was that subjects in this study were paid at the end of the working period. They were told in advance that during the bonus period they would be given coupons redeemable for canteen items. Work units completed per hour served as the dependent variable. The task consisted of counting pages to make scratch pads. The bonus procedure significantly increased group productivity above that previously attained under nonbonus conditions and differentially maintained productivity at values consistently higher than those attained during temporally adjacent nonbonus periods. The authors suggest that verbal instructions given in conjunction with the procedures could have accounted for some of the results.

Zimmerman, Stuckey, Garlick, and Miller (1969) applied a token reinforcement system to study effects on the productivity of multiply handicapped clients in a sheltered workshop. The task performed by 15 of the 16 subjects was a Western Electric terminal board assembly. The sixteenth client folded Goodwill bags. Assembly involved inserting 49 small U-shaped metal terminals into slots of a perforated plastic connector block which is part of a telephone set. The bag-folding task required folding a bag five times, placing a rubber band over the folds, and throwing the bags into a box. The experiment included the following sequence: (1) 7 weeks of base line performance under standard workshop conditions; (2) 2 weeks of a practice condition in which verbal information about production, and nonredeemable points were given daily; (3) 2 weeks of a points condition in which verbal information about production was given daily, and clients received and could spend point cards; (4) 2 weeks of alternating conditions (2) and (3) daily, in which the type of consequence available at the end of each day, identified via instruction, was given at the beginning of each day; (5) 2 weeks of return to base line condition. The results were that (a) productivity increased significantly when the base line condition was replaced by the practice condition; (b) productivity increased significantly again when the condition was replaced by the points condition; (c) the productivity on point days was significantly higher than the practice days during the alternate period; (d) productivity under the final base rate condition was significantly lower than under conditions in which points could be earned; and (e) productivity was somewhat higher under the second base line condition than under the initial base line condition. Although the authors state that 14 of the 16 subjects in the study were mentally retarded, no information was given as to the degree. The instructions utilized suggest that the clients might have been borderline or mildly retarded. The tasks used were of a fairly simple and repetitive nature. Nevertheless, the impressive information provided, that systematic control of reinforcement contingencies produced predictable changes, has implications for sheltered workshop productions with all levels of retardates and with more complex tasks. The authors stress the importance of controlling and measuring the effects of work conditions.

In another study, Zimmerman, Overpeck, Eisenberg, and Garlick (1969) used seven clients from the Zimmerman, Stuckey, Garlick, and Miller (1969) study and six other clients, and the same tasks described in that study. The use of isolation-avoidance procedures and production-contingent work reinforcement to stimulate productivity were studied. The isolation-avoidance procedure consisted of using production rate to determine whether or not the client could participate with other trainees on the following day. That is, if the client failed to meet a production goal on one day, he was isolated from the group on the following day. The procedure demonstrated was highly effective with the clients and tasks used. Production-contingent work reinforcement consisted of utilizing choice of work as a reinforcement for meeting production goals. The two subjects who were exposed to this condition showed significant increases in performance as a result of this procedure. A description of the application of the procedures developed by Zimmerman and his colleagues may be found in the article by Campbell (1971).

Screven, Straka, and Lafond (1971) report a program of research designed to provide clients with an understanding of the relationship between money received and work output. Simple tasks such as filling a tray with 12 red and 12 black checkers and putting them into a cardboard box, and filling a counter board with 50 golf tees and bagging them are used. They have examined the effects of various mechanical reinforcement devices, goal setting, and various sequences leading from immediate, contingent reinforcement to weekly pay and report good results. For example, in one of the studies for which data were reported, rate increases of from 50 to 100% were obtained using bonus pay procedures and manipulating the schedule of reinforcement. Because of the considerable amounts of equipment, space, and staff time required for their procedures, the feasibility of applying their techniques to other settings needs to be demonstrated.

Another program of research on the development of training procedures for trainable retarded students in public school settings is being directed by Lou Brown. In the first study reported (Brown & Pearce, 1970), the use of feedback, modeling, and reinforcement procedures similar to those used by Zimmerman and his colleagues were assessed. Using three students and an envelope-stuffing task, they found considerable individual differences, but, in general, found all variables to be sufficiently effective to warrant further study.

The next experiment (Brown, Johnson, Gadberry, & Fenrick, 1971) utilized six trainable students performing the same task to study the effects of individual versus assembly line production and social versus social plus tangible reinforcement. The four possible procedures were administered in a series of 36 15-minute periods. Tangible reinforcement consisted of tokens which, collectively, were redeemable for components of a "banana split." Typical verbal social reinforcers were used randomly. Feedback, which involved writing and explaining production figures on the chalkboard, was given to all students throughout. Individual performance consistently exceeded assembly line performance. Performance under the tangible reinforcement condition increased an average of 60% for individual performance and 49% for assembly line performance. Pacing and balancing problems of assembly line production were discussed. The authors emphasized that the study was done in a classroom by classroom teachers, and that such positive results suggest more use of these procedures in classroom settings.

A third study (Brown, Van Deventer, Perlmutter, Jones, & Sontag, 1972) examined the effects of charting and pay on production rate. Eighteen trainable students collated a four-page catalog, representative of most simple, repetitive tasks which require little or no training to perform and which are the mainstay of subcontract work found in sheltered workshops in this country. After reaching a criterion of three consecutive correct trials, students produced under the following five conditions: (1) base line, consisting of three 10-minute periods; (2) charting, consisting of showing students the relationship between productivity and a line on a graph and having them produce and chart in 10-minute periods until production stabilized; (3) repeat of condition (1); (4) repeat of condition (2); and (5) charting and money, consisting of paying each client 5 cents for each 10-minute period in which production exceeded previous performance. Teacher performance was used to establish a norm against which to compare. Using typical workshop practices, productivity was labeled work activity level (low), competitive sheltered work level (medium), or competitive employment level (high) on the basis of the highly questionable normative performance of teachers in the school.

During the first base line period, all students performed within the work activity range (0–39.6 units per 10-minute period). The first charting condition produced increases for all students, but the amounts of increase varied widely (3.2–59 units per 10-minute period). The second base line condition and chart condition produced mixed results. The introduction of money produced substantial increases. Three students reached competitive levels of productivity, as defined (over 46 units per 10-minute period). Most of the other students had some periods in which they produced within the competitive range but averaged somewhat lower. Only one student failed to produce above the minimum work activity level. Errors decreased over sessions and were virtually eliminated by the end of the study. A similar study was done by Logan, Kinsinger, Shelton, and J. M. Brown (1971).

The fourth study involved quality, quantity, and durability of work performance (Brown, Bellamy, Perlmutter, Sackowitz, & Sontag, 1972). Four students were taught to assemble packs of cards using what appeared to be highly verbal training procedures. Following acquisition of the task the following sequence of manipulations was performed: (1) base line, during which time no feedback or reinforcement was given; (2) weekly payment, during which time students were told in advance that they would receive, at the end of the week, a penny for each accurately assembled pack; (3) session payment, which involved payment every 15 minutes and feedback on accuracy; (4) high rate contingency, during which payment was contingent on productivity exceeding that of any previous period; (5) daily payment, which included removing the high rate contingency and giving feedback on quality; and (6) weekly payment, as in the second condition.

Student performance was again compared to the performance of four teachers, who were considered to have produced at a normal rate. Quality of performance increased over sessions for all students. All students showed substantial quantitative growth, and two of the four students reached competitive production range, as defined by teacher performance. Durability, defined as maintenance of high and accurate performance levels during the weekly payment schedule, was attained by two of the students.

While these studies do not provide a clear cut description of an effective workshop or prevocational pay system, they do lay the groundwork for the development of such a system, which is described further in Section III, B, 2. The kind of programmatic research done by Brown and his colleagues, in addition to its content value, exemplifies the potential for cooperation between researchers and practitioners.

An interesting attempt to utilize clients to administer reinforcements to other clients is reported by Kazdin (1971). Successful applications included increasing appropriate conversation by clients giving each other tokens for talking; a client learning to walk with his head erect, instead of on his shoulder, by giving tokens to other clients who praised him when he held his head correctly; and a client decreasing talking and laughing to himself, and increasing talking with others, by his giving and receiving tokens for social interaction. Kazdin points out the preliminary nature of his data, which were not reported, and mentions several advantages of using clients to administer reinforcements.

In summary, research on modifying rates of behavior has produced a small but impressive groundwork on which to base future efforts. In addition to the varied procedures and degrees of effectiveness shown, there are two other findings which are evidenced across studies: (1) Procedures designed to elevate performance levels seem to have some effect on the quality as well as the quantity of performance. (2) Verbal directions appear to be powerful controlling variables of performance but have not been systematically investigated, at least not in workshop settings.

b. Facilitating the Acquisition of New Behaviors. The literature on facilitating the acquisition of new behaviors is, indeed, sparse. There are hundreds of articles describing training programs, which do not delineate the specific manipulations made which facilitate development. Instead they describe clients, facilities, activities, and other aspects of the milieu in which training is supposed to occur, but not the training itself. The studies reported here were selected because they specify the manipulations made and because they fit the definition of training used in this review.

One of the most fruitful areas of training research is the use of autoinstructional techniques. Such techniques in the field are a recent occurrence (Bitter & Bolanovich, 1966; Eldred, 1965). The studies reported here include the development of both hardware and software specifically for such use.

Screven *et al.* (1971) describe their adaptation of a commercially produced machine. Features of the adapted versions include match-to-sample press panels; controlled audio feedback and response-contingent pacing; and slide projector and movie projector hook-ups. Software includes the use of both audio and visual materials; taped vocal reinforcement and feedback; programs using printed material, symbols, and pictures; and programs to name and to discriminate colors, to make small change, to listen, to train clients to use the machine; and some basic reading programs. Their experience with this equipment has generated the following opinions regarding the use of autoinstructional equipment: (1) The use of such devices increases the likelihood of carefully organizing and sequencing materials. (2) Materials can be reworked efficiently. (3) Such devices are replicable. (4) Operating the equipment is sufficiently reinforcing, in itself, to sustain attention for long periods. (5) The use of automatically dispensed reinforcers draws clients' attention away from the stimulus materials. (6) Where added reinforcement is needed, it can be programmed into the visual and audio presentations in the form of verbal praise or visual cartoons. (7) Machine presentation appears to be superior to nonmachine presentation of the same materials in terms of client error rate, frequency of nontask behavior, and number of reruns needed to reach criterion performance. While the data to support these statements were not presented, their observations seem consistent with the rest of the programmed instruction literature.

Blackman and Siperstein (1967) describe the use of an autoinstructional device to train educable retarded individuals to plug solder. The device used coordinated slides and tape. Considerable reworking of both the slide sequences and the instructional tapes was suggested, although the procedure was considered more efficient than alternative conventional procedures in terms of holding client attention, reducing distractability, standardizing instruction, and individualizing instruction. The program developed incorporated the following: (1) a detailed task analysis; (2) systematic review of previous steps; (3) brief, easily understood directions; and (4) the integration of supervisor feedback and machine presentation.

Blackman and Siperstein feel that their procedures should be further studied, and that marketable skills appropriately taught to the retarded, using such procedures, should be identified.

The most extensive program involving the use of autoinstructional devices for the field was conducted at the Devereux Foundation (H. Platt, J. Cifelli, & W. Knaus, undated). At least three new devices were designed in the program in addition to the adaption of already existing equipment. The software described is very verbal and intended for use with mildly retarded individuals. Numerous studies designed to test the efficacy of the autoinstructional devices and programs developed were reported in detail. The authors concluded the following: (1) In most cases higher achievement test scores were obtained using autoinstructional devices. (2) Autoinstructional devices were most effective when used in conjunction with material introduced by the teacher. (3) Performance on proficiency tests was lowest with students who were exposed only to the machine method. (4) The use of autoinstructional methods reduced learning time. (5) Programmed instructional material facilitated retention. The program at Devereux also includes a large dissemination component which consists of frequent presentations at conferences and at universities, the distribution of written materials, and the manufacture and sale of their devices.

In summary, the literature on the use of autoinstructional devices is impressive. Even within the limited scope of the research described, the practical possibilities are encouraging.

Programming, in the operant sense, is certainly not limited to use with autoinstructional devices. Programming of the total sheltered workshop environment is the focus of the research carried on under the direction of

James Crosson (Crosson, Youngberg, & White, 1970). This research differs from the other operant work reported in this article in that the emphasis is on the acquisition of new behaviors rather than on the modification of existing rates of behaviors. The initial report (Crosson & deJung, 1967) describes a study in which a group of severely retarded males were successfully trained to perform three simple workshop tasks, using principles of shaping, operant discrimination, and chaining. The value of the study is not that severely retarded individuals can acquire such behavior, but that the task was analyzed and presented effectively. This involved defining the correlated response topographies and redefining each task in terms of operants. Each component of the task was then taught using modeling, verbal, and nonverbal assistance and physical assistance (priming). The experimenters gradually removed (faded) assistance as the task was learned. Reinforcements, which consisted of candy and verbal praise, were also faded over trials until reinforcement was given only at the end of each session. The effects of the procedures used were reported in detail and provide a valuable resource for further use of operant techniques to facilitate acquisition of new behaviors. In addition to the acquisition study, a 2- and 12-month retention study was performed (Crosson, 1969) which yielded retention of over 90% of the discriminations by all subjects.

In a more recent publication, Crosson et al. (1970) expanded the techniques and theories encompassed in the studies reviewed to an entire workshop environment. They use the term "transenvironmental programming" to describe a workshop program based on an awareness of the functional relationship between behavioral and environmental events. Training objectives for the program include specification of criterion performance for successful completion of the program, specific skills to be learned, the sequence in which the behaviors are to be learned, and the specific training procedures to be used. They emphasize the importance of response measures and give an excellent description of the kinds of data and methods of collection used. In addition, an idealized sequence for moving clients from immediate primary reinforcement to the normal reinforcement systems found in work settings is described.

The basic model was based on the following hypotheses: (a) The deficient repertoires of retarded clients are largely a function of inappropriate or deficient responses to "natural" programs which occur, for the normal child, throughout the developmental period. (b) Remediation of the deficient repertoires can be rapidly accomplished through "compression" of critical elements of the "natural" developmental program through careful selection of target behaviors and refined programming procedures. Data were obtained on nine of 26 clients enrolled in the program. Of the nine, four were involved in the prevocational phase, and five were in community placement programs. Of the four clients in the prevocational group, all of whom were being trained on various components of in-house custodial tasks, three demonstrated significant acceleration in correct performance rates. The five clients in the community placement program were trained for specific preanalyzed job placements in the local county through a two-stage process of simulated in-house preplacement programming, and subsequent on-the-job training. All clients demonstrated rapid acceleration of correct performance in both the simulated and on-the-job conditions (D. Jacobson, unpublished manuscript, University of Oregon, 1972; C. D. Youngberg, unpublished manuscript, University of Oregon, 1972). Generally speaking, program effects were more rapidly established in the community placement group. The prevocational groups demonstrated considerably greater degrees of performance variability under progress conditions, a finding which was thought to be partially due to imprecise programming. The results of the pilot effort, while not considered conclusive, were thought to lend support to the "compression" hypothesis (J. E. Crosson, personal communication).

The development of vocational skill training procedures is also the goal of a program of research being conducted by the author (Gold, 1972) at Children's Research Center, University of Illinois. More broadly stated, the research incorporates the many biases evidenced in this review in an attempt to elevate the skill functioning of the retarded and the expectancies of the society in which they live. Gold (1969) utilized task analysis, nonverbal training, and concepts and procedures from the Zeaman and House (1963) Attention Theory to facilitate the acquisition of a complex assembly task by retarded adolescents. Sixty-four moderately and severely retarded adolescents enrolled in four sheltered workshops were trained to assemble a 15-piece (training task) and a 24-piece (transfer task) bicycle brake. One-half of the subjects worked with the parts of the training task brake as they came from the factory, having to make discriminations using the shape of each part (form dimension). The others worked with parts that were color-coded (color and form dimensions). Coding consisted of painting that surface of each part that is facing the subject when it is placed in the proper position for assembling. All groups worked with the parts of the transfer task brake as they came from the factory (form dimension only). Sixty-three out of sixty-four subjects reached a criterion of six correct out of eight consecutive trials on both brakes. One subject reached criterion on the training task brake only. The addition of the color cue resulted in the color-form group learning the task in half the trials required by the form-only group. In addition, a significant transfer effect was obtained. One year later, 53 of the original 64 subjects were rerun, with half of the subjects doing the 24-piece brake first. With no interim experience on the brakes or on tasks differing from the subjects' experience before the experiment, highly significant retention effects were obtained (Gold, 1972). The principles and procedures demonstrated have been described subsequently in terms of classroom application (Gold & Scott, 1971) and have led to a program of research now in progress. Another study completed involved a replication in which no difference between institutional and noninstitutional subjects was found (M. W. Gold, unpublished). In another study, 20 subjects, some from the first study, produced the 15-piece brake individually, 1 hour per day for 10 days, with no social or other reinforcements given, except a brief salutation at the beginning and end of each session. Mean production for the 200 hours was 24.9 brakes per hour per subject, with a 6% error rate. Individual subject performance ranged from a mean of 17 per hour to a mean of 60 per hour. The correlation between trials to criterion during acquisition and mean units completed per hour was .26. This raises some questions regarding the validity of conventional work samples and suggests further study of the relationship between acquisition and production. Studies planned or in progress are discussed in Section III, B, 2.

One of the goals of this research is that the techniques can be used by first-line service personnel without much training. Experimenters are chosen with this in mind. They are recruited from among volunteers in the workshops and acquaintances of workshop personnel. None have had any formal training or paid experience working with the retarded. Training consists of from two to six 2-hour group training sessions followed by 1 week of independent practice, then actual data collection with gradually decreasing supervision. Excellent results have been obtained. No experimenter effects are evidenced in the data. Several of the data collectors have been subsequently hired as shop floor supervisors.

C. Summary of the Present

The field is undergoing many changes. Many service agencies have reached the point where energies formerly devoted to establishing organizations and communications have been fruitful and can now be directed toward programs. This change in focus is, in part, facilitated by the beginnings of a technology of instruction, which is developing from research conducted in service agencies by, in most cases, university-based researchers.

Much of the work that has been done was directed at prediction and evaluation. The work on evaluation, particularly work sample theory, has provided us with some meaningful information to use as a basis for further development. The work on prediction, in the view of the author, has resulted in little usable information.

The development of training procedures is a recent addition to the field. Even the relatively small proportion of energy expended to date has resulted in a substantial body of information awaiting large-scale dissemination and further development.

III. THE FUTURE

The discussion now turns to the future, with the intention of providing impetus for debate. The first two parts of this section follow up on the descriptions given of the present. The third part, prospective involvements, focuses on literature from outside the field which has exciting potential for application. In the third section authors are explicitly identified to maximize the impact of their observations.

A. Recommendations for Service Programs

The field has recently concluded an era marked by a tremendous proliferation of school and workshop programs, initiated in most cases through federal and state support. The emphasis has necessarily been directed toward organizational development, funding, and other exigencies of creating new facilities and agencies. Most agencies served as their own prototype in the absence of proven models. At present communities either have programs of their own or have access to information which will eliminate most of the trial and error which has previously been so common.

Now it is time to focus on program. The author contends that agencies have necessarily directed the majority of their energies toward the development of organizational structures within which programs operate, but have spent little energy on the programs themselves. Staff, schedules, equipment, and activities do not constitute a program. A program exists only when these resources interact in a setting which results in measurable day-to-day development in habilitants. If the field is to proceed, a technology of habilitation, developed through the cooperation of researchers and practitioners, must emerge.

There is a large gap between laboratory research on learning and application. There are several reasons for this gap: (1) Few researchers or practitioners study the relationship between principles of learning and the teaching of skills. (2) Laboratory research examines variables for their theoretical interest rather than immediate practical use. (3) There is an absence of research designed to replicate and validate laboratory findings in applied settings. (4) Few attempts have been made to translate the jargon of the laboratory researcher into a form understood by the practitioner (Deno, 1970; Gold, 1968). (5) There is a lack of awareness of, and communication with, resources outside the field (Younie, 1967). (6) There is resistance on the part of both researchers and practitioners to change.

Part of the solution is the development of "middle-road researchers" whose function would be to combine the control, methodology, design, and hypothesis testing from basic research with an interest in the solution of applied problems leading to the development of training procedures (Crosson, 1969; Gold, 1970). Such researchers would be responsible for the development and implementation of an applied technology through direct involvement with service agencies, and professional and governmental organizations. Their responsibility would also include the identification of applied problems in need of study. Few programs exist, at present, to train such researchers, or to do this research.

Concurrent with the development of middle-road research programs, there must be research on the dissemination of information emerging from this research. The limitations of existing technology are magnified by the virtual wall between available information and current practice. In most fields the available literature lags behind the state of the technical art, making it difficult for other practitioners to acquire the latest techniques available (Marangell, 1971). The lag is indeed large in this field. Valuable information, which has been available for years, has yet to find its way into practice in all but a very few programs.

Another factor in need of attention is the relationship between researchers and practitioners. For an excellent description of some of the causes for difficulties between researchers and practitioners in rehabilitation the reader is referred to Rusalem (1969). Most of Rusalem's comments, however cogent, are not applicable to the kinds of research emphasized throughout this article. His comments refer primarily to research on adjustment, placement, diagnosis, and counseling, whereas this review focuses on skill training. He encompasses the entire field of rehabilitation, and not specifically the retarded, and seems to be referring, primarily, to within-rehabilitation researchers rather than researchers from other disciplines who are applying their skills to the field of rehabilitation.

Rusalem (1969) feels that for rehabilitation research to be truly productive, researchers should be allowed to proceed on their own, without having to attend to the needs and demands expressed by service personnel in the field. For the research emphasized in the article, the author disagrees. Applied researchers do have a responsibility to address the problems of the practitioner. This is not to suggest that researchers bounce from problem to problem at the dictates of practitioners. However, addressing problems of skill training and the establishment of appropriate work behaviors do not necessarily require longitudinal or other lengthy experiments. The preponderance of lengthy experiments found in rehabilitation can probably be attributed to the emphasis on correlational rather than experimental psychology, which has permeated the field (Cronbach, 1957). Using paradigms from experimental psychology and, in fact, information already acquired using these paradigms, many of the immediate problems of the practitioner could be solved quickly, expediently, and inexpensively.

The need is to facilitate meaningful, perpetual, and direct communication between researchers and practitioners. Such a relationship has been inferred before: ". . . it is possible not to perceive that the arts and manufactures of the country are intimately connected with the progress of the severer sciences; and that, as we advance in the cause of improvement, every step requires, for its success, that this connexion should be rendered more intimate [Babbage, 1832, p. 270]." One possible way to expedite communication is for service agencies to support research in their facilities. This means administrative interest, space, access to clients, and some personnel. Much of this kind of support could be absorbed within existing agency expenditures while greatly reducing need for grant support to the researcher. The benefits to the agency would include: (1) continuous input to the researcher regarding critical areas in need of study; (2) continuous exposure of staff to techniques and procedures used in the research, but equally applicable for service through formal in-service training and informal coffee chats; (3) participation by clients in activities designed to facilitate change in their functioning; (4) agency prestige through research involvement; (5) access to sources of information not normally available to service agencies because of service load. Benefits to researchers would include: (1) an opportunity to identify relevance at a time when it is becoming increasingly relevant to do so; (2) financial support; (3) a way to maintain a realistic perspective; (4) an opportunity to implement and test findings beyond the experimental level; and (5) increased opportunity for validity testing.

The establishment of such a movement might be encouraged through the dissemination of the description of such relationships. Since fall, 1970, such a relationship has existed between the Children's Research Center at the University of Illinois at Urbana-Champaign, and several service agencies in the Midwest. In each instance, agencies provide research space, access to clients, and some labor as part of a consultation contract. Children's Research Center provides consultant reports, seminars, scheduled staff observations, and access to a comprehensive library. These relationships have resulted in significant changes in both the agencies and the research. For the agencies, changes have included methods of evaluating clients, production design, material flow, client training, record keeping, and reinforcement systems. Changes in the research program include addressing problems not previously considered and a major change in focus which is discussed in Section III, B, 4. Parenthetically, the ongoing dialogue between the practitioners and the researchers has been very enjoyable and seems to be a strong reinforcer for continued interaction.

For the future, then, the field should actively pursue the establishment of ongoing, in-depth relationships between researchers and practitioners.

B. Recommendations for Research

If the field is to proceed maximally, its research must provide a leading edge. Statements regarding accountability, dissemination, client evaluation, training, and new input need to be made, challenged, and addressed if research is to assume a meaningful role. Below is one attempt at such a statement.

1. Accountability

The resources devoted to research must yield more return than if expended some other way. Unless those in the field are reinforced for research its resources will continue to be utilized for more and more of the same thing. Most practitioners have little reason to consider research a part of the field. Their only contact with it has been vicarious, through coursework or lecture, with little or no information coming to them which is both usable and identifiable as coming from research. If practitioners do not get substantial return for their involvement with researchers, in terms of new information and the implementation of existing information, there will continue to be little or no meaningful interaction, and, eventually, funds for research will dry up. Some researchers feel this process has already begun.

To the present, a researcher has been held accountable only in terms of grant reports and publications. This may be sufficient for basic research, or for very esoteric applied research. But for the research emphasized in this review, accountability should go much further. Such research must be evaluated by those for whom the research is designed to provide information. This would contribute to the solution of problems regarding translation and implementation.

2. Dissemination

Information obtained from research must be widely disseminated. The criterion for successful dissemination should be the direct observation of the information disseminated being correctly utilized in agencies not directly connected with the research. The efficacy of current dissemination practices such as courses, publications, convention presentations, and one-shot consultations should be evaluated and revised and new practices developed which involve more bidirectional than unidirectional exchange.

The process of dissemination should receive considerable attention in its own right. Research projects designed to disseminate information from other projects are already in operation, but seem to be using conventional and thus far ineffective processes rather than seeking alternatives. Without major changes in the existing dissemination process there is little value in collecting more information, merely to have it sit, unused, on library shelves or administrators' desks.

The research program conducted by Gold (1972) includes considerable emphasis on dissemination. In addition to consulting activities, and the usual publishing and convention presentations, the program has developed a less extensive library on vocational training of the retarded. The library grows constantly, through continuous perusal of reference lists and journals and contains, presently, close to 1500 entries, which are cross-referenced and categorized for efficient accessibility. On an increasing basis, personnel from throughout the Midwest are coming to the center to utilize this resource. This is seen as an integral part of the "middle-road" research program which is discussed in Section III, A, 1.

3. Prediction and Evaluation

Research on evaluation should move away from prediction. The voluminous literature reported attests to the monumental failure we have experienced trying to develop valid predictors. Interestingly, the attempts of industry and the military to develop predictors have yielded statistically significant correlations comparable to the work in retardation, but are far more valid and utilitarian because they are used almost exclusively to predict success on a particular job or task (Fleishman, 1965). When this is the case, all of the types of validities and reliabilities can be tested. Even under such ideal conditions, which we could never hope to approach, ultimate decisions still often rest on performance on the task itself rather than on the predictor (Jones, 1966). It should also be pointed out that prediction, outside of the field, is used primarily as a means of screening individuals out of something, rather than as a means of determining how to keep them in.

So long as the emphasis remains on generalized training and placement is on menial tasks, prediction should be discarded as a useless drain on our resources. However, if there is a move in the direction of placements which require skill and training, and toward occupational groupings which provide a reasonably stable pool of jobs, then prediction may be possible, necessary, and expedient. Until then, evaluation should concentrate on description rather than prediction. Research on descriptive evaluation must result in procedures which yield demonstrably useful information. Present evaluation procedures result in information which is either very dependable and of little use, or very descriptive but undependable because of semantic ambiguities. What is needed is very dependable and very descriptive information.

In Section II, B, 1, numerous criticisms of existing evaluation procedures were discussed with suggestions for change. The basic concept of work samples appears to provide the most fruitful approach to evaluation. However, major changes in present usage are necessary. Acquisition and production must be separated. The length of time and conditions necessary to learn various tasks should be separated from how fast the production is after the tasks have been learned. If both acquisition and production data are obtained, on a variety of tasks and levels of difficulty, then highly reliable and descriptive data will be obtained and *training* will necessarily occur, simultaneously with evaluation.

Other variables, such as following directions, working with others, pressure, etc., can all be systematically included. The result would be a matrix of work sample tasks which might constitute the majority of a transitional client's experience and would yield quantifiable and yet descriptive information and demonstrable changes in behavior. Such an approach would also insure a more realistic relationship between evaluation and training.

4. Training

Research on training must have as its goal the development of procedures which can be implemented in the absence of sophisticated equipment, large sums of money, and highly trained first-line service personnel. For the existing information described in Section II, B, 2, this means further research to adapt, translate, and disseminate what is already known. This has been discussed above. But most of the technology is yet to be developed.

a. Increasing Rates of Existing Behaviors. A variety of techniques have been presented, all of which have some merit. The effects of the various procedures, over time, on a variety of tasks, and with all levels of clients should be determined. If possible a comprehensive reinforcement program for client productivity should be developed which would have sufficient clarity and alternatives to be universally applicable. Definitions, language, data collection, criteria for the various levels of reinforcement in the sequence, and where to go for help would have to be dealt with very carefully. Although this sounds like an unapproachable panacea, the operant literature does seem to have the necessary basic set of rules for such an accomplishment.

Utilizing the same basic rules, a completely separate system should be developed for nonproductive behaviors. Different reinforcers in a different system should be used for eliminating inappropriate behaviors, and establishing appropriate nonproductive behaviors such as self-help, and social and language skills. Although these behaviors obviously interact with productive behaviors (actual job tasks), it is contended here that separate systems and reinforcers would be much better for both clients and staff. In addition, a clearer picture of the relationship between productive and nonproductive behaviors might be obtained.

b. **Facilitating the Acquisition of New Behaviors**. In light of the perspective given in this review, the small beginnings of a technology for facilitating the acquisition of new behaviors are surprising. The few studies done evidence the potential impact of this research on the field.

The work on autoinstructional devices has a good start. Further work on the development of reasonably priced, flexible hardware is needed. But the development of software will require the greater effort. Verbal and nonverbal programs for basic skills and more common occupational skills should be developed along with explicit procedures for using such materials. The effective use of autoinstructional devices could become a major force in the field. In addition, it might prove even more valuable if data collection were programmed in such a way that information from all agencies using the same programs could be collectively analyzed and reported.

The use of transenvironmental programming was discussed. With some translation and more detailed explanation, such a system might be effectively implemented by workshop personnel not familiar with the terminology and the operant perspective. Research utilizing stimulus control procedures, nonverbal techniques, and an emphasis on attentional variables was described. This program of research has just begun. Preliminary data and feedback from service personnel suggest several areas in need of examination: (1) the relationship between task complexity and inappropriate behavior; (2) the effects of extraneous irrelevant stimuli on production and the control of such effects; (3) the effects of various training procedures on transfer and retention; (4) the height of skill achievement obtainable by the retarded at all levels; and (5) ways in which this information can be used to achieve the goals of the field.

An integral part of this research is the utilization of information and techniques not previously applied to the field. The next section deals with some of this information.

C. Prospective Involvements

The section on prospective involvements requires some explanation. The areas discussed are not often turned to as resources for the field. While there are occasional isolated reports in the literature, little has been done to utilize these resources. It is intended here to describe these areas briefly for the following reasons: (1) to make the reader aware of information which is available and immediately applicable to both service and research; (2) to indicate potentially fruitful areas for research; and (3) to show the commonalities between these areas and the field.

The literature described is but a sampling. Perusal of these areas reveals many relevant topics which are not dealt with here because of space limitations and author bias. For example, the personnel literature abounds with articles on motivation, incentives, organizational efficiency, and other topics of interest.

Another fascinating discovery is the literature specifically on the handicapped, written by management for management, which has not found its way into the habilitation literature. Some of this is discussed below.

1. Industrial Management

The area of management dealing with personnel is replete with professional journals, e.g., *Personnel, Personnel Journal, Personnel Practice Bulletin.* A wide variety of topics is discussed in these journals. The sampling described here includes (a) the handicapped, (b) training, (c) the disadvantaged, and (d) productivity.

a. The Handicapped. Industry has long been interested in the handicapped (e.g., Gilbreth & Gilbreth, 1953). Professionals in the behavioral sciences, however, have been remiss in their attention to this interest. Placement of the retarded into industry is justified by quoting figures, citing articles, and using vocabulary and techniques all from the field. In addition, industry is usually regarded as a customer rather than a partner.

The literature of industry evidences an awareness and willingness to participate. Joseph P. Monge, Vice President and Treasurer of International Paper Company, calls for industry to face its responsibility, to revise its job specifications, and to hire the handicapped (Monge, 1969).

Lawrence N. Loban (1968), Training Supervisor at Crown Zellerbach Corporation, San Francisco, California, describes the problem of imposed handicap. With considerable insight, Loban describes the practice of industry to keep handicapped individuals from certain jobs, not because of their inability to perform the job adequately, but just because the handicap exists. He discusses the problem of arbitrarily imposed educational requirements. Especially of interest is his perception of the result obtained when industry ignores its obligations to the handicapped. Using an industrial rather than social mode of expression, he says that industry must eliminate unnecessary barriers itself if it is to remain free from legislation which will mandate hiring practices and reduce freedom of selection. This is a logical position, understandable to industry, and probably far more cogent than the same position as it might be expressed from within the field. If business does not assume responsibility for its power, someone else will (Davis & Blomstrom, 1966). Davis (1967) also feels that once a power is lost to government, it is lost for a long time. This provides us with a powerful tool for getting industry to participate in the habilitation of the retarded. This is, do it on your own and retain control before you are forced to do it and lose control. For further discussion of the social responsibility of industry, the reader is referred to Carrington (1970), Carrol and Pati (1970), and Petit (1967).

Describing the employment of handicapped individuals in Australia, Howe (1965) points out that physical or mental impairments should be considered as handicaps only as they serve to reduce prospects of employment. Through selective matching of individuals and positions, most impaired individuals can find employment.

One of the most valuable aspects of the industrial management literature is the description of the performance of handicapped workers, written by management. W. G. Firth (1965) is the Managing Director of P. J. Firth Ltd., Enfield, New South Wales, which employs over 200 individuals. Among his observations are: (1) The production of retarded workers is comparable to that of other workers. (2) Retarded workers are more consistent in their work. (3) They move around and talk less than nonretarded workers. (4) They fit in well with other employees. (5) They are practical. (6) They tend to be more stable then nonretarded employees in areas involving simple repetitive tasks where high labor turnover is normally experienced. Firth also describes briefly how his company got involved with the retarded through his attendance at a service club meeting. At the time the article was written, 13 retarded individuals were employed at the plant. The information provided by Firth is not new to the field. But the validation by industrial management provides invaluable support for promoting the placement of retarded individuals in industry.

Kelly and Simon (1969), business and management professors, surveyed company experience with retarded workers. They found plant managers concerned about issues regarding productivity, training, speed, supervision, endurance, and safety. To obtain information on these issues, they held interviews with supervisors of all retarded employees who had been rehabilitated and placed in competitive employment situations in the Greater Denver Metropolitan Area. Their findings concurred with those of Firth, despite differences in cultural and geographical setting, and in the backgrounds of the authors. Reports such as these from industry must be found, publicized, and used effectively if the field is to achieve its goal.

b. Training. Use of the word *training* in the vocational habilitation of the retarded was discussed in Section I, B. Current research on training of the retarded, as defined in this review, is discussed in Section II, B, 2. Training, as the term is used in industry, usually refers to specific skills taught for specific jobs (Ackerman, 1968; Broadwell, 1966; Whitesell & Pietrus, 1965). Considerable energy has been expended to develop techniques for training, many of which are relevant for use with the retarded.

The literature exemplified here evidences several trends which might well be duplicated by the field. First is the attempt to define the role and objectives of training. For industry, training means closing the gap between existing and desirable conditions (Prieve and Wentorf, 1970). This requires describing the desired state of the organization. According to McGehee and Thayer (1961) this involves: (1) organizational analysis, i.e., an examination of the whole organization; (2) operational analysis, i.e., examination of the task requirement for specific jobs; and (3) manpower analysis, which concerns the skill, knowledge, or attitudes needed by each employee. Prieve and Wentorf (1970) point out the need to include individual differences and attitudes in the analyses in order to effect meaningful training, even though objectives are ultimately tied to organizational efficiency rather than to personal fulfillment.

The issue of personal fulfillment versus organizational efficiency is a topic of debate in industry. Some feel that the objectives of training are related solely to organizational efficiency (e.g., Denova, 1968; Hennessey, 1967), while others believe that individual and societal goals are equally important (e.g., Ackerman, 1968; Turrentine, 1968; Weir, 1971). These issues have their parallel in the habilitation field. Sheltered workshop staffs often debate the relative importance of production and habilitation. It is contended here that good habilitation procedures will facilitate good production. It is interesting that there is a movement in industry toward social responsibility and personal fulfillment (e.g., Ackerman, 1968; Loban, 1968; Monge, 1969), and a movement in the field toward organizational efficiency (e.g., Chione & Snyder, 1968; Crosson et al., 1970; Screven et al., 1971). These movements could result in the elimination of two major barriers to the habilitation of the retarded: (1) resistance on the part of industry to participate; and (2) the present inability of the field to provide clients with marketable work skills.

Until training objectives are specified in terms of specific, general, and salable skills for either competitive or sheltered employment, meaningful training programs will not emerge. Industry can provide a model. For an in-depth study of how industry develops objectives for training the reader is referred to the works of Ackerman (1968), McGehee and Thayer (1961), Whitesell and Pietrus (1965), and Prieve and Wentorf (1970).

A second trend in the industrial training literature relates to the identification and evaluation of training devices. The use of devices and techniques requiring considerable verbal facility is common in industry, but adaptations to the retarded seem feasible. For example, programmed instruction (Hennessey, 1967) and audio-visual machines (White, 1968), both of which have been used in the field (see Section II, B, 2), are used in a variety of ways not familiar to the field. For a survey of the use of training aids in industry the reader is referred to Chin-Quan and Eastaugh (1969).

A third, and perhaps the most relevant trend in the industrial training literature, is the description of specific company training programs. Companies share training successes with one another, despite their competitive nature, whereas programs in the field seldom benefit from each other's efforts.

F. A. M. Mackay (1966), Training Officer at Fibremakers, Ltd., Bayswater, Victoria, describes learning principles underlying their training program. Included are the following: (1) Preliminary exercises will facilitate learning for some tasks; (2) Learning of complex tasks by breaking them down into a series of simple tasks; (3) The simple tasks are best combined progressively with particular attention paid to the transitions; (4) Awareness of criteria will facilitate learning; (5) Spaced practice is better than massed practice; (6) Provisions must be made for gradual development of stamina. Mackay also discusses task analysis of each operation to determine sensory and manual skill requirements, bottlenecks in production, and faults in production procedures. This information is used to develop a training manual for the training program. Mackay justifies the program in terms of reductions in training time, wastage, and wages paid to trainees, and, most significantly, in terms of the company being enabled to meet the demand for skilled labor. All of his points are directly applicable to the field and need little, if any, modification to be implemented.

A similar program is described by P. Smith (1968). As Manager of Staff Training and Development for Arnott-Brockhoff-Guest Pty. Ltd., Burwood,

Victoria, Smith trains operators involved in highly repetitive manual jobs related to the manufacture of biscuits. He describes training for wrapping and packaging operators and gives details of how training is scheduled so as to minimize fatigue and maximize efficiency. Training includes basic exercises to prevent muscle strain, the development of judgment of length, the use of equipment, hygiene, introduction to the plant, weighing, bagging, quality control, safety, and wage structure. The training schedule and most of the topics are highly relevant to the field. He also notes that people of lower intelligence often take longer to train but are more reliable in performance, and find job satisfaction where others tend to lose concentration.

Further discussion of industrial training practices may be found in the discussion on the disadvantaged which follows.

c. **The Disadvantaged.** The literature on training programs for the disadvantaged and hardcore unemployed has literally exploded in the last few years. This literature is germane to the field for several reasons: (1) Those populations labeled either retarded or disadvantaged are by no means mutually exclusive, if for no other reason than the fallible assumptions of the labeling process; (2) The socioeconomic status of the retarded and the disadvantaged are, in most cases, the same; (3) Societal and industrial barriers exist for both categories; (4) Educational experiences in both categories are similar; (5) The area of training the disadvantaged has received considerable attention and support; (6) Many individuals with expertise outside the field have applied their skills to the area; (7) There is increasing pressure from government for those presently serving the retarded to address the problems of the disadvantaged.

The literature here is only a small sampling of what is available, but should suffice to indicate the potential for further inquiry. For an historical review of federal programs for the disadvantaged the reader is referred to Levine (1970). He contends that training must be for the highest possible occupational achievement if favorable cost-benefit figures are to be obtained, and if individuals are to receive maximum benefits of training, both economic and personal. Levine calls for more effort in evaluating the human gains resulting from these programs. A similar effort is needed in the field, one which also utilizes a cost-benefit approach. Doing so might facilitate better recognition of successes and failures and direct attention to critical issues of training and organization.

Largely as a result of federal pressure and funds, industry is turning its attention to the problems of the hardcore unemployed. It is impossible to discern, in most cases, whether this results from genuine interest in the problem as a human one or only as it serves corporate interests. In any case, maximum advantage must be taken of this interest. This means the inclusion of that segment of the hardcore population additionally labeled retarded. Some companies are involved in large-scale efforts to provide much more than just vocational training. For example, Pitney Bowes participates in a program which includes identification and recruitment, counseling, training of basic academics, and even the building of integrated, moderate-income housing (Turrentine, 1968). Eastman Kodak contracted with the Board for

Fundamental Education, one of numerous nonprofit organizations established to raise the living standards and aspirations of the undereducated
(Gassler, 1967). Their program consists of basic courses in reading, con-
sumer skills, and arithmetic. Classes are characterized by noncompetitive
situations, seminar-type interactions, much reinforcement, high-interest
material, and no presuppositions regarding entering skills of students, all
characteristics relevant for use in the field.

In another program, called New Careers (Riessman, 1968), companies
such as General Foods, Oxford Chemical Corporation, and Supermarket
General Corporation are hiring workers with minimum education, without
training or experience, and are providing basic training from the start. For a
critical analysis of these kinds of programs the reader is referred to Weir
(1971) and to Sloan (1970), whose perspectives are equally applicable to
programs in the field. Programs such as these can serve the field in at least
two ways: (1) by servicing clients, and (2) by providing models for training
and for working cooperatively with industry and government.

d. Productivity. The industrial literature on worker productivity has
heavy emphasis on motivational factors (Ackerman, 1970, Herzberg, 1968),
and does not contain, in the author's opinion, particularly useful information
for application to habilitation programs. However, perusal of this literature
would provide the reader with an understanding of what clients will be exposed to if they enter competitive employment.

For descriptions on industrial approaches to motivation, the reader is
referred to Ackerman (1970), Brethower and Rummler (1966), and Herzberg (1968). For excellent descriptions on industrial worker productivity,
see Groff (1971) and Lupton (1971).

2. Industrial Engineering

Problems relating to production line efficiency and. worker performance
on assembly lines have long been the concern of industrial engineers. As
the habilitation field develops, these concerns will become increasingly a
part of the picture. The two areas of the literature sampled here should demonstrate the value of further study.

a. Job Design and Job Enlargement. The industrial revolution and subsequent developments have resulted in a pattern of job design characterized
by task specialization, low-level skill requirements, very specific job content,
procedures and use of tools, repetitiousness, and minimum control by the
worker of the production process (Bucklow, 1967). The job design literature
is heavily influenced by the work of L. E. Davis (e.g., 1957, 1966; Davis &
Canter, 1956). The references cited provide a wealth of information on
industrial practices regarding production design. The one specific aspect to
be covered here is the contention of Davis that job enlargement is an important concept for industry which, from the author's view, has considerable
application to the field. The reader is referred also to Conant and Kilbridge
(1965), Guest (1957), Pauling (1968), Stewart (1967), and Tuggle (1969).

Job enlargement refers to increasing the responsibility of workers, quantitatively and/or qualitatively. It differs from conventional job design in that

workers become responsible for their own pace, quality control, rectification of mistakes, machine set-up and repair, and choice of method. The result of job enlargement is to produce jobs at a higher level of skill (Hulin & Blood, 1968). Hulin and Blood feel that job enlargement is overrated and base their findings on a comprehensive review of the literature. Hulin (personal communication) feels that the use of job enlargement, as presented below, does appear valid and is not subject to the criticisms he and Blood raise. The concept of job enlargement seems almost to epitomize the direction inferred from this review, especially for lower-level retarded individuals. The retarded should be doing much more complex work. If the effects of job enlargement transfer, it could be hypothesized that retarded individuals would evidence less of the behaviors that have precipitated such labels as short attention span, distractible, hyperactive, etc. In addition, increased habilitative value and increased potential for placement would result from increased skill training and greater responsibility. The job enlargement literature should be carefully studied by the field. If the concepts and criticisms are understood, it could become a valuable resource.

   b. **Methods—Time Measurement.** Methods—Time Measurement (MTM) is another controversial area of industrial engineering. The procedure, developed for use in industry, is based on the early work of the Gilbreths on motion study (e.g., Gilbreth, 1911; Gilbreth & Gilbreth, 1917, 1953) and Frederick W. Taylor on time study (e.g., Taylor, 1895, 1903, 1911). The MTM system, first published in 1948, analyzes manual operations into their required basic motions and assigns a fixed, predetermined time standard to each motion. The time standards are determined on the basis of voluminous data, and take into consideration the nature of each motion and its context (Maynard, Stegemerten, & Schwab, 1948). MTM is one of several predetermined motion-time systems. These systems, which are designed to determine work time standards, are restricted to operations whose performance times are affected only by the workers. They are characterized by their ability to arrive at a time standard in advance of the operation actually being performed (Rohmert, 1971). Criticisms include a lack of regard for individual operator characteristics, e.g., sex, age, height, degree of fatigue, degree of practice of skill, and motivation; no regard for working conditions, e.g., light, noise, temperature; and no regard to work place layout, e.g., height, degree of fatigue, and presentation of articles being worked on (Rohmert, 1971). Of these systems, MTM is seen as the most relevant for use in workshops and with the retarded for the following reasons: (1) Performance ratings are not necessary; (2) Only one sample of the product is necessary to determine a standard; (3) MTM is familiar to industry; (4) Good production procedures can be established before production begins (Stroud, 1970).

   The basic unit of movement in MTM is the Gilbreth Basic Element, or therblig. These units have also been referred to as basic divisions of accomplishment (Lowry, Maynard, & Stegemerten, 1940). Gilbreth is credited with identifying 17 basic elements, or therbligs (Holmes, 1945; Maynard *et al.*, 1948). Since his original work, the list has expanded and contracted several times (Honeycutt, 1963; Morrow, 1946). At present, MTM uses the following nine basic movements: reach, move, turn and apply pressure, grasp, position, release, disengage, eye travel time and eye focus, and body, leg, and foot motions.

The unit of time used in MTM is the Time Measurement Unit (TMU), which equals .00001 hours, or .0006 minutes, or .036 seconds. The decision to have the basic unit as such was based on the established industrial practice of expressing production standards in terms of decimal hours, and the need for small units of time to measure the minute therbligs.

TMU values are assigned to each therblig according to the conditions under which it occurs. Several variables contribute to each value. *Distance moved* has the most significant effect on performance time. It affects TMU values for reach, move, and body, leg, and foot motions. Distances up to 30 inches, about as far as is practical to move without body movement, are accommodated in the tables. *Types of motion* before and/or following the therblig, are taken into account for reach and move. The three types of motion are: (1) at rest when therblig begins and ends; (2) in motion at beginning or end; and (3) in motion at beginning and end. *Weight allowance* is a variable for move. Tables contain weight allowances for up to 47.5 pounds and take into consideration actual weight of object moved, effects of resistance, e.g., brushing thick paint onto a surface, and the effect of premovement muscular tension. *Symmetry* is a variable for position and considers the amount of rotation a part might require for positioning. *Ease of handling* is a variable for position and for disengage and is divided into easy or difficult to handle. *Class of fit* is a variable for position and for disengage. It refers to the amount of pressure needed to insert or separate parts. Categories include loose, close, and exact or tight.

Level of control is a variable for reach, move, grasp, release, and body, leg, and foot motions. This variable receives considerable attention. Dimensions of control which contribute to the TMU values include muscular, visual, and mental control and level of motion, e.g., automatic, moderate accuracy, and much accuracy.

To put the system in some perspective, Rohmert (1971) describes the average length of one motion element as .005 minute. A working cycle which takes 1 minute might be split up into some 200 motion elements, each of which is defined by perhaps five variables. Thus about 1000 data items might be needed in order to set up the time standard for one operation of 1 minute duration. The time needed to carry out the analysis for such an operation would be between 150 and 300 minutes.

There are significant implications for using MTM in sheltered workshops, in research on skill training, and perhaps in research on all types of motor learning. At the most practical level, the use of MTM in sheltered workshops is good business. In one of the few reported instances (Chione & Snyder, 1968) the gross income of the workshop doubled, as did the income of the trainees. Within 6 months the figures had tripled. Chione and Snyder applied MTM methods to several aspects of workshop operation. First, to physical layout, rearranging work stations and eliminating unnecessary steps. Second, MTM was used for bidding. The effect was to provide accurate data on which to base estimates of output rate, and consequently, more competitive bidding. Third, it was used to compare individual client performance with that of average workers, using percentage ratings. Fourth, it provided an accurate means of paying commensurate wages, that is, normal pay for that portion of the normal labor rate produced. Lastly, it was used to identify and eliminate those basic motions that a client could not perform.

There are other possible uses of MTM in the vocational training of the retarded. In evaluation, application of MTM to the work sample movement (see Section III, B, 3) might facilitate a large increment in its value. For instance, work samples could be compared or equated on the basis of their therbligs, and the classes and conditions of each. In training, therbligs could be systematically added to facilitate acquisition and faded out prior to production.

It should be noted that the use of predetermined motion—time systems is not universally accepted in industry and receives considerable criticism. However, these criticisms do not appear to be directed toward the kinds of applications suggested, but rather to labor—management issues.

IV. CONCLUDING COMMENTS

The field of the habilitation of the mentally retarded, as it exists today in the United States, has been described. It exists within a context where the population with whom it deals is perceived by almost everyone as being far less capable than is really the case. Long-standing expectancies, which have recently been shown to be inappropriate, are slow to change. The majority of efforts expended have been on the development of organizational structures, leaving little for actual program. But this is beginning to change as a result of established structures and an emerging technology. The goal of the field was expressed as maximum opportunity for growth. The following is a summary of the debatable recommendations made throughout this review, intended to help facilitate that goal.

1. The focus must change from organizational considerations to the development of program (Section III, A).

2. The field must develop middle-road researchers (Section III, A).

3. Service agencies and research agencies must establish ongoing relationships (Section III, A).

4. Resources devoted to research must yield more return than if expended some other way (Section III, B, 1).

5. Research must be evaluated by those for whom the research is designed to provide information (Section III, B, 1).

6. Information obtained from research must be widely disseminated (Sections III, A and III, B, 2).

7. Research on evaluation should move away from prediction (Section III, B, 3).

8. Research on evaluation must result in procedures which yield demonstrably useful information (Section III, B, 3).

9. Research on training must have as its goal the development of procedures which can be implemented in the absence of sophisticated equipment, large sums of money, and highly trained first-line service personnel (Section III, B, 4).

10. A comprehensive, universally applicable reinforcement system for productivity should be developed (Section III, B, 4).

11. The field should identify and adapt relevant information from other disciplines (Section III, C).

12. Training objectives must be clearly defined (Section III, C, 1).

13. The application of MTM and job enlargement should be investigated (Section III, C, 2).

The basis for a technology is established. The resources are available, and the field is ready for change. A number of recommendations have been made with the intention of helping to stimulate the dialogue which must ensue if the personnel are to meet their responsibility to those in their charge.*

POSTSTATEMENT

It is surprising how little things have changed. We have not come far in 7 years. There are some notable exceptions to this and also some nonchanges worth noting. We are still a capitalistic society, we still have a surplus labor force, we are still using that surplus labor force as an excuse for not finding quality jobs for people labeled retarded and handicapped. But we are also in transition on this issue. In the last few years, even with a fairly high unemployment rate, more and more people with significant handicapping conditions are finding meaningful positions in business and industry. That was not the case in 1973, and therefore this represents the beginnings of a major change.

The stance I took regarding Farber's position is one that I still hold. Attempts to revise institutional arrangements are certainly far more active now than they ever have been. Although we still cannot claim that the retarded have fully taken their place in society, significant numbers of persons with mental retardation, including the more severely retarded, are moving into society and toward a quality existence. At the time the chapter was written

*Preparation of this paper was supported by the National Institutes of Health, U.S. Public Health Service, through Grants MH 07346 and HD 05951.

Some of the writing and secretarial work was also supported by the Department of Special Education, California State College at Los Angeles, for which the author is grateful.

this movement was in its infancy. We are now very strongly into this transitional period, but we are clearly not yet where we should be. In my discussion of service programs I make the statement that "existing service programs
can still be classified as school or workshop programs." Since that time there
has been a significant proliferation of community-based residential programs.
That certainly represents a big change in a short time.

Another interesting and welcome change involves the relationship between special education and vocational education. The chapter describes the
relationship between special education and vocational rehabilitation. I am not
aware of many strong relationships between special education programs in the
schools and departments of vocational rehabilitation. It is the case, however,
that the same people who were involved in that movement, for example,
Donn Brolin, Bill Younie, Gary Clark, Charles Kokaska, and others have since
become very interactive with people from the field of vocational education
and have greatly expanded what had originally started out as a relationship
with people in vocational rehabilitation.

In rereading this chapter I noticed the complete omission of any reference to work activity centers. Unbelievable! They were in existence then just
as much as they are now. Such organizations are now serving individuals with
much more significant handicapping conditions than they were even 7 years
ago. But to have put this chapter together and not so much as mentioned
their existence is really quite surprising. Had I covered work activity centers,
I would have made comments about like those on sheltered workshops. What
I would add, however, is that work activity center certificates, by and large,
are really licenses to do even less than people are doing in sheltered workshops.
Our experience and our data suggest that work activity center clients are, in
most cases, capable of producing considerably more than most people now
produce in sheltered workshops. We knew that then, and we know it now.
The low levels of productivity found in work activity centers today are no
more excusable now than they were then. This low productivity is changing
in some places.

I still agree with Dubrow (1958) that extended care workshops (and
work activity centers) should be largely self-supporting. He made that statement 22 years ago. It must be added, however, that I have had a number of
years to prove my point and am still having trouble doing it. To my knowledge, the several isolated examples in which the work part of an agency was
self-supporting have been temporary because of various circumstances such
as contract availability, funding, and staff turnover. I can legitimately be
criticized for not yet having demonstrated on a large scale and permanent
basis that such agencies can be self-supporting. But I am still trying. The
argument would be closed if efforts at placement into competitive industry
became so successful that they made obsolete the conventional concepts of
sheltered workshops and work activity centers. We will probably continue to
have such entities, but they should evolve into integrated agencies, including production workers labeled both normal and handicapped. They should
expand to include a significant number of individuals earning competitive
wages. Under this condition I would feel much more comfortable about

their continued existence. If we include in the scheme of things a wide variety of other options such as semisegregated work forces within industry, job stations in industry, etc., we can have a full range of options and still stay away from the unacceptable concept of large-scale, totally segregated, nonproductive holding tanks.

Automation laid an egg. Pocket calculators cost about one-tenth of what they used to, lots of home computers have come into existence at reasonable prices, but we do not seem to be much closer to efficient, effective use of automation in programs for the handicapped. Some of the systems developed for people with severe physical and multiple handicaps are exciting. They are, however, still expensive and not readily available to many individuals. I hope that we keep pursuing this area in the field, but I am not as confident of its importance as I was when I wrote the paper.

The section on prediction and evaluation could be written today with the same conclusions. I have spent hundreds of hours since then talking to people, being asked to endorse various evaluation and assessment devices and products, and debating the issue of prediction and evaluation. I am more critical of work samples today. But there is a viable alternative now—criterion referenced assessment. Criterion referenced assessment involves tests that are related directly to the actual skills which the trainer wishes the learner to have. The assessment consists of teaching the person until she demonstrates competence, with that competence being the assessment. Criterion referenced assessment is a viable and meaningful way to describe performance. It resolves most of the criticisms leveled against conventional forms of assessment, including work samples.

Since that chapter came out, several organizations developing work samples claim to have addressed the criticisms in this chapter and designed tests and evaluation batteries that fit in with my suggestions. Although I have not examined all of them in great detail, what I have seen falls far short of what I could endorse. I would hasten to add that this may be true in part because my thinking has changed in the direction of criterion referenced assessment. That may not be fair, but it is my present thinking.

In the last 7 years there have been many articles on the use of reinforcement systems. It is still the case, however, that few service agencies have well-developed, effective reinforcement systems. Overuse and misuse of reinforcement systems are still rampant in the field. In sheltered workshops and work activity centers it is rare to see a well-thought-out and systematically utilized reinforcement system. This can be partially explained by high staff turnover and lack of training, a dual problem that is as prevalent today as it was in 1972. Perhaps this staff problem exists partly because reinforcement systems for staff are no better developed than those for clients.

Well, how has the future discussed in the chapter actually been unfolding? First, few communities have really benefited from the errors made by other communities. Organizations such as the National Association for Retarded Citizens have certainly helped in the sharing of experiences, but there have been too many repetitions of creating the wheel. This is still going on and probably will continue. Second, we are not any closer to focusing on program content than we were 7 years ago. The emphasis is still on program expansion and new organizational structures rather than the activities in which clients and staff engage to change the quality of existence for people labeled clients.

I still have a commitment to middle-road research as a viable strategy for connecting what has been learned in the laboratory with the field. Personally, I have chosen to move completely out of laboratory research and into the community. My current activities, described in terms of research, involve studying strategies for creating significant change in social service organizations. My colleagues and I systematically collect data on our activities, but I really don't feel it appropriate to label that research.

I still believe that service agencies should connect with university personnel for mutual benefit. In those instances where this has happened, every possible result has occurred, including happiness or frustration on the part of one or both sides. But I still think this is useful and should continue.

Under recommendations for research in the chapter it was predicted that funds would dry up for research if practitioners did not get substantial return. This has come to pass. It is getting harder and harder to obtain financial support for pure laboratory research in the area of mental retardation. Most of the people who used to be involved in such research are now doing studies having application to service settings, as part, if not all, of their research endeavors.

In the discussion on increasing rates of existing behaviors the development of a comprehensive reinforcement system was suggested. Something very important was left out of that discussion. The use of such a system should not be brought into play until job stations are efficiently designed, production workers are taught cycle constancy, and the work being done—when done efficiently and correctly—can generate a decent wage. Without these prerequisites, the use of strong reinforcement programs is inappropriate, at best.

In the comments on facilitating the acquisition of new behaviors, five areas in need of continued research were suggested. As you will see from some of the other studies reported here, my colleagues and I got into some of these issues but really resolved none of them. Research in all of these areas is still important and should be done.

Under the discussion of prospective involvements a body of literature was described. There has been very little use of this literature to date. The comments made there still apply and should be addressed. The field is still afraid of industry, labor unions, and the world out there. Until that becomes a major focus of our attention we will not accomplish our goals.

I find it very interesting to note the statement that industry should develop programs for the handicapped and retain control before they are forced to do it and lose control. That statement was written just a few months before the passage of the Rehabilitation Act of 1973, which did just that. Seven years later, however, industry is still far short of meeting the law or its subsequent revisions. We would have been better off, in the long run, to have industry focus on the capabilities rather than the handicaps of people so labeled.

Since the chapter was written many companies have begun to hire people with mental retardation and other handicapping conditions. That is, there have been the beginnings of a move to hire people with severe handicapping conditions including mental retardation. We need expanded documentation of this. The advertising industry and public interest groups have disseminated this information to some extent, but they should capitalize much more on the successes and competencies that have been demonstrated recently. We should drop forever the slogan "Hire the Handicapped" and replace it with the slogan "Hire the Competent and learn what competence means."

After the chapter was written, I had the opportunity to go through training in Methods—Time Measurement. The Maynard Corporation in Chicago which teaches this system allowed me to go through training without receiving the blue card and without having to pay a fee. The agreement was that if I thought the system was valuable and worth putting into agencies, I would promote its use. I went through the training and found it interesting, but I did not feel that the money and energy needed to obtain and use the system was worth it. This chapter gives a pretty good description of the basic concepts involved in the system. The concepts are extremely helpful in looking at tasks, but I do not believe the molecular use of the system warrants the energy in settings where the production force is primarily people labeled handicapped. I might be wrong on this issue, especially if having someone trained in the system can be used as a basis for establishing credibility with industry. At the present time, then, I am not inclined to recommend MTM training for personnel, although I believe people should have a familiarity with the system and a conceptual understanding of what it does.

I still support the recommendations made at the end of the chapter. There has been progress toward some of them, but much work is still needed in all these areas. In light of our greatly increased focus on community-based residential programs and on the mandatory education for all handicapped individuals, however, this chapter falls far short of calling for what is needed to match where our society now seems to be and seems to be going. That, indeed, is encouraging.

CHAPTER 8

An Adaptive Behavior Philosophy: Who Needs It?

Marc W. Gold

PRESTATEMENT

When this paper was presented, several experiments had been conducted beyond the original study with the bicycle brakes. The research was beginning to develop interest, but it was still seen as fairly left field. I was surprised and pleased to be invited by Bob Gettings, the executive director of the National Association of Superintendents of Public Residential Facilities, to speak at their workshop. Looking back on the meeting, I recall that I met several people who have been good professional colleagues and friends ever since. Not too long before that meeting the American Association on Mental Deficiency came out with their Adaptive Behavior Scales, and these were becoming very popular for use in residential settings. It's important to remember that this paper was presented when alternative community residential facilities were just beginning. Several of the people at that meeting, in fact, are still in the forefront of the development of alternatives and in the movement away from large-scale residential settings.

Present concern about adaptive behavior should go beyond the AAMD Adaptive Behavior Scale. Adaptive behavior needs to be addressed in terms of the context in which institutionalized retarded individuals find themselves moving from institutions into communities. The adaptive behavior of community, parents, and professionals in fields dealing with the retarded is at least as critical as that of the retarded themselves. It is not difficult to get the retarded to adapt. Where things bog down is in getting society to adapt, move, and change.

How does one tell a group of superintendents that they must find ways of eliminating their jobs as they presently exist? Being the director of a com-

This paper originally appeared in the Proceedings of the National Association of Superintendents of Public Residential Facilities, Region V, Interaction Workshop on Community Living for Institutionalized Retardates, Chicago, May 1972. Reprinted by permission of the publisher.

munity residential program is different from being the director of a large institution and requires a major modification in job description and functioning. That takes a tremendous amount of adaptive behavior.

Training professionals to train moderately and severely retarded individuals to assemble electronic parts so they can earn good money on the open labor market, getting society to hire the retarded, getting unions to accept the retarded for membership—these changes require adaptive behavior. Yet, we go along with our adaptive behavior checklist and whom do we check off? We check off the retarded.

Why are we not checking off the labor unions and management, parents' organizations, institutions, and directors of institutions? They are the ones supposedly more equipped to adapt. By definition, the retarded are not able to adapt, and yet they are the only ones expected to do so. It is not that they cannot. They have all the flexibility to adapt and are just waiting to do so. It is the rest of us who are not adapting, and that has to change. One way to effect this change is to expose some of the inappropriate expectancies for the retarded which many members of society share. Many of these inappropriate expectancies are based on the fallacy of requisite intelligence.

What is the difference between a person who is five years old for one year and someone who is five years old for many years? Do they think the same? Do they act the same? Should we expect the same behavior from both of them?

When someone is labeled mentally retarded and diagnosed as performing at the mental level of a five-year-old, the tendency is to expect him to perform like a five-year-old. We must change that expectancy.

What do you suppose a normal five-year-old could do if he could stay five for more than just one year? He could learn to do new things in that added time. And, if he happened to be large for his age, say five-foot-eight, he could learn even more.

Consider some very specific activities such as morning routines, travel to and from work, and work itself, and ask these questions: Which activities require intelligence? Which ones require training, but not much intelligence? Which ones require both training and intelligence? Most activities which we assume require intelligence do not. Activities such as basic cooking, housework, bench assembly work, auto parts assembly, and disassembly work are all good examples. They require training. Intelligence is required to organize the activity and to do the training, but the tasks themselves can be performed without requiring much intelligence.

Why then do we perpetuate the fallacy of requisite intelligence? One reason is that we like to think of ourselves as intelligent beings doing intelligent things. We have been conditioned to think this way and so, for no real reason, it is uncomfortable to find out that much of our time is spent doing what any five-year-old could do if he were trained.

Another problem is the expectancy cycle which we perpetuate. For a century now, those working with the mentally retarded have described their limitations. When working with the retarded, we operate with the expectancies generated by our own work. We prove that we are right and the expectancy cycle goes on. Since normal folks can do things that the retarded cannot do, we assume that those things must require intelligence. The retarded are not expected to do them and the cycle continues.

Another reason for limiting the retarded is society's need to maintain the status quo. As long as six million people are kept out of the mainstream of society by our saying they do not have what it takes, not only do we avoid having to make room for them, but we also provide a lot of other people with work taking care of the retarded and keeping them out of the mainstream.

Farber and Lewis use the term *progressive status quoism* to describe a situation where systems having two very specific characteristics are established. The first characteristic of the system is that it gives the impression that considerable effort is being expended to solve a societal problem. The second characteristic is that the problem is not being solved by the system. The education system in this country is a good example. When a black man seeks a loan to start a business and is turned down, we give him more education instead of forcing the banks to lend him the money. When a Puerto Rican is not able to get into the carpenter's union to become a carpenter, we say he needs more education instead of doing something about the carpenter's union that will not admit him. A Puerto Rican can have a Ph.D. in wood, and still not be admitted. A large structure is set up, spending much time, energy, and manpower, all of which is designed to solve the problem, but it does not. What happens instead is that we absolve ourselves of the real responsibility of helping people get good jobs. And we do exactly the same with the retarded. The same political and economic structures in the country allow us to absolve ourselves of the responsibility for solving the problems of the retarded.

The position taken here is based on experiences at Children's Research Center, University of Illinois, where research is being conducted on the development of a technology of instruction for the vocational habilitation of the mentally retarded. The technology has developed to the point where a housewife with no prior experience with the retarded, one day of instruction, and one week of practice can enter a sheltered workshop and work individually with moderately and severely retarded individuals. With an average of two hours of client instruction, she can give trainees sufficient skill to do work worth a minimum wage. Attempts to implement the technology have brought to focus the adaptability of the retarded and the rigidity of everyone else.

This and the other research must be utilized to facilitate change in government. For example, import laws and labor laws must be modified so that much of the electronics business that is now being farmed out to Taiwan, Korea, China, and other places can be profitably brought back into this country for the retarded and the handicapped. By bringing back to the U.S. a small fraction of the hand labor and bench assembly labor that our industries are now sending overseas, every retarded individual in this country could be kept busy for the rest of his life earning a very good wage. If this is to happen, labor and management must be involved. We have found them very willing to help. The Bendix Corporation, Magnavox, and General Electric have given us large amounts of time and have opened their most private files to show us quality control data and methods time measurement data. They seem willing to do anything they can to assist. They indicate a willingness to work with labor toward getting the retarded into their organizations or getting work out of their organization.

And what about labor? Who has asked them? The next time you are talking to the Board of Directors of some agency for the retarded, ask for a show of hands of people on the board who are members of labor and see what you find. Labor is seldom involved in our work and it is not their fault. It is ours. If we are really going to change things, we must get to labor, too.

A note on housing. Many believe that changing the housing of the retarded is somehow going to solve their problems. That is only a small, small piece of what has to happen. What are you going to do with the retarded when you get them out there living in groups of two and three unless you affect the entire context in which they live? This means the community, families, professionals. Where you live is not normalization. Normalization is not defined by where you live but how you live.

Some specific examples of our research might help to describe the application of some of the foregoing position statements. In one study, a group of 64 moderately and severely retarded adolescents from sheltered workshops for the handicapped located throughout Illinois learned to assemble a 15-piece bicycle brake, accurately and consistently. This is a task which almost no one could do without some training or practice. The average time required to learn each task was just over two hours.

In another study, 16 severely retarded individuals were trained to sort bolts. The criterion task was sorting 7/8-in. long from 1-in. long bolts. They had to sort the pile once without any errors which meant 25 of the 7/8-in. bolts were placed in one pile and 25 of the 1-in. in another pile. A maximum of 750 attempts were allowed, that is, 15 sortings of the pile. Eight subjects worked only on the 7/8-in. from 1-in. discrimination. None of them reached criterion in 750 trials. All eight subjects trained using an easy-to-hard sequence learned all three tasks, averaging less than 400 trials to criterion.

In a large production study, moderately and severely retarded individuals assembled the bicycle brakes either one hour or three hours per day. Average hourly production was over 22 brakes per hour per person. The overall error rate was under 5 percent.

Another relevant aspect of our research relates to the issue of IQ. We get zero order correlations between IQ and ability to learn these tasks, suggesting that one cannot predict from IQ how people are going to learn a task, at least if it is nonverbal and manipulative.

The data presented are just the beginning. We hope to go to Social and Rehabilitation Services in a couple of years with a stack of W-2 Forms belonging to severely retarded individuals who are earning four or five thousand dollars a year and ask why their vocational rehabilitation was not funded. We will be told it was because they were diagnosed incapable of being habilitated.

We are proposing that a terminal extended-care sheltered workshop could be set up where individuals who will probably never succeed competitively could make two and a half to three dollars an hour in a non-competitive situation.

To conclude, when thinking about adaptive behavior, think of it as applying to others more than to the retarded. Everyone will have to give up some of what he has held near and dear for a long, long time, break loose, and try another way.

The instructional technology used in the studies mentioned is certainly an important recent development, but more important is the break we have made in the expectancy cycle. As society, parents, and professionals become increasingly aware of the kinds of accomplishments described above, they will change their expectancies and give the retarded their inherent right to full participation in society.

POSTSTATEMENT

Since 1972 there have been numerous attempts to design instruments and strategies for looking at the context into which people labeled retarded find themselves. PASS 3* is one example. The PASS System has received much attention, both positive and negative. The principle negative reaction seems to be occasioned by how some of its adherents administer the procedures.

We are still a long way from really addressing the issues of context either in terms of the characteristics of the agencies which service people labeled handicapped or in terms of the generic services and communities in general where these individuals live or will live. Until we do so, we are not going to make a big difference in people's lives. The opening paragraph of this paper establishes a basic position that will show up very strongly under the alternative definition of mental retardation (Chapter 14).

Several of the components of what we now describe as the philosophy of the Try Another Way System were first presented in this paper. They include the fallacy of requisite intelligence, the expectancy cycle, and progressive status quoism, the concept labeled and developed by Bernard Farber and Michael Lewis.

The word *retardate* showed up again. This time it was in their title, rather than mine. I also noticed the word *housewife*. That was the correct label then, but present levels of consciousness dictate that a different word should have been used.

There was a suggestion in the paper that import and labor laws would

---

*Wolf Wolfensberger & Linda Glenn. *PASS 3: A method for the quantitative evaluation of human services, Handbook* (3rd ed.). Toronto: National Institute on Mental Retardation, 1975.

have to be modified. What seems to be happening now is that other countries are gradually catching up with us in terms of the wages they pay, so more of the work is being done here in the country. There is still plenty going on abroad, but the natural laws of supply and demand seem to be resolving this issue. It also seems possible that the Iranian Crisis of 1979–1980 and other international tensions could stimulate a level of nationalistic spirit that would promote home production.

In rereading this paper, I was very favorably impressed with two of the sentences: "Where you live is not normalization. Normalization is not defined by where you live but how you live." I also noticed proposing a terminal extended-care sheltered workshop. I don't think we should set up any more sheltered workshops. But certainly many of those that are already in existence could and should become more remunerative and should be integrated in terms of their production force, that is, nonretarded individuals should be included.

The Learning of Difficult Visual Discriminations by the Moderately and Severely Retarded

Marc W. Gold and Craig R. Barclay

PRESTATEMENT

The concept of middle-road research was described in some detail in the chapter on the present and future habilitation of the mentally retarded (Chapter 7). The present study represents a clear example of middle-road research. It attempts to combine laboratory control and theoretically based constructs with the solution of problems found in real settings.

This was the first experiment in our research program that did not involve the bicycle brakes.

Sorting tasks are very common in school and workshop programs for the retarded. In schools, trainable retarded children learn to sort on many dimensions including size, shape, color and category. The use of systematic training rather than merely exposure is, however, seldom found. The level of difficulty, in addition, is usually kept very low.

In sheltered workshops and work activity centers, sorting is usually done as a subcontract. When the required discriminations are perceived by staff as difficult, one of two alternatives is usually followed: either the subcontract is rejected on the grounds that it is too difficult for the clients, or a jig is made to insure the correct decision. (A jig is a device used as a guide or template.) For example, to sort piles of bolts which are identical in every way except one-eighth inch difference in length, the board with a hole the depth of the shorter bolt might be used. The sorting decision would be made on the basis of whether or not the bolt went all the way down in the hole. The position taken here is that the use of jigs in sheltered workshops and vocational training programs often results in reducing the habilitative value of the con-

---

This article originally appeared in *Mental Retardation*, 1973, *11* (2), 9–11. Reprinted by permission of the publisher.

tract. Instead of teaching clients the discriminations and movements required to perform the task, they are allowed to complete the contract using skills already in their repertoire. In addition, jigs are often slower because of the added movement (Maynard, Stegemerten & Schwab, 1948). One other reason for the frequent use of jigs in habilitation programs is that professionals would not expect the retarded to be able to accurately and consistently sort a pile where the difference between bolts was one-eighth of an inch, especially if the professionals had attempted the task and experienced difficulty.

There were several purposes to the present study: (1) to demonstrate the ability of moderately and severely retarded individuals to learn a difficult visual discrimination; (2) to apply a piece of information from basic learning research to a task found in applied settings; and (3) to demonstrate the effectiveness of the particular training procedure. The procedure used was based on information from the Attention Theory of Zeaman and House (1963). According to the theory a series of easy-to-hard discriminations is learned more quickly than a hard-only discrimination (House & Zeaman, 1960; Shepp & Zeaman, 1966; Zeaman and House, 1963). For a practitioner-oriented description of the theory the reader is referred to Gold and Scott (1971).

The independent variable was procedure (easy-to-hard sequence or hard task only). Criterion for learning was defined as one errorless sorting of the pile on the one task, for the Hard Group, and on each of three tasks for the Easy Group. The dependent variable was trials to criterion, where the decision on each bolt constituted a trial.

METHOD

Subjects

Sixteen moderately and severely retarded adolescent and adult individuals were randomly selected from the population of a work activity center located in an industrial midwestern city of about 40,000 residents. The mean IQ score for the sample was 47.5; the age range was from 17 to 59. Following selection, subjects were randomly assigned to one of the two groups. A replication of this study was conducted subsequently, using mildly and moderately retarded clients from a workshop in Peoria, Illinois. For this group, the mean IQ score was 58; the age range was 20 to 57.

Materials

The apparatus was a 2 by 3 foot plywood base with three trays—one for the mixed and two for the sorted Cap-Screws-Hex Head bolts. Twenty-five of each of four length bolts were used—one and one-half inches, one inch, seven-eighths of an inch, and three-quarters of an inch. All were one-quarter of an inch in diameter.

Procedure

Each subject was seated at a table on which the apparatus was placed. The experimenter sat across the table facing the subject. The experimenter picked up one bolt, looked at it, and placed it in one of the two empty trays; then he picked up a bolt of the other length and placed it in the remaining empty tray. The experimenter then said to the subject, "Now, you do it." When the subject made an error, the experimenter removed the bolt from the wrong tray, handed it back to the subject and said, "Try another way," while pointing to the correct tray. No other verbal directions or cues were provided.

Subjects in the Hard Group were brought to the criterion of one errorless sorting of a pile of 50 bolts containing 25 each of one inch and seven-eighths inch bolts. Subjects in the Easy Group were brought to criterion on each of three piles, starting with one and one-half inches and three-quarters of an inch, then one inch and three-quarters of an inch, and ending with one inch and seven-eighths of an inch. Subjects failing to reach criterion by 15 sortings of the pile (750 trials) were stopped and given a score of 750. For the Easy Group this meant having to learn all three tasks within 750 trials. An independent groups design was used.

RESULTS

For the moderately and severely retarded work activity center clients, no subjects in the Hard Group learned the task. All subjects in the Easy Group learned all three tasks; their mean trials to criterion for the three tasks combined was 394, the range was 200-750. The difference was analyzed using a single classification Analysis of Variance, and found to be highly significant ($F_{1,14}$ = 32.72, $p < .001$). All of the subjects in the Hard Group were subsequently re-run using the easy-to-hard sequence. Two subjects still failed to reach criterion. The other six reached criterion, with a mean of 358 trials (Range = 250-450, not including the two failures).

For the mildly and moderately retarded subjects in the replication study, the mean trials to criterion for the Hard Group was 281 (Range = 50-750). Mean trials to criterion for the Easy Group was 413 (Range = 200-750). The difference was not significant ($F_{1,14}$ = 1.47, n.s.). Two subjects in the Easy Group and one subject in the Hard Group failed to reach criterion. None of the subjects in the replication study were re-run.

DISCUSSION

For clarity, the replication data will be discussed first. The replication data contained considerable variance and no indication of treatment effect. This is especially interesting in light of the magnitude of the difference found in the first study. The interpretation presented here is that the sheltered workshop population from which the replication sample was drawn may have contained considerable heterogeneity on variables, such as attention span, motivation or coordination, which were not assessed, but which could affect performance on the task.

The same problem has been noted with institutionalized populations on other, more complex tasks. That is, between-subject variance was great, and statistically significant differences were not found. New studies are in progress on the problem of determining the nature of qualitative rather than quantitative differences between populations. This phenomenon has been found in several studies, however, which suggests that the data from the first study can still be used with confidence.

For the work activity center clients in the first study the effectiveness and efficiency of the easy-to-hard sequence was clearly demonstrated. Had the conventional approach been used where the learners were exposed to the criterion task only, the conclusion could have been that they were not capable of learning the task. Such a conclusion is often made in the absence of alternative methods of instruction. The performance of the Hard Group on the easy-to-hard sequence, following failure, further supports the procedure and suggests something else. Two of the subjects never reached criterion. The other six took approximately the same amount of time as the Easy Group, even after 750 trials on the third of the three tasks. This is interpreted as an example of failure set. Failure set refers to a situation where the retarded individual, having experienced prolonged failure on a problem which he cannot solve, finds it difficult to solve very simple problems, which he could solve, prior to the failure experience (Zeaman & House, 1963). The data presented here might be interpreted to suggest the importance of selecting a training procedure in advance of training, rather than after the learner has experienced a procedure and not learned the task. This means identifying and having some idea of the relative strength of applicable procedures. This study and the works by Brown and Foshee (1971), Gold and Scott (1971), Gold (1968, 1973), and Touchette (1968, 1969) provide information on a variety of training procedures.

An important implication of this study relates to the difficulty of the discriminations acquired by the subjects. Discriminating differences on one-eighth of an inch, without having a sample against which to compare, has been demonstrated to be an initially difficult task for normal individuals. The position taken by the writer is that intelligence is related to the time it takes to identify what the problem is, but not to the discrimination itself. Therefore, moderately and severely retarded individuals should be expected to make the same visual discriminations as normal individuals, but require more assistance in guiding their attention to the relevant aspects of the problem. The procedure described in this report might have application to other situations where visual or other sensory discriminations are required, such as letter recognition, cooking, and bench assembly work.

This study also suggests several possible changes in current sheltered workshop and work activity center practices. Perhaps tasks which are presently refused or "jigged" because of presumed difficult discriminations would be more habilitative and remunerative if the discriminations were taught. A study is in progress to provide further clarification on this issue.

In the present experiment, the procedures were administered using a one-to-one relationship (teacher-student). The easy-to-hard procedure could also be used effectively in small groups. However, many individuals need the supervision and feedback available only in a one-to-one situation in order to learn this and other tasks. Workshop and work activity center personnel seldom set up systematic one-to-one training programs because of staff shortage and client load, and also because they have been successful doing what training they have done in group settings. As expectancies rise and techniques develop, we will have to move to one-to-one instruction for much of the training to be done. What has been a luxury for teaching simple tasks will be a necessity for training on more complex tasks.

The level of complexity of tasks found in work settings for the moderately and severely retarded must be scrutinized for their non-habilitative nature (Gold, 1973), with the intent of moving to more fulfilling tasks. Studies such as this one should cause us to question all of the assumptions which underlie apparently inappropriate expectancies. Revised expectancies and an emerging technology of instruction should result in a significantly improved outlook for the moderately and severely retarded.*

POSTSTATEMENT

The problems that this study addresses still exist. It could be argued that this article had little, if any, impact on solving those problems. The suggestions in the article for training individuals on sorting tasks remain useful since there are still many sorting tasks in sheltered workshops and work activity centers. If workers were paid a decent piece rate on such projects, I would be much more comfortable about suggesting ways of significantly increasing their productivity. As it stands now, in many sheltered workshops and work activity centers norms for standard productivity are set so high that workers are paid very poorly per piece, no matter what the rate. For a vivid description of such conditions, as of 1979, the reader is referred to the *Wall Street Journal*, October 17, 1979.

There is a wonderful lesson for a researcher to learn from this article: publish before you replicate. We had a perfect study. All subjects in the experimental group learned. All subjects in the control group did not. A researcher's dream. Then we replicated using a different population and found no significant differences between the two treatment conditions. Should we have published just the first experiment? I do not think so. Should we have not done the second study? Who knows? The discussion section of the article does a poor job of trying to clarify what happened. Trying to provide a better explanation today is proving to be no easier.

---

*This study was supported in part by NICHHD Program Project Grant No. HD 05951 to Children's Research Center, University of Illinois at Urbana-Champaign.

Appreciation is expressed to Progress School, Decatur, Illinois, and Community Workshop, Peoria, Illinois.

Perhaps the most useful statement in the article is found near the end. "As expectancies rise and techniques develop, we will have to move to one-to-one instruction for much of the training to be done. What has been a luxury for teaching simple tasks will be a necessity for training on more complex ones."

CHAPTER 10

The Effects of Verbal Labels on the Acquisition and Retention of a Complex Assembly Task

Marc W. Gold and Craig R. Barclay

PRESTATEMENT

This study was originally designed to "prove" that verbal labels used in train-ers' instruction did not work with people considered moderately and severely retarded. I am a little ashamed to admit that we thought we could *prove* this. It is a basic part of research methodology that one cannot prove that some-thing does not exist—one cannot "prove the null hypothesis." A researcher can prove a difference when she gets it because she did get it. That approach is called "rejecting the null hypothesis." When she does not get a difference, all she can say is that she did not get a difference. Researchers are supposed to know that. Many of us, however, still overlook this very basic piece of scientific method.

This article was published in the *Training School Bulletin*, a journal of fairly limited circulation. The journal, however, has been in existence for many years.

This was our first study using the bicycle brakes in which we did not use the two shoes. There were two reasons for this: (1) There was a great deal of difficulty with the manipulations involved in inserting the shoes in the pre-vious studies and (b) since this study had to do, primarily, with discrimin-ations rather than manipulations, this change seemed appropriate. Both of these points should have been made in the article. Incidentally, when we began using this task with blind individuals, we changed the method for in-serting the shoes, thus solving those problems.

The use of labeling, as a teaching tool, is an integral part of every classroom and workshop. Usually, labels are used indiscriminately. That is, the trainer does not systematically decide which skills are best taught or retained using labels. The labels are usually taught simultaneously with the tasks or dis-

This article originally appeared in *Training School Bulletin,* 1973, *70* (1), 38–42. Re-printed by permission of the publisher.

criminations being labeled. In most situations the trainer assumes that there is a natural, logical and recognizable relationship between the label and what is being labeled. For example, if the trainer says "The flat part goes up" it is assumed that "flat" communicates something, that the trainee knows the difference between flat and not flat, and can meaningfully relate the label to the discrimination being made. One of the problems resulting from such an arbitrary strategy is that, when a trainee fails at a task, it is usually assumed he cannot perform the task. However, it may be that, had the trainee understood the labels and directions, he could have done the task. Seldom is this second interpretation investigated.

The research program, of which this study is a part, emphasizes the use of non-verbal training procedures and has demonstrated that moderately and severely retarded individuals are capable of learning to do complex assembly work, using such strategies (Gold, 1972). The present study is the result of a series of discussions in which the facilitating effects of the non-verbal procedures, as opposed to other aspects of the methodology, were questioned. The literature on verbal mediation (e.g., Harter, 1965; Zigler & Balla, 1971) and memory (e.g., Belmont, 1966; Shepp & Turrisi, 1966) is confusing and does not provide a clear perspective of the problem.

The present study was designed to specifically study the effect of labeling each discrimination, or part, while retaining the essentially non-verbal procedures for correcting errors. This is the first study in the research program which utilized or manipulated verbal cues. Consequently, the decision was made to limit the study to the effect of labels as they would be used in a typical classroom or workshop setting. That is, no pretesting for meaningfulness of the labels was done, and labels which "seemed" to provide information were used. There was no intent to control for meaningfulness but rather to obtain an initial indication of the effect of labels as they are typically used in service settings.

The purpose of the study was to compare the effectiveness of verbal labels with no verbal labels on the acquisition and retention of a complex assembly task. The independent variables were Cue Condition (verbal labels or no verbal labels) and Learning/Retention. Dependent variables included trials to criterion, discrimination errors to criterion, and manipulation errors to criterion.

METHOD

Subjects

Subjects were sixteen moderately and severely retarded (mean IQ = 43) work activity center clients. Descriptive data for the sample are presented in Table 1.

The sample was drawn randomly from the shop populations, with the only restriction being that subjects had sufficient visual and motor capabilities to see and hold the parts of the assembly. Subjects were randomly assigned to one of the two groups. The data presented are for 14 subjects because two subjects in the No Verbal Cue Group were unavailable for the retention phase of the study.

Materials

The apparatus consisted of a wooden tray with compartments for a small quantity of each part and a divider which allowed for one of each part to be moved forward so that one set could be segregated and sequenced for assembly.

The task was a Bendix, RB-2 coaster brake with the shoes removed. Previous studies have conclusively demonstrated the ability of moderately and severely retarded individuals to learn to assemble the complete brake (Gold, 1972).

The verbal cues for the Verbal Cue Group are found in Table 2.

Procedure

The general procedure for demonstrating the task, correcting errors, recording data, and giving reinforcements is described in detail by Gold (1972). The assembly was demonstrated once by the experimenter to show the subject how to respond to the correction procedure, then the subject assembled the unit until a criterion of six correct assemblies out of eight consecutive trials was reached. One complete assembly of the brake without error or assistance con-

Table 1
Descriptive Characteristics of Subjects

Group	IQ			CA (years)		
	Mean	SD	Range	Mean	SD	Range
Verbal Cue	44	4.73	37-51	24	10	12-38
No Verbal Cue	42	5.12	36-49	24	4.9	19-33

Table 2
Verbal Labels and Cues for Verbal Cue Group

Part	Verbal Label and Cue
axle	—
expander	The square goes up.
bearing	The flat part goes up.
cap	The little end goes up.
arm	The letters go up.
nut	—
sub-assembly	The lines go up.
hub	The little hole goes up.
bearing	The flat part goes up.
drive	The big end goes up.
bearing	The flat part goes up.
cone	The flat things go up.

stituted a trial. Subjects failing to reach criterion by 55 trials were stopped and given a score of 55.

When a subject made a discrimination error, that is, started to put a part on upside down, the experimenter said, "Try another way," and then, "Good," when the subject turned the part over. "Good" was also said at the completion of a trial and was the only intentionally administered reinforcer. The difference between the two groups in the present study was the addition of the verbal label for the Verbal Cue Group. For example, when a subject in the Verbal Cue Group made an error on the expander, the experimenter said, "The square goes up. Try another way," and for the bearings, "The flat part goes up. Try another way." The No Verbal Cue Group got, "Try another way," only.

The retention interval was six months during which time subjects were not exposed to the task. Subjects were retrained to the original criterion. During retraining subjects in the Verbal Cue Group were not given verbal cues so that the effects of the verbal cues used during original learning could be assessed for retention.

RESULTS

A 2 x 2 (Cue Condition X Learning/Retention) analysis of variance was performed on each of the three dependent variables. Cue condition was the between-subjects variable and Learning/Retention was the within-subject variable.

The only reliable effect for the trials to criterion dependent variable was the main effect due to Learning/Retention, in favor of retention ($F = 17.78$, $1/12$ df, $p < .01$), indicating that the mean number of trials to criterion was significantly less for retention (12.21) than for original learning (34.14).

The mean number of manipulation errors to criterion was less for retention (1.00) than for original learning (27.71), the difference being highly significant ($F = 21.68$, $1/12$ df, $p < .01$).

Reliable effects for the discrimination errors to criterion dependent variable included main effects for Cue Condition, and for Learning/Retention. The Verbal Cue Group had fewer discrimination errors (mean = 21.38) than the No Verbal Cue Group (mean = 49.50) ($F = 16.68$, $1/12$ df, $p < .01$). There were fewer discrimination errors for retention (mean = 8.79) than for original learning (mean = 58.07) ($F = 19.98$, $1/12$ df, $p < .01$). The interaction between Cue Condition and Learning/Retention was not significant ($p < .07$).

DISCUSSION

The highly significant retention effect, found for both groups and all three dependent measures was consistent with the one year retention study done using essentially the same task (Gold, 1972). These data support the long term retention literature (Belmont, 1966) which indicates that retention is related, in part, to the degree of original learning. Six correct out of eight consecutive trials is considered here to be a strong criterion. In the present study it is interesting to note that retention was strong for both the manipulative and the discriminative steps of the task. Such reliable and replicated effects have implications for those service personnel who frequently report that the individuals with whom they work learn things and then forget them. Perhaps if the criterion for learning was increased, for instance, from one to two correct trials to eight or more depending on the task, then retention would be better.

No reliable differences were found between the two groups on retention. The only reliable effect attributable to Cue Condition was the overall superiority of the Verbal Cue Group on discrimination errors, for both original learning and retention. The data suggest that the addition of the verbal cue facilitated both acquisition and retention of the discriminations. If the data generalize, then, moderately and severely retarded individuals can utilize verbal labels in the acquisition of the kinds of visual discriminations required for the tasks utilized in the present study.

However, before assuming generalization several methodological issues need clarification. All of the criticisms raised by Belmont (1966) related to methodological problems of long term retention studies apply to the present study. Additionally, the small sample size of the present study precludes confidence and suggests the need for further clarification of the effect of verbal cues on retention.

Apart from these issues, some changes in the procedures seem warranted. Subjects who reach 55 trials should not be included in the data as undifferentiated from subjects who reached criterion. In the present study and previous studies using the Bendix brake, 55 was arbitrarily used as the terminating point, and was necessarily applied in only a few cases. In the present study three subjects, all in the No Verbal Cue Group, went 55 trials without reaching criterion. Interestingly, all reached criterion during retraining, in 7, 7, and 20 trials. This suggests that the magnitude of difference between the two procedures might have been much more visible had a larger sample size and/or higher termination point been used. In future studies subjects failing to reach criterion by 55 trials will be replaced for the parametric analysis, run clinically, using whatever is needed to bring them to criterion, and reported on separately in the same publication as the data analyzed parametrically. This should clean up some of the variance due to methodological factors and enhance the applicability of the procedures. It is still felt that allowing subjects to go beyond 55 trials would create the risk of disproportionate heterogeneity and decrease the meaningfulness of the data.

The intention of the research program, of which this study is a part, is to provide a technology of instruction for use in applied settings. The above changes seem consonant with that goal. The present study represents another step in the development of that technology.*

---

*This study was supported in part by NICHHD Program Project Grant No. HD 05951 to Children's Research Center, University of Illinois at Urbana-Champaign.

Appreciation is expressed to Progress School, Decatur, Illinois, Peoria Association for the Retarded, Peoria, Illinois, and to Paul Touchette, E. K. Shriver Center, Waltham, Massachusetts, for his methodological insight.

POSTSTATEMENT

The use of verbal cues did not affect the overall learning time in original learning, but it did affect the number of discrimination errors made in original learning. The verbal cues did assist in making the discriminations but did not assist in the overall efficiency of learning the task. Those same verbal cues, however, seem to have provided the learners who had them in original learning, but not in retention, with enough assistance to make a significant effect on discriminations in the retention phase.

This finding is helpful in clarifying a statement that is on the film *Try Another Way,* * is also in this study, and is still used frequently to describe the Try Another Way Approach. In the film the comment is made that the Try Another Way Approach is "essentially non-verbal." In the article it says that our research program "emphasizes the use of non-verbal training procedures." We believe that the use of verbal cues and verbal instructions is valuable and helpful some of the time. In most of the task analyses in our task analysis bank, some verbal cues are included in the training procedures. What can also be found in most of those task analyses are procedures and assists that do not require the use of verbal labels or verbal statements. The important thing when working with people who find it difficult to learn is to plan in advance what cues and statements are to be used and to make sure that the learners either know the cues already, that learning them is part of the training, or that they can learn the task without having to know the verbal cues or statements. What this study really suggests is that many individuals can use specific labels for specific parts or steps if these labels are used consistently and systematically. The study says nothing about the use of sentences of general verbal instructions.

In rereading the articles for this book, I have found various statements about studies that are going to be done. We did a few of them. Most never got done. I do not regret their not being done, but I am somewhat embarrassed about having said we were going to do them and then not following through. Our research went in directions that made those studies less interesting or valuable, within our values, than the ones we did.

Within the research program this was the second study involving a retention phase over a long period of time. The fact that we got highly significant retention effects on both studies does begin to build a nice case for the ability to remember of people labeled moderately and severely retarded. Of course, the qualifications regarding the task and the training procedures have to be considered. But since retention studies of this length are not frequently found in the literature, these studies should be used to promote trainers' confidence in the ability of persons labeled mentally retarded to

---

*Glenn Roberts (Producer). *Try Another Way*. Indianapolis: Film Productions of Indianapolis, 1975.

remember things that they have learned, where a strong criterion was used for original learning.

In the last paragraph of this article the research program is described as having the intention of providing a technology of instruction for use in applied settings. In looking back at these studies, it is interesting to note our apparent interest in variables relating to retention, color coding, verbal cues, etc. While these studies were going on, we were not fully aware that the technology we were developing was a system of task analysis and that the variables we were studying, in many ways, were really quite incidental to the instructional strategies we were developing. The particular event that focused our attention on the importance of developing the task analysis system was a site visit from the National Institute of Child Health and Human Development for the grant that supported the research. On that site visit Don Baer, University of Kansas at Lawrence, was assigned to observe what we were doing and critique it. What he said, in essence, was that we should stop fooling around with all of the variables we were reporting in the studies and concentrate on the system of task analysis we were using. He realized that it was really the center of what we were doing. After that visit we began to emphasize task analysis.

CHAPTER 11

Factors Affecting Production by the Retarded: Base Rate

Marc W. Gold

PRESTATEMENT

This study was intended to be an important step in the sequence of studies which constituted our research program. It was the first attempt to look at production from a nonreinforcement perspective. Having criticized the field very strongly for the body of literature on production by the retarded done only within the context of simple tasks, we were making our first effort to investigate production of a complex task.

From a research perspective the study was successful. It resulted in some impressive production data and added another small disclaimer to the relationship between intelligence and productivity and to the relationship between learning ability and production ability. This again brings up the topic of the null hypothesis which was mentioned in the prestatement of the last chapter. One of the basic constructs of the scientific method is that a difference can be proven, but no difference cannot be proven. The null hypothesis can be rejected or held tenable. It cannot be proven. In this experiment the null hypothesis would be that there is no significant correlation between intelligence and production rate. Had there been a significant correlation between these two variables, the null hypothesis would have been rejected, proving that a correlation exists. At least within the confines of the methodology (the use of subjects and tasks in the experiment) the nonsignificant correlation obtained from these data held the null hypothesis for this study to be tenable. That is, the data did not show any correlation between the two variables. That is much different from saying that we proved there is no correlation. A person reading the experiment and interpreting the data can use his own judgment about results. When many experiments with sound methodology hold a particular null hypothesis tenable, the evidence becomes fairly convincing. A single study cannot do this.

This base-rate study was an attempt to begin building a body of evidence. We felt that this experiment could be capitalized upon to develop strong arguments against the use of intelligence tests as predictors. But we also

---

This article originally appeared in *Mental Retardation*, 1973, *II* (6), 41-45. Reprinted by permission of the publisher.

knew that evidence would have to come from a series of studies, rather than a single project.

The productivity of mentally retarded individuals, as defined by their performance in sheltered workshops and vocational training programs throughout the United States, is considerably less than that of normal individuals doing similar kinds of work. The retarded are relegated to mundane, unskilled, menial jobs. The reason may lie in the inability of the retarded to perform above present levels, or that higher level contracts or jobs are unavailable to them. Farber (1968), Gold (1973), and Heiny (1971) believe that basic societal expectancies and the previous experiences of professionals in the field are the principal limiting factors.

Whatever the reasons for the present status of the retarded, a wide discrepancy exists between what the retarded do, vocationally, and what they are potentially capable of doing both qualitatively (Crosson, 1969; Dolnick, 1971; Gold, 1972), and quantitatively (e.g., Brown, Johnson, Gadberry & Fenrick, 1971; Zimmerman, Stuckey, Garlick & Miller, 1969). Studies on the quantitative aspects of productivity of the retarded have focused almost entirely on the manipulation of reinforcement contingencies (e.g., Evans & Spradlin, 1966; Zimmerman, Stuckey, Garlick & Miller, 1969), and have dealt with productivity of the retarded only on tasks of the simple, repetitive type typically found in workshops.

None of the studies found in the literature acknowledge a possible relationship between task complexity and productivity, nor do they study this relationship. The impression is that the findings apply to all tasks rather than just simple tasks. It is contended here that virtually all of the assumptions presently held, related to how the retarded function vocationally, must be questioned, or held as tenable only within the context of performance on simple tasks.

Before assessing the differential effects of various environmental manipulations on simple and complex tasks, it is necessary to establish a clear picture of base-rate performance, that is, production in the absence of intentionally administered reinforcements or other systematic changes of the work environment.

The present study was to obtain base-rate data (nonreinforced production) on moderately and severely retarded individuals producing a complex assembly. A complex assembly is subjectively defined as one for which a retarded individual requires individualized and extensive training in order to perform the assembly. The assembly used consisted of 14 pieces, 12 of which were different; it is further described under "materials." Comparatively, the task requires a larger number of different visual discriminations and motor movements than is the case for knob-pulling (Evans & Spradlin, 1966), counting pages (Hunt & Zimmerman, 1969), assembling connector blocks (Zimmerman, Stuckey, Garlick & Miller, 1969), or bagging golf tees (Screven, Straka & Lafond, 1971). Huddle (1967) used 16 pieces, but three of the pieces and operations were repeated five times. The tasks reported in the literature which appear to be more complex are the relay panels reported by Tate and Baroff (1967) and also by Schroeder (1972). However, the actual task, as performed by each retarded individual, was not described, nor was the training procedure.

In the research program of which this study is a part, a distinction is made between acquisition and production. Acquisition refers to the process of learning a task to some criterion of errorless performance. In the case of the task used, the criterion was six correct out of eight consecutive assemblies of the task. Errors during acquisition are interpreted as an indication that the task has not been learned. There are no rate requirements for criterion on acquisition. Production is defined as performance following acquisition, where rate is the primary measure. Production errors are interpreted the same way as in industry, where it is assumed that the worker knows the task but "just made an error," rather than that the worker does not know the task.

Two separate base-rate studies were conducted: a 1-hour study in which 20 worked 1 hour per day for 10 days and a 3-hour study in which 16 participated 3 hours per day for 10 days.

ONE-HOUR STUDY

Method

Participants

Participants were 20 retarded individuals enrolled in three sheltered workshops. Descriptive data for the sample are presented in Table 1. Workshop directors were asked to suggest their lowest performing clients for use in the study. It was not until the study was completed that the inclusion of two individuals with IQ scores of 87 and 97 was noticed. They are included because their overall performance both in and out of the experimental situation in no way distinguished them from the others.

Materials

The apparatus consisted of a Sempco® #1424 Bench Frame on which were mounted the appropriate number and size of bins to house quantities of each part. The unit is typical of the type found in factories where bench assembly work is done. In addition to the bins, boards with 25-7/16 inch holes were used to hold the assembled units.

The task was Bendix, RB-2 coaster brake, consisting of 14 parts.

Table 1
Descriptive Characteristics of Subjects

Group	IQ			CA		
	Mean	SD	Range	Mean	SD	Range
1-hour	50.4	17.2	25-97	25	5.7	17-39
3-hour	46.7	8.1	33-67	24.7		15.8-37.5

Procedure

Workers were first trained to assemble the brake. (A detailed description of the brake and the training procedure is found in Gold, 1972.) They were brought to a criterion of six correct out of eight consecutive assemblies prior to production. Those who had learned the task as part of previous studies were rerun to criterion. Then they made the transition from the flat tray used for training to the production bins, and were brought to a criterion of two consecutive correct assemblies.

On the first day of production, workers were told that they would not lose any pay for being away from their regular job. This was intended to minimize the probability of time away from their regular work serving as a negative reinforcer for performance in the study. No one indicated any desire not to participate. They were told to "work until the bell goes off and to then return to your regular work station."

The experimenter did not sit or interact with individuals during the production period. No feedback on productivity was provided. The only external reinforcement was a thank-you at the end of each session. Following each production period, the experimenter counted the completed assemblies. Errors (any incorrectly assembled brake) were counted and recorded as the experimenter disassembled each brake in preparation for the next worker. Disassembly was done in the absence of any workshop clients so as to control motivational variables which might result from individuals seeing their work undone.

Results

Production data are shown in Table 2. One-hour figures are based on 200 hours of production (20 subjects $\times$ 10 hours). Grouped performance over days is shown in Figures 1 and 2. Overall error rate was 6.3% for the 1-hour group.

Correlations were computed to determine the relationship between acquisition rate and mean hourly production rate—between how quickly the task was learned and how fast it was produced. For the 1-hour group, the correlation was .26 (n.s.). Correlations were also computed to determine the relationship between IQ score and mean hourly productivity. For the 1-hour group, the correlation was .30 (n.s.).

THREE-HOUR STUDY

Method

Participants

Sixteen retarded individuals enrolled in three workshops were chosen for this study. Four had participated in both the 1-hour and 3-hour studies, with several months between their 1-hour and 3-hour production blocks. Table 1 includes descriptive data for those who worked in the 3-hour study. The four are included in both groups.

Materials

Materials were the same as for the 1-hour study.

Table 2
Production Data

Group	Hourly Production Rate		Hourly Error Rate	
	Mean	SD	Mean	SD
1-hour	24.9	7.21	1.58	1.01
3-hour	20.35	5.50	.39	.77

Procedure

The procedure was the same as for the 1-hour study. In addition, those in the 3-hour study were given a 15-minute break following 90 minutes of production.

Results

Production data are shown in Table 2. Three-hour figures are based on 480 hours of production (16 subjects × 30 hours). Grouped performance over days is shown in Figures 3 and 4. Overall error rate was 3% for the 3-hour group. A correlation of -27 (n.s.) was found between acquisition rate and mean hourly production rate. For mean hourly production rate and IQ score, the correlation was .29 (n.s.).

DISCUSSION FOR BOTH STUDIES

The brake is normally assembled in a 2-step assembly process. Each of the two different job stations utilizes a pneumatic vice, impact and torque wrench, and units are greased as they are assembled. Consequently, a realistic comparison of productivity and error rate is not possible, especially since the task is so much slower and more difficult to perform in the absence of the power tools and the grease.

A different comparison can be made. The performance reported appears to far exceed, both qualitatively and quantitatively, any performance of the mentally retarded reported in the literature. The rate and quality of the labor of the present study, in the absence of pay, appears to be worth a high hourly wage, even where strong reinforcement systems were utilized. (No attempt was made to organize for maximum efficiency, for instance, by using a jig to hold the assembly, to use a two station assembly line, or even to arrange the bins for motion efficiency, giving further support for interpreting the base-rate data as highly conservative.) The data, then, suggest that more should be done to increase the level and value of the work the retarded do instead of trying to develop bigger and better reinforcement systems for simple, low paying work.

The data also raise some questions about the assumption presently held in the field that pay, in some form, and praise are the only reinforcers available for work. Figures 1 and 3 show a general increase in productivity for both studies over the 10 days. Although the figures represent grouped data, individual production curves closely resemble the group curves. With money considered the principal reinforcer in a work setting, one might consider the data as being obtained during extinction conditions. It appears that something more than a Hawthorne (halo) Effect is operating. The position taken here is that the task has strong reinforcing properties for the workers. Figures 2 and 4 illustrate that error rate dropped very low, very quickly, in absence of any feedback on quality or reinforcement for correct assemblies.

Another important finding is the non-significant relationship found between acquisition and production. Current methods of evaluating the skill ability of the retarded are based on the assumption that a strong relationship exists between learning ability and production ability. None of the popular evaluation batteries—e.g., Tower System (Rehabilitation Institute for the Crippled and Disabled, 1967); Philadelphia System (U.S. Department of Labor, 1968)—separate acquisition from production. The present data suggest that current evaluation procedures result in a misleading underestimate of the performance capabilities of the retarded (Gold, 1973), and fail to provide the kind of information needed to design individual training programs. The statistically non-significant relationship between IQ and production raises more questions about the limiting effects of current diagnostic and evaluative procedures.

Table 3 shows the production and error rates for the four workers in both tasks. Their mean production rate went from 19.6 in the 1-hour study to 21.1 for the 3-hour study, with only one worker showing any decrement in production rate. These individuals worked a total of 40 hours without pay, praise, or feedback.

CONCLUSIONS

The data suggest that the mentally retarded are capable of producing, qualitatively and quantitatively, at a level far above what is presently found, even in the absence of conventional reinforcement systems. The current trend toward an emphasis on incentive systems was questioned. Implications of the reinforcing properties of complex tasks were discussed as possible alternatives to current trends. Current evaluative tests and practices were characterized as limiting and misleading.

A study is in progress to investigate the relationships between task complexity, reinforcement and productivity.

Table 3
Production Data for Four Subjects Included in Both
1- and 3-Hour Groups

Subject	Hourly Production Rate		Hourly Error Rate	
	1-hour	3-hour	1-hour	3-hour
1	17.1	20.3	12%	3%
2	19.2	19.4	15%	2%
3	20.1	15.0	2%	2%
4	22.0	30.0	6%	1%

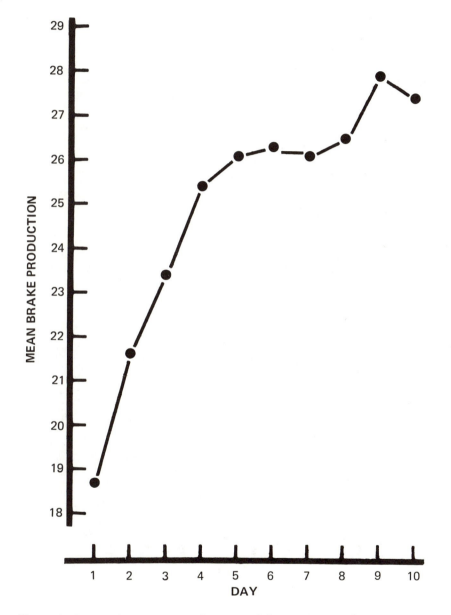

Figure 1. Each point represents the mean daily production for 20 workers producing for 1 hour.

131

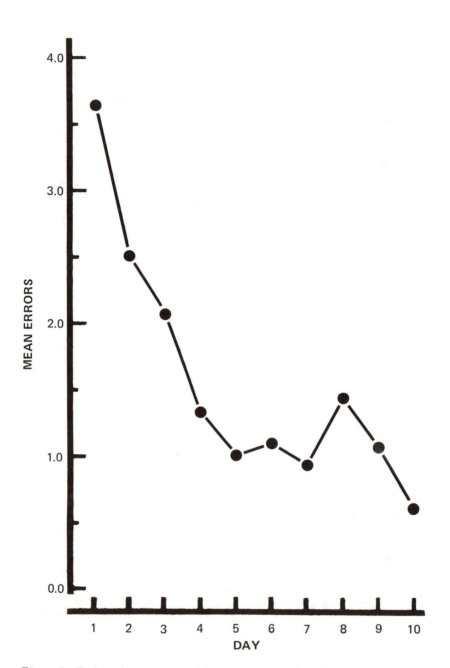

Figure 2. Each point represents the mean errors for 20 workers producing for 1 hour.

132

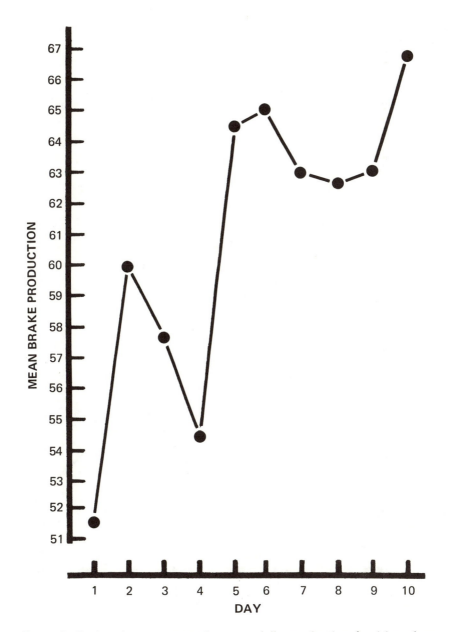

Figure 3. Each point represents the mean daily production for 16 workers producing for 3 hours.

133

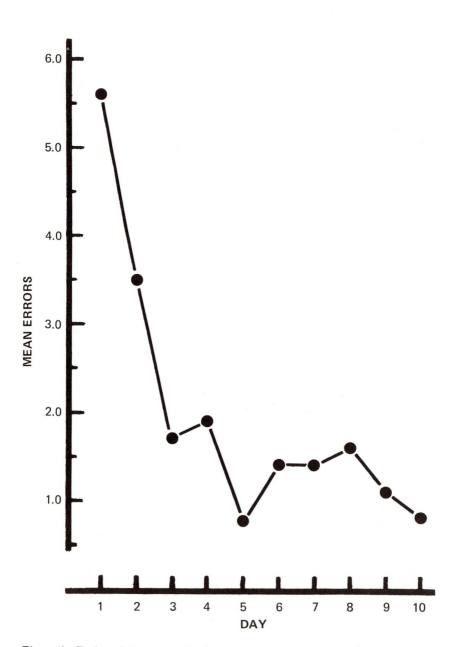

Figure 4. Each point represents the mean errors per session for 16 workers producing for 3 hours.

It is hoped that the present study will serve to stimulate research and service personnel to re-evaluate existing perspectives regarding the capabilities of the retarded, and the techniques used to evaluate and develop those capabilities.*

POSTSTATEMENT

One of the significant contributions of this study was to draw attention to the distinction between learning tasks and doing tasks. In the Try Another Way System we now talk about Criterion I environments, which are the learning environments, and Criterion II environments, which are the doing environments. This study, from our perspective, strongly supports treating those environments separately from the standpoint of strategies for training and criteria for performance.

In the description of the participants two individuals with IQ scores of 87 and 97 were mentioned. Their inclusion was an accident, but it certainly supports the points we were trying to make regarding the relationship between intelligence and productivity. The two subjects constituted sort of a reverse case for what we were showing, but this situation did contribute, nevertheless.

From my present knowledge of current vocational test batteries, I think the criticisms of the evaluation systems extant in 1972 are as relevant today as then. Although some companies have attempted to include more training in their systems, I still find them falling short of providing genuinely meaningful data on which to base decisions regarding people labeled retarded. These criticisms do not apply to local agencies that develop criterion referenced forms of testing relative to the specific products and tasks involved. While I still am open to the possibility of someone coming up with a generalized evaluation battery that might be useful with this population, I have not seen it yet. My commitment at this time is to the criterion referenced form of testing which involves tasks that the agency wishes its clients to know and which evaluates only within the context of training on those tasks.

After this study we did another one on production in which we paid clients. There were some methodological problems with the study and the conclusions were, by our estimate, not worth publishing. Incidentally, we did not get any significant differences between people who were paid and those who were not paid for producing the bicycle brakes. This was also the case for production on a bolt sorting task. As with some of our other research we became involved in production of real tasks in sheltered work-shops and industry and therefore stepped away from this particular line of

*This study was supported in part by NICHHD Program Project Grant No. HDO5951 to Children's Research Center, University of Illinois at Urbana-Champaign.

Appreciation is expressed to Developmental Services Center, Champaign, Illinois, Peoria Association for the Retarded, Peoria, Illinois, Kennedy Job Training Center, Palos Park, Illinois, Progress School, Decatur, Illinois, Johnny Appleseed School, Fort Wayne, Indiana, and to Craig R. Barclay, Research Associate.

research. Data from organizations we have been involved with have clearly shown, in real settings with real tasks, that people labeled moderately and severely retarded are capable of producing, reliably and consistently, up to 115% of industrial norms. These figures can be very misleading because industrial norms are not sacred; in fact, they are more politically than scientifically determined. In any case, there are now considerable data obtained under real work conditions, rather than experimental conditions, which show the productive capabilities of people labeled severely handicapped. It would be nice to have some of this under laboratory controlled conditions, but I believe the data which are available can stand on their own and under close scrutiny would retain their credibility.

CHAPTER 12

Redundant Cue Removal in Skill Training for the Retarded

Marc W. Gold

PRESTATEMENT

The original study using the bicycle brakes showed very clearly that the use of a cue redundancy in the form of painting half of each part red was a powerful cue for teaching the discriminations of that task. Having done that, we were anxious to show how to eliminate the color cue for those tasks that did not inherently have color as a cue. We were very pleased with the three strategies we devised for eliminating the color coding and thought that they would be helpful to teachers who so frequently use color cues to teach things that are not naturally color coded (e.g., tying shoelaces).

This article was published in *Education and Training of the Mentally Retarded,* the teacher-oriented journal of the American Association on Mental Deficiency. The emphasis in our research program by this time had begun to shift toward useful information for practitioners, rather than research for consumption primarily by other researchers.

The use of a cue redundancy—color—to facilitate the acquisition of a complex assembly task was clearly demonstrated in an earlier study (Gold, 1972), in which subjects with color coding available learned to assemble a 15 piece bicycle brake in half the trials needed by the subjects without color coded parts.

The theoretical support for this procedure is from the "Attention Theory" of Zeaman and House (1963). According to this theory, the more relevant and redundant the cues, the more efficient the learning. This means, for instance, that if a problem can be solved using cues from both the color and the form dimensions, it will be solved more efficiently than if the only cues available are on the form dimension (Gold & Scott, 1971).

With the efficiency and effectiveness of cue redundancy in aiding task completion previously demonstrated, the purpose of this study was to investigate means of fading it out in such a way as to make color coding an efficient

This article originally appeared in *Education and Training of the Mentally Retarded,* 1974, *9,* 5-8. Reprinted by permission of the publisher.

learning procedure on tasks where the coding must be removed following acquisition and prior to production. This is often necessary since in many tasks color coding cannot be used in production because of the cost and impracticality of painting every part.

METHOD

Subjects

The subjects were 36 adolescent and adult sheltered workshop clients. Descriptive data for the sample are presented in Table 1. The sample was drawn randomly from the workshop populations, the only restriction being that subjects had to be able to see and hold the parts. Twelve subjects were randomly assigned to each of the three groups: (a) complete removal group, (b) incremental removal group, and (c) forced choice group.

Materials

The apparatus was a tray containing 15 compartments. A divider runs parallel to and 3 inches from the front of the tray. The purpose of this divider is to separate the parts that are being used for a particular trial from the parts to be used in subsequent trials (Gold, 1972). The parts of the assembly are sequenced in the tray, rather than having the subjects learn the sequence. This is consonant with industrial procedure, where parts are stored in a sequence most conducive to assembly rather than randomly or in a pile.

The task was a Bendix RB-2 coaster brake. In the earlier study (Gold, 1972) the complete 15 piece assembly was used. For this experiment the assembly consisted of 12 pieces. The three parts left out were a lock nut and two shoes.

The cue redundancy consisted of painting (red) the surface of each part that is facing the subject when it is placed in the proper position for assembly. Ten of the 12 parts can be put on two ways, one of which is correct. The addition of a color cue to one of the two alternatives to this two choice problem means that attention to the cue can provide solution.

Table 1
Descriptive Characteristics of Subjects

Group	IQ			
	Mildly Retarded		Moderately Retarded	
	Mean	SD	Mean	SD
Complete Removal	62.50	10.80	29	11.83
Incremental Removal	57.90	7.53	31	9.66
Forced Choice	59.80	8.53	34	11.12

Procedure

The general procedure consisted of one demonstration of the task by the experimenter, showing correction of errors and reinforcement procedures (Gold, 1972). The experimenter assembled the unit once, then the subject assembled the unit until a criterion of six correct assemblies out of eight consecutive trials was reached using the noncoded parts. A correct trial was one complete assembly of the brake without error or assistance. The subject did four trials per day until the criterion was reached.

Three procedures for fading the color coding were used. Subjects in the complete removal group were brought to six correct out of eight consecutive trials on the cue redundant brake (color coded parts) and then brought to criterion on the noncoded brake. Subjects in the incremental removal group started out on the cue redundant brake. Color coded parts were replaced with noncoded parts following three consecutive correct discriminations, and were reinstated following three incorrect discriminations, not necessarily consecutive, on that part. Trials were considered correct when no errors were made and only noncoded parts were used. Subjects in the forced choice group were first brought to six correct out of eight consecutive trials on the cue redundant brake. They were then transferred to the form only brake (no cue redundancy).

When a discrimination error was made, the assembly was taken from the subject and placed on the table; then the following procedure was used with the part on which the error was made:

1. A color coded part was placed in front of the subject, noncolor side up.

2. Three form only parts were given to the subject with instructions to place them on the table in the same position as the color form part (a match to sample discrimination task), forcing the subject to solve the problem using the form dimension.

3. The procedure was repeated with the coded side of the part up.

4. The subject then continued on the partially completed assembly until criterion was reached.

Subjects in any group who failed to reach criterion by 55 trials were given a score of 55 and terminated. Their data were included in the analyses.

RESULTS

An independent groups design was used. The reliability of the effects was assessed via one way of analyses of variance using trials, manipulation errors, and discrimination errors to criterion as dependent measures. No effects approached significance. The data are presented in Table 2.

DISCUSSION

The principle value of this study is to demonstrate three techniques for

Table 2
Group Means and Standard Deviations

	GROUPS					
	Complete Removal		*Incremental Removal*		*Forced Choice*	
Measures to Criterion	Mean	SD	Mean	SD	Mean	SD
Trials	32.33	16.36	20.83	10.37	26.08	11.16
Manipulation Errors	10.08	10.07	5.66	4.37	7.33	10.94
Discrimination Errors	35.16	34.75	27.92	20.87	28.83	34.54

eliminating color coding on a task where it has been added for training purposes. The different procedures might provide sufficient variety so that various tasks and various children could be efficiently taught. With color coding a common phenomenon in educational settings these techniques would appear to be of use.

For this particular task and sample population, inspection of the data shows considerable within group variance, suggesting the possibility of large individual differences related to the relative effect of each procedure. The present design did not allow administering more than one procedure to a given subject. In the absence of a clear-cut hierarchy of training procedures, however, the data do suggest a strategy for training on tasks where a cue redundancy can be added temporarily for training. One could begin with the incremental removal procedure. If the subject requires the reinstatement of color more than three or four times, suggesting that the cue redundancy is not facilitating the use of the form cue, switch to one of the two alternate procedures, both of which require that the subject first reach the criterion of six correct out of eight consecutive trials on the entire task before the cue redundancy is removed. Some individuals might acquire the task more efficiently this way.

In the present study, three of the 36 subjects completed 55 trials without reaching criterion, two in the complete removal group and one in the forced choice group. The methodology of the present study precluded giving them additional trials or different training. Procedural flexibility should be kept to a minimum in the experimental setting (and where group designs are used). But in the applied setting flexibility is a necessity. Several changes should be made in our procedures related to subjects who fail to reach criterion. First, their data should not be included in the parametric analyses. These subjects should be replaced. Second, they should be run clinically. That is, procedures from other groups in the experiment or completely different procedures should be used until the subjects reach criterion on the task. The procedures for these subjects should be reported separately from the group data but included in the same publication. This would provide both experimental and clinical data resulting in increased applicability for the practitioner.

Subsequent experiments will include the above methodological changes and will investigate the use of other color coding and fading procedures on the acquisition of bench assembly tasks with the intent of contributing to a much needed expanded technology of instruction for the retarded. Data from the research program described give strong support for the benefits of such a technology. The data also point up the disparity between what the retarded are capable of doing vocationally and the low level to which the retarded have been relegated by our society and our profession (Gold, 1973).*

POSTSTATEMENT

Within the present Try Another Way System the use of color coding would be considered artificial informing. One of the characteristics of artificial informing is that it has to be removed before a person can reach proficiency in the natural environment. This removal, of course, was the essence of this piece of research. On that basis the study was a failure in the sense that it did not result in a method of arriving at the natural environment in an efficient way, or at least in a way that was any more efficient than not having used the color coding in the first place. As it turned out, none of the three strategies was superior to the other two. In addition, the number of trials required to remove the color cue, when added to the number of trials to reach criterion using the color cue, ended up being virtually identical to the number of trials to learn the task without any color in the first place. What a shocker! This particular use of attention theory was supported in one sense but not in another. Whether or not to use the color cue became a question of efficiency.

We did not use time as a dependent variable in this study. We might have seen some significant differences in time between the various procedures. If we had seen such differences, the efficiency issue could have been addressed. This was a major error in this piece of research. If we were looking for the most efficient way of using color cues, time should have been the most important variable, and we ignored it completely. The study suggests that others who want to try color cues should employ them, use one of the elimination strategies described in the paper, and record the difference in training time with and without the cues. If one of the color cue procedures works much faster in terms of training time than not using color at all, I recommend using it. In short, this study should not be interpreted to mean that the use of color as an artificial method of providing information to the learner should be thrown out.

This article still reflects our blindness to the task analysis system that we were developing. The training strategies we were developing and using were not covered in the article. While the use of color coding was emphasized in

*This study was supported by NICHHD Program Project Grant No. HD05951 to Children's Research Center, University of Illinois at Urbana-Champaign.

Appreciation is expressed to Community Workshop, Peoria, Illinois, and to Craig R. Barclay, Research Associate.

this project, obviously many other training strategies were also being used in the study.

CHAPTER 13

An End to the Concept of Mental Retardation: Oh, What a Beautiful Mourning

Marc W. Gold

PRESTATEMENT

By 1973 it had become obvious that the technology my colleagues and I were developing, and for that matter any technology, could not exist outside of a philosophy and a set of values related to the existence of people with handicapping conditions in society. When Don Moss, the executive director of what was then called the Illinois Association for the Mentally Retarded, asked me to do the opening address for their annual conference, I decided to devote the entire presentation to nontechnical, philosophical issues. I was really just beginning to develop strategies for consciousness raising and introspection and was experimenting with different techniques for doing this.

One way of looking at public speaking is in terms of content and delivery. For this particular presentation I decided to experiment with delivery, specifically, choosing to do the entire presentation with absolutely no humor. The purpose was to see what the effect would be on the audience and to try to develop control of that particular dimension in my presentations. On another occasion I did a presentation (in Topeka, Kansas) which was filled with as much humor as possible.

This poem was delivered at the end of the presentation to the Illinois Association for the Mentally Retarded. All of the concepts represented in the poem were discussed in nonpoetic fashion during the course of the presentation. This included elevating expectations for the capabilities of the retarded, seeing the retarded as people first, criticizing the use of tests as debilitating rather than helpful, and promoting an optimistic view that when some of these changes took place, people would find the mentally retarded to be much more capable and equal to the rest of us than current perceptions would indicate.

This poem was originally presented as the conclusion to a presentation given to the Illinois Association for the Mentally Retarded, April 1973, Springfield, Illinois.

An End to the Concept of Mental Retardation:
Oh, What a Beautiful Mourning

If you could only know me for who I am
    Instead of for who I am not,
There would be so much more to see
    'cause there's so much more that I've got.

So long as you see me as mentally retarded,
    Which supposedly means something, I guess,
There is nothing that you or I could ever do
    To make me a human success.

Someday you'll know that tests aren't built
    To let me stand next to you.
By the way you test me, all they can do
    Is make me look bad through and through.

And someday soon I'll get my chance,
    When some of you finally adapt.
You'll be delighted to know that though I'm MR,
    I'm not at all handicapped.

POSTSTATEMENT

The presentation went very well. At the end of it many people in the audience were crying. I will never do that again, but it was an important experience. There is a tendency in our field for people to present material dryly or nonemotionally. This is a mistake. It is certainly a mistake to go out and try to put an audience in tears; however, to be conscious of the value of motivating people, exciting their emotions and their attitudes, is important.

    The poem has been very popular ever since. It is also the opening of the sound track to the film *Try Another Way.** I still feel very comfortable with what the poem says and believe that its message is as relevant today as it was then. I also believe that the "someday soon" described in the poem is much more "now" than it was then, although we have not even begun to show the capabilities of people labeled retarded.

---

*Glenn Roberts (Producer). *Try Another Way.* Indianapolis: Film Productions of Indianapolis, 1975.

CHAPTER 14

An Alternative Definition of Mental Retardation

Marc W. Gold

PRESTATEMENT

In January, 1974, a lengthy and fruitful relationship began between our research group and Unit X of the Dixon State School, which later became the Dixon Developmental Center. Roger Hoffman, the director of the unit at the time, had received a National Significance Grant from Developmental Disabilities in Washington for a program which included vocational training of people with severe and profound mental retardation who were also blind and, in some cases, deaf. Until that time all of our research had been with people labeled moderately and severely retarded; most of them were sighted and had hearing. Virtually 100% of them had learned to assemble the bicycle brakes, which was the only task we were using at that time, with the exception of the bolt sorting previously reported (Chapter 9).

We had already developed the concept of power. The present definition of power, as the term is used in the Try Another Way System, is: The amount of intervention, assistance, or direction required by the trainer in order for the learner to reach criterion. We felt that our techniques were very powerful because everyone learned everything. Of course, we were essentially using only one task and were not working with people with profound multihandicapping conditions. The first thing we discovered in working with Unit X at Dixon State School was that we did not have very much power.

My second trip to Dixon was on April 2 and 3, 1974. During that visit several of the staff were being shown some of the techniques we had developed. A tray and the bicycle brakes were sitting on a table in the shop area. While I was explaining, a gentleman walked by carrying a young man. I asked if I could work with the young man for a minute to demonstrate some of the techniques being discussed. He said the young man would not be able to do anything. After a brief discussion he allowed me to sit the young man next to me and work with him for about 3 minutes. The young man was Bill Widmar, a person whose records indicated an I.Q. of 7 and who was described as profoundly retarded, deaf-blind, severely self-destructive, and severely aggressive. The gentleman who was carrying him was his father, who was visiting Bill. After working with Bill, I thanked both of them. His father carried him away, and I then asked the people standing around what was causing their anxiety, which I could definitely sense. One of the staff members said that I could have been very badly hurt, that she had had surgery after Bill had bitten her severely. She said that they had never seen him sit and do anything with someone for any period of time. Roger asked if I would be willing to work with Bill again the following day so that other staff could see and so that they could videotape it for use within the unit. I agreed to do so.

The next day we worked together for approximately 17 minutes. The tape of that session has been shown several thousand times by now; there are numerous copies in existence. It has given people a feeling of optimism about the potential for individuals with the labels that Bill had.

On the tape I said I felt very inadequate in working with Bill because our techniques did not have the power needed for someone who found it as difficult to learn as Bill. I had a lot to think about when I left Dixon that day. I could not understand why Bill showed such phenomenal capabilities, considering who he was supposed to be. The next day in my office I tried to put my thoughts together and in the process of doing so generated the alternative definition of mental retardation presented here. What is presented in this book is actually a several-times revised edition of the original statement, but the essence is the same. This definition is presented as a counter definition to that of the American Association on Mental Deficiency because the AAMD definition seemed to be in total contrast to Bill's behavior and to our other findings on the capabilities of people with significant mental retardation. At the time I was not particularly antagonistic about the AAMD definition; I could simply see the need to propose alternatives which could be considered by people in the field.

At the AAMD annual meeting in June, 1977, Herb Grossman, who had been the one responsible for the 1973 edition of the Association's *Manual on Terminology and Classification in Mental Retardation,* spoke to me about the alternative definition. He indicated that the committee would be meeting soon to develop the 1977 edition and asked for a copy and some information about it so that it could be discussed at the meeting. He was given a copy of the definition and some additional details. Two months later I received a letter dated August 8, 1977, in which he said, "Thanks for sending the definition, which was considered by the T&C Committee and was most helpful. Look forward to talking to you in the near future about this." I was very pleased and felt that it could be an important addition to the manual in terms of providing practitioners with some optimism for working with persons with significant mental retardation. I was also aware that this definition would probably have to be used as an adjunct since there is a heavy focus on psychological and medical issues in the manual whereas this is clearly a sociological definition.

Several months later the new manual was published. Nothing was mentioned about a sociological perspective of mental retardation or any of the perspectives that would generate from this alternative definition. It was additionally disappointing to find that the definition in the manual had not changed one word from the 1973 edition and that the supporting material had not changed significantly, either. Herb and I have not since talked about the deliberations of the committee. Perhaps someday we will.

In trying to assess my response to the situation I must admit to some degree of personal resentment, but more than that, I am disappointed in the AAMD for moving so slowly toward a more beneficial stance regarding the full participation of people labeled retarded in society. The current definition and manual reflect that slow pace.

The Try Another Way System is currently being used with a wide variety of people who find it difficult to learn. The original development of this system involved people labeled mentally retarded. As this technology developed, it became clear that the current accepted definition of mental retardation provided no help in conceptualizing those individuals in a manner consistent with the capabilities they were demonstrating. It became necessary, therefore, to react to the current accepted definition of mental retardation and to propose an alternative.

CURRENT DEFINITION OF MENTAL RETARDATION

The current definition (since 1973) accepted by most governmental bodies and by most professionals is:

Mental retardation refers to significantly subaverage general intellectual functioning existing concurrently with deficits in adaptive behavior, and manifested during the developmental period. (Grossman, 1977).

This is the definition published by the American Association on Mental Deficiency in 1973 and reconfirmed in 1977.

The following assumptions are implied in the AAMD definition:

1. Retardation is a general phenomenon.
2. Intelligence, as defined by tests, is permanent.
3. Defined intelligence is sufficiently general to describe all functioning and to imply potential.
4. Adaptive behavior includes both spontaneous adaptation and trained adaptation.
5. There is no such thing as the developmental period for all people.
6. It is useful to catalogue individuals according to their tested intelligence and tested adaptive level.
7. Mental retardation is most meaningfully conceptualized as a psychological phenomenon, existing within the individual, rather than as the context in which the individual operates.

ALTERNATIVE DEFINITION OF MENTAL RETARDATION

The following alternative definition provides a much more optimistic perspective of mental retardation, a reaction to the currently accepted definition in the field, and a perspective that represents the philosophy of the Try Another Way System:

> Mental retardation refers to a level of functioning which requires from society significantly above average training procedures and superior assets in adaptive behavior on the part of society, manifested throughout the life of both society and the individual.

The mentally retarded person is characterized by the level of power needed in the training process required for her to learn, and not by limitations in what she can learn.

The height of a retarded person's level of functioning is determined by the availability of training technology and the amount of resources society is willing to allocate and not by significant limitations in biological potential.

The following assumptions are implied in this alternative definition:

1. Mental retardation is not a general phenomenon. Every person labeled retarded has areas of normal capability, developed or undeveloped.

2. Intelligence, as defined by performance on tests, is a concept of little use.

3. No behavior clearly defines potential. Prediction describes what the person predicting knows about the environment in which the person labeled retarded will exist.

4. Adaptive behavior can be assumed for all persons.

5. Development is lifelong.

6. When testing and evaluation are the focus of attention, training is not likely to occur. When training is the focus of attention, evaluation must occur. So, train, don't test.

7. Mental retardation is most meaningfully conceptualized as a sociological phenomenon, existing within society, which can only be observed through the limited performance of some of the individuals in society.

THE CONCEPT OF POWER

The term "power," as used in the alternative definition, represents an important concept in the Try Another Way philosophy. *Power* refers to the amount of intervention, assistance, or direction required by the trainer in order for the learner to reach criterion. Power lies in the strategies and procedures the trainer utilizes in order for the learner to acquire the task. The more capable the learner, the less power is needed. Assists for the more capable learners could include verbal directions; for those who need more power, different assists which rely less on the capabilities of the learner are used, such as demonstration of the task; and if it is likely that even more power will be needed, the trainer can use more powerful assists such as direct manipulation of the learner's hands, etc. Within each of these dimensions of assists, there is a wide range of power available.

Within the Try Another Way philosophy the expectancy is that any individual, given prerequisites, powerful training procedures, and time, can be brought to criterion on any piece of learning. No one is thought to be incapable of learning. This does not deny that all individuals have limits, some more than others, but it does promote a recognition of the impossibility of evaluating limits in the absence of powerful training.

POSTSTATEMENT

The seven assumptions implied in the AAMD definition are increasingly questionable. The fact that thousands of retarded citizens are taking their places in communities, adapting and getting along, but are still labeled retarded by AAMD and by society, is but one example of the need for the definition to change. The 1977 manual still describes the developmental period as occurring until approximately age 18. The general consensus throughout the field of psychology is that this period lasts at least into the mid-twenties; some psychologists feel that it goes considerably beyond that. This becomes a more critical issue with individuals for whom the developmental period does not proceed unhampered. It seems important, therefore, for the AAMD definition to reflect the most recent trend so that the association can work toward maximizing the opportunities for and perceptions of the mentally retarded.

One of the changes that occurred in the 1973 definition was including the existence of concurrent deficits in adaptive behavior, along with significant subaverage general intellectual functioning. No distinction was made then, and none has been made since, between spontaneous adaptation and trained adaptation. Most individuals in institutions have, in fact, shown tremendous ability to adapt to an extremely difficult environment. Many of those same individuals have shown their ability to readapt as part of a transinstitutionalization process whereby they are put into smaller institutions within communities. Additionally, many persons labeled retarded are now holding jobs, using money, and existing successfully in various community settings. A lot of this has been the result of training by staff. But the label remains.

That the AAMD definition is a psychological one is no suprise. That the association still has failed to acknowledge and describe the impact that sociological variables play in the behavior and performance of people labeled mentally retarded is a surprise. The alternative definition is intended, in part, to focus attention on the role that environment plays on the performance of people labeled mentally retarded.

This perspective, however, is to be distinguished from the historical distinction made between endogenous and exogenous mental deficiency, sometimes expressed as the nature-nurture controversy. The position taken here is that individuals with retardation, regardless of the cause or extent, are capable, given strong environmental support, of significant learning and of full participation in society.

If the 1977 AAMD definition and this alternative definition are taken as hypotheses to be tested, then the AAMD definition, as a hypothesis, can be substantiated most by the field's and society's doing less and less for those labeled mentally retarded. Conversely, the alternative definition can be substantiated most by the field's and society's doing more and more to challenge the limitations of the definition itself and of the population it describes. In that regard the alternative definition provides an opportunity for optimism and expectations that can be evaluated only within the context of a great deal of effort.

Approximately 2 years after the videotape of Bill Widmar was made, he passed away from respiratory problems. Many more individuals having handicaps of comparable severity still wait for their opportunity to learn. By recognizing the alternative definition, or at least the issues it raises, the AAMD could become a powerful force in moving out to challenge the limits—in giving more people, including those like Bill, greater opportunities to learn and participate.

CHAPTER 15

Marcron, Inc.: A Request for a Program Related Investment

Marc W. Gold and Ron S. Torner

PRESTATEMENT

This is a document few people have seen, but many people have heard about. We were so excited about this concept that we talked about it in many presentations while we were pursuing the idea. Many people shared our excitement and have been asking what happened, ever since.

When this concept was developed early in 1973, we thought it would be "the solution." It represented something completely outside the experiences and activities of the field. This proposal was actually written in 1975 after we had tried some alternative ways of capitalizing the factory. The concept of a Program Related Investment was exciting to us because it seemed to be what we needed. Federal law prohibits foundations from granting funds to profit corporations. With the civil rights movement of the 50s and 60s, however, Congress passed legislation allowing foundations to use some of their capital to stimulate small business development in urban communities. The concept of a Program Related Investment allowed them to capitalize these businesses without violating their not-for-profit status. The Marcron concept fit nicely with efforts in urban areas to establish businesses that would provide job opportunities for people who were currently part of the surplus labor market.

I. Introduction

This document is a request by Marcron, Inc. for a Program Related Investment (PRI). Marcron does not yet exist. At the suggestion of our legal consultant, Leonard Flynn, of Franklin, Flynn, and Palmer, Champaign, Illinois, we are postponing incorporation until we know the source(s) of the funds to capitalize the corporation. The corporation will be owned by us—Marc Gold and Ron Torner. The background section describes some of the experiences we have had during the last 18 months as we detailed this concept. These experiences have led us to feel that private ownership and control is important because of the complexities of the specific training procedures and job design techniques needed and because of the importance of the relationship between task characteristics and production employee characteristics.

A. **Objectives** - The magnitude of this concept requires specification of three levels of objectives—immediate, intermediate and long range.

1. **Immediate Objective** - The initial central focus of the corporation is an electronic assembly factory where 50 production employees, all moderately or severely retarded and some with additional disabilities, will do subcontract printed circuit (P.C.) board assembly. These employees will be subject to the same rules, regulations, and laws as are any employees of any corporation. For example, they will all be paid the current minimum wage or more. Their wages will be subject to FICA, federal and state unemployment compensation deductions, and other taxes. They will have major and minor medical insurance, life and accidental death benefits, and will participate in profit sharing. There will be no special licenses from the Department of Labor, nor will there be any other special considerations that would distinguish the labor force in this factory from any other. All nonproduction considerations (e.g., housing, transportation, counseling) for production employees will be handled by them or through existing public social service agencies. The factory is a factory.

The quality of skill and level of productivity manifested will, we believe, far exceed anything now found in places where moderately and severely retarded individuals work. The idea of such individuals working in a place that is not a sheltered workshop or some other situation utilizing special certificates from the U.S. Department of Labor permitting special (low) wages is one that has often been discussed but never implemented in the manner intended here. We have been referred to many supposedly similar attempts throughout the country only to be disappointed. Every one either utilized high-level mildly disabled workers, was strongly subsidized, or both. None showed a net profit derived exclusively from worker productivity.

The immediate objective of Marcron, then, is to create a successful subcontract factory. The two criteria for measuring attainment of the immediate objective are solvency and stability. Solvency is defined here as producing a net profit and a positive cash flow simultaneous with an appropriate rate of debt reduction. Stability is defined as solvency existing for a minimum period of 6 months, with accounts receivable and contract bids showing strong likelihood of continued stability.

2. **Intermediate Objectives** - The factory will have several functions— intermediate objectives—in addition to the overall goal. One is documenting the competence of this previously untapped labor force. It will also serve as a model for the kinds of business and industrial practices needed for the moderately and severely retarded to have full economic participation in society. These practices include new forms of training and job design in addition to utilization of existing business and industrial procedures that are available but often ignored or overlooked by most corporations.

Equally significant, the factory will serve as the base, or medium, for the development of a national training program for people who work with the retarded. This means franchising or regionalizing the factory and setting up management and training agreements with existing agencies. Training programs will be located adjacent to each factory but will not use or drain factory resources. The quality of skill and level of productivity in the factory will be so much more advanced than any current endeavors that a national training program is sure to be received enthusiastically by the field. Since March, 1973, Gold and Torner have mentioned the concept in their lectures and travels throughout the United States and Europe. It has also be mentioned in an Associated Press article. Professionals, the public, and the press have actively pursued further inquiry. There is no question about the impact the concept will have. Already, appropriate officials of several states, on the basis of a sketchy description of the factory, have indicated a strong interest in contracting services and setting up a factory and training center in their states. The need for effective staff training programs is acute. The Right to Education litigation currently going on in many states and the precedent set in Pennsylvania for mandatory education for every child have magnified the need for such training programs.

There are only two programs in the United States which, in our opinion, are doing anything decent in terms of giving people skills with which to effectively train the severely retarded. One is Dr. Lou Brown's program at the University of Wisconsin-Madison. The other is Dr. Jim Tawney's program at the University of Kentucky-Lexington. Neither of these programs is designed to train people to work with adults or to train complex work skills.

The intermediate objectives will not be implemented until the immediate objective is reached.

3. **Long-Range Objectives** - The ultimate long-range goal is a major societal reconceptualization of the retarded that, in brief, could be expressed by the following long-range objectives: (1) Retardation would be viewed as a condition that describes the amount of training needed for full participation in the work force, and not a condition that necessarily describes what level of participation can be attained. (2) An individual in the surplus labor force would be selected for an available job on the basis of his ability to successfully perform the required task, rather than his ability to talk, fill out an application, or take a test, as is now the case. An in-depth discussion and numerous experiments addressing this issue are contained in the appended materials.

In conjunction with these long-range objectives, a demonstration of real economic viability by the moderately and severely retarded would create major conceptual and operational inconsistencies with the way society presently "provides" for them. This situation would almost certainly cause considerable change in public policies related to housing, care, training, and advocacy. When it is demonstrated that the moderately and severely retarded can fully participate in the economy, society will hopefully be forced to reexamine virtually all the present expectancies, policies, organizational structures and laws related to them.

B. Background
The social and pedagogical perspective which underlies Marcron, Inc. can be found in a chapter entitled "Research on the Vocational Habilitation

of the Retarded: The Present, The Future," which appears in *International Review of Research in Mental Retardation,* Vol. 6 (Gold, 1973b). That perspective was generated from a program of research which began in 1968 and was first described in 1972 by Gold. The first study documented the ability of 64 moderately and severely retarded individuals to learn, in an average time of 105 minutes, to accurately and consistently assemble a 15-piece and then a 24-piece bicycle brake. Studies since then have replicated this work, generated more training technology, and expanded it into production studies as well (Gold & Barclay, 1973a; Gold & Barclay, 1973b; Gold, 1973a; and Gold, 1974). This work has clearly demonstrated the ability of the moderately and severely retarded to learn complex assembly work and to produce that work with high quality and reasonable quantity (Gold, 1973a).

In 1972 Gold began research on P.C. board assembly training. This task was chosen for several reasons: (1) It is naturally color-coded (Gold, 1972; 1974). (2) The similarity of one P.C. board to another, in terms of assembly skills needed, is considerable (Merwin, 1973). (3) There is a very large market for P.C. board subcontract work (We have been told by several people in the electronics industry that, even without considering the work done overseas, there is a $30 million market). (4) There is no stable work force to do the work. Even with the current high unemployment rate in Chicago, for example, electronics firms there have as much as a 400% annual turnover on bench assembly jobs, making training and downtime costs exorbitant.

Two P.C. board studies have been completed and are being prepared for publication. Several pretraining procedures utilizing slide presentations of common objects, geometric forms, pictures of resistors, and pictures of P.C. boards were administered prior to training individuals to assemble two different 12-component P.C. boards. The two boards used in the first study each had 280 holes and 12 two-lead components (Merwin, 1973). Learning was defined as five consecutive correct boards without assistance. That meant 60 consecutive correct insertions of components on one task and then on the other—a very rigid criterion for learning, especially with so many holes in the boards. Eighty-nine percent of the institutionalized retarded individuals (every level of retardation was included in the study) completed the experiment in an average of less than 3 hours of training per person. Most of the trainees made few or no errors on the second board, showing that the skill learned on the first board transferred to the second board very well.

The second P.C. board study was just completed. Preliminary analysis of the data suggests that our revised procedures are even more efficient.

In March, 1973, following the first P.C. board study, Gold began seriously formulating the concept of the factory. Besides capital, two important issues needed resolution. One was verification that the moderately and severely retarded could do quality and quantity production of electronic component assembly work in a shop setting (rather than acquisition of complex skills in an experimental setting). The other issue was finding a partner who knew the business and operational aspects of a shop, electronic assembly, and the retarded. Even more important, the person had to have the integrity and commitment to pursue such a complex venture. Gold and Torner met when Gold spoke to the staff of the workshop directed by Torner, where moderately and severely retarded individuals were in fact doing electronic assembly work, often earning an average of more than $2 per hour. Some of his workers were producing at more than the industrial norm. It was clear that Gold and Torner collectively had the combination of skills needed for the factory. One of our principal skills that has subsequently become evident is the ability to recognize our own skill deficiencies and obtain information from appropriate sources.

In coming to the decision that the concept was a viable one, we took the following into consideration as related to the moderately and severely retarded: (1) They already have demonstrated their ability to work essentially full work days in sheltered workshops and work activity centers throughout the country, doing menial, unreinforcing garbage work for little or no remuneration (Gold, 1973b; Wolfensberger, 1967). (2) Their productivity can be influenced through money (e.g., Brown & Pearce, 1970; Evans & Spradlin, 1966; Schroeder, 1971). (3) They can learn to do complex work and produce it reliably and consistently (Gold, 1973b; Schroeder, 1971; Torner, personal experience). (4) They obviously enjoy and often prefer complex tasks over simple tasks (Gold and Torner, personal experience). (5) When they are doing complex work, most inappropriate behaviors go away spontaneously (Torner and Gold, personal experience). These experiences and data, along with many more subjective observations, give us the confidence to proceed.

In October, 1973, Torner accepted a position as field representative with the Joint Commission on Accreditation of Hospitals in their Accreditation Council for Facilities for the Mentally Retarded. He was hired specifically to design and field test the survey procedures by which the Standards for Community Agencies Serving Persons with Mental Retardation and Other Developmental Disabilities would be applied. The position was accepted with the understanding that he would leave when the factory materialized.

In March, 1973, we began negotiating with a large corporation for funds to capitalize Marcron. In light of poor progress, we terminated those negotiations in April, 1974.

We have also investigated a Small Business Administration (SBA) loan through the Amalgamated Bank of Chicago. After two meetings we were encouraged to submit an application but decided not to pursue this source of capital because SBA requires personal rather than corporate liability. Neither of us is in a position to assume personal liability for a large amount of money.

The other source of funds investigated briefly was the sale of debentures or promissory notes. If funds are solicited from more than 25 individuals, papers have to be filed with the Federal Securities and Exchange Commission and the equivalent Illinois commission. This would be an extremely long and expensive process. If funds could be borrowed from a single source, we could avoid "going public" and begin operations.

Program Related Investment, then, certainly seems to be the way to go. Basing our understanding of PRI on the description presented in *Foundation News* (Rein, 1973), we see eight factors involving the PRI concept and Marcron. *First,* we wish to demonstrate that the moderately and severely retarded can contribute to, and assume a role in, the world of work. That means no subsidy. Being a for-profit corporation is important for this reason. *Second,* the population constituting the production force certainly could be classified as a minority group, one which has been severely discriminated against and one for which paternalism, in one form or another, has been total. *Third,* while some aspects of our concept have been tried elsewhere, to our knowledge there has never been an endeavor such as this to achieve real economic viability for any group so strongly perceived as incapable. *Fourth,* if our concept works, the target population can serve itself without having to rely on welfare, public aid, departments of mental health, or any other governmental or philanthropic paternalism. *Fifth,* it is projected that the factory itself will be profitable. In addition, the training program and other activities related to training staff of agencies throughout the country and the world should be highly profitable. *Sixth,* the electronics industry badly needs printed circuit board assembly work done (for both peaceful and military uses) but cannot acquire or maintain the labor force to do it, even through manpower programs and even during high unemployment periods such as now. *Seventh,* extensive discussions with people in finance, business, law, social services, and industry lead us to believe our concept to be viable from all standpoints. *Eighth,* we have postponed incorporating until we decide which source of capital to use, so we are still completely flexible from that standpoint.

We are, therefore, submitting this proposal for a Program Related Investment of $300,000.

II. Operating Plans

Incorporation will take place as soon as there is reasonable assurance of the nature of capital to be used. When Marcron, Inc. is capitalized, Torner will be the full-time manager of the factory. His first responsibilities will be to find and lease a building, order equipment, recruit nonproduction employees, and begin taking in potential contracts for bidding. Once these things are done or at least underway, Torner's general role as plant manager will include running the operation, hiring and supervising all employees, procuring, bidding and supervising all contract work, and supervising the physical plant. This will involve his enhancing relationships he has already cultivated in the electronics industry, developing new ones, and establishing Marcron's technological base in the industry. Torner already has verbal commitments from several firms wishing to do business because of the high quality work done by the shop he directed.

Gold will retain his position at the University of Illinois. Because of the following reasons this should be the most facilitative way to proceed: (1) He has a 100% research appointment which gives him complete flexibility concerning time. (2) This venture is directly related to his work and, in fact, is the logical extension and application of that work. (3) He presently spends approximately the maximum allowable time traveling, so converting that time to the factory instead of consulting would create no changes in his present university role and function. (4) His administrators and colleagues are well aware of the venture, approve of it completely, and are highly supportive, within the confines of his university responsibilities, which are apparently satisfactorily met (Gold received tenure this year). (5) The university position provides support for continued research on skill training, most of the personal financial support for Gold, and important ties with the field. (6) Gold has summers free, a sabbatical coming up, and leave of absence possibilties, should Marcron require such large amounts of his time.

Gold's responsibilities in Marcron will include training the supervisory staff, providing the training procedures for the production workers, working with Torner on contract procurement, bidding, and designing production, and handling public relations. He will not supervise employees but will act in a consultative role where needed. Gold will have major responsibilities for the Staff Training Division when it is developed (see Section IIIG).

A. Staff - All employees will receive all normal benefits including life, accidental death and dismemberment, and basic and major medical insurance. In addition, all employees will participate in a profit-sharing plan. Wage increases for all employees will be based on merit and corporate productivity.

1. Production Employees - Fifty moderately and severely retarded individuals will constitute the initial production force. They will be recruited from one or two public or private sheltered-care homes or institutions. The factory will be located on a public transportation route convenient to the facilities where the workers live. The screening procedure will be simple interview, not necessarily oral since some or many workers may not have language. No IQ or other data will be considered.

Initially, individuals who evidence severe emotional problems will not be hired. Individuals with physical disabilities (in addition to the retardation) and deaf (retarded) individuals will be hired. No blind individuals will be hired until a training technology for them has been developed. Production employees will include only individuals who, by conventional approaches, would be most unlikely to participate in the normal labor pool.

Production employees will go through an average of 62 hours of training, working approximately 2 hours per day for approximately 6 weeks. That is more than 20 times the amount of training described in Section 1B. This will be criterion-based training, so there will be considerable individual differences. Employees will be paid during training. Individuals for whom the procedures are ineffective in terms of bringing them to criterion will be terminated. Gold's research, where identical screening procedures are used, has had an overall success rate exceeding 90%. Following training, production employees will begin production half time and will be graduated into full-time production on an individual basis, each taking an average of 1½ months to move from half- to full-time work (see Section III). Production employees will start at the current minimum wage. This proposal assumes a minimum wage of $2.20 per hour. Since we do not know when Marcron will commence, this figure covers current projections of existing laws.

2. **Foremen (4)** - There are no specific job prerequisites for foremen, but they will probably be high school graduates with experience in the electronics industry and/or with the retarded. Their major responsibility will be supervision of production lines, with minor responsibility for production worker on-line retraining, only to the extent that it does not interfere with production line supervision. Each will receive a starting wage of $4 per hour.

3. **Trainers (2)** - Prerequisites for trainers are the same as for foremen. Their major responsibilities will be to train production employees on new jobs, retrain where the need goes beyond the appropriateness of assistance from the foremen, and assist in setting up new lines. They will have major responsibility for production, but only as it relates to production employee performance. Each trainer will receive a starting wage of $4 per hour.

Six individuals will be hired to fill the positions of foremen and trainers. All will receive identical training. All will participate in the training of the first group of production employees (see Section III). During this time decisions of who will train and who will be foremen will be made, based on performance and preference.

4. **Secretary/Receptionist** - The secretary/receptionist will be selected from individuals with prior relevant experience. That person will receive a starting wage of $3 per hour.

5. **Bookkeeper/Office Manager** - The bookkeeper/office manager will be selected from individuals with prior relevant experience in full-charge bookkeeping including payroll, disbursements, and sales. That person will receive a starting wage of $4 per hour. We also plan to utilize business consultants to assist in setting up the accounting and bookkeeping system.

6. **Delivery/Maintenance Person** - The delivery/maintenance person will be selected from individuals with prior driving experience in the Chicago area. That person will receive a starting wage of $3 per hour.

7. **Quality Control and Job Design Person** - The person to handle quality control and job design will be selected from individuals who are retired from the electronics industry, who have experience in quality control and job design, and who still have plenty of gusto. That person's responsibilities will be to provide the electronic expertise needed to complement Torner's and Gold's knowledge of electronics, to be responsible for general quality control, and to assist with bidding and job design. We see this position as a necessity, not a luxury. The person in this position will receive a starting wage of $4 per hour to supplement his retirement income.

B. **Facility** - An industrial building of approximately 10,000 square feet will be leased. This figure is based on a commonly used formula allocating 200 square feet per production worker. In the suburbs west of Chicago such buildings lease for approximately $2.40 per square foot or $24,000 per year. The building will need 220-volt lines, a loading platform, and good lighting, but no other special considerations, with the exception of the location (discussed in Section IIA).

III. **Time Table**
  A. **First Quarter**
  1. Identify production employee population pool.
  2. Search for factory site.
  3. Write up requisitions for equipment.
  4. Take option/lease building.
  5. Hire foremen, trainers, secretary, and quality control person to begin work second quarter.
  6. Begin bidding contracts.
  7. Begin screening production employees.
  8. Contract for fringe benefits to begin second quarter.

  B. **Second Quarter**
  1. Set up factory.
  2. Obtain contracts.
  3. Train foremen and trainers.
  4. Design production lines.
  5. Hire delivery/maintenance person and bookkeeper to begin work third quarter.
  6. Hire 40% of production employees (20) to begin training third quarter.

  C. **Third Quarter**
  1. Begin training of 40% of production employees (20), with each training an average of 2 hours per day.
  2. Refine training procedures.
  3. Initiate production second half of third quarter, with 40% of production employees working half time and graduating to full time by end of third quarter.
  4. Differentiate foremen from trainers and move two foremen into production.

  D. **Fourth Quarter**
  1. Train 60% of production employees (30), with each training an average of 2 hours per day. (This will necessitate some pairing of trainees by the four people still doing training. With 2 months of practice in training, this should present no problems.)
  2. Reach 100% of production employees producing—40% full time; 60% graduating from half time to full time during fourth quarter.

  E. **Fifth Quarter**
  1. Attain full production (50 production employees full time).
  2. Begin retraining where necessary.
  3. Obtain new contracts.
  4. Train new production employees (necessitated by attrition).
  5. Expand job design methodology.

6. Begin raw material acquisition. (Up to this time materials supplied by the customer will be used.)
7. Become solvent and stable.

F.   Sixth-Eighth Quarters
1. Gradually increase productivity and income.
2. Gradually increase payroll and expenses. (We expect productivity to increase more rapidly than payroll as a function of employee efficiency and technological growth.)

G.   Ninth Quarter - When the immediate objective is reached (see Section IA1), detailed plans for the Staff Training Division will be developed. With the factory opening wide the inconsistencies between what the moderately and severely retarded can do and what they presently are doing in agencies throughout the country, Marcron will offer a comprehensive program to governmental and private agencies and institutions to train their staffs in the techniques validated by the success of the factory.

The Staff Training Division will not impede the operations of the factory. It will have separate staff, budget, and location. No capital for the Staff Training Division is requested in this proposal. Cost and income are not projected, but such programs can be highly profitable. The factory is seen as being profitable, with the profits being shared by the employees. The Staff Training Division, on the other hand, is viewed as developing from the success of the factory. We intend for it to be profitable for us, as owners of Marcron. Alternatively stated, we as owners do not intend to reap personal profit from the productivity of the factory, but we do plan to profit from the Staff Training Division.

The market for the Staff Training Division has already been well established. Numerous agencies have expressed strong interest and even verbal commitment to participate when the program is ready. Our strategy is to create, through the factory, a condition where it becomes increasingly uncomfortable (or economically fatal) for sheltered workshops, work activity centers, or vocational programs to operate almost solely through governmental or other subsidy.

Further discussion of the Staff Training Division is not needed for this proposal, but it is relevant to describe and show its importance as related to Marcron's long-range goals and objectives.

IV. Evaluation
The nature of Marcron makes evaluation an integral part of the program. As with any business—in contrast to social science projects—the books do the talking. There will be no need to develop special evaluation instruments to assess financial success.

While the general measure of success is obvious, a variety of consultants will be utilized to provide ongoing feedback and evaluation on all aspects of Marcron. Throughout the planning period we have met with a banker, an accountant, a lawyer, and two businessmen each time a major decision point arose. In each case the final decision was the amalgamation of all the input. Our confidence as businessmen is growing, but we intend to work closely with these consultants and others for some time. It is also hoped that a PRI would carry with it the professional resources of the lending institution.

V. Budget

Monthly figures are based on a 40-hour week; 52-week year; 3 weeks paid vacation and holidays; and 49 weeks of productivity.

A. Income - Projections are based on the following considerations: (1) A mean individual worker productivity of 50% of normal worker production is estimated. Our production data suggest that 50% is a conservative estimate of potential productivity. (2) P.C. boards which have been looked at are going at a labor (plus overhead) rate of from $5 to $9 (1973 rates). A $6.50 board is used here for a conservative projection. (3) Normal production on the $6.50 board is 9 boards per hour by 6 people, generating $58.50 per hour, or $9.75 per normal worker per hour. (4) Fifty percent of normal productivity equals a projected generated income by Marcron production employees of $4.88 per person per hour.

PROJECTED INCOME FOR FULL PRODUCTION (STARTING FIFTH QUARTER)	*Monthly*	*Quarterly*	*Annually*
50 production employees x 40 hours per week x 49 weeks x $4.88 mean hourly income per worker	$39,853	$119,560	$478,240

(By comparison, if production employees average 70% of normal productivity instead of 50%, projected income would be $669,340.)

B. Expenses

1. Salaries and Wages - Salaries and wages are for full production (beginning fifth quarter).

	Hourly	*Monthly*	*Quarterly*	*Annually*
Production employees (50)	$2.20	$ 381	$ 1,144 (50)	$ 4,576 (50)
Foremen (4)	4.00	693	2,080 (4)	8,320 (4)
Trainers (2)	4.00	693	2,080 (2)	8,320 (2)
Secretary/Receptionist (1)	3.00	520	1,560	6,240
Bookkeeper/Office Manager (1)	4.00	693	2,080	8,320
Delivery/Maintenance Person (1)	3.00	520	1,560	6,240
Quality Control Person (1)	4.00	693	2,080	8,320
Marc Gold		900*	2,700	10,800
Ron Torner		1,800*	5,400	21,600
TOTAL SALARIES AND WAGES FOR 62 EMPLOYEES		$28,353	$85,060	$340,240

*These amounts are liberally commensurate with Torner's present salary and Gold's present consulting income, both of which would cease.

2. Fringe Benefits Approximations for 62 Employees

	Monthly	*Quarterly*	*Annually*
a. FICA @ 5.85% of salaries and wages	$1,659	$ 4,976	$19,904
b. Unemployment Compensation @ 3.2% of salaries and wages (limit $4,200)	694	2,083	8,333
c. Workmen's Compensation and employer liability @ 1.64%	465	1,395	5,580
d. Employee insurance			
i. Life @ $2.00/person/month for $5,000/person	124	372	1,488
ii. ADB and Dismemberment @ $.30/person/month for $5,000/person	19	56	223
iii. Basic and Major Medical @ $13.32/person/month	826	2,478	9,910
TOTAL FRINGE BENEFITS	$3,787	$11,360	$45,438

e. Profit Sharing – The formula and form of profit-sharing have not yet been worked
out. Federal maximum limit is 15% of salaries or wages.

3. **Travel and Transportation** – Torner will be spending some time, especially during the first two quarters, in the field procuring contracts. Gold will do some but much less of this. Gold will be traveling to the factory, probably one trip per week. Initially, this will be for several days each time. Transportation will be the only cost (340 miles round trip). There will also be some travel costs for consultants and for some public relations by Torner and Gold.

	Monthly	*Quarterly*	*Annually*
Travel costs for Torner and Gold	$400	$1,200	$4,800
Truck operation	300	900	3,600
TOTAL TRAVEL AND TRANSPORTATION COSTS	$700	$2,100	$8,400

4. **Equipment and Remodeling** – Equipment costs were computed early in 1974 and, therefore, probably should be boosted 6–10%. Equipment is a one-time expense.

Remodeling and Setup		$7,000
Gummed tape sealers (3)	Derby Model 152 - T	240
Scale (2)	Pennsylvania counting, Model C 25, double ratio, 25-lb. capacity, on platform	680
Pallet truck (2)	Thor Uniflo hydraulic, 3000-lb. capacity, 48-in. fork length, 27-in. width	530

Stationary compressor (1)	Jacuzzi Model S2H331A, 110/220-v., 1-phase, 2-cylinder actual delivery, 7.40 CFM, 20 gal. air receiver size	700
Clecomatic screwdriver (2)		700
Workbenches (25)	Equipto, steel, 6-ft. length, 33-in. height, 33-in. depth	1,025
Stools (50)	Equipto, steel seats & backs, adjustable 22–25-in. legs	460
Gliders (200)	Equipto	180
Shelves (20)	Equipto, iron grip, closed end-open back, 7-ft. 1½-in. height, 3-ft. width, 18-in depth	965
Lockers (50)	Lyons: units of 3, 12 x 18 x 72 (used)	500
Pick racks (4)	Equipto Model 30666	514
Step ladder (2)	I.D. Cottermann 4 step-guard rails, 26-in. base, 24-in. step	169
Truck (1)	Ford 1½-ton, steel-bed, aluminum shell, hydraulic lift gate	6,500
Solder station (50)	Weller with 700° screwdriver tips	200
Wave soldering system (1)	Hollis Consoline (TDC) Automatic, 10-in. wave	6,000
Vapor degreaser (1)	London Chemical	1,800
Pallet rack (1)	8 bays	760
Electric rider truck (1)		2,000
Drill press (2)	Sears Craftsman	320
Magnifiers (5)		450
Steel flat trucks (3)		300
Banding equipment (2)	Signode Strapping Kit	80
Time clock (1)	Simplex Model 87KAA, fully automatic reconditioned 115/60	300
	1 Model 4017-42 Bell, 4-in., 115/60	17
	2 Type 2208 Card Racks, 25 cap.	19
Fluorescent lighting		1,000
P.A. system		1,000
Insertion masters (25)	G.D. Patrick Model 1000	750
TOTAL COST OF EQUIPMENT AND REMODELING		$35,159

	Monthly	Quarterly	Annually
5. Facilities			
Lease on building	$2,000	$6,000	$24,000
6. Telephone-communication expenses	150	450	1,800
7. Utilities			
Heat, electricity, and water	1,000	3,000	12,000
8. Supplies			
a. Office supplies	150	450	1,800
b. Shop supplies	400	1,200	4,800
c. Small tools	100	300	1,200

9. Other expenses

	Monthly	Quarterly	Annually
a. Depreciation on equipment*	$ 300	$ 900	$ 3,600
b. General insurance	200	600	2,400
c. Repairs*	300	900	3,600
d. Promotion*	200	600	2,400
e. Annual corporation costs, franchise fees, tax, legal, etc.	83	250	1,000
f. Business consultants	200	600	2,400
TOTAL (3–9 above, except 4)	$5,783	$17,350	$69,400

*These expenses will probably commence the fourth quarter.

C. **Budget Summary for First through Fourth Quarters** – Projections represent fractional amounts of full production based on time table. For training and graduated production of production employees (third and fourth quarters) a mean of 20 hours per employee per week is used, even though workers will be working 40 hours per week by the end of the quarter in which they are trained.

For the first four quarters, which are confusing because of the phasing in of production employees, 62 days (approximately 49 working weeks ÷ 4) is used for computation for each quarter. This makes for some small inconsistencies in the budget.

	First	Second	Third	Fourth	Year 1 Total
Income	$ 0	$ 0	$12,102[a]	$ 66,564[b]	$ 78,666
Expenses					
Salaries & wages	8,100	24, 220	18,153[c]	75,640[d]	126,113
Fringe benefits	574	2,210	7,690	9,631	20,105
Overhead	6,575	11,250	13,450	17,350	48,625
TOTAL	$15,249	$37,680[e]	$51,395	$169,185	$ 273,509[e]
DEFICIT AFTER FIRST YEAR					$−194,843[f]

[a]20 workers × 4 hours/day × 31 days

[b]20 workers × 8 hours/day × 62 days plus 30 workers × 4 hours/day × 31 days

[c]includes 20 workers × 62 hours of paid training plus the same 20 workers × 124 hours of production

[d]includes 30 workers × 62 hours of paid training plus the same 30 workers × 124 hours of production plus 20 workers × 496 hours of production

[e]exclusive of equipment purchasing

[f]includes equipment purchasing and remodeling ($35,159)

D. Budget Summary for Full Production (Fifth Quarter)

	Monthly	Quarterly	Annually
Income	$39,853	$119,560	$478,240

	Monthly	Quarterly	Annually
Expenses			
Salaries & wages	28,353	85,060	340,240
Fringe benefits	3,787	11,361	45,438
Overhead	5,783	17,350	69,400
TOTAL EXPENSES	$37,923	$113,771	$455,078
PROJECTED NET INCOME EXCLUSIVE OF DEBT REDUCTION	$ 1,930	$ 5,789	$ 23,162

VI. Loan Request

To the best of our knowledge, the projections given represent liberal estimates of expense and conservative estimates of income. As projected, Marcron in full production can fully support its employees, provide them with liberal fringe benefits, and cover its overhead, less debt reduction. We have no doubts that real income, barring unforeseen economic or political catastrophes, will far exceed the projections made in this proposal. If the projections should turn out to be correct, as conservative as they are, the Staff Development Division will be justified and should certainly generate sufficient profits to cover debt reduction and growth. On the basis of these projections, Marcron shows a positive cash flow starting the first quarter of the second year. We expect our audited financial statement at the end of the first year to show a net loss of approximately $194,843. Start up (initial inefficiency) and training costs are somewhat higher than normal, but equipment and operating capital, which constitute much of the net loss, seem quite reasonable.

We are therefore requesting a loan of $300,000 which would cover payroll and overhead for 2 years, given no revenue the first year, less revenue than anticipated in the second year, and even reasonable delays in accounts receivable. This request assumes a direct relationship between income and expense. That is, there is no possibility that Marcron would maintain a full labor force over any period of time that was not either showing earnings exceeding expenditures or showing strong growth in that direction. The amount of capital requested represents, to us, a reasonable balance between coverage for possible underestimates of cost projections and overestimates of income projections on the one hand, and overkill on the other.

Marcron can provide the impetus for full participation in society by the moderately and severely retarded. In light of the setback the retarded in our society would experience if we try, and fail, we have attempted to comprehensively plan our strategy and our operations. We are now eager to proceed.

Marc W. Gold   Ronald S. Torner

POSTSTATEMENT

Marcron never happened. We were not able to generate the needed capital. At one point we could have done it by putting up our own homes as collateral. At the time this did not seem like a wise decision, in terms of our families, so we did not. After we submitted the proposal to one foundation, the electronics industry began to go into a significant slump; we pulled back on our attempts to capitalize Marcron. Approximately 1 year later when the electronics industry began to come around again, our interests had changed somewhat. Ron Torner, by then, was involved in some other things, and I was beginning to question the idea of a segregated organization of any kind. The intention to use retarded persons *exclusively* in the production force was an error. Any labor force involving handicapped people should be well-integrated, employing people who have been labeled normal, as well as those who have been labeled handicapped or retarded. The concept thus modified is still intrinsically good, but various economic and sociological factors have made it less attractive.

The basic economic logic of the proposal is still valid. Obviously, the costs of equipment, operating, etc., have gone up considerably. The minimum wage is a lot more than it was then, but so is the labor rate charged for such work. As a matter of fact, the need for such labor is at least as strong as it was then. This need, combined with increased awareness and activity on the part of society, as evidenced, for example, by Section 504 of the Rehabilitation Act of 1973, and the continued existence of sheltered workshops and activity centers make this modified concept still relevant. Marc Gold & Associates, Inc., in early 1980, entered into a contractual relationship with several electronics organizations to provide recruitment and training of workers in their factories. These workers included people with significant handicapping conditions. From the perspective of job stability this is certainly the way to go. If substantial numbers of opportunities can be found in large, stable companies, this would seem to be the best possible solution. This does not preclude the development of subcontracting factories or organizations in certain places under certain conditions. Both of these possibilities should be available, in addition to modified forms of what are now called sheltered workshops and work activity centers. In fact, sheltered workshops and work activity centers might modify this proposal for establishing the work part of their operation as a self-sustaining, nonsubsidized business.

CHAPTER 16

Vocational Training

Marc W. Gold

PRESTATEMENT

This chapter was written at the invitation of Joseph Wortis, an MD at Maimonides Medical Center in New York who has edited a series of volumes entitled *Mental Retardation and Developmental Disabilities*, published by Brunner/Mazel. These volumes have not had much circulation among practitioners in the field, but they have been read and well received by the research community in mental retardation. Most of the points made in the chapter still need to be made to people who work in service programs for individuals labeled retarded. Perhaps this reprinting of the chapter will receive wider attention within the service community.

   This chapter was the first publication of three components of the philosophy of Try Another Way. They are the competence/deviance hypothesis, the expectancy cycle, and the expectancy spiral. The wording of the competence/deviance hypothesis at that time still included just the word *him*, showing how recently we began trying to use nonsexist language.

INTRODUCTION

Mental retardation has always been perceived as a phenomenon that exists within individuals. If we, as members of a discipline or group of disciplines, are to make the necessary changes and adaptations to bring about successful existence for people labeled mentally retarded, it should be recognized that their behavior and performance are more a function of the context in which they exist than of their innate capabilities. Because this chapter is on vocational training the comments made will be within that context. It is intended that these comments will be generalized by the reader to all aspects of mental retardation.

   The societal context in which the retarded presently find themselves differs from anything that has been in the past. For one, the United States is now experiencing an age of awareness and advocacy (Diamond, 1974; Rosen

This chapter originally appeared in J. Wortis (Ed.), *Mental retardation and developmental disabilities: An annual review*, Vol. 7. (New York: Brunner/Mazel, 1975). Reprinted by permission of the publisher.

& Soloyanis, 1974; Whitten, 1974). In mental retardation the initial impetus in the United States began via the efforts of the executive branch of the Kennedy administration. Following an initial period of funding resulting from the personal involvement of President Kennedy, the legislative branch of the government assumed responsibility in the form of the development of the Bureau for the Education of the Handicapped (Gallagher, 1968), the Vocational Rehabilitation Acts (Boggs, 1972), and other legislation such as the Developmental Disabilities Act, and more recently, the Rehabilitation Act of 1973 (U.S. Department of Health, Education, and Welfare, 1973; Whitten, 1974). In the last few years the judicial branch of government has provided the prime source of movement and direction through court cases designed to alleviate chronic problems in the field (e.g., Bailey, 1972; Laski, 1974; Rowan, 1972). The three principal areas of litigation have been right-to-education, right-to-treatment, and peonage. The right-to-education court cases, such as the one in Pennsylvania, have resulted in legislation requiring that public education systems provide services to all school-aged individuals. Numerous states now have mandatory education for all children as a function of this kind of legislation. Other cases are pending. The second category of litigation, right-to-treatment, will not be covered in this chapter.

The third category of litigation is peonage. This litigation, for the most part, concerns individuals in institutions who have been required to perform services needed to maintain the institution where their pay is not consistent with current wage laws nor commensurate with the productivity stemming from their work. While the specific cases are of no particular concern to this chapter, the conceptual issue which is of importance relates to the inherent assumption underlying much of the institutional peonage that has gone on: that the retarded are incapable of a quantity and quality of work which would necessitate paying them a normal wage. This assumption has been supported by the low level performance of retarded individuals at work, in and out of institutions, under conditions where no attempts were made to provide skills and attitudes which would allow them to produce significantly above current levels of expectancy.

Low expectancy on the part of society is perhaps the single most critical deterrent to progress in our field. We have established an expectancy cycle which perpetuates low levels of success and low functional employment capabilities. From the early work of Binet (Binet & Simon, 1948) and Itard (1801) right on through to the current writings of Goldberg (1971) and Kirk (1972), people working with the retarded have decided, on the basis of their own experiences, the performance capabilities of the retarded. They then went out and, as a self-fulfilling prophecy, proved themselves to be right. That is, the retarded did no more than what they were expected to do. This gave early workers the confidence to tell their successors of the capabilities and limitations of the retarded and, in cyclical fashion, their successors went out and again proved that the retarded could be just what they were expected or not expected to be. This cycle continues so that today the retarded still accomplish exactly what is expected of them where the expectancies the people in the field have are basically the ones handed down by their predecessors.

Two factors, however, make today different than any other time: (1) data are now available showing the abilities of moderately, severely, and profoundly retarded individuals to perform tasks or exhibit behaviors totally inconsistent with previous expectancies for such individuals (Foxx & Azrin, 1973; Gold, 1972; Merwin, 1973; Schroeder, 1972a); and (2) there are now emerging a variety of technologies, developed in laboratory settings and previously unavailable in service settings, designed to help individuals who find learning difficult. Examples of these technologies include discrimination learning (Gold & Scott, 1971; Zeaman, 1965), attention-retention theory (Fisher & Zeaman, 1973), behavior modification (Gardner, 1971; Kazdin, 1973; Panda & Lynch, 1972; Schroeder, 1972a & b), and such specific techniques as match-to-sample (Bijou, 1968; Merwin, 1974), oddity (Brown, 1970), clustering (Bousfield, 1953), fading (Touchette, 1968), and shaping (Brown, Bellamy, & Sontag, 1971; Brown, Scheuerman, Cartwright, & York, 1973; Brown & Sontag, 1972; Brown, Williams, & Crowner, 1974). These two factors give the support, justification and, in fact, the mandate for breaking into the expectancy cycle so that we begin to completely revise what will be accepted as appropriate, successful, or even minimum performance from those individuals labeled mentally retarded. The role of expectancy is given considerable weight here because without revised expectancies, all of the technology available will go unnoticed in the absence of individuals having reason to believe that the retarded are capable of significantly more than they presently show (Gold, 1973b). This chapter will discuss several practices which have resulted in the perpetuation of existing inappropriate expectancies, and will indicate how current practices might be modified to break the expectancy cycle to achieve full participation by the retarded in society.

FOLLOW-UP STUDIES

The field has a long history of follow-up studies on the vocational training and placement of the retarded (Fairbanks, 1933; Keys & Nathan, 1932). Examination of this literature shows several consistencies. Virtually all studies indicate that when retarded people fail on a job, it is not because they cannot perform the task, but because of the social interactions involved. The jobs described in these studies are almost all characterized by low levels of remuneration and placement at the bottom of the perceived job hierarchy in the work setting. None of the studies investigates the relationships between task complexity, job sophistication, self-perception, and the perceptions of others. These interactions provide significant weight to the performance of normal persons in work settings (Hulin & Blood, 1968; Scott, 1973) and might be relevant to the retarded as well (Bishop & Hill, 1971).

It seems oversimplified to say that the retarded fail for social reasons, simply because they are inept, and leave it at that. Several factors might contribute significantly to the problem. Korman (1970) points out that people have a chronic level of self-esteem, but that self-esteem is also influenced by a particular task at hand. The reality on which self-esteem is based comes from the expectations and feedback from others. The chronic level of self-esteem for most retarded individuals is quite low and comes principally from the feedback of others, especially in the work setting, where the retarded do the lowest level work. It is hypothesized here that a significant upgrading of the kinds of jobs performed by the retarded would result in a different reality on which to base their self-esteem. That reality would generate from a change in the way they are perceived by others, as a function of their newly demonstrated competence. Alternatively stated, replace the expectancy cycle with an expectancy spiral.

A test for such a hypothesis requires a shift away from the correlational strategies typical of most research done in vocational training of the retarded and toward experimental strategies where the focus is more on the effects of training than characteristics (Cronbach, 1957). Such a shift has begun to occur in vocational training (Close, 1973; Gold & Barclay, 1973; Schroeder, 1972c; Screven, Straka, & Lafond, 1971). The areas of self-esteem in the retarded and changing societal expectancies as they relate to work have not yet been investigated. Follow-up studies could provide a means for evaluating change on these and other variables if the follow-up data were part of an experimental design instead of the usual correlational, retrospective or descriptive approaches (Brolin, 1972; Olshansky & Beach, 1974; Stabler, 1974). In most cases, follow-up studies have not been able to describe what was being followed up. In the absence of clearly defined and measured training programs and procedures, those studies have, at best, described the successes and failures of the retarded as related to the organizational structures in which their early experience was obtained (Brolin, 1972; Gibson & Fields, 1970; Olshansky & Beach, 1974). At worst, their failures have been attributed to cause and effect relationships which were inappropriately inferred from correlational information (Rosen, Floor, & Baxter, 1972; Rosen, Kivitz, Clark, & Floor, 1970). Training programs should operate under the assumption that demonstrations of vocational skill competencies in individuals currently perceived as permanent members of the surplus labor force (Farber, 1968) will provide the *sine qua non* for positive social change. Vocational skill competence is defined here as skills not found in any untrained member of the work force, working or surplus. Retarded individuals should hold jobs where their removal would require training someone else, even a normal individual, and would result in down time for the work place. In this society gainful employment and the nature of a man's work still provide the most reliable means for obtaining the basic privileges and acceptances (Jones & Azrin, 1973; Parker, 1971). When the retarded can be judged as they function following carefully designed training programs, which include training of community expectancies and attitudes as well as work and social skills, full participation in society should be forthcoming.

THE TESTING MOVEMENT

"If test technology is not greatly improved, long before the applied experimentalists near their goals, testing deserves to disappear" (Cronbach, 1957).

This statement by Lee Cronbach is as meaningful today as it was in 1957. In fact, the research done before and since then on testing in the vocational areas of retardation has been almost completely devoid of practical significance and utility. For comprehensive reviews of this literature the reader is referred to Patterson (1964), Wolfensberger (1967), and Gold (1973b). These reviews need not be duplicated here; however, a current example of the testing literature will serve to clarify some issues.

Perhaps the most ambitious and creative effort to develop predictive instruments is the recent work of Rikard Palmer (1974). He has systematically expanded the general strategies used by Elkin (1967), Gibson and Fields (1970), and others who have operated under the assumption that the potential ability of someone must be known or guessed in advance in order to fully develop it. The correlations reported between predictor variables and criterion variables are reminiscent of earlier studies by Wagner and Hawver (1965) and Tobias and Gorelick (1960) where many predictor and criterion variables shared considerable common variance. But with sheltered workshop performance used as the criterion variable, why predict at all?

The Palmer studies also share several problems in common with other prediction research. The samples were not drawn randomly from the available population. Variables such as previous success in vocational training and level of socially acceptable behavior were used to establish criteria for selection. These variables were also included in the prediction and criterion measures, thereby systematically biasing the data and limiting its generalizability.

Gold points out that all previous work on prediction involved simple tasks for the retarded to perform (Gold, 1973b). Palmer validly suggests that the use of more difficult tasks might improve predictability, but his data do not support such a position. He uses percent error in production as a measure of task difficulty. The position taken here is that percent error in production is more a measure or a function of job design and the criteria used for initial training. The variables studied by Palmer are not predictive at all; they are descriptive of the training strategies, instruction capabilities and expectancies of staff.

Palmer mentions that parents of clients in the workshop where his studies were conducted took the position that the workers should be trained, not tested. As Palmer also mentioned, this author strongly agrees with the parents, and interprets Palmer's work as supportive of that position.

Even in the military, in industry, and in the related academic fields of industrial psychology, human factors and ergonomics prediction are far from clear-cut issues. Edwin A. Fleishman, the foremost researcher on prediction of skills, after more than 20 years of systematic study, reported as recently as 1972 that his work had not yet resulted in a battery of standardized tasks which could be generalized to new tasks (Fleishman, 1972). His work with normal individuals suggests that nonmotor abilities contribute more to performance during early stages of learning and less as proficiency is obtained. If such is the case with normal individuals, one might expect even greater differences with the retarded, where attainment of proficiency is so much more contingent on powerful training procedures.

Data from the author's research seem to support the possible application of this finding to the retarded (Gold, 1973a). Gold found correlations of .27 and -.27, neither significant, between acquisition rate (trials to criterion) and mean hourly production rate in two different production experiments. This suggests that, at least for the task used, early performance was not predictive of subsequent production on the same task. Current vocational testing practices become suspect in light of such data. It becomes increasingly naive to believe that a person's initial performance on a small variety of tasks will allow prediction of eventual job success on a potentially infinite variety of tasks and settings. In the two experiments discussed above, correlations of .30 and .29 were found between IQ and production rate. Initial experiments in electronic circuit board assembly training yielded correlations of .03 and -.19 between IQ and acquisition rate (trials to criterion) where IQs ranged from 23 to 92 (mean = 55) and 18 to 77 (mean = 39.66), respectively (Merwin, 1973, 1974). These data suggest that IQ, acquisition rate and production rate share little common variance for the population and tasks used.

From a vocational perspective, mental retardation should be conceptualized in terms of the power needed in the training procedures required for someone to reach proficiency. Prediction and testing promote a reliance on screening out individuals who are difficult to train instead of developing training procedures with sufficient power to meet the needs of all trainees. If Fleishman's work was completed, and adaptable to the retarded at all levels, if powerful training procedures for a wide variety of tasks and settings were available, and if society had a commitment to a broad-based participation by all levels of the retarded in the world of work, then prediction and formal testing might be facilitative. Until then, this author is opposed to further use and development of formal predictive and diagnostic instruments specifically in the vocational aspects of retardation.

THE COMPETENCE-DEVIANCE HYPOTHESIS

In an effort to provide a social perspective justification for the philosophy evidenced in this chapter the following is hypothesized: the more competence an individual has, the more deviance will be tolerated in him by others. Deviance is used here to mean aspects of an individual which cause negative attention. Competence is defined as attributes, skills, etc. which not everyone has, and which are appreciated and needed by someone else. Using work skill as an example, the Competence-Deviance Hypothesis would posit that if someone successfully performs a job task which is essential to the organization, and which no one else could perform without considerable training, that individual must exhibit considerable deviance before dismissal would be considered. Each individual who remains in society does so, more or less successfully, as a function of the balance between his competence and his deviance.

Teaching someone to toilet, to use public transportation, or to eat with utensils is to eliminate deviant behavior, since these skills are expected of everyone in our society. Deviance and competence can be graphically represented as two halves of a line separated by a zero point which represents neutrality. If the mean of an individual's competence-deviance relationship in a situation (work, marriage, community) is above zero, as perceived by those with decision making power, then the individual can remain, and if below zero, then he is out.

In our field the overwhelming emphasis has been on the elimination of deviance, rather than the development of competence, as the terms are used here. The goal seems to be to bring individuals up to zero. This results in the all-too-frequent situation where a retarded individual who is existing successfully in the community, or on the job, commits some minor infraction, such as picking his nose, swearing at someone or showing up late, and is fired or institutionalized. Clearly, this would not be the effect of such infractions if there was competence to maintain a positive balance. But with a mean of zero, the slightest deviance might precipitate exclusion.

The profession must recognize that normalization means competence as well as the elimination of deviance. And vocationally, the retarded at all levels have already demonstrated competence. We must capitalize on current training technologies to give all retarded individuals sufficient competence to maintain a positive balance and a place in society.

CONCLUSION

In a society which places considerable value on a person's work and worth perhaps the most fruitful approach to helping someone find acceptance is to facilitate his vocational competence. To accomplish this requires a shift away from prediction and testing and toward training, under the assumption that potential competence is a given for all individuals, and that people differ in how much power is needed to train them. The demonstration of competence by the retarded should be the precipitating mechanism for eliminating imposed handicaps such as hiring and testing practices, preconceived notions of intellectual requisites, and low expectancies which have so severely handicapped us all.*

POSTSTATEMENT

This chapter presents a strong argument against common testing procedures. But lots of people with far fewer resources and skills than Fleishman are still trying to develop the perfect instrument.

I laughed when I reread this chapter. In the section on follow-up studies I used the expression *sine qua non*. I have not the slightest idea why I used it. In rereading it I did not even remember what it meant. I guess I was trying

*The preparation of this paper was supported by the National Institute of Child Health and Human Development Program Project Grant No. HD05951.

to impress somebody. In any event, Joe Wortis caught it and several other of my attempts to sound academic. After he received the chapter, he said in a letter, "I generally hold the view that clear thinking correlates highly with clear writing, but your writing is often unnecessarily complex. For one thing, as a nonacademic personality you get bogged down too much in academic vocabulary; for another, your syntax is sometimes tortured. Say it simply!" He was right on all counts, especially the part about my being a nonacademic personality. I had a good laugh when I got the letter and have tried since to write more simply and not try to impress people. You can judge whether the rest of the prestatements and poststatements reflect that resolve.

CHAPTER 17

Work Skill Development

Sidney M. Levy, David J. Pomerantz, and Marc W. Gold

PRESTATEMENT

When the American Association for the Education of the Severely/Profoundly Handicapped (now called The Association for the Severely Handicapped) came into existence, one of the first things they did was to go into the publishing business. As part of that effort, they solicited chapters for a series of volumes, *Teaching the Severely Handicapped*, edited by Norris Haring and Lou Brown. Sid Levy, who was working on the concept of job enlargement, put together a paper on it. Dave Pomerantz had begun to apply some of our research group's techniques to younger children, and I was very much involved in expanding the work that Mary Merwin had done when she was a part of the group. This chapter gave us the opportunity to put our thoughts down in these three areas and synthesize them into something useful for the association.

INTRODUCTION

This chapter is designed to provide a current account of the research on work skill development of the severely handicapped which has been going on at Children's Research Center, University of Illinois at Urbana-Champaign, since 1969. Those activities which have been described in other publications or are currently being prepared for publication will not be included. The focus of attention here will be on pilot activities and recent developments which are not likely to find their way into publication in the near future. The three separate areas to be covered include pilot work on skill training with young children; pilot work on the acquisition of the necessary skills to assemble printed circuit boards with many components; and a detailed discussion of the concept of job enlargement from the industrial psychological literature, which provides some insights into worker motivation and productivity which might be of use to our field, and perhaps some information which can provide strategies for the inclusion of the severely handicapped into existing industrial organizations.

This chapter originally appeared in N. G. Haring and L. J. Brown (Eds.), *Teaching the severely handicapped: A yearly publication of the American Association on Education of the Severely/Profoundly Handicapped,* Vol. II (New York: Grune & Stratton, 1977).

MANUAL SKILL TRAINING OF CHILDREN

Until 1974, research activities in work skill development were carried out with adults only. The rationale for this was that studies of manual skill development would be clearer if a developmental effect was minimized by avoiding the use of younger individuals, where such a factor would have to be accounted for. We felt that the information generating from that research would be applicable to younger children, even though adults were used to obtain the information and to generate the strategies. Anecdotal information from the field has tended to support that position. Many public school personnel are using our procedures and, according to their verbal reports, have found the techniques useful. This past year, we began working with younger children in an attempt to more systematically assess the applicability and limitations of our procedures with school-age children. Part of this decision related to a long range goal of developing a prevocational training program for public school use.

Two general attitudes underlie the work conducted by this program. First, we recognize the primary importance of a technology of training developed from basic and applied research. Data from such research can provide educative agencies with the instructional expertise required to give to the severely handicapped the skills needed to live with dignity within their home communities. The second philosophical foundation of our work is a bit more disturbing. Developing effective ways of teaching the retarded is not in itself an adequate strategy for solving their problems. In fact, many of these problems can be most meaningfully conceptualized as existing outside of the handicapped individual (Gold, 1975). They are reflected by inappropriately low levels of expectation commonly held in society and a general tendency to exclude deviant people from the mainstream rather than to adapt to their special needs. If we are to engineer meaningful change, farsighted social action strategies in addition to pedagogic skill are essential.

One such intervention plan focuses on economic reality. If the severely handicapped can be molded into a labor force able to meet industrial demands, the chances would significantly improve for them to be assimilated into the social structure as productive citizens. In the past, our research has attempted to demonstrate the potential of the retarded for economic viability. The studies have utilized 14- and 24-piece bicycle coaster brakes, as well as electronic circuit board assemblies. These represent considerably more difficult tasks than are usually associated with the severely handicapped, and are therefore useful for demonstrating the large discrepancy between the current level of functioning and unknown potential of retarded persons. The assemblies are also useful as research tools because they have considerable face validity. Watching subjects produce bicycle brakes or circuit boards, one sees a clear example of the retarded engaged in activity that is typically wage-generating.

The subjects who participated in the majority of studies of vocational skill development were sampled from unscreened populations of moderately and severely handicapped adolescents and adults. After an average of less than 2 hr cumulative training time, they were demonstrating a vocational competence, as indicated by high quality performance in production of complex tasks. It is clear that the severely retarded can acquire skills under appropriate training conditions. If their level of functioning can be dramatically elevated after 2 hr of intervention, what are the possible outcomes of well-planned, comprehensive training opportunities provided consistently from an early point in the lifespan? Most severely handicapped persons do receive some form of special educational or professional "helping" services during childhood. If such services were characterized by an orientation toward training and building of skills, application of powerful instructional techniques, and accountability for positive behavior change, clients would display much larger repertoires of competencies by adolescence than they do at present.

It is within this context of unfulfilled potential that the goals and techniques of this program are being extended to younger age ranges within the population of severely handicapped persons. Five- through 12-year-olds from trainable classes in the public schools have received training on complex vocational assemblies. These studies represent an effort to assess the modifications in training procedure and strategy that are necessary for intervention with younger children. Also, this expansion of research involvement should provide momentum for the development of prevocational components for public school curriculum planning and programming. Society appears to be accepting its responsibility to provide quality services to the severely handicapped, and much of this responsibility is being delegated to the public schools (Brown & York, 1974). The clearest indications of change are the judicial and legislative actions of several states guaranteeing to all children the right to public education (Gilhool, 1973). If economic viability is to be considered a long range objective of educational services, the schools will have to provide a systematic progression of prevocational experiences over an extended period of time. Researchers will have to begin looking at the many unanswered questions associated with prevocational training. What kinds of experiences will be most facilitative for future vocational training and placement? The rapidly changing nature of the vocational structure in a technologically advanced society, as well as the great degree of variability across work situations make these issues quite complex. Deficiencies in knowledge and experience characterize much of the prevocational area at the present time, and are particularly evident in reference to elementary curricula. Baroff (1974) has proposed a set of basic objectives for elementary prevocational programs. These include (1) developing manual skills, (2) making small objects, (3) developing concern for the quality of tasks performed, (4) creating an awareness of the importance of task completion, and (5) strengthening work-related personality characteristics. Although the training described in this chapter is conceived as a preliminary search for information and not a prevocational program, it could be considered an appropriate activity for working toward all of these objectives.

Originally, our plans called for the use of the 14-piece coaster brake in studies with young children. This assembly was considered ideal for pilot research because of our extensive experience with it. A high degree of task familiarity serves to emphasize the particular needs of a subject population. Also, it facilitates flexibility on the part of the trainer, so that the procedures can be readily adapted to meet these needs. The well-developed level of organization of bicycle brake training techniques was indicated in previous extensions of our research involving institutionalized deaf—blind severely retarded, as well as profoundly retarded persons. Although the original training method included 24 steps in the content task analysis, it was readily apparent that further refinement, in the form of other, intermediate steps, had to be added in addition to changes in the kinds of feedback that were given. Experimenters were able to isolate the precise junctures where modifications were needed, and have alternative methods available because they knew the task well. Thus, the pilot studies with trainable children were conceived as a further broadening of the scope of the vocational skill development program in terms of populations involved. An effort was made to hold other parameters of the research environment (e.g., setting, basic format of training, and task) constant. Information regarding generalizability of our methods in reference to other parameters is equally important, and research concerning these issues has been included in our plans. A careful progression of study should provide a basic understanding of the factors important in effective training of the severely handicapped.

The following anecdotal data are based on a pilot study conducted over a 7-mo period. Twelve school children (mean chronological age = 8.5 years, mean IQ = 40) from two trainable classes served as subjects. Within the first 2 days of training, it became evident that there were serious architectural barriers to manual skill training of small children in school. It was difficult to find a table-chair combination that was size-appropriate. Despite numerous attempts to circumvent the problem (including seating subjects on the trainer's lap), it was never adequately resolved. From our perspective, this kind of difficulty is quite important. The training techniques employed in these studies of vocational skill development stress stimulus control, or manipulation of response probability, through arrangement of antecedent conditions in the training environment. The physical format of training is a major determinant of efficiency. If such physical limitations of the instructional setting are common in public school classrooms, they could obstruct the development of high quality elementary prevocational training programs.

A large proportion of the procedural modifications attempted were necessitated by the size of the learners' hands. It was most difficult for the children to hold up the brake while performing the fine manipulations involved in its assembly. One remedial strategy relied on the trainer to support the weight of the task, and to gradually reduce his assistance as the learner's proficiency and/or strength increased. Under these conditions, the two choice discriminations involved in the bicycle brake were learned relatively quickly, but manipulative skill never developed to the desired level. It seemed that the children had been taught too well to depend on the trainer, and that this pattern was most difficult to reverse. The withholding of physical assistance led to slower rates of acquisition (i.e., learning the discriminations), but higher quality skills resulted in the final analysis. A promising alternative method is to use simple jigs to support the brake as the child works on its assembly. These kinds of data illustrate the importance of flexibility in the task analyses for application to different populations. Even during its original formulation, an instructional plan must consider alternative ways to break down a task.

In terms of the system developed within the research program described in this chapter, training format and feedback procedures are considered in the process task analysis. Format refers to the manner in which instruction is sequenced and to the layout of materials. In the usual brake training procedures, the parts are arranged in a left to right order. Identical pieces are grouped together in a compartment of the assembly tray, and the learner must bring one piece from each compartment to the front of the tray before starting the assembly. Commonly, retarded individuals have learned to perform this aspect of the task very rapidly, after observing one demonstration. Although the tray was uncomfortably large for all of the children involved, format adaptations were needed for only two of them. These particular children tended to grab randomly at parts in the tray, seriously disrupting the continuity of the training process in its early stages. Control over the situation was increased by leaving the parts of only one brake at a time in the tray. Physical prompts toward the correct piece successfully eliminated the disruptive behavior, so that many more trials per session were possible. After gradual fading of the prompts, the children consistently approached the task in correct sequence.

Much of this research effort has been directed toward determination of the kinds of feedback that will facilitate skill acquisition by trainable children. The instructional techniques which provided encouraging acquisition data with adolescents and adults were relatively nonverbal in nature. Trainers relied mostly on modeling and manipulation of the learners' hands, rather than spoken instructions and reinforcement. One verbal phrase, "try another way," was consistently used to cue the necessity of a correction, and appropriate task responses were met with silence. The rationale for such a strategy had several aspects. First, the majority of individuals participating in these studies exhibited extreme deficiencies in their language repertoires. Many attempts to teach severely handicapped people combine remediation of language deficits with skill instruction. In our view, this practice results in inefficient development of stimulus control over both classes of target behavior involved. There is a lack of clear communication to the learner of what he is expected to do in these situations, and failure often results. The general rule proposed is that language and skill training should be provided separately, with verbal cues included in the instructional process only so far as they are inherently involved in the target behavior. Several qualifications about this rule are needed. The vocational tasks described in this chapter are ideally suited for nonverbal training because criterion performance involves no receptive or expressive language. In most tasks, there is more ambiguity concerning the extent to which language is involved. Also, under certain conditions, verbal cues can function efficiently in training. Caution should be taken, however, to insure that they consistently control the responses that they are intended to control.

The second aspect of the rationale for a nonverbal emphasis comes from a literature commonly called analyses of social reinforcement (Stevenson, 1965). Many studies have investigated the effects of positive and negative verbal feedback (usually presented to children by adults) on rate of simple motor responses, persistence at relatively simple tasks, and discrimination learning. Such feedback can exert a great deal of control over behavior, but it has generally not had strong effects in studies that employ measures of discrimination learning (Cairns, 1967; 1970). Intuitively, it seems probable that high frequencies of praise and criticism lead to increased reliance on the trainer at the expense of active formulation of general problem solving strategies. Zigler (1966) indicates that retarded persons, due to their histories of failure in evaluative situations, are much more likely than matched MA normals to depend on external cues for solving discrimination problems. By minimizing the amount of feedback (particularly verbal) that is provided in training, we hope to force the learner to confront the "rules" of the task. Another consistent and relevant finding of social reinforcement studies is that negative feedback has greater impact on rate, persistence, and learning than do positive evaluative comments (Stevenson, 1965). One explanation for this phenomenon is that criticism is delivered less often, more contingently, and with greater reliability for predicting further consequences than is praise in the social environment (Paris & Cairns, 1972). Finally, this literature indicates that children interpret adult nonreaction as positive or negative feedback if it is alternated with either praise or criticism alone (Spence, 1966; Hill et al., 1974). Thus, learners in the bicycle brake training situation should interpret silence as an indication of good performance.

The third basis for designing nonverbal instructional procedures was the kind of atmosphere that resulted in the training setting. The quiet, business-like nature of the sessions may have helped communicate the kind of social interaction that we tried to offer. The learner is treated as a dignified adult developing vocational competency, and is expected to act accordingly. Constant praise for correct task responses was seen as violating this unspoken agreement.

Judging by the quality of acquisition data accumulated in brake training studies (Gold, 1972), the feedback strategy was effective in providing information to the learner and maintaining on-task work behavior. Adolescents and adults tended to "ask for" feedback during the early trials by looking up at the trainer and hesitating after each correct response. Such behaviors rapidly extinguished because trainers continued to look down at the task and did not return eye contact. The learners appeared to genuinely enjoy working on the brake assembly, and disruptive behavior problems were rarely encountered. In general, the children's performance was excellent in the early stages of training. Although their teachers reported that they had deficient attention spans and would not sit still during classroom activities, the children remained consistently on-task throughout the relatively long assembly cycle (cycles ranged from 5 to 12 min), and were able to complete two or three cycles per session. One child did not respond well under the original training procedures. He did not stay seated for more than a minute at a time, and he did not maintain the constant manipulations needed to complete the assembly task. However, this pattern was reversed by providing play time with the trainer contingent upon completion of a full cycle assembly. Eventually, this subject would finish two cycles (approximately 20 min of work) without interruption before the play opportunity was provided. In general, we recommend reliance on natural contingencies in vocational and prevocational training in order to enhance transfer to many diverse work situations. Extrinsic reinforcers are programmed into training only when their necessity has been demonstrated.

Several significant problems were encountered in the later stages of training. Typically, children learned the discriminations, and most of the manipulations involved in the task, but did not improve on one or two crucial manual responses. Although the troublesome manipulations were not identical across subjects, they all were related to inability to hold the brake still as it became uncomfortably larger and heavier with the addition of each part. As the number of trials without improvement increased, the children began to consistently make errors on parts of the assembly that they had clearly learned much earlier in training. Also, at this point in the training process, a significant increase in inappropriate, off-task behavior was noted. These data have led us to search for alternative tasks for which prevocational training techniques can be developed. Such tasks will retain the characteristics of the bicycle brake that we consider important. They will involve detailed, complex assemblies which can be disassembled so that they can be used in ongoing training programs. The assembly cycle will be shorter and the task itself smaller and lighter than the brake.

JOB ENLARGEMENT AND THE SEVERELY HANDICAPPED

If the adult severely handicapped are to succeed in the sheltered or unsheltered world of work, that world must be understood by those who prepare them. The discussion below is meant to contribute to that understanding. The issues which are relevant to the concept of job enlargement are central to both the training of the severely handicapped and to their integration into the labor force.

Gold (1973b) has already pointed out the possible relevance of the job enlargement concept and literature to the vocational habilitation of the retarded. In that chapter, a brief description is given of the concept and a few of the findings from that literature. With the recent trend towards the habilitation of the severely handicapped (Rehabilitation Act of 1973), the concept seems to take on additional meaning: There is now, for the first time, an organized, explicit movement toward their inclusion into the labor force. An optimistic conceptual framework might help such a movement. The concept of job enlargement is reviewed in detail here for several reasons: (1) to provide the reader with some background in an area of industrial psychology that can provide some meaningful "buzz words" and issues for consideration; (2) to point to the complexity of motivational systems, discussing affective as well as cognitive variables; (3) to provide the reader with an expanded in-depth awareness of the context into which the severely handicapped find themselves when entering competitive employment; and (4) to discuss directly the application of the concept to the severely handicapped. If we are going to efficiently and effectively integrate the severely handicapped into industry, we must know a great deal about industry, how it works, how it thinks, and perhaps more importantly, an awareness of recent literature in industrial research so that we can keep up with advances in technology.

The trend in industry since early in the Industrial Revolution has been to simplify jobs. The process of simplification that developed from the scientific management approach of Frederick Taylor (1895, 1903, 1911) still prevails in many industries. The method involves the analyzing and breaking down of jobs into their simplest components. Jobs are standardized and made routine with workers limited to performance on small components of the total job. This procedure was thought to be the most efficient and economical way to produce.

Management's function under this system is to break the task down and to establish the production process. The worker provides the energy to run the system. As a result of simplification, jobs are reduced to elemental components requiring less skill from the worker, are highly repetitive, and allow little or no flexibility or autonomy from the routine.

The process of job simplification has been linked to worker dissatisfaction by many industrial investigators (Argyris, 1964; Davis, 1957; Guest, 1955; Herzberg, 1966; Kornhauser, 1965; Walker, 1950; Walker & Guest, 1952). The position taken is that simple, routine, nonchallenging tasks remove supposed intrinsic sources of personal satisfaction from the job leading to worker dissatisfaction. This, in turn, results in undesirable behaviors, from a management point of view, such as absenteeism, personnel turnover, and lower productivity.

An explanation for worker motivational problems resulting from simplification can be found in the writings of Maslow (1943). Maslow developed a hierarchy of needs beginning with lower level physiologic needs such as hunger, thirst, and sleep, and progressing towards higher order needs which include achievement and self-actualization. It is suggested that in today's society, most workers have their lower level needs satisfied and are motivated toward the fulfillment of their higher level needs. One way of attaining the desired results is through the work situation. A complex responsible job might allow the worker to experience a feeling of achievement and self-actualization, while a simple repetitive job would not. Workers not fulfilling their higher order needs would become frustrated and dissatisfied.

Argyris (1964) proposes that the organization that follows the simplification model causes frustration, a feeling of failure, and conflict in the individual worker. He believes the individual should be integrated into the organization. Evaluating factory workers for mental health, Argyris found them to score low on his positive mental health dimension (richness of self, self-acceptance, growth motivation, investment in living, unifying outlook on life, regulations from within, independence, and adequacy of interpersonal relations). The results confirmed his expectations leading him to conclude that simplified jobs contribute to poor mental health. The state of the workers' mental health before entering employment was not determined, thus obscuring his interpretation.

In another study, Argyris (1959) compared highly skilled workers to semiskilled and unskilled workers. He found that semi- and unskilled workers expressed less aspiration for high quality work, less need to learn more about their work, more emphasis on money, lower estimates of ability, less desire for variety and independence, fewer friends on the job, and less creative use of their leisure time. His position was that their needs and attitudes were a result of the workers' maturity being stifled by their jobs. An alternate point of view would be that individuals brought the needs and attitudes into the work situation, rather than the job causing them. Since a pretest of the workers' attitudes before they began their jobs was not made, it is difficult to attribute the effects to job simplication.

Kornhauser (1965) maintains that poor mental health may be attributed to the simplification process. He defines mental health as "those behaviors, attitudes, perceptions and feelings that determine a worker's overall level of personal effectiveness, success, happiness, and excellence of functioning as a person." Adhering to the Protestant work ethic principle that work is the most prominent factor in men's lives, he believes that fulfillment must be achieved through the job. Kornhauser doubts whether other aspects of workers' lives, such as their family relationships and recreational activities, could compensate. He questions whether workers who are satisfied with a simplified, repetitious job are experiencing good mental health. After interviewing 655 factory workers, he determined that there was a decrease in good mental health and satisfaction commensurate with decreases in job level. Kornhauser concluded that the simplified job was the cause of the workers' poor mental health, and generalized from the sample to all blue collar workers. His definition of good or poor mental health involved the value judgment that striving for personal betterment is important, whereas a realistic evaluation of one's situation may not be. The assumption that all people should have the common goals of a desire for material possessions, social esteem, influence, and security is unfounded. People differ greatly in their value structure. To place a high value in a job content that allows for greater use of ability is surely a characteristic of some people, but not all. To say those who do not value it are experiencing poor mental health is not justified. Despite the criticisms, there was enough interest in the statements that Kornhauser and others were making to warrant industrial action.

In an effort to combat the presumed effects of job simplification, a contrasting organizational structure called job enrichment has developed. One form of job enrichment frequently used is job enlargement. There are many definitions of job enlargement (Ford, 1969; Guest, 1957; Hulin & Blood, 1968). The definition of Hulin and Blood (1968) seems to incorporate most of the conceptualizations of the other definitions, and is most universally used. They define job enlargement as "the process of allowing individual workers to determine their own working pace (within limits), to serve as their own inspectors by giving them responsibility for quality control, to repair their own mistakes, to be responsible for their own machine setup and repair, and to attain choice of method." The purpose of job enlargement is not simply to increase the individual's duties, but to allow him to do work that requires a higher level of skill. It is designed to incorporate a varied amount of work content and a relatively high degree of autonomy.

Lawler (1969) suggests that jobs can be enlarged along two dimensions, which he terms horizontal and vertical. When a job is enlarged on the horizontal dimension, the number and variety of the operations that a worker performs is increased. Enlarging the job vertically increases the degree to which the individual controls the planning and execution of his job. The amount of participation that the worker is permitted in the determination of company policies would also be included in the vertical dimension. Lawler proposes that for job enlargement to be successful in increasing a worker's motivation, both dimensions must be enlarged. There has been a paucity of studies investigating jobs enlarged on only one dimension; therefore, it is difficult to verify Lawler's proposal.

An aspect of horizontal job enlargement that is of particular interest to this chapter is the task. The question to be considered is how significant is the task itself in motivating workers? Ford (1969) considers this issue in his definition of job enrichment. He defines it as "changing the task itself so that it becomes a source of motivation." A discussion of why the task could be a source of motivation will be addressed later in this chapter.

In an attempt to eliminate the high rate of absenteeism, turnover, and lower productivity, industry has turned to the job enlargement concept as a possible solution. There have been numerous studies reporting positive effects from job enlargement (Biganne & Stewart, 1963; Conant & Kilbridge, 1965; Davis & Werling, 1960; Ford, 1969; Guest, 1955, 1957; Pelissier, 1965; Walker, 1950; Walker & Marriott, 1951).

Walker (1950) reported on a job enlargement program at IBM. Four small and distinct jobs that were currently being done in their general machine shop were combined into one enlarged job. The reported results were improved quality, less idle times, and increased worker satisfaction. The study failed to present adequate data to support the findings, and, as in many of the studies to be presented, there was no control for a Hawthorne effect.

Using an interviewing procedure, Walker and Marriott (1951) interviewed 976 men from two automobile assembly plants and one metal mill. The results showed that, in one automobile assembly plant, 35 percent of the workers complained of boredom, and, in the other, 35 percent also had the same complaint. In the metal mill, only 8 percent of the workers complained of boredom. The difference in worker satisfaction between the two types of plants was attributed to the metal mill having very few repetitive jobs. They also found that, within the automobile plants, workers on conveyor-paced jobs were less satisfied than workers who were not. They interpreted the results as a strong argument against repetitious and simplified work, suggesting that it leads to a higher degree of dissatisfaction. The authors failed to acknowledge the possible differences between the work forces as a contributing factor, rather than differences in production techniques. Also, the fact that two-thirds of the automobile workers did not complain of boredom was not emphasized.

Another study investigating job enlargement in an industrial setting was reported by Biganne and Stewart (1963). Intensive and comprehensive attitude surveys of workers at the Maytag plant in Iowa were carried out prior to enlarging jobs. Subsequently, 25 job enlargement projects were carried out over a 6-year period. The results of the projects were improved quality, lowered labor costs, relatively quick majority acceptance of enlargement, and initial costs recovered by tangible savings within 2 years. Some of the positive effects of job enlargement were seen to be improved job satisfaction, additional responsibility, quality improvements, uninhibited pace, and versatility of skills.

The majority of empirical studies considering job satisfaction as it relates to job size have been attacked by Hulin and Blood (1968) as being poorly controlled, and by MacKinney, Wernimont, and Galitz (1962), who maintain that studies indicating detrimental effects of job simplification are methodologically weaker than research to support simplification.

The assumption that job simplification universally leads to worker dissatisfaction is unfounded. MacKinney, Wernimont, and Galitz (1962) maintain an individual difference point of view and take exception with those who believe all workers will react in the same way to an enlarged job. They feel that satisfaction with a job is more than a function of the job itself. Rather, it is a function of both the man and the job, or, the man–job interaction.

Smith (1955) found that feelings of monotony were not merely a function of job content, but were related to characteristics in the worker. Workers who were content with a repetitive task generally were characterized by "placidity" and possibly "rigidity," but were not "stupid" or "insensitive." They appeared to be accepting of things as they were. Smith's study establishes an awareness of individual differences, and of the interaction between job content and personal characteristics of the worker.

Results have been reported that link simplified and repetitive tasks to high worker satisfaction (Kilbridge, 1960; Smith & Lem, 1955; Turner & Miclette, 1962). In their paper, Turner and Miclette (1962) describe an industrial setting where less than 20 percent of the workers complained about being bored on an extremely repetitive job. They reported that they derived satisfaction from the work itself.

Baldamus (1961) has also suggested that highly repetitive work may have a positive motivating effect. He proposes a traction effect, a feeling of "being pulled along by the inertia inherent in a particular activity," resulting in a pleasant feeling. This view has been verified experimentally in an industrial setting by Smith and Lem (1955).

It appears that some work populations respond to job enlargement and others do not (Hulin & Blood, 1968; Scott, 1973; Susman, 1973; Turner & Lawrence, 1955). Turner and Lawrence (1955) tested the job enlargement hypothesis on a sample of 470 workers. They investigated 11 industries who provided data on 47 different jobs and found nonsignificant results between level of job and satisfaction. Analysis of the data showed a number of curvilinear relationships which led Turner and Lawrence to conclude that the workers studied had been drawn from two separate and different populations. They interpreted their data to mean that workers from urbanized factories responded differently to similar jobs than workers from small town factories. The workers from small town factories responded positively to job enlargement, while workers from the urban factories did not.

Hulin and Blood (1968) argue that workers in large urban industrialized communities are alienated from the middle-class work values and respond negatively to an enlarged job. They contend that workers from small communities with low standards of living but with few slums would accept middle-class work values and respond positively to job enlargement.

It appears that a wide range of individual differences exists in regard to what workers find satisfying about a job. Not all workers react in precisely the same way to the same job. Some may find a particular job highly satisfying; to others, the same job may be boring, repetitious, and nonchallenging. Shepard (1972) points out the necessity to determine empirically those characteristics that differentiate workers who will respond to job enlargement from those who prefer more simplified tasks. From the perspective of one concerned with the integration of the retarded into industry, an alternative approach to the study of individual differences is desirable. Rather than studying the characteristics of workers, we might focus on the characteristics of training and intervention programs needed to bring each retarded individual up to acceptable levels of motivation and performance.

Another area of inquiry which might prove fruitful is the relationships between task characteristics and worker motivation. One line of research that has concentrated on the task as a determinant of satisfaction and performance is called activation theory. Having its foundation in physiology, the theory explains task behavior in terms of stimulation of the reticular formation (Scott, 1966). The reticular formation is a dense network of neurons involved in general stimulation of the cerebral cortex. It does not provide the cortex with information, but it helps to maintain the organism at a high level of arousal or activation. According to the theory, individuals who are subjected to repetitive, simplified, dull tasks experience low levels of arousal and will tend to seek stimulus inputs to raise their level of activation.

Variables that are thought to affect activation level are stimulus intensity, variation, complexity, uncertainty, and meaningfulness. Properties such as complexity and meaningfulness are difficult to deal with, since they vary greatly with the individual's perceptions and interpretations of external stimuli. A highly complex interaction between the external properties of stimuli and the individual's cortical processes appears to exist.

Activation theory predicts that when tasks are simple, unvarying, and require the constant repetition of a very few responses, certain behaviors can be anticipated. After an individual learns the responses of a simple repetitive task and becomes familiar with its setting, a decrease in activation level will probably occur. If the individual is forced to stay in the situation, he will develop a negative affect and attempt behaviors that will increase the activation level and decrease the negative feelings. The effect on task performance would be a decline in productivity.

In that situation, the individual may attempt to leave the task setting or engage in other behaviors to increase activation level. He may engage in daydreaming activity or attempt movements such as changing positions or stretching. Leaving the work situation frequently to get a drink or visit the restroom might also be indications of attempts to increase activation level. Another way to increase the activation level is engaging in social activities with fellow employees, such as conversations or horseplay. These behaviors are frequently observed with mentally retarded workers in sheltered workshops, where the tasks are almost always of a highly simplified and repetitive nature. It would appear that, if greater variety and complexity were incorporated into the task, long-run productivity might be sustained and satisfaction for many workers increased.

Hulin and Blood (1968) question the attempt to generalize the theory from studies conducted with vigilance tasks in controlled settings to industrial tasks in factory settings. The different types of stimuli impinging on workers in industrial settings, such as noise, lighting changes, and the interaction and movement of other people do not present the same conditions as the controlled laboratory. They suggest that the tasks used in the vigilance studies are so different from industrial tasks that attempts to link industrial work motivation to a physiologic basis could create a valid theory, but further investigation with industrial tasks in industrial settings is warranted. A possible environment for studying these problems is sheltered workshops for the handicapped. In that environment, the research could investigate industrial tasks in a quasi-industrial setting, while maintaining greater control of the variables. Workshops also would allow for more flexibility than industry.

A look at sheltered workshops for the mentally retarded reveals a situation in which workers are relegated to a simplicity previously unheard of. The tasks are almost always the most menial found in any work situation. The work demands placed upon workers are minimal, and nonproductive behavior can be observed in most shops.

When considering the retarded, the assumption usually made is that their limitations only allow them to engage in simplified tasks. Gold (1969, 1972) clearly demonstrated that moderately and severely retarded individuals are capable of performing much more complex work than has ever been thought possible (e.g., bicycle brakes and electronic circuit boards). Gold's research strongly suggests that, with the proper training techniques, severely retarded people can acquire skills necessary to produce complex industrial assemblies, and not only under conditions involving very short cycle times.

People working with the mentally retarded have not, even conceptually, made use of the job enlargement concept. Perusal of the literature reveals only one study that investigates job enlargement in a sheltered workshop environment. Bishop and Hill (1971) were concerned with enlarging job content as opposed to merely changing it. They also attempted to determine the effects of enlargement and change on contiguous but nonmanipulated jobs and the function played by worker status. The dependent measures were job satisfaction (determined by the use of the Job Description Index), job performance (quality and quantity of output), and tension (measured by the Anxiety Differential Test, used to identify a possibly underlying correlate of changes in job satisfaction and performance).

The simplified task consisted of sorting either nuts or bolts, while, with the enlarged task, subjects were asked to sort both nuts and bolts. In addition to the sorting, the enlarged groups were also asked to assemble the nuts and bolts and place them in a container. The job change consisted of assigning bolts to subjects that were sorting nuts and vice versa. The task chosen is another indication of the expectancies society has for the retarded. Assembling nuts and bolts does not seem to constitute an enlarged or complex task.

The results showed no changes in quantity of output for the three tasks, but a decrement in quality with the enlarged task. Bishop and Hill suggest that error frequency was a partial function of a greater complexity of the enlarged task. The authors present no information regarding how subjects were trained on either task. With retarded people, the quality of their production is often a function of their initial learning. If they are trained to a rigid criterion, then errors in production are minimal (Gold, 1973a). Without additional information, the assumption could be made that they never really learned the enlarged task. Bishop and Hill further conclude that change is as effective in influencing production and satisfaction as job enlargement. They also determined that manipulated groups (receiving experimental treatment) showed positive effects, while nonmanipulated groups demonstrated negative effects.

Although there are questions as to whether the study truly investigated job enlargement at all, Bishop and Hill's discussion of the population and work setting for future investigations is relevant to this discussion. They acknowledge the problem of generalizing the experimental results from a special workgroup to a more normal one. Our concern here is in the other direction, that is, how the notions of job enlargement and the findings in the literature might generalize to the population of concern in this chapter. One might postulate that many of the tasks now performed by normal workers, if performed by the severely handicapped, would constitute, in a sense, the epitome of job enlargement. That is, severely handicapped persons working on tasks which are dramatically enlarged from their current work might show all of the benefits shown by normal workers on enlarged jobs. The retarded, given the opportunity to perform tasks of a much higher complexity and cycle time than they have ever done, might prove to be an ideal labor force. This possibility has significant implications for both sheltered workshops and industry. While there have been no systematic attempts to look at job enlargement with the severely handicapped performing on complex long cycle tasks, subjects working on production in our research program consistently show a willingness and interest in working at the task, even in the absence of external reinforcers such as pay, food, or social praise (Gold, 1973a). The job enlargement concept, then, might provide us with a conceptual basis for further investigation of complex work by the severely handicapped, and also a mechanism for opening up meaningful dialogue with industry for the inclusion of the severely handicapped into their labor force.

ELECTRONIC PRINTED CIRCUIT
BOARD ASSEMBLY TRAINING

Related to the concept of job enlargement is the issue of community perceptions of an individual and how they develop. In our society, what a person does vocationally and how much he earns often determines his value and the level of respect he holds with its other members. The severely handicapped have rarely participated in the labor market because they were thought incapable of making a significant contribution to it. They have been perceived as a surplus, along with the aged, hardcore unemployed, and others (Farber, 1968), without the training or skills necessary to fill existing jobs. Consequently, the retarded constitute one of the largest segments of the nonemployed population with a great deal of energy and money spent on their maintenance. Gold (1972) states, "Some of the energies presently used for *maintenance* of this unproductive portion of the population should be directed toward *training* the retarded to somehow effectively compete in the labor market with other members of the surplus population who are not additionally stigmatized by the label 'retarded.' "

Many of the procedures developed in our program and those of others, such as those described throughout this text, are being successfully employed by agencies serving the retarded. Most of the work tasks currently available to the retarded, however, are of a highly simplified and repetitive nature and do not require sophisticated training techniques. Studies to develop training procedures for one particular kind of complex work task which could be available as real subcontracts for rehabilitation agencies are currently being undertaken. The tasks are electronic printed or etched circuit boards (P.C. boards). P.C. boards were selected because of their apparent feasibility as a source of highly remunerative work for this population. Preliminary studies by Merwin (1973, 1974) indicate the ability of moderately and severely retarded persons to perform this type of work.

Merwin investigated the effects of pretraining upon the training and transfer of P.C. board assembly utilizing a match-to-sample training procedure. The initial study utilized 45 adult residents of a state institution. Their mean IQ was 55 (range 23–92).

Learning to assemble a circuit board is considered to be primarily a discrimination task. Form, size, and color of the individual components, as well as their position on the board, are the relevant dimensions to be learned. Consistent with the Attention Theory of Zeaman and House (1963), the purpose of the pretraining was to help direct the subject's attention to those relevant dimensions. It was believed that prior knowledge of the relevant dimensions might enhance the learning and transfer of the discrimination skills required in assembling the boards.

Conditions of visual discrimination pretraining was varied for three groups, using an automated multiple-choice visual discrimination apparatus (Scott, 1970). After completing the pretraining, all subjects were trained on the assembly of two similar P.C. boards.

In pretraining one group (group I) was asked to solve match-to-sample problems containing multidimensional junk stimuli (e.g., pictures of a dog, tree, etc.). The purpose of the junk stimuli problems was to familiarize the subjects with match-to-sample type problems, and was not intended to systematically direct attention to the color and form dimensions. After pretraining, they began training on the board itself. The second group (group II) also was trained to solve junk stimuli problems. After learning the junk problems, they were presented with problems involving electronic components as stimuli, and finally sets of problems of P.C. boards with increasing numbers of components. When they were able to discriminate pictures of boards containing 12 different components, training on the actual boards was begun. The purpose of the problems containing the components was to direct the subjects' attention to the color and form dimensions. The P.C. board problems included the dimension of position, as well as color and form.

The final group (group III) first received problems consisting of geometric form stimuli which differed in color and form. After learning the geometric form problems, the subjects were presented with the component problems, followed by the circuit board problems. The intention of the geometric form problems was to make the dimensions of color and form more salient.

Thirty-nine of the 45 subjects, 88.6 percent, learned to assemble both the training and transfer P.C. boards each to a criterion of five consecutive correctly assembled boards (60 consecutive correct insertions). The mean number of trials to criterion across both boards was 16.5, and the mean total time for pretraining, training and transfer was 170 min. The effects of pretraining on task assembly training were inconsistent. In accordance with the theoretical assumptions of the pretraining, group III (geometric forms) had superior performance in training and transfer, as predicted. Since group II received identical pretraining, except for the junk stimuli problems in place of the geometric form problems, it was predicted that their performance would be close to group III. Group II had the poorest performance, with group I (junk stimuli only) falling between groups II and III. Although differences between groups occurred, the differences did not reach statistical significance.

Suggested interpretations are that the geometric forms pretraining had a slight effect on assembly acquisitions, that experience with match-to-sample problems is facilitative in learning the circuit board task, or there was no pretraining effect at all, and direct training on the board would have been as facilitative. Since there was no control group that received only direct training, the latter interpretation could not be addressed.

A significant transfer effect on the second board was obtained for all groups. Whether this was due to pretraining effects, to the training on the first board, or to the combination of the two could not be resolved from those data.

In her next study, Merwin attempted to resolve the unanswered questions. The second study utilized 60 institutionalized adults. Their mean IQ was 40, with a range of 18-77. As with the first study, the type and amount of pretraining were varied between groups. The first group received only direct assembly training on a 12-component circuit board. Following criterion, they were presented with a second board with different components in different positions (transfer). The second group was given matching pretraining in the form of match-to-sample slide problems (components and circuit boards), which was followed by training and transfer. The third group received the matching pretraining (the slide problems), followed by placement pretraining, and finally training and transfer on the two boards. Placement pretraining consisted of manipulation and insertion of six of one type of component in a board. By using identical components, color and form dimensions were held constant, with only position allowed to vary.

Forty-eight of the 60 subjects, 80 percent, reached criterion on both boards. The data failed to show a significant pretraining effect. It appears that direct training on the task is as effective and efficient as the forms of pretraining employed in the study. As in the first study, a strong transfer effect was found for all three groups. Since most P.C. boards are similar with regard to the relevant dimensions (color, form, position) for the discriminations necessary for assembly, the generalizability of the transfer effect to most other P.C. boards seems probable. The mean total time for all three groups to reach criterion was 246 min.

The training techniques generated from these two studies indicate that retarded workers can learn to insert electronic components into a P.C. board using a match-to-sample strategy. The procedure consists of picking up a component, matching it to its counterpart on the sample board, finding the correct holes on the board being assembled, orienting the component (not reversing it), and placing the leads in the holes. The P.C. boards assembled in the electronics industry usually contain many more components than subjects in the prior studies were required to do, although job stations in industry sometimes call for insertion of only 10 or 12 components. The assembly of the boards also entails additional steps such as bending, cutting, and crimping the leads, and in some cases soldering the components in place. The Merwin studies provide sufficient encouragement to investigate whether retarded workers can do these other steps and how many components they can assemble.

Pilot work addressing these issues has been started using a circuit board consisting of 45 components. The P.C. board task being used is one that is currently produced by an electronics company in the Midwest. The components include resistors, capacitors, and diodes. For each component, two leads must be bent, inserted in a specific place on the board and in a specific position, and cut and crimped. In addition to the insertion components, there are parts that must be mounted and riveted into place, and others that require mounting with small screws and nuts.

Four subjects from a sheltered workshop in Champaign, Ill., have been selected to pilot our procedures: (1) a 25-year-old male with an IQ of 48; (2) a 28-year-old female with an IQ of 35; (3) a 22-year-old female with an IQ of 45; and (4) a 19-year-old male with an IQ of 45. The etiology of three of the four is Down's syndrome; the fourth is unknown. All subjects were chosen because they were described by their supervisors as functioning in the trainable range with no gross motor or sensory problems, and as being cooperative individuals. It was decided that individuals with those characteristics would best serve to answer the initial questions being asked in the pilot work.

A question being investigated is, can they learn to assemble a large number of parts, using the match-to-sample training procedure? The initial task consists of the insertion of 32 prebent components into their appropriate positions on the board. In this task, they are also required to insert the parts with the markings on the components in identical positions, as found on the sample. Some parts have letters, or numbers, or both facing in a specific direction. Some of the other components have color bandings. If a part is inserted upside down, it is considered an error and the subject must correct it. In actuality, many components function appropriately with either lead in either hole, but, because the markings on some of the components must be readable and some components do have specific polarities, we must require constant positioning of all components.

At the present time, two subjects have reached our criterion of five consecutive correct assemblies of the part of the board assembled in Job Station 1 (32 components), that is, 160 consecutive insertions without error or assistance. The total amount of trials (boards) to reach criterion for subject 1 was 19, which took seven training sessions, one per day. The total time to criterion was 141 min, averaging 7 min 44 sec per trial. The subject was run 19 trials past criterion to determine the validity of our criterion, consistency, and also to get a feel for production. In the 19 trials, which consisted of 608 insertions, he made four errors. The mean time per trial was 5 min 32 sec, decreasing over trials.

An interesting incident took place with this subject during the postcriterion trials. On the table where the subject was engaged in the task was a correctly assembled circuit board with all 45 components. After completing his work, the subject, who is almost nonverbal, pointed to the completed board. He was told that he would soon learn to assemble the rest of the board in addition to the parts he already knew. The subject then proceeded to point to each of the new parts on the complete board and correctly showed the experimenter where they went on his board, without ever having been directed toward it.

Another interesting event occurred during the postcriterion period. While assembling a board, he got out of sequence and had six parts in wrong places. He seemed to know something was wrong and expressed concern. The experimenter said, "That isn't correct, Francis, fix it." Using the sample board as a guide, he proceeded to correct the mistakes.

Subject II has not yet reached criterion. She has had 83 trials to date, and her number of position errors has gone down from approximately 18 per trial to one or two on her last three trials. The time per trial has also decreased from over 20 min initially to about 10 min currently. Her problem is in attending to the writing or color coding on the parts (reversal errors). If reminded to attend, she will insert the part correctly; if not, the part will go on correctly, or incorrectly, depending on how it was picked up. Use of a magnifying glass did not decrease these errors.

Subject III reached criterion in nine trials. On her first trial, she made no position errors and two reversal errors. That is, with one partial demonstration trial by the experimenter, she proceeded to place all 32 components into their proper places the first time she attempted the task. On trials one through four, she made one position error on all four trials combined, while committing one to two reversal errors per trial. On trials five through nine, she was errorless. Her total time to criterion was 90 min 16 sec, with times per trial decreasing from 15 min to approximately 8 min. She was run three trials past criterion, during which she remained errorless, and her time decreased to under 5 min 30 sec.

Subject IV has had 46 trials to date. His initial trial took over 39 min and decreased gradually over succeeding trials. His current time is approximately 10 min. Errors over trials have dropped from 28 to 3. This subject had difficulty with the fine motor movements required to insert the parts. As his experience with the task increased, his dexterity improved and insertion no longer presents a problem.

All subjects learned the sequence and positions of the components relatively easily. With two of the subjects, letter and number discriminations (reversal errors) were difficult to achieve. New and more powerful training procedures are being developed in an attempt to facilitate learning.

Two experiments and work with four pilot subjects have been discussed. These data strongly suggest that additional investigation is warranted. Current plans include: (1) the running of additional subjects to verify the findings to date; (2) developing training procedures for lead bending, small tool usage, and soldering; (3) doing the circuit board used in the present pilot work as a remunerative subcontract; (4) obtaining several other subcontracts and training workers in order to validate the training procedures; and (5) creating an electronics factory for the purpose of documenting and marketing the skill competencies of the severely handicapped.

The severely handicapped should be granted the right to full participation in society. An important area of participation is work. Determining their true capabilities in this area and giving them the means for reaching those capabilities is providing an option previously not available. Whether or not they will be able to exercise that option remains to be seen. Today's society will have to undergo major modifications for the full integration of the handicapped to occur. Helping them to develop sophisticated manual work skills may be the most effective means to accomplishing that goal.

CONCLUSION

Data have been presented to document the competency of the severely handicapped in terms of their ability to do high quality complex work. The concept of job enlargement has been presented in detail to provide a conceptual base for their inclusion into industry as a previously untapped labor force with, perhaps, some characteristics that are needed but presently unavailable. In addition, pilot work with younger children was presented to indicate the feasibility of pursuing the development of complex work skills in younger children. All of this is seen as providing the field with a highly optimistic stance towards the full development of the skills of the severely handicapped.

For this to happen, we must first be convinced that they are, in fact, capable, and then we must get rid of the many barriers that seem to hold us back. Current testing and evaluation practices, preconceived notions about intelligence, poor preservice and in-service training programs for teachers and other service personnel, and continued reliance on heartstring diplomacy must all give way to the development of sophisticated training procedures, and a commitment to genuine major change in the skill functioning and life functioning of the severely handicapped. As competence by the severely handicapped is demonstrated, current expectancies and benevolent feelings should give way to genuine respect and revised expectancies so that, at some point, virtually all severely handicapped individuals will be given the training and support to become our peers instead of our charges.*

POSTSTATEMENT

The first thing I noticed upon rereading this chapter in preparation for this book was the poor editing we did. There are any number of sentences that needed revision.

I was surprised to see the terms *potential* and *unfulfilled potential* in this article. As discussed elsewhere in this book, these words should not be used in connection with mentally retarded people.

On the positive side, descriptions of parts of the task analysis system occur in our work for the first time. Until this point, we had discussed different kinds of variables and effects. Here, for the first time, we are talking about some of the intricacies of making decisions about training. This theme will develop further throughout the book.

The point is made in this chapter that natural reinforcement (contingencies) is very important in prevocational training programs "in order to enhance transfer to many diverse work situations. Extrinsic reinforcers are programmed into training only when their necessity has been demonstrated." This point has become an increasingly important part of the Try Another Way System. In the field there is still an overreliance on the use of reinforcement contingencies for controlling learner behavior. In the vocational realm there are such wonderful natural contingencies available that we should be very hesitant to draw too heavily on artificial reinforcement systems. We can use artificial reinforcements sparingly and move quickly into the natural reinforcements that exist in the work environment.

---

*Preparation of this paper was supported by NICHHD Program Project Grant No. HD-05951 to Children's Research Center, University of Illinois at Urbana-Champaign.

CHAPTER 18

Some Thoughts on Training

Marc W. Gold

PRESTATEMENT

I was surprised to receive the invitation to present a paper at the Fifth Annual Meeting of the National Society for Autistic Children. Although I had some experience with individuals labeled autistic, I felt pretty ignorant about the area. I especially felt inadequate to present to a group of people knowledgeable on the subject. I was asked to cover the instructional strategies we used and to be motivational. That sounded fine, but when it came time to writing the presentation, I thought it was not very much to do in the allotted time. My strategy, as you will see in the paper, was to grasp for any bits and pieces that might be helpful to parents and professionals involved with people labeled autistic. I used a lot of qualifiers to make sure that they knew I was not sitting there feeling like an expert. And I certainly was not.

Topics in this presentation including labeling, talking about handicapped children's problems in front of them, the difference between learning something and being able to do it in the natural environment, the difference between *what* one teaches and *how* one teaches, the importance of practitioners looking at different theories of how people learn, and issues related to inservice training and diagnosis.

What I would like to do for the next hour is cover many small issues; some perhaps not so small. I will not be spending a great deal of time on any one topic, because I want to cover a lot of material; give you some food for thought. My responsibility here, according to the people who asked me to speak, was twofold. First, I was asked to describe to you some of the concepts I have developed in my training programs that could be of use to you in your work, and, second, to try if possible to convey to you some of my optimism regarding service delivery and training programs for severely handicapped individuals. I will attempt to meet both of these responsibilities in my presentation to you this morning. I am not an expert in the field of autism, or any other specific handicap. I have studied, trained, and worked with individuals who have many different kinds of handicaps. Recently, I

This paper originally appeared in *The education and management of the behavior-disordered child*, Proceedings of the 5th annual meeting and conference of the National Society for Autistic Children, St. Louis, Missouri, June 1973.

have been involved in a research project to develop training procedures for the handicapped, and to teach professionals these training methods.

To begin with, I would like to take just a minute or two to draw an analogy between the people who work with the handicapped and a giant from Greek mythology, Procrustes. Procrustes was a man who wanted to make sure that everything fit into place properly. If someone came to visit him, and he was a little too tall for the bed Procrustes had for him, Procrustes would cut off his legs so they would fit; if the person was too short, he would stretch him out so that he would fit properly. From his name comes the adjective, procrustean, which is a word used to describe someone who is very particular about things being in place, and fitting properly into that space. Since everyone here knows at least a little bit about the attitudes of many professionals, I don't need to explain further why I compare them to Procrustes.

In the field of mental retardation, for example, we have a definition that says that mental retardation refers to subnormal general intellectual functioning which originates during the developmental period, and results in impaired mental capacity and an inability to function normally. Then, we take a group of handicapped people, examine them in various ways, and state that all of them that test out a certain way are to be labelled mentally retarded. So, we have made a box called "mental retardation," and we attach this label to all of the people in this group. Thereafter, we assume that anyone who has the label must fit into that box, that is, our definition of mental retardation.

The term or group of characteristics that are called "brain-damaged" or "brain-injured" are a perfect example of procrusteanized thinking. Nearly all of you professionals could, if I asked, give me a list of characteristics of a brain-damaged child. It would then be a very simple matter for me to find one individual or a group of individuals who exhibited those characteristics and, by virture of your list, would be labeled as being brain-damaged. Upon examination of one of these lists, you might have stated that such a person would be hyperactive, have a short attention span, be distractable, have poor eye-hand coordination, and figure-ground problems, your assumption being that if an individual bore that label, "brain-damaged," he must manifest all of those symptoms. Then, to use a popular expression, the old "self-fulfilling prophesy" comes into play. Thereafter, you make very sure of just what this brain-damaged individual will accomplish. You don't give him a chance to have a long attention span because you know he doesn't have one. Why even try?

My guess is that in the field of autism, a very similar situation probably occurs. You may consider this as a big "cop out" on my part, to absolve myself of knowing anything about autism. Just remember, if I say anything you don't agree with, I told you I didn't know much about the specific subject of autism. In my work, I am not so concerned about labels and the symptoms that are supposed to go with those labels as I am about how individuals function.

I would imagine that those individuals who were a part of my research study who came to me with the label "autism," and who allegedly had many of the characteristics that were regarded as being "autistic" needed careful and objective reevaluation. We who work with the handicapped have a continuing responsibility not to accept labels, and not to accept characteristics that are "hanging tools" that we can use to make sure that the individual stays functioning at the same level.

I have noticed a few interesting things in working with families of autistic children. I've talked to many parents of autistic children, and while we were speaking, their autistic children were present. I noticed a very blatant inconsistency in their attitudes and responses to their handicapped child. They would tell me how much receptive language their child really had, and they would also, right in front of the child, talk about autism, about his characteristics and symptoms, what he could and could not do. If those parents really believed that their child could understand what they were saying, they should have realized that it was very wrong to discuss him and his problems in front of him and another person, a stranger. So why don't we all do this; why don't we believe that they all have receptive language, and stop telling them, even in an indirect way, all the ways we expect them to behave; stop discussing all the things they do that you and I consider to be "autistic." I would guess that many of you parents are quite convinced that the receptive language capabilities of your child are fantastically above what he can demonstrate, and I tend to agree with you; this has also been my impression.

Another thing I wish to discuss with you has to do with the business of making eye contact. In our research study one of the things we taught our data collectors to do during their very extensive training was not to make eye contact with the subjects during the time that they were performing a task. What I taught them was that if there was anything to be learned in my face, then I'd want them to look at my face, but since what I wanted them to learn was out there in front of them, in their hands and on the table, where was the efficiency of having them always look at my face? And, so, by not looking back at their face, it took only a very short period of time for them to learn not to look at my face, but to look at what was going on in front of them. I visit sheltered workshops frequently, and staff people often tell me that I won't be able to watch the people work normally, because, when someone walks in, they stop working because you are there. When I visit a facility I walk in without talking to the people; I don't make eye contact with them; I stand next to them, watching their hands. They stop, turn around, smile, and make some comment to me. In a very soft and informal way I tell them to continue with their work, that I would like to watch them work, without making eye contact. It's rare that they don't immediately go back to work. They are encouraged to be very involved in what their hands are doing, because that's where I am looking.

I'm not suggesting that eye contact is not important, but I think that what many people working in your field have done is to confuse the issue. Eye contact is a piece of learning that really relates to certain kinds of social interaction. They often fail to recognize that eye contact is something that very obviously stands in the way of a lot of learning that needs to take place. My suggestion to you, therefore, is that it may prove very helpful if you, in your teaching, make a distinction between those occasions where eye contact is required, such as during social interaction, and lessons where it can be detrimental to the success of the task being taught, such as work requiring eye-hand coordination. Again, let me remind you that I warned that my lecture would be broken up into short discussions of bits and pieces gleaned from my research and experience that I thought would apply to your specific field of interest.

Another subject I would like to discuss is education and learning. I want to make sure you recognize the difference between learning to do something, and doing it. Education in a sense is defined as creating a special environment so that learning can occur, the inference there being that the environment necessary for acquiring a task is somewhat different than the environment under which that task will ultimately be performed. What we must do, then, is try to create an environment which will maximize the probability that a person will acquire a task; will learn something. We call this environment a classroom, or a variety of other names. Of course, we need classrooms. But we must remember the distinction between learning a task, and then performing that task without the support of the original learning environment. Having a behavior manifest itself under these special classroom conditions that we created for learning that behavior is not complete; we cannot assume that the behavior is then automatically going to manifest itself in the individual's natural environment outside the classroom. This, of course, is where it must ultimately occur for your teaching to have been successful.

For example, you can create a special environment to teach a child to brush his teeth. You can even take data, check off the days, and find that he's apparently learned to brush his teeth. Yet when he opens his mouth at the end of the month, you may find that he still has tartar on his teeth. If his tooth brush isn't wet every morning when he leaves for school, what difference does it make what he does under that special environment in the classroom? I could give you many different examples, but the essence of the comment is that if you are teaching something, if you're trying to establish a behavior, you must first decide on the behavior you want, and then you must ask yourself why it is that you want this behavior. This is no small issue. Asking yourself why you want it should also tell you where and when you expect that behavior to be used. You can create a special environment for teaching that behavior, but don't call yourself a success until you have made the transition of seeing that behavior manifest itself under the conditions where you ultimately want it to occur. If you can do this, you have really taught something. Until you have achieved this with your students, you are kidding yourselves thinking that you have taught them some useful behavior.

I once saw a teacher in a classroom doing some arithmetic drills with her students. She said, "What is three times four?" One youngster raised his hand and said, "Twelve." The teacher said, "Very, very good. All right, that's all of our arithmetic lesson for today." Then she turned to the boy who had just answered her question, and told him to check to see how many chairs there were over in the back of the room because some student teachers were expected to visit that day. In the back of the room there were three rows of chairs with four chairs in each row. The child went back and counted, "1, 2, 3, 4, 5, 6, 7, 8, 9, 10, 11, 12." The back of the room was where the real lesson was; the arithmetic lesson had not ended, in fact it had failed. What possible good was there in the child knowing that three times four equaled twelve? The teacher had not thought through the reason for teaching that arithmetic fact to the children. If she had recognized why she was teaching it, and had gone that extra step, she could have given the children a complete and practical lesson in mathematics.

My next point is the distinction between content and process. Content refers to that which the learner is going to have when you finish; process is what the teacher or trainer goes through to ensure that the learner obtains the content. The content, then, is the thing that you are teaching.

For example, let us look at one simple task, that of teaching someone to tie his shoelaces. Let's use an arbitrary figure, and say, "The content is the twenty-seven steps involved in tying shoelaces." The process for tying shoelaces is whatever steps you plan on going through to get those twenty-seven steps of content into the person you're working with. Next, it is important that you analyze the children you are working with and determine their needs before you decide what you want to teach them. And you must ask yourself as explicitly as need be for the children in front of you how many pieces the chosen task should be broken down into to make it possible for it to be learned.

For instance, let's take the task of picking up and folding a piece of paper into two equal parts. In our work we had to break that task down into twenty-four steps because, for some of the people we work with, that's how many steps it takes to teach it. We also have eight, ten, or fifteen process steps we use to teach these same pieces of content; we use the process that seems to work best for each individual.

Another thought on "process": actually, another distinction, that is, the distinction between power and efficiency. When you decide on a technique you are going to use, it may consist of using a verbal procedure; you may also give a demonstration, or use a non-verbal procedure. The non-verbal procedure could be your modeling the task or your putting his hands through it, or your showing him a sequence such as demonstrating an act that he is supposed to match at his own desk or bench. It could also consist of using a shaping procedure where you put him in an environment, and keep reinforcing him as he moves closer to the things you want him to do.

As a generality I think you will find an inverse relationship between power and efficiency, that is, the more efficient the process you use (process meaning the training procedure), the less power he has; and the less efficient the process, the more power. So, if you said to a child, "Give me the tape recorder," and the child reached over and picked it up and handed it to you, you would have found that he was able to respond to that verbal command; that the process you used was fantastically efficient. You merely asked him, that taking about one second, and he did what you asked, showing that he had the behavior you wanted him to have under that circumstance. As far as power is concerned, there is very little actual power in nothing more than a verbal command.

To demonstrate, in teaching, you usually start by using the most efficient, the quickest techniques you see that work. Then, if you become convinced, after one, two, or three trials, that your efficient low-power decisions aren't working, one of the things you can do is further subdivide the task until you have the behavior or task broken down enough so that the individual can assimilate and learn it. There is little efficiency in many teaching strategies, but sometimes we must sacrifice efficiency for power in order to teach a task or behavior. You would find very little efficiency in a procedure that might take an hour, a day or longer to teach, but you would have a procedure that had in it a great deal of power. Sometimes you must break down a task into a whole series of pieces of learning, working from recognition to differentiation, from there to labeling, to coming under verbal control, etc. You would have broken the task down into a series of simple pieces so that your process would then have had a lot of power, which had been achieved at the expense of efficiency. Before you begin to work with an individual, then, you must decide on a whole series of strategies, both verbal and non-verbal ones.

The next distinction I would like to make is the distinction between humanistic psychology and behavioral psychology. Many of you have been caught up in the controversy over the relationship between the "human engineers" and the "shrinks"; between the people who are "behaviorists" and the people who are "psychoanalytic" or "personality" oriented. Still another way to state it is those individuals who look at behavior as being a symptom of something going on inside the person, and those individuals who look at behavior as a separate entity standing by itself, so that there is no immediate concern about what is going on inside the person, inside his head. I believe that the proper perspective is somewhere in between, and I'm sure I'm not the first person to arrive at that conclusion.

There is a tendency among some professionals who have a certain background, who have studied and embraced a specific theory or belief, to take a very "hard-nosed" position about this issue. Often these are the "ivory tower" research people, university people who teach, lecture, write, and who have a responsibility to study and promote their own point of view. Generally, these people don't know too much about any work except their own point of view in the field. They tend to spearhead the movement in terms of their own theories, frequently doing so by attempting to undermine and destroy the theories of other workers in the field. From the standpoint of intellectual debate and academic involvement this can be stimulating, but you and I have to live with and help people grow up. We cannot afford the luxury of attaching ourselves to one particular belief unless we believe completely that that theory can solve all the problems we will run into. I feel that it is much better to be multi-theoretical, and not tied to any specific belief or approach.

Even though he may not realize it, the successful analytical psychiatrist or personality psychologist is obtaining favorable results not because he is looking at behavior as symptomatic, but because he's unknowingly, perhaps, a good behavior modification man. He presents such strong and convincing arguments, he is able to persuade people to move in the direction he wishes.

Conversely, the successful behavior modification person is one who has the human feeling, sensitivity, and insight to know just where and when to interject the reinforcer. Nowhere in the extensive writings on behavior modification does it specify just exactly how much you smile, when to smile, how much reinforcement to give when, how often to give a pat on the back, etc. Human feelings and sensitivities must be an integral part of the use of applied behavior modification technology. A therapist can have all the feelings and sensitivity in the world, but if he does not also have technology, he is selling his patients short; on the other hand, you could have all the schedules of reinforcement, even own your own chocolate factory, and you will be unable to change people if they don't "buy" you.

Until fairly recently, people working in professions that served the severely handicapped had a "bag of tools" that included love, affection, longevity, perseverence, patience, and sweat. If you had your child in a class where the staff had all of those "tools of the trade," you were pretty happy, and your child was probably happy, too. That used to be enough, but, today, if a child is in a classroom with a teacher who has those tools but nothing more, his parents are beginning to complain; I certainly would if I were such a parent. In recent years, we have begun to develop a fantastic technology of instruction, one that is still changing, growing, improving. New concepts, strategies, structures, and techniques are being developed, and a parent should demand that the professionals who work with his child avail themselves of the many new techniques and tools for teaching children that exist today. The best technology should be made available in the instructional programs for your children.

In exercising your "parent power," the power you have over the agencies that serve your children, don't forget that in their budgets there should be mandatory continuing in-service training for staff members, and that the agency should be picking up the tab for it. The agency should also make sure that there is ample staff time to pursue such in-service training. In-service training is important, and if you demand it, six months from today your teachers will be able to do things that they could not do today, and, more important, six months from today your children will be doing things that they could not do today. Still, in-service training usually gets shoved aside as "an expense we can't afford right now." Administrators hire whoever comes in, and just assume that they know all there is, or that they will take their Saturdays and Sundays to study; this is not right.

This brings us to another issue, the issue of effective utilization of staff time and the training of parents. Most agencies probably operate with eighteen staff members running around in twelve bodies, and that just isn't efficient. Many people teach all day, then run a parent group or two in the evenings. This is selling parents short, selling the staff short, and it's selling the children short. How can you prepare to do lessons for tomorrow's class if you're busy training parents in the evenings? How can you effectively teach parents if you're preparing for the children's class? How can anyone have the time and energy to do a good job at both of these tasks?

We need things like parent training, but it shouldn't be "added on." We're the most "add on" business in the world! Any time someone comes up with a good idea of something we can do, we add it on. When do we subtract? You're all going to get some really good ideas at this convention! OK, go back home and decide which ideas are really important and should be implemented. When you do, decide exactly how much time you expect it to take you to do it, and then identify some activity presently in your curriculum, something that's really not helping much, and dump it. If you don't dump something, guess what's going to happen? The overall program will suffer; if you keep increasing quantity, you will keep decreasing quality, and your whole purpose is defeated.

I've discussed several aspects of the technological advances that have been made, now let's talk about optimism, and how it relates to diagnosis and evaluation. The position I take on diagnosis and evaluation is a very one-sided dogmatic one. I think that diagnosis is useless, and that the concept of prediction or prognosis is fatal. Evaluation in its present form tends to be very limiting. In most instances we take individuals who we know have problems, and we spend so much of our resources, money, and staff time proving that we are right, that there is nothing left to do anything about it; we're already all tired out when we have reached the point of saying "You know, he really does have something wrong!"

Another thing that we do when we have any kind of conventional diagnosis or evaluation is tend to find ways of confirming all of those things that he cannot do, though we know we can't do anything with what he cannot do, only with what he can do. Think about it. You can't work with behaviors he doesn't have, this is impossible. You can take behaviors he does have, and capitalize on them, expand them into behaviors that he doesn't now have.

When he's sitting in front of you, you must accept the fact that he can't read; you can't use reading skill to help this child. Then you discover that when you clap your hands he will jump, or that if you stroke the left side of his face, his head moves that way. Those responses are the beginnings of something; you've got some behaviors that you can work with and build on.

In an evaluation, instead of listing all the things a person cannot do, I think a more viable strategy would be to come up with information that says not only what he can do, but gives some ideas on how he acquires learning. If an evaluation gave some information such as "Under these sets of circumstances, he acquired the following behaviors," we would be off to a running start in helping him. We would eliminate the present separation of evaluation and training, and the evaluation would lead to change and improvement. At the present time, you present an evaluation to the client, and he comes out the same as he went in. For that matter, how useful is it to us?

For example, in an evaluation, the team meets to discuss the person, and the social worker says, "This child's family is in very bad shape; they're not cooperative and they just aren't together at all; they aren't very reliable." The psychologist says, "This person is severely retarded, brain-damaged, has a rather severe perceptual disturbance, and tests out at about 29 IQ." The physician says, "This child is difficult for me to work with; I think he should be on the following medication." They all say, "What'll we do now?" The doctor writes out a prescription, and they come up with a consensus opinion; they recommend trial placement in a sheltered workshop.

Introducing the next case, the social worker says, "This family is quite well-informed. They understand the problem, they're willing to do anything, they have the time and money and resources, and they're a pleasure to work with." The psychologist reports, "This young man tests out at a 75 IQ, is very cooperative, mildly retarded with obvious symptoms of brain damage. I think he's going to do very well." The physician says, "I see no clinical symptoms that would indicate the need for medication." Their consensus opinion and recommendation in this case is the same as the previous one, in that they advise placement in a sheltered workshop.

This might seem humorous to some, but consider the amount of time, money, and professional energy that is expended every day all over the country just to come up with all this useless "stuff." And yet we insist on it before we even consider trying to make a plan of what we're going to do for an individual.

What we decide to do for a person, and the label that we give him, is much more a function of where he got the label than how he is actually functioning. You can take a child into a learning disabilities laboratory, and, not surprisingly, he's diagnosed as being "learning disabled with emotional deficits." The prescription in this case would probably place the emphasis on work to correct or ameliorate the learning disability. You can take the same child into a clinic for emotionally disturbed children, and he will come out with the label "emotionally disturbed with academic deficits." The recommendation, then, would be for psychiatric treatment, with little or no attention being given the learning problems.

Don't you agree with me that we would be making much better use of our time and energies by taking the bulk of our resources and putting them into training and designing programs? Then, the day the child walks in, something is going to start to happen to him, and, as he proceeds through various learning experiences, if there's anything you want to know about him, you'll be certain to find out about it. As he proceeds through organized learning experiences, what he does know becomes quickly obvious, and what he doesn't know, he learns, so you have combined an ongoing evaluation with actual learning experience.

I would like to leave one thought with you concerning the actual training of the children; why some teachers succeed and why some don't have much success despite good training and background. If one doesn't have an assumption or a belief down inside himself that the person with whom he's working really can learn a behavior or task, he's not going to work very hard to get him to do it. This may sound very unscientific for a scientist to say, but that was the single most important thing we learned in our research. We have severely, profoundly retarded people in our program who are learning to assemble quite complex circuit boards in one-hundred seventy minutes of training. I would have to state that the most important thing going on in our research, the critical factor, is expectancy. How can one measure expectancy or record it on a graph? As scientists, we back up that nebulous factor with a tremendous amount of technological involvement, techniques, and strategies. But that one vital ingredient, expectancy, is something no one can give or teach to you; it must come from inside you; you must really believe that they can learn, and that feeling should provide the impetus for figuring out how to teach them.

Now, I want to describe the factory project to you. If plans materialize, in November, 1973, a factory will open here in the Midwest. It will be an electronic assembly factory that produces electronic circuit boards. There will be approximately sixty employees in the factory; approximately ten non-production line workers, and fifty production line workers. The people working in the factory will have the kinds of things normal workers have, that is, full minor and major medical coverage, will pay FICA, unemployment compensation, Social Security, and, in addition to that, there will be profit-sharing for all the employees in the factory. The only difference between this factory and any other will be that all the employees in this factory will be moderately or severely retarded. The wages in the factory will begin with minimum wage and go up from there, so it will not be anything like a sheltered workshop.

We have no intention of trying to be all things to all people with this project. We are not a rehabilitation agency, so a person who does not make it in our factory will be fired, no question about it. In our research we have worked with well over five hundred individuals, teaching them to assemble bicycle brakes, electronic circuit boards, and similar kinds of tasks. We drew at random from the population of handicapped, so we have worked with all kinds of individuals, including cerebral palsied, autistic, schizophrenic, and retarded, and we find we're running about 95% successful.

In hiring our initial workers for the factory, there will be no special criteria used, that is, we will take people as they are recommended. There is an institution from where we will be getting people originally; then, by virtue of their performance and consistency in the situation, they will either make it, or not.

There won't be any social workers or speech therapists in the factory; you don't see such people in ordinary places of work. Perhaps more significant, within approximately two years' time, according to our prediction, the average income of the fifty production workers in the factory will be in the neighborhood of $5,000 a year. This will generate, according to our figures, a total annual employee income of a quarter of a million dollars; a gross corporate income of three-fourths of a million dollars; a personal income tax liability of $32,000; and a corporate income tax of a quarter of a million dollars.

In the relatively small community where these people will live, they will represent a significant economic force. I think that in order to retain the substantial business that could be available from that source, the merchants of the community will probably go to considerable lengths to make sure that no one gets the impression that anyone is being cheated in their place of business. I think they will take care to see that the workers are given the time and cooperation they need to shop in comfort and dignity.

Whether we like it or not we live in a capitalistic society. Most of us enjoy it, but when it comes to delivering a service to people, like our children, the present system, by virtue of its organization and structure, causes us to withhold dignity in lieu of economic power. With most of our handicapped, the best we can do is to create group homes, give them decent clothing, and keep them out of institutions. We still make nearly all of their decisions for them, "we" being professionals, agencies, and/or parents. On the other hand, some of you parents may eventually find yourselves in the position of relying completely on the productivity and performance of your children for your existence. Then, by virtue of our existing system, those children will command dignity and respect. The same holds true with our handicapped. If we enable them to achieve financial independence, their position in society, the way people treat them, will greatly improve.

I will soon begin a lecture tour of Europe, and one of the things I expect to investigate there is the difference I think occurs between available service and general treatment of the handicapped in various countries. From what I have heard, in one of the Scandinavian countries, the probability of a severely handicapped individual being able to walk amongst his fellow man with true dignity, not pity or disgust, is much greater than it is under our system in the United States.

In closing, I hope that you will remember that you should emphasize training rather than diagnosis or evaluation in your programs; that you should make assumptions that your children can learn to do all of the things you want them to do, and that perhaps the only reason they're not doing these things is you, not them or their handicap.*

POSTSTATEMENT

The presentation went quite well. Since then, I have presented several times for the National Society for Autistic Children, have felt comfortable doing so, and have also done more work with people labeled autistic. I have not found autistic children to be a homogeneous group. Adolescents and adults labeled autistic, as a group, are even less homogeneous than that.

I still have the same opinion about eye contact. It is also the case that people, such as Lois Blackwell, the executive director of the Judevine School in St. Louis, Missouri, differ greatly on the topic and know a lot more about people labeled autistic than I do. We have debated this issue over the years and have so far failed to convince one another.

The point about the difference between learning environments and doing environments is a critical one for individuals labeled autistic. It is easy to think

*The preparation of this paper was supported in part by NICHHD Program Project Grant No. HD05951 to Children's Research Center, University of Illinois at Urbana-Champaign.

of the person labeled autistic as having to always remain in a closed environment. The goal of training should be their performance on any task, trained in a manner so that performance is acceptable under natural circumstances.

The section on power is very confusing in this paper. The discussion of the alternative definition of mental retardation (Chapter 14) provides a clearer presentation on power.

Near the end of this presentation I mention a trip to Europe. I did not find some of the things I thought would be there. There was definitely a nicer feeling about the handicapped in the Scandinavian countries, but I did not find the dignity they were given to be any greater, really, than that found here. This, hopefully, has improved both there and here. The last line in the presentation is terrible. It sounds as if blame is being placed on parents, which is something I never wish to do. It should have said that we as parents and professionals have the responsibility and the resources to assist children in attaining more acceptable, usable skills, and if we do so, they will change. It did not come out that way in the manuscript, and that was a mistake.

There is one concept not covered in this paper that is worth adding. The concept is what I call *masking*. Masking is what happens when a person's deviant behavior draws so much attention that her competencies go unnoticed or undeveloped. For example, when we work with people labeled autistic, the behaviors that bring negative attention are so overwhelming and overpowering that we work on them, attending to those behaviors to the exclusion of developing positive skills and competencies in these students. A number of years ago, Craig Barclay worked with a young man in Fort Wayne, Indiana, who had many of the behaviors that usually elicit the label autistic. Craig taught him to assemble the bicycle brakes. The young man learned to do the task very well, but in a very strange way. He would pick pieces up and walk about the room making strange noises, flailing his arms, crawling under tables, and climbing over tables. After he reached criterion on the task, Craig had him work in a room with a two-way mirror, alone, with components of the bicycle brake available in bins on a table. He worked 1 hour a day for 10 days. During this time he was observed. Even though we were interested in his production on the bicycle brakes, almost the entire time our attention was directed to his strange behaviors. It was not until we went in at the end of each hour and looked at what was on the table that we realized that, in fact, production had occurred. At the end of 10 days he had produced an average of 25 brakes per hour, with no errors. If my memory serves me correctly, it was after this experience that I came up with the concept of masking. It was very clear that our attention was drawn almost exclusively to his deviance, even though we were specifically trying to develop competence.

There are two implications of the concept of masking. First, we should not wait until the deviant behaviors are gone before starting to develop and build competence. Second, when we see someone with very strange behavior, we should work hard at trying to also notice the less conspicuous but no less important skills and competencies that the person has.

CHAPTER 19

Vocational Training for the Mentally Retarded

Marc W. Gold and Kathryn M. Ryan

PRESTATEMENT

One day I got on a plane in Champaign, Illinois, and happened to sit next to two women who had been in Champaign for a conference on social psychology. I could not help but hear them discussing the conference, and at one point I inquired about what kind of social psychologists they were. The woman sitting next to me introduced herself as Irene Frieze and said that she was an attribution theorist. I asked her to explain what attribution theory was and asked a number of questions as she described the basic concept of that specialty. At one point in the discussion she said, "And what do you do?" I said my work involved taking people who were perceived as having very low capabilities and who perceived themselves as having low capabilities and creating events that caused them to be perceived as having much greater capabilities and to perceive themselves as having much greater capabilities. I had purposely described my work in the terms she had just used to explain attribution theory. She looked very surprised and said, "That's attribution theory. We are having a symposium at the American Psychological Association this year on applied attribution theory. Would you be willing to present?" I said if she would teach me enough about attribution theory to present without embarrassing myself that I would be more than happy to try. Irene sent literature on attribution theory, and I began to write the paper for the symposium. As it happened, I spent that summer in Los Angeles. Bernard Weiner, the person who initially developed attribution theory, was at UCLA. When the first draft of the paper was done, I called him, asked to meet, and went over the paper with him. He was extremely helpful and provided an expanded perspective that I had not gained from reading his work and that of others. Considerable assistance was also provided by Carol Dweck back at the University of Illinois in Urbana-Champaign.

The paper and the symposium were received very well at the APA. Those of us who participated in the symposium got together and at the suggestion

This chapter originally appeared in I. H. Frieze, D. Bar-Tal, and J. S. Carroll (Eds.), *New approach to social problems* (San Francisco: Jossey-Bass, 1979). Reprinted by permission of the publisher.

of Irene Frieze and Daniel Bar-Tal agreed to contribute to a book on applied attribution theory.

I expanded the paper into a chapter and sent it to Irene. She was very unhappy with the result and asked if I would be willing to allow a student of hers, Kathryn Ryan, to rework the chapter, retaining the content, adding support material, and doing a better job of putting it on paper. Kathryn did a fine job, and I am pleased with the chapter.

Intelligence is an important and desirable personal characteristic in modern society. Intelligence has been found to produce a generally positive impression in others (Solomon and Saxe, 1977) and to result in greater social acceptance (Dentler and Mackler, 1962). Conversely, lack of intelligence—especially extreme lack of intelligence, or mental retardation—is thought to be an undesirable characteristic that produces a generally negative impression in others. Mental retardation has been defined by the American Association on Mental Deficiency as "significantly subaverage general intellectual functioning existing concurrently with deficits in adaptive behavior, and manifested during the developmental period" (Begab, 1975, p. 5). This definition indicates the association between low levels of intellectual functioning and maladaptive behavioral functioning. It also implies two reasons for potential rejection of the mentally retarded: their lack of intelligence and their disruptive behavior.

Mental retardation is usually stereotyped by the general public in its most extreme form (Gottlieb, 1975; Mercer, 1973), and it is frequently confused with mental illness (Gottlieb, 1975; Latimer, 1970). Thus the mentally retarded are considered to be, among other things, inadequate, helpless, and abnormal (Guskin, 1963). The mentally retarded are in reality, however, a very heterogeneous population. The vast majority of persons labeled *retarded* score between 55 and 70 on intelligence tests. These individuals, referred to as *mildly retarded*, are thought to be most affected by the *mentally retarded* label, because, for the most part, their behavior and appearance are normal, so they would probably be accepted by others if they were not so labeled. The mildly retarded are usually labeled early in their school careers because of poor performance on intelligence tests, and they are generally segregated into special classes for the Educable Mentally Retarded (EMR) because of this label (Mercer, 1973). Thus, a deleterious consequence of the *mentally retarded* label is segregation (MacMillan, Jones, and Aloia, 1974). Later in their lives, the mildly retarded are frequently able to escape the *mental retardation* label and to lead fairly normal, useful lives (Baller, Charles, and Miller, 1967; Edgerton, 1967; Guskin and Spicker, 1968).

A much smaller group of individuals are labeled *moderately* or *severely retarded*. They score between 25 and 55 on standardized intelligence tests. School programs for this group are called *TMR classes* (for the Trainable Mentally Retarded). Persons scoring below 25 on intelligence tests are referred to as *profoundly mentally retarded*. Only recently have public schools begun serving this population, and the label for such programs differs from place to place throughout the country. Persons labeled *moderately, severely,* and *profoundly retarded* generally behave and appear distinctively, so they are likely to be rejected, with or without the *mental retardation* label. Thus, they are thought to be less affected by the *mentally retarded* label than the mildly retarded. These individuals are, however, still quite affected by attributional and expectational implications of the *mentally retarded* label. This is apparent, for example, in the lack of adequate vocational training (and the consequent inability to find work) for most of these individuals due to the erroneous belief that they cannot learn.

Having remunerative employment is important in modern America for a variety of reasons: because self-worth is largely measured by occupation and wealth, because self-identification is largely through one's work role, and because of the Protestant Ethic. The mentally retarded, especially the moderately, severely, and profoundly retarded, are excluded from remunerative employment for two basic reasons, their lack of competence (useful skills or ability) and their deviance (unusual and distinctive behavior and appearance). Both of these characteristics can be conceptualized as stable, internal, unintentional causes of maladaptive behavior. Thus, the individual's incompetence and deviance are thought to be stable characteristics that are caused by the retardation and are incapable of being changed or controlled. Farber (1968) believes, in the context of mental retardation, that incompetence refers to a personal problem and that deviance refers to a social problem. Further, Farber proposes that educational institutions focus on incompetence, whereas social agencies focus on deviance. It could be argued, however, that many mildly retarded children are first examined for mental retardation because they present behavior problems (Braginsky and Braginsky, 1971; MacMillan, Jones, and Aloia, 1974). Thus, assumed deviance is a central focus of much institutional treatment for the mentally retarded, in spite of the fact that intelligence tests are generally used to define mental retardation (Mercer, 1973), especially for the mildly retarded.

It is our contention that to focus on deviance and to expend a great amount of effort to terminate deviant behaviors leads one to neglect basic inadequacies resulting from the lack of adequate educational, social, and vocational training. This notion will be elaborated on later in the chapter. A second major contention deals with the deleterious attributional and expectational patterns that result from labeling an individual *mentally retarded*. In fact, mental retardation can be thought of as an attributional excuse for poor academic and social performance. This excuse may or may not be appropriately used, and it may or may not be a beneficial attribution for the retarded individual. Finally, this excuse can have different implications, depending on whether the excuse is invoked by the retarded individual or by persons dealing with this individual.

ATTRIBUTIONAL AND EXPECTATIONAL IMPLICATIONS
OF THE MENTALLY RETARDED LABEL

Weiner and his colleagues (1972) proposed an attributional framework for achievement behavior that can be constructively applied to the mentally

210 TRAINING FOR MENTALLY RETARDED

retarded. The Weiner framework included a two-dimensional categorization of the attributed causes of an individual's successful or failing performance. The two dimensions were the locus of the cause (whether the cause stemmed from within the individual or outside the individual) and the stability of the cause (whether the cause was something that was present for a long duration or something present for a short duration). Later, a third dimension, intentionality (whether the cause was something intended and controlled by the individual or whether it was unintended and uncontrolled by the individual), was added by Rosenbaum (1972). The first two dimensions, internality and stability, are related to affect and expectations, respectively. An internal cause (such as ability or effort) makes an individual feel more pride after his or her success and more shame after his or her failure than an external cause (such as task difficulty or luck), and a stable cause (such as ability or task difficulty) increases an individual's expectations after his or her success and decreases expectations after his or her failure more than an unstable cause (such as effort or luck). The last dimension, intentionality, is related to the individual's level of responsibility. An individual is held more responsible for a success or failure when the cause was intentional (such as effort) than when it was unintentional (such as ability).

Weiner's framework can be productively applied to mental retardation, because it illuminates an attribution-expectancy cycle that may well harm retarded individuals. Mental retardation, in accordance with popular stereotypes, leads to low expectations for the retarded person's competence and high expectations for his or her deviance. Many times, both of these expectations are inappropriately extreme (Gold, 1972) and may affect the individual's performance. For example, expectations concerning a retarded person's ability may be inappropriately low, and he or she will not be encouraged to perform to his or her potential. Present expectations can also affect future expectations, because different attributions are made for expected versus unexpected outcomes, and these attributions affect future expectations (Valle and Frieze, 1976; McMahan, 1973). Expected outcomes are attributed to stable factors, and unexpected outcomes are attributed to unstable factors. Thus, unexpected outcomes are discounted, whereas expected outcomes are inflated.

For retarded individuals, this means that poor performance and disruptive behavior will be attributed stably (to the retardation), and good performance and normative behavior will be attributed unstably (for example, to effort, the situation, or another person). In other words, a retarded person is thought to do poorly because of his or her retardation and to do well in spite of the retardation (because of external facilitating circumstances). So, a retarded individual generally feels very poorly about his or her failure, because failure is commonly attributed internally, and he or she rarely feels good about success, because success is commonly attributed externally. Also, the retarded person is expected to do poorly in the future, because stable attributions are made for his or her poor behavior, and unstable attributions are made for his or her good behavior. It is apparent that this is a harmful and unproductive attributional pattern, because it perpetuates low expectations and adversely affects performance. A possible cause of this attributional pattern may be a common belief that ability (and lack of ability) is a global, inclusive characteristic (Heider, 1958, p. 93). That is, it may be believed that, if someone fails at a task because of lack of ability, he or she will be unable to perform another task, even if it is unrelated to the first.

This attributional pattern may also be explained by using some of Kelley's (1967, 1973) notions concerning causal schemata. Kelley believes that individuals attribute causality according to a covariation principle. That is, individuals decipher the causal source of a behavior by analyzing the behavior for potential correlates. Potential correlates that are examined are: consensus (Do others behave the same way?), distinctiveness (Is this the only task that is affected?), and consistency (Does this happen all the time? Does this happen for all of the task-related behavior?). When a consistent correlate is found, the behavior is thought to be caused by that correlate. There may be a common belief that mental retardation is sufficiently low in consensus (most people do not have it), low in distinctiveness (it affects a large portion of tasks), and high in consistency (it affects most of the task-related behaviors a large portion of the time), so that mental retardation can be used as a brief and efficient causal explanation (or schema) for bad behavior. Mental retardation is a person-oriented schema because of its location on the consensus, distinctiveness, and consistency dimensions. Because mental retardation is person-oriented and high in consistency, the *mental retardation* attribution again leads to expectations for poor future performance. We shall separately review research concerning expectations, consequences of those expectations, and attributions for a retarded person's performance for observers and for the retarded.

OBSERVERS' EXPECTATIONS FOR RETARDED INDIVIDUALS' PERFORMANCE

Teachers' Expectations

Teachers have low expectations for their mildly retarded students, and they commonly attempt to segregate those students from normal students. The generally accepted rationale for segregating mentally retarded students is that, if these students are not segregated, they are likely to be unable to keep up with the rest of the class and so become frustrated and unwilling to learn. This rationale proposes that the purpose of segregation is to protect the retarded student. An equally important but often unstated rationale for segregation is that the retarded student often disrupts the class and requires a large portion of the teacher's time and effort, so adequate instruction of the rest of the class is often hindered by a retarded student's presence. This rationale proposes that the purpose of segregation is to protect the retarded student's nonretarded classmates and his or her teacher. Underlying both rationales is the assumption that retarded students cannot learn at the same speed as normal students and that they must be taught more slowly and meticulously because of this. It is also frequently assumed that retarded students cannot even learn the same types of things that normal students learn.

Once students are segregated, the assumptions concerning their low learning potential undoubtedly direct instructors to prepare lessons at a very low level. The assumptions may also affect teachers' expectations and behavior concerning the amount of learning to require from these students. Jones (1966) reviewed current research (including many unpublished studies) on special education teachers and special education teaching procedures. Guskin and Spicker (1968, p. 263) interpreted Jones' research review as suggesting that teacher orientation toward a mentally retarded student is more likely to be maternal than achievement oriented. Kurtz and others (1977) found that education students engaged in more nonverbal immediacy when reading to a child labeled *mentally retarded* than when reading to a child that was not so labeled. This result could be interpreted as further evidence of a maternal orientation. Beez (1968, as reported in Guskin and Spicker, 1968, p. 264) found that teachers working with a pupil who was expected to do poorly covered a mean of 5.66 words in instructing the student, whereas teachers working with a pupil who was expected to do well covered a mean of 10.43 words in instructing the student. Also, Sperry (1974) found that teachers planned higher-level instructional materials for students who were expected to do well than for those who were expected to do poorly. Thus, there is some evidence that expectancies can affect the amount and type of material a teacher attempts to cover. And, finally, Farina and others (1976) found that confederates labeled *mentally retarded* were shocked with less intensity and duration for failure at a learning task than confederates labeled *mentally ill* or *normal*. Farina and others interpreted this result to mean that individuals hold lower expectations for the performance of a mentally retarded individual. This research also supports the notion that the mentally retarded are less likely to be punished for failure than the nonretarded.

Much expectancy research has been done as a result of Rosenthal and Jacobson's (1968a, 1968b) famous study, in which falsely high teacher expectancies were said to lead to increased student performance in the lower grades (first and second grade) for all types of students. Most of the subsequent research that dealt with expectations for mentally retarded students (Badad, 1977; Gozali and Meyen, 1970; Schwartz and Cook, 1972; Soule, 1972) found no significant effect of teacher expectations on student performance. However, within these studies, there were two labeling effects operating— the student's initial label (EMR, TMR, mental retardate) and the experimental label (the manipulation of the student's potential for improvement). The initial label is, of course, a very potent factor that may have dominated and nullified any effects the experimental label may have had.

The effect of the initial label is also important, because a student's performance may be measured differently, depending on whether he or she is labeled *mentally retarded* or *normal*. That is, the frame of reference for retarded and nonretarded students is quite different, and this affects whether a given performance is perceived as good or bad. The frame of reference for a retarded student includes the performance of other retarded students or the performance of a stereotypical retarded student. The frame of reference for a normal student includes other normal students or the performance of a stereotypical normal student. Teachers' expectations for a retarded student's performance affect teacher-student interactions and the amount of material covered, probably because different frames of reference are held for normal and retarded students. These different frames of reference may also affect a teacher's attributions and his or her reward allocations to students. For example, a retarded student may be rewarded more than a normal student for a mediocre performance, because he or she is thought to be performing closer to his or her level of ability, putting forth greater effort, and working with a task that is more difficult for him or her to perform than a normal student.

Trainers' Expectations

Frequently, moderately and severely retarded persons are served in programs where the emphasis is on manual tasks. The rationale in these programs is usually to prepare the retarded for adequate social functioning. Teachers or trainers in such programs frequently hold very low expectations for the retarded person's ability. Changing these expectations is very important. It has been repeatedly demonstrated (Gold, 1975) that even severely retarded individuals are able to perform difficult tasks—for example, assembling bicycle brakes, electronic printed circuit boards, locking gas caps, spring-loaded hinges, and milking pumps. Most individuals working with the retarded, however, still do not believe that their clients are able to achieve success with these quite difficult tasks.

Gold (1972) engaged in an experiment in which four sheltered workshop directors were asked if any of their clients would be able to assemble a fifteen- or twenty-four-piece bicycle brake. All directors said that their clients would not be able to learn these tasks, even if the clients were allowed to form an assembly line, in which each individual would only be required to assemble one or two pieces. Each director was then asked to select the sixteen most limited individuals in the agency, and these individuals were trained on a one-to-one basis. Half the subjects were trained using the form of the pieces as the only discriminant learning cue, and the other half were trained using the form and color of the pieces as redundant learning cues. Every one of the subjects (N = 64) successfully learned to assemble the fifteen-piece bicycle brake. In addition, all but one subject successfully learned the 24-piece bicycle brake. Several follow-up tests indicated that performance capability continued for a very long time—one year and five years (Gold and Close, 1975). This experiment successfully demonstrated the tremendous discrepancy between directors' expectations and the actual performance ability of retarded individuals. This phenomenon, which has been repeatedly demonstrated by Gold's research, is thought to be one of the greatest deterrents of sufficient training for the retarded.

Consequences of Low Expectations

As a consequence of the expectation that the retarded have low ability and the belief that repeated failure frustrates them, teachers and trainers may spend too much time teaching the retarded easy tasks, they may overreward

the retarded for easy successes, and they may not attempt to teach the retarded more difficult skills that may be useful in the future. These activities
seem to be quite popular solutions to the problems concerning the retarded,
yet each of them may lead the retarded to learn harmful and unproductive
attributional responses.

When retarded persons spend too much time learning easy tasks, they
do not learn the causal linkage between effort and ability, and they do not
realize that effort must be expended to increase skills. Also, they do not
learn that success at a worthwhile and challenging task demonstrates ability
and achievement (Bailer, 1961).

It is possible that future unsuccessful experiences will be handled poorly
by an individual who is inexperienced with failure. Also, overrewarding a
student for success may undermine his or her intrinsic motivation to learn
(Lee, Syrnyk, and Hallschmid, 1976; see also Chapter Ten), and it may lead
the retarded student to believe that his or her teachers have very low standards.
The most deleterious consequence of low expectations, however, is likely to
be the lack of proper training in useful and essential vocational skills. This
leads to future unemployment and all the personal and social problems
associated with unemployment, such as lower self-concept, higher depen-
dency, and higher crime rates.

OBSERVERS' ATTRIBUTIONS FOR THE
PERFORMANCE OF THE RETARDED

Little direct research has been done on observers' attributions (rather than
expectancies) for the successful and failing task performances of the retarded.
One could expect, considering the arguments presented earlier, that observers
would attribute retarded individuals' success to unstable, external causes
(luck, effort) and their failure to the stable, internal cause of lack of ability.
Severance and Gasstrom (1977) tested this hypothesis in a study in which
attributions concerning the cause of a hypothetical individual's performance
and expectations for his or her future performance were solicited. Results
revealed that a retarded individual was attributed significantly greater lack of
ability for failure than a nonretarded individual. However, a nonretarded individual was *not* attributed significantly greater ability for success than a retarded individual. It was also found that a retarded individual was attributed
significantly more effort for success and significantly more task difficulty for
failure than a nonretarded individual. Severance and Gasstrom concluded that
observers of a retarded person's performance attribute failure to lack of ability
and task difficulty and attribute success to effort.

The expectancy measure in Severance and Gasstrom's experiment revealed that a nonretarded individual's success led to high expectancies for the
future, whereas a retarded individual's success led only to moderate future
expectancies. This result is in agreement with the attributional results, because more unstable attributions (to effort) were made for the retarded
individual's success than for the nonretarded individual's success. However,
there was no significant difference found for expectancies for a nonretarded

and a retarded individual's performance after failure. This is in spite of the fact that more attributions of lack of ability and task difficulty were made for a retarded individual's failure than for a nonretarded individual's failure. Perhaps this nonsignificant difference for expectancies after failure was because the individual, for whatever reason, was incapable of succeeding at the task. Thus, the individual was not expected to succeed in the future. In conclusion, the expectancy measure showed that expectancies for a retarded individual's future performance are modifiable by observed success but that these modifications are not to the same degree as those for a nonretarded individual.

These general laboratory findings are supported by observations of people actually evaluating the performance of the retarded. It is Gold's experience that, with surprising frequency, when visitors observe individuals with severe retardation successfully performing a complex task, their comment is, "You are certainly excellent trainers." Thus, directly observed competence of the worker brings about attributions of ability, but not for the worker! Apparently, the biases found by Severance and Gasstrom are strong enough to require even more than direct observation of competence. Perhaps the direct observation of competence on a variety of complex tasks by numerous retarded individuals would alter attributions and replace the attribution-expectancy cycle, in which attributions lead to low expectations, and low expectations in turn lead to harmful and unproductive attributions.

This experience with observers suggests an attributional category, *training*, that is not frequently mentioned by attribution theorists. Training is a temporal interaction between the individual and another person, and it requires ability and effort on the part of both participants. The addition of training as a category of perceived causality requires a closer inspection of the nature of ability. If ability is internal to the performer and stable, then it must be assumed, given Gold's research results, that even the most limited individuals may be capable of demonstrating considerable ability when powerful training procedures are available. The word *power* is used here to mean that the trainer must utilize ability and effort for the learner to acquire the task at hand. From our perspective, the difference between individuals is the amount of power (ability and effort) needed in the training process rather than any differences in *what* they can ultimately learn. The more difficult it is for someone to learn a task, the more power the trainer must utilize. Also, the more difficult the task is, the more effort the individual must exert to learn it. Thus, it is assumed that sufficient ability for the task is given, and training processes are seen as unstable and therefore modifiable.

Training plays an important role in the relationship between the difficulty of a task and the person's ability. The distinction between *can* and *try* made by Heider (1958) fails to acknowledge this. Weiner (1974, p. 6) acknowledges the difficulty of "explaining perceived improvement or learning [within the attribution theory perspective], inasmuch as both the determinants of "can" (ability and task difficulty) are conceptualized as "fixed." The addition of the causal attribution of training requires no change in existing categories in the Weiner framework, but it allows for the recognition of a

distinction between manifest and potential ability. Manifest ability is demonstrated, measurable performance, and potential ability is a testable hypothesis
concerning an individual's capability of acquiring a new skill or behavior. It
may be that focusing on the individual's potential rather than his or her
manifest ability is what is needed to change the expectational and attributional biases of the observer of a retarded person's performance.

RETARDED INDIVIDUALS' EXPECTATIONS
FOR THEIR OWN PERFORMANCE

Because most retarded individuals have had a past history of repeated failure,
they are thought by many to have low expectancies for success and high
expectancies for failure. Tymchuk (1972) concluded that previous research
has shown this to be true. MacMillan and his colleagues (Keogh, Cahill, and
MacMillan, 1972; MacMillan, 1969; MacMillan and Keogh, 1971), for example,
have found that retarded students are more likely than normal students to
blame themselves for failure to complete a task. They found that this occurred,
even when the task interruption was previously defined as a success, and they
found that self-blame increased with increasing grade level. These results
support the notion that retarded individuals have a higher expectancy for
failure than normal individuals. The general acceptance of this belief, in fact,
has led to the common practice of constructing tasks so that the retarded
individual experiences only success, to reduce frustrations.

Other research, however, has shown that the retarded do not have a higher
expectancy for failure than normals. Revi and Illyes (1976), for example,
found that TMR children had higher expectancies for success than normal
children. This, however, could have been caused by the type of task they
used, a relatively easy motor task that may have been similar to other tasks
the children had been given previously. MacMillan (1975) found no expectancy differences for EMR and normal children's initial success predictions
and concluded that this result failed to support the "past history of failure"
notion. In this study, experimentally induced success and failure were found
to significantly affect expectancies for both groups of children. Success was
found to increase performance expectancies, and failure was found to decrease performance expectancies. Schuster and Gruen (1971), in a similar
study, found that mentally retarded children initially had higher expectancies
for success than their same-age peers. In this study, it was also found that all
the children raised their performance estimates after success and lowered
them after failure.

Issues concerning expectancies of the retarded are more complicated
than originally thought. For example, retarded individuals' expectancies may
differ according to the type of task, the setting, the trainer, and the adequacy
of the training procedure. Task characteristics would be especially important
in determining expectancies, because past experience with similar tasks is
used by an individual as evidence of his or her ability or inability to perform
the present task. Thus, a retarded individual's expectancies for success or
failure may widely vary according to the type of task.

CONSEQUENCES OF LOW EXPECTATIONS

An important issue concerns the effects a retarded individual's low expectations have on his or her performance. Cromwell (1963) proposed that retarded individuals' expectations for failure and normal individuals' expectations for success lead each group to adopt a different strategy in approaching a task. According to Cromwell, the retarded are "failure-avoiders," that is, they perform a task so as to minimize their chances of failing, whereas normal people are "success-strivers," that is, they perform a task so as to maximize their chances of succeeding. To support this notion, Cromwell cited a probability-task study (Shipe, 1960), which revealed that retarded subjects always guessed the predominant item in order to be correct on most of the trials (or fail the least number of trials), whereas normal subjects switched their guesses in order possibly to be correct on *all* the trials. Cromwell also noted that the assumption that the retarded are failure-avoiders led to research that presented evidence that retarded individuals enter situations with a performance level that is lower than what they are capable of, they are less affected by failure than normals (presumably because they are less surprised by failure), and they are less likely than normals to increase effort following failure. Also, retarded children have been found to attribute less negative affect to their teachers following failure than do normal children (Hayes and Prinz, 1976). These consequences may, in part, be due to harmful and unproductive attributions.

RETARDED INDIVIDUALS' ATTRIBUTIONS
FOR THEIR OWN PERFORMANCE

It has been proposed that mentally retarded individuals do not learn the causal relationship between effort and success and lack of effort and failure, and thus they do not feel responsible for their own performance (Wooster, 1974). This would lead one to assume that retarded individuals would not attribute their performance to effort or to any other intentional causes. One could also assume that other harmful and unproductive attributions may be made by these individuals because of their tendency to blame themselves for failure. For example, one would expect retarded individuals to attribute their failure to their retardation, which would lead these individuals to feel very bad and to stop trying. Moreover, given the previous arguments, one would also expect retarded individuals to attribute their success to external, unstable causes.

However, research has shown that the mentally retarded make attributions for success and failure that are similar to those made by normals. For example, EMR junior high school students were found to make more external than internal attributions for failure situations (Panda and Lynch, 1974). Also, EMR adults have been found to make more effort and luck attributions for failure than for success and more ability attributions for success than for failure (Horai and Guarnaccia, 1975). However, Horai and Guarnaccia's findings are suspect. Because attributions were elicited verbally from the subjects, socially desirable responses may have been given. Also, because the success manipulation included the statement "You did better than any I have tested so far" and the failure manipulation included the statement "Most of the people I have tested so far did at least ten more than you" the manipulations included base-rate information. This may have activated social-comparison processes (Festinger, 1954), with other retarded individuals as the frame of reference, and affected the subjects' attributions. Finally, Horai and Guarnaccia did not analyze the attributions within the success and failure conditions. By examining the means, it appears that there were no differences between the attributions for success (on a scale between 0 and 3, Task-Difficulty mean = 1.7, Ability mean = 1.5, Luck mean = 1.4, and Effort mean = 1.35), whereas there were differences between the attributions for failure (on a scale between 0 and 3, Luck mean = 2.15, Effort mean = 1.85, Task-Difficulty mean = 1.3, and Ability mean = 0.70). In conclusion, it would seem that retarded individuals are able to attribute their failures favorably, but they have not been shown to attribute their successes favorably.

Another interesting question concerns the effects a retarded individual's attributions have on his or her performance. Hoffman and Weiner (1978) examined the effects of manipulated attributions and outcomes on subsequent performance of TMR adults. The design was a 4 (ability, effort, task difficulty, or no attribution) X 2 (success or failure outcome) factorial. The independent variable was a success or failure experience combined with an appropriate attribution (or no attribution), and the dependent variable was subsequent performance on a second trial of the same coding task. Results revealed that an attribution of ability in the success condition enhanced the retardate's subsequent performance relative to the other attribution (and the no-attribution) conditions. No significant differences were found between the attribution conditions within the failure situation. Hoffman and Weiner interpreted these results as suggesting that retarded adults respond to attributions in a manner that is similar to normal adults and that their performances can be enhanced by proper attribution-outcome combinations.

Wooster (1974) was able to show that the retarded may be taught to attribute their performance optimally by having them repeatedly observe their responsibility for success and failure. So, it seems that a beneficial and productive attributional pattern can be learned by the retarded and that this attributional pattern is then used by them to enhance their performance. However, this attributional pattern is not habitually employed without such learning.

THE ATTRIBUTION–EXPECTANCY CYCLE: CONCLUSIONS

It has been demonstrated that the retarded and their instructors have low expectations for retarded individuals' ability. Consequently, they underestimate the kinds of tasks that can successfully be performed, and they do not give the retarded person deserved credit for success. Thus, successes are attributed to factors other than ability, which means that observations of a retarded person's manifest ability do not affect estimates of his or her potential ability. Failures are attributed to the retardation, so it is assumed that the retarded individual's inability to perform is both stable and unintentional. The latter factor implies lack of responsibility for failure, which may or may not be beneficial for the retarded individual. If the retarded individual does not have the potential ability to succeed at the task, the unintentional factor may be beneficial, because he or she is not punished for an inability that cannot be controlled. However, if the retarded individual does have the potential ability to succeed at the task, the unintentional factor may be harmful, because the individual will not be trained, and he or she will not try to succeed at something that can be done. Since it is impossible to assess the individual's potential, the appropriate strategy is to assume that the person is able and to place responsibility for nonattainment of criterion performance on the trainer.

We feel that the attributional process itself must become more conscious, so that implications of various attributions are recognized and a deliberate decision is made concerning the relative payoff of allowing individuals an excuse for failure versus allowing them hope for success. Training should become a key attributional precursor to ability for the retarded. This attribution could allow for greater fulfillment of each individual's goals for a full life.

THE RELATIONSHIP BETWEEN COMPETENCE AND DEVIANCE

Hollander's (1958, 1960) theory of idiosyncrasy-credits states a fundamental relationship between competence, conformity, and deviance in a group. Competence, according to Hollander, refers to an individual's ability, especially his or her ability to perform activities that reward the group. Deviance refers to an individual's eccentricities, which are negatively evaluated by the group. And conformity refers to an individual's conventionalities, which are positively evaluated by the group. Hollander theorized that an individual's perceived competence and his or her past conformity creates a "credit balance" within a group, called *idiosyncrasy-credits*. This credit balance allows the individual to deviate later without group censure. This is because the individual is of value to the group, and his or her value affects how his or her behavior is perceived and whether it will be punished. The perceptual component can be seen to fit the attributional framework discussed earlier. That is, behavior consistent with past behavior (present conformity and past conformity) is considered to be stably caused, and behavior inconsistent with past behavior (present deviance and past conformity) is considered to be unstably caused. Moreover, because the past behavior probably occurred at different times, in different contexts, and with different individuals, consistent behavior is likely to be perceived to be due to the individual, whereas inconsistent behavior is likely to be perceived as externally caused. So, consistent conformity is rewarded, consistent deviance is punished, and inconsistent behavior is treated intermediately. The punishment component is intuitively plausible, because one can readily see that other group members will not want to lose a potentially valuable group member.

COMPETENCE AND DEVIANCE OF THE RETARDED

Hollander's theory of idiosyncrasy-credits can be restated as, "The more competence an individual has, the more deviance will be tolerated in that person by others" (Gold, 1975, p. 260). This hypothesis is readily applicable to the mentally retarded, because these individuals are likely to function concurrently as both incompetent and deviant. Thus, the retarded individual has two separate but related behavior problems.

It has been shown that expectancies for a retarded individual's competence are low. Foster and Ysseldyke (1976) demonstrated that expectations for a retarded individual's deviance are high. In this study, teachers were assigned to one of four label groups, and the members of each group were asked to list the behavior they expected of a hypothetical normal, EMR, learning disabled, or emotionally disturbed child. Then, each teacher observed a videotape of the same normal boy, who was supposedly a representative of the labeled group. Results showed that the teachers held negative expectancies for children categorized with a deviant label and that they maintained these expectancies, even when confronted with normal behavior. In addition, it was found that the lowest expectancies were held for the EMR child.

Traditionally, trainers and teachers of the retarded have focused on their deviance. This may be because deviance is more apparent than incompetence, because modern tools (such as group teaching or behavior modification) are more applicable to deviance than to incompetence, or because it is believed that one must eliminate deviance to augment competence. The result of this focus is that the retarded individual's competencies are so low that any deviance can readily result in group sanctions. This is especially harmful, because a retarded individual's deviance may be more readily apparent than his or her competence, because there is a common discrepancy between a retarded individual's potential ability and his or her manifest ability, and because of the expectancy-attribution cycle previously mentioned.

We do not believe that a retarded person's deviance should be ignored; rather, his or her competence should be given more attention. Attending to the individual's competence, we believe, increases his or her employment potential, increases his or her self-confidence and self-worth, decreases his or her deviant behaviors, and breaks the deleterious attribution-expectancy cycle. It is self-evident that training the retarded will increase their job potential. Self-worth can also be increased by employment, because employment is an important goal for most retarded people (Edgerton, 1967) and for the society in which they live. Employment also increases buying power and the ability to enjoy the goods and activities available in this society. Also, because deviant behavior is sometimes incompatible with competent behavior, it can be assumed that increased competence may decrease deviance. In fact, Gold (1975) has found this to be the case for many of the retarded individuals in his training program. And, finally, it is felt that training the retarded individual will eventually lead to the elimination of the deleterious attribution-expectancy cycle described earlier.

POTENTIAL SOLUTIONS

Mainstreaming

A currently popular solution to the problems of retarded children in the public schools is to transfer retarded students from special classes back into regular classes. This solution derives from the belief that the *mentally retarded* label does more harm than good, especially because the label results in segregation. Budoff and Gottlieb (1976) found that mainstreamed EMR children were more internally controlled and had more positive attitudes toward school than their segregated peers. In addition, it was found that the more able EMR children benefitted more from mainstreaming than the less able EMR children. Most importantly, able EMR students were found to change their self-concept of ability and their beliefs concerning how competent others perceived them to be. Strang, Smith, and Rogers (1978) found that half-time mainstreaming (mainstreaming for half of the school day) optimally augmented EMR children's self-concepts. They felt that this was due to the fact that half-time mainstreamed students were able to compare themselves with students in special classes or regular classes, and, depending on the comparison item, they were able to enhance their egos with one or the other comparison. It appears that mainstreaming can allow EMR students to regain their self-concept of ability can lead to beneficial attributions and expectancies. Thus, able EMR students that are mainstreamed are frequently able to show better performance.

The issue of mainstreaming more severely retarded students is more complicated because of the amount of time and effort needed to teach retarded students to form better attributions and expectancies and to perform to their fullest capacity. Regular classroom teachers do not have the time, and they may not have the skills to motivate and train retarded students properly.

Training

In Gold's instructional system (Gold and Pomerantz, 1978), it is believed that the severely and profoundly retarded can be trained to form healthier attributions through successful vocational experiences. It is also believed that this system may change trainers' attributions concerning their clients' abilities. In this system, the task is divided into teachable units, which are modified for each learner. This method results in high rates of acquisition for most learners, although there are differences in the rate of acquisition. Thus, each learner experiences much success from the beginning of the training process. This training procedure should not be misinterpreted to suggest that errorless learning is desired. On the contrary, errors and the reduction of errors are seen as important in developing a retarded person's ability to deal with errors (Dweck, 1975) and to recognize the importance of effort in the learning process.

It is common practice in most programs for the retarded to be reinforced for any and every little positive behavior. An unstated assumption is that these individuals have little if any ability, and so any positive actions must represent effort rather than ability. The present position is that reinforcement given for low levels of success results in support for the retarded individual's low self-concept. In other words, the individual believes that, if he or she is reinforced for very simple tasks, then others believe that he or she has very low ability. An alternative strategy is to provide little or no reinforcement for simple, positive behavior. Also, it is believed that silence can have reinforcing qualities, when the trainer is clearly paying attention to the learner. In this situation, when the trainer is not commenting, the learner learns that "no news is good news." Each time an error that has been made before is corrected, the trainer provides enough information to correct that error but less information (and frequently different information) than in the last correction. This approach combines many factors that will promote ability attributions for success and discourage lack of ability attributions for failure, and this type of training may lead the retarded to fulfill their substantial potential.

One final observation from Gold's program stems from anecdotal information collected during training sessions. It has been repeatedly observed that many of the clients who had been previously described as having severely deviant behavior displayed none of these behaviors during the training session. It could be that conventional extinction procedures were working throughout the session to extinguish these behaviors. However, it may also be that the clients were not deviant, because they were not *expected* to be deviant. This is felt to be a crucial component in adequate vocational training for the mentally retarded. The learner must be expected to perform the task competently, and he or she must not be expected to behave deviantly. Thus, trainers of the retarded must cease to form deleterious attributions and expectancies, and this will lead retarded individuals to form more beneficial attributions and expectations for themselves.

CONCLUSIONS

We believe that two basic problems currently inhibit efforts to provide adequate educational and vocational training of the retarded. These are a deleterious attribution-expectancy cycle and an almost exclusive focus on the retarded individual's deviance. Both of these problems are related to general expectations that the retarded individual should lack competence and be deviant. The attribution-expectancy cycle leads to the ascription of performance failure to the retardation and performance success to external, unstable factors. In this way, the cycle operates to perpetuate low expectations for the ability of the retarded. The focus on deviance leads to situations in which the retarded are fired from jobs or alienated from family and friends because of their limited ability to reward others. Retarded individuals today are taught so few skills that any deviance is punished quite severely. We believe that the focus of future training of the retarded must be on their competence. Also, there must be a concerted effort to change attributions and expectancies of those associated with the retarded and thus an effort to change attributions and expectancies of the retarded themselves. This may be done through a conscious effort to restructure attributions, or it may be done on a less conscious level by mainstreaming, at some level, all retarded individuals. By focusing on each retarded individual's potential ability through the teaching and training processes, retarded individuals can be allowed to fulfill their great social potential.

POSTSTATEMENT

The concept of attribution theory represents, to me, a very nice middle ground between humanistic and behavioristic psychology. It acknowledges the concept of reinforcement contingencies but goes on to describe them within the framework of peoples' feelings about the things that happen around them and to them. The attribution theory perspective is very refreshing and has considerable potential use for conceptualizing developing training programs for people labeled handicapped. A first reading of attribution theory may leave you confused about who is feeling what about whom, but as you get into it more, you will begin to recognize some of the relationships and their utilities in program development.

One of the suggestions made in this chapter is the addition of the attributional category "training." It is mentioned here only to reemphasize my feeling of its importance.

Another issue in this paper that needs discussion is the concept of manifest and potential ability. As indicated earlier, the word potential is not helpful when used in regard to the retarded and the handicapped. Potential is something that we should assume for all individuals. Further, when somebody demonstrates a capability to perform a task that she could not perform before and that was beyond the expectations other people had of her, we must be very careful not to think that she has somehow arrived at her potential. The development of new skills should go on and on. Trainers should never believe that they have even come close to arriving at someone's potential. The distinction between manifest and potential ability was made to separate the terms conceptually in dealing with attributions. At the end of the section entitled Observers' Attributions for the Performance of the Retarded this statement occurs: "It may be that focusing on the individual's potential rather than his or her manifest ability is what is needed to change the expectational and attributional biases of the observer of a retarded person's performance." I would much prefer that we had discussed focusing on the training of tasks that were currently beyond what was expected of the individual.

Another sentence in this chapter says, "This type of training may lead the retarded to fulfill their substantial potential." This is another comment about potential that I wish had not shown up in my writing, but it did. Just to be redundant, I do not think anyone is capable of "fulfilling" his potential.

All any of us can do is to keep adding to what we have in terms of capabilities. We can acknowledge that potential did indeed lie beneath a particular achievement, but we cannot predict the depth of that potential—a reservoir to be explored.

In reviewing this chapter, I was amazed when I saw the word *retardate* again. I went through the chapter carefully before it went to press. Sorry.

I first read about Hollander's theory of idiosyncrasy-credits in this chapter when it came back from Kathryn. As you probably noticed, it is a fairly close parallel to my competence/deviance hypothesis, and since it came out in 1958, it predates the competence/ deviance hypothesis by at least 10 years. I have always wondered about the ethics involved in coming up with an idea, publishing it as your own, and then later finding that someone else had published essentially the same idea at some other time. I was once accused of having stolen the competence/deviance hypothesis from Bernard Farber. I have looked through Farber's work and have not been able to find from where I might have stolen it. Hollander's concept is, on the other hand, similar to mine. In any case, being the positivist that I am, I would prefer to think of Hollander's work as supportive. His concept contains some components that the competence/deviance hypothesis does not and, in fact, adds to a conceptualization that is useful for looking at the perceptions that people have of the performance of individuals labeled handicapped.

CHAPTER 20

Five-Year Retention of an Assembly Task by the Moderately and Severely Retarded

Marc W. Gold and Dan W. Close

PRESTATEMENT

When Dan Close and I began this study, we were extremely eager to find out what would happen. When the study was completed, we were excited about the results. Because of our commitment to scientific process, we analyzed the data using what we felt were the best techniques. We also gave careful attention to devising sound methodology. Retention is a touchy issue in psychological research. The entire field of psychology has never really established clean, discrete ways of studying retention; however, we felt we had done an acceptable job in setting up the study to get a good look at how well the subjects remembered. The raw data seemed to stand by themselves. The statistical analyses also seemed to support what we felt the raw data were saying.

We also thought it was significant that 11 of the 16 individuals in the workshop were still there 5 years later. To us, this meant that they represented a stable work activity center population and that, therefore, this study was descriptive of the performance of persons labeled moderately and severely retarded.

In a previous study (Gold, 1972) data were reported on the acquisition, transfer, and retention of a complex assembly task. The acquisition and transfer data were obtained during the fall of 1968; the retention data were collected 1 year later. In the original study 64 moderately and severely retarded individuals who were enrolled in four sheltered workshops learned to assemble a 15-piece bicycle brake and were then tested for transfer to a 24-piece bicycle brake. Training procedures utilized the concept of cue redundancy (Zeaman & House, 1963). Half of the subjects worked with the parts of the training task brake as they came from the factory (form-only). The others worked with parts that were color-coded (color-form). Coding consisted of painting red the surface of each part that was facing the subject when it was placed in the proper position for assembly. Half of the subjects learned the 15-piece bicycle brake, which was the training task, to a criterion of 6 correct out of 8 consecutive trials; the other half performed 20 trials beyond criterion (overlearning). All groups worked with the parts of the transfer brake assembly as they came from the factory (form-only). Color-Form

Groups learned the training task brake significantly faster than the Form-Only Groups. Overlearning did not affect transfer. Details regarding the population and the procedures used for the training may be found in Gold (1972).

Fifty-three of the subjects were available for the retention study 1 year later. The procedures used were the same as those in the original study, except that half of the subjects started on the transfer task brake so that an unconfounded retention measure could be obtained for both tasks. Also, there was no demonstration of the task on the first day. The 1-year retention study yielded highly significant retention effects for all dependent measures. The contracts on which the subjects performed in the workshop during the interim period were, essentially, no different from those on which they performed prior to the acquisition study. The contracts were also essentially the same during the 5-year period between the 1-year retention study and the data reported here.

The purpose of this study was to show for retention what has been shown for acquisition in other studies generated from our research program. That is, the retarded, especially the moderately and severely retarded, are capable of learning and remembering to a degree far in excess of what preconceived notions have restricted us to teaching them. In addition to contributing to the technology of instruction for the retarded, these data are intended to greatly expand the range of expectancies which govern all the activities in which we allow the retarded to participate.

METHOD

Subjects

Subjects were 11 of the 16 adults from one of the four sheltered workshops that participated in the original study. In that study the workshop was included as an independent variable. No significant main effects of, or interactions with, this variable were found. It seems, therefore, reasonable to conclude that the present population was representative of the total population in that first study. Further support for this may be found in comparisons between the total group of subjects in the original study and the subgroup which comprises the subject population in the present study. The mean IQ for the 11 subjects in the present study was 47.74 (range = 37-57). The mean IQ for the entire population of individuals in the original study was 47.19 (range = 37-59). On the coaster brake, which was the one used in the present study, mean trials to criterion for the entire population was 26.09, with a range of 8-51. For the 11 individuals in the current study the mean trials to criterion in acquisition in the original study was 27.00, with a range of 12-39. In the 1-year retention data mean trials to criterion for the 53 subjects who participated was 14.31, with a range of 7-40. For the current subjects mean trials to criterion was 12.90, with a range of 7-17. All but one of the current subjects participated in the 1-year retention study.

Materials, Experimenter, and Procedure

Only the training task (coaster) brake was used in this 5-year retention study. It was felt that the information sought could be obtained without addition of the second task. The experimenter for the present study did not participate in the original study or in the 1-year retention study.

The one other modification in the procedures from the original study and also from the 1-year retention study was that all subjects worked with the form-only brake. This meant that six individuals who had learned originally on the color-form brake and also relearned using the color-form brake on the 1-year retention study were given the form-only brake for this study. This was an oversight not discovered until the data had already been collected.

The training procedure was identical to that used in the original study and in the 1-year retention study. Subjects were worked with individually. The subject was seated at a table on which the acquisition tray (Gold, 1972) was placed. Parts for four brakes were placed in correct assembly sequence within 14 compartments of the tray. The experimenter sat to the left of the subject. A total task procedure was used; that is, the subject assembled an entire bicycle brake each trial, with the experimenter providing feedback when necessary. The total task procedure is in contrast with chaining procedures in which subjects learn just the beginning or the end of a task until they know it and then work with more and more of the task. When discrimination errors were made, the experimenter said, "Try another way." When a manipulation error was made, the experimenter reached in and repositioned the subjects' fingers. Subjects performed an average of four trials (brakes) per day.

RESULTS

Table 1 shows mean and F ratios (or t values) for the 11 subjects in the present study for original learning, 1-year and 5-year retention in respect to trials, manipulation errors, and discrimination errors to criterion. Significant retention effects were obtained for trials to criterion, t (10) = 5.26, $p < .001$ and manipulation errors to criterion, t (10) = 2.80, $p < .02$. Discrimination errors to criterion did not reach significance, t (10) = 1.79, n.s. The data were very similar to those obtained for the 1-year retention study. With criterion being six correct out of eight consecutive trials, subjects on the average were making no errors after the seventh trial.

Time to criterion was not measured for the original study or for the 1-year retention study, although estimates were reported on time to criterion for the original data. It was estimated that the average time taken to reach criterion on each of the two tasks in the original study was less than two hours. The trials were timed for the present study. Mean minutes to criterion was 33; the range was 19–60.

DISCUSSION

Five years is a long time. The failure to find any differences between the 1-

Table 1
Mean and F Ratios (or t values) for Original Learning,
1-Year and 5-Year Retention

Measure	Original Learning	1-Year Retention	5-Year Retention	F (Original Learning/ 1-Year)	t** (Original Learning/ 5-Year)
Trials to Criterion	27.00 (26.09)*	11.80 (14.31)	11.91	(66.55)	5.26
Manipulation Errors to Criterion	37.09 (33.47)	7.50 (6.18)	3.27	(66.16)	2.80
Discrimination Errors to Criterion	37.45 (35.05)	7.30 (9.21)	12.55	(95.53)	n.s.

*Numbers in parentheses are for all subjects in original and 1-year retention studies.
**Comparisons are between current performance and performance of the same subjects on original learning.

and 5-year retention interval suggests that the material was as available 6 years after training as after 1 year. It might be argued that the retraining after 1-year complicates the interpretation of these data.

In addition to remembering the overall task (trials) and hand manipulations, the subjects also showed strong retention of the correct response to the expression "Try another way" and demonstrated the proper use of the acquisition tray. Upon entering the room and seeing the acquisition tray with the brakes in it, one subject exclaimed, "The bicycle brakes!" He then sat down, picked up the first two parts, held one of them in his hand, looked at it and said, "Try another way," turned the part over, and installed it correctly on the axle.

Although the size of the sample in the present study is small, it seems appropriate to assume some generalizability of these results in light of the degree to which the subjects typify the larger group of individuals in the original study of which these subjects were part. The means listed in parentheses in Table 1 are for all subjects in the original and 1-year retention studies. The means listed to the left, not in parentheses, represent the means for the 11 present subjects in the original study and the 1-year retention study. As can be seen, their performance almost exactly matched the means for the entire subject population for all measures.

An extremely interesting aspect of the present data is the performance of those individuals who, prior to the present study, worked only with the color-form brake. Mean discrimination errors to criterion for the 11 subjects was 12.55. For the five subjects who had always worked with the form-only brake the mean was 11.20, and for the subjects who had previously worked only with the color-form brake the mean was 13.67, almost the same. For the same subjects on discrimination errors to criterion on the 1-year retention study the means were 10.80 for the Form-Only Group and 3.80 for the Color-Form Group, where each group was working with the brake that those subjects had learned previously. It appears that the color-form subjects utilized the cue redundancy available for the 1-year retention study but, in its absence, performed as well as the form-only subjects for the 5-year study.

This is especially interesting in light of previous efforts, utilizing the same task, to find ways of removing the cue redundancy (Gold, 1974). In that study, 36 adolescent and adult sheltered workshop clients each received one of three different procedures for removing the color cue. No significant difference was found between procedures. In addition, trials to criterion approached trials to criterion for the form-only subjects in the original study. Alternatively stated, the use and subsequent removal of a cue redundancy took approximately the same number of trials as if the cue redundancy had not been used at all. Since three rather different procedures for removing the color cue were tried, the data were interpreted to suggest that color coding is an effective means for teaching a task, but in those cases where the color coding has to be removed, it would be just as efficient not to use it at all.

Apparently, there was at least one other procedure that we did not try in the 1974 study: Teach the task using color; wait 5 years, and then retrain without the color. In the redundant cue removal study (Gold, 1974) one group (complete removal) was brought to criterion on the color-form brake, then on the form-only brake. This was the same as for subjects in the present study who previously had the color-form brake, except for the 5-year interval and the 1-year retraining in between. They performed as follows: Mean trials to criterion, 32.33; mean manipulation errors to criterion, 10.08; and mean discrimination errors to criterion, 35.16. The group of six subjects in the present study who previously had experience only on the color-form brake had present means of 12.16, 4.83, and 13.67, respectively. Combining these with means for the present subjects for original learning (color-form to criterion, 1968, plus form-only to criterion, 1974) we get the following means: trials to criterion, 32.49; manipulation errors to criterion, 46.66; and discrimination errors to criterion, 38.00. Their performance was almost identical to the Complete Removal Group for those dependent measures which reflect the effects of the cue redundancy (trials and discrimination errors to criterion). These data reflect a surprising stability. Using mean trials to criterion to exemplify this stability, we find the following: form-only (original study), 33.00; color-form, then form-only (Complete Removal Group of cue removal study), 32.33; and color-form, 1-year retraining, then 5-year retraining with form-only (present study), 32.49.

Another interesting aspect of the data involves time to criterion. There were no data on time to criterion for the original study or the 1-year retention study; however, comparisons can be made to the production studies done by using subjects from the original study (none of the present subjects), working on the same tasks (Gold, 1973). Gold reported a mean hourly production rate of 24.90 for subjects working 1 hour per day for 10 days, and 20.35 brakes per hour for subjects working 3 hours per day for 10 days. Production data were collected by using subjects who had already reached criterion on the task. A mean production rate of 24.90 brakes per hour yields a mean time per brake assembly of 2.40 minutes; and for a mean hourly production rate of 20.35 brakes per hour, there is a mean per unit time of 2.95 minutes per brake. The mean time per assembly for the present study was 2.88 minutes. While direct comparisons between acquisition and production are not possible, these data strongly suggest that the subjects in the present study, in addition to showing strong retention effects for the quality of their performance, were also performing at a rate (quantity) consistent with the production rate of their peers who produced the assembly shortly after reaching criterion in the original study.

CONCLUSIONS

The data presented here represent another example of the competencies of the moderately and severely retarded. Their ability to retain the necessary skills to perform a difficult assembly task was clearly demonstrated. Support was also evidenced for retention of rate of assembly. The present data were compared with several other studies for trials, discrimination errors, elimination of the cue redundancy, and rate. These comparisons show an extremely stable performance across subjects and studies, suggesting that acquisition and retention capabilities of the moderately and severely retarded, as demonstrated by these studies, can be expected.*

POSTSTATEMENT

We submitted this study to the *American Journal of Mental Deficiency*. It was rejected for methodological reasons. At the time of rejection I had mixed feelings. Although I believed this was an important study which would be useful to the field, I did not feel qualified to contest the judgment of the reviewers regarding methodological problems with the study. In any case, I reread it for possible inclusion in this book, and I feel comfortable publishing it here. I would be happy to discuss the study with readers who have questions regarding its relevance to their own interests.

*This study was supported in part by NICHHD Program Project Grant No. HD05951 to Institute for Child Behavior and Development, University of Illinois at Urbana-Champaign.

CHAPTER 21

Task Analysis of a Complex Assembly Task by the Retarded Blind

Marc W. Gold

PRESTATEMENT

This experiment attempted to directly test the system of instruction that was developing within our research program. This clearly involved a test of the concept of power and the loop system of revising training decisions as a function of the existing interactions between training procedures and learner performance. This was also the first time that a description of our task analysis system appeared in the literature.

The research program in which the present study was conducted has documented the capabilities of moderately and severely retarded individuals to learn and to produce on complex tasks (e.g., Gold, 1972; Gold & Barclay, 1973; Gold, 1974; and Merwin, 1974). Individuals with physical, aural, emotional, neurological, and language handicaps, in addition to their mental retardation, have also participated.

The most important product of this research program is a system for training called *task analysis*. In order to validate and expand this particular system, two lines of application are being pursued. The first is to apply the system to a different task: electronic printed circuit board assemblies (Merwin, 1973, 1974; Levy, Pomerantz, & Gold, 1977). The second application is to a population more difficult to train than those with whom the system was developed. The populations chosen for this are the severely and profoundly retarded blind and deaf-blind.

Historically, blind retarded individuals have been among the most ignored individuals in institutions and agencies serving the retarded. Perusal of the vocational training literature revealed no description of programs or research for this population. The present study was a first step in the development of a skill training program. The working hypotheses were that: (a) blind retarded individuals could be taught to assemble one of the tasks used in research with

Reprinted from *Exceptional Children* by Marc W. Gold by permission of The Council for Exceptional Children. Copyright 1976 by The Council for Exceptional Children, 1920 Association Drive, Reston, Virginia 22091.

sighted retarded individuals; (b) specific training techniques for the present population could be developed using the task analysis system which was generated from our work with sighted retarded persons; and (c) commitment to a zero-reject model would result in all subjects reaching criterion on the task.

TASK ANALYSIS

Definition

Task analysis is defined here as all the activity which results in there being sufficient power for the learner to acquire the task. *Power* refers to the strategies and procedures the trainer must use in order for the learner to acquire the task. The concept of power is intended to give the trainer responsibility for the student's reaching criterion. The more difficult it is for someone to learn a task, the more power the trainer must use. The data described in this study expand the boundary conditions of this statement. The term *task analysis* is used differently in various situations by different task analysts. The particular form of task analysis described here has been designed specifically for developing training procedures for the moderately retarded, severely and profoundly retarded, and multiply handicapped. It should be noted that where the term task analysis is used in this article, it refers to this specific form of task analysis. This article describes the basic structure of this particular task analysis system and validates its usefulness and power using data from work with the severely and profoundly retarded blind and deaf-blind.

Components

There are three major components in task analysis: method, content, and process. These components are employed in 7 phases.

Phase 1.

Method refers to the way in which the task is to be performed. There are several different methods, for example, of putting on a coat. One is to start by inserting an arm into a sleeve and bringing the coat around to the other side; a different method starts by placing the coat on the table, inserting the arms into the armholes of the coat, and then bringing the arms up and dropping the coat over the head. For production-line tasks there are almost always numerous alternatives for how the job is designed, each one being a different method.

For a particular task a subjective decision is made by the person doing the task analysis (task analyst) as to which method, of the methods available, is the best one. The alternative methods considered are a function of the creativity and experience of the task analyst. It is usually considered more difficult to identify alternatives with familiar than unfamiliar tasks. For example, when designing a task analysis for putting on a coat, care must be taken not to restrict the alternatives to the method which the task analyst uses for putting on his own coat. With an unfamiliar task such as the assembly of a milking machine pump, however, the task analyst has no preconceived method and so can explore alternatives without prejudice.

In a task analysis, a statement regarding the method should be used only in those cases where it adds clarity to the analysis. For example, a task analysis on the use of a knife and fork might include a statement that the European method will be used. Anyone knowing the European method will immediately know how the knife and fork are to be positioned. In most instances, however, the method is described through the content task analysis.

Phase 2.

Content refers to the steps into which the method is divided. Content is what the learner acquires or is expected to do. *Content task analysis* means breaking a task down into teachable components. *Teachable* refers to a judgment made by the task analyst regarding the size of the components into which the task will be divided. Procedures for correcting inappropriate decisions here are described in Phase 6. In a content task analysis the steps are numbered and described in detail. The content task analysis is similar to a set of instructions that one might obtain with something that was purchased unassembled. The description of the steps, however, are only for the trainer's understanding. Nothing is mentioned in the content task analysis regarding the trainer function or the interaction between the trainer and the learner. What the trainer does is described in the process task analysis.

Phase 3.

Process refers to the way in which the task is taught. *Process task analysis*, which means designing strategies for teaching the content, has three subdivisions: format, feedback, and procedure.

Format refers to the presentation of the content. Examples of format for single pieces of learning include match-to-sample, which consists of presenting an object (stimulus) and having the learner select the one that matches from a group of objects (response), and oddity, where the learner selects the one that does not match from a group of objects. Examples of format for multiple pieces of learning include: backward chaining, where the last part of the task is taught until the learner knows it, then the next to the last part, and so on, until the entire task is learned; forward chaining, where the first part of the task is taught until the learner knows it, then the next part along with the first part, and so on until the entire task has been learned; and total task presentation, where the learner performs the entire task every trial and where errors and assistance diminish over trials until the task has been learned.

Feedback refers to how the learner knows what is wanted and if he is achieving it. Feedback concerns the way in which the trainer provides the learner with information that is conveyed to the learner prior, during, or subsequent to action by the learner. Examples of broad categories of feedback would include stimulus control procedures, where the emphasis is on the organization of materials and environments in advance of learner behavior (e.g., Gold & Scott, 1971; Gold, 1972; Merwin, 1974; and Zeaman, 1965); reinforcement control procedures, which emphasize positive, negative, or neutral consequences following action by the learner (e.g., Gardner, 1971; Kazdin, 1973); and the perspective of the information theorists related to knowledge of results, which conceptualizes feedback as much more than the elevation or reduction of need states (e.g., Holding, 1965). From this last perspective, reinforcement is one subcategory of feedback.

Feedback, both in terms of instructions and consequences, may be verbal or nonverbal. Verbal feedback, especially in terms of instructions, is efficient, when it works. That is, telling someone what is wanted of him is usually much faster than showing him or manipulating his hands. For some learners, however, limitations in language skills restrict the amount of information obtainable through language. The use of verbal consequences, in the form of information provided after action on the part of the learner, or verbal reinforcement, is suspect with these learners for the same reason. Examples of nonverbal feedback include color-coding (Gold, 1972, 1974); fading (Dweck, 1975; Gold & Scott, 1971); imitation (Steinman, 1970); direct manipulation; and silence (Gold, 1975a).

In a task analysis general statements regarding feedback are given. Examples of such statements include: "Try another way," "The flat part goes up," and "Pick it up here." The entire task will be demonstrated once by the trainer; the learner will be allowed to select one reinforcer from among a group of them at the end of each training session. The general strategy for integrating feedback and content is described in the procedure.

Procedure refers to a description of the proposed training plan. The intention of the procedure section is to provide the trainer with sufficient description of the interaction between content and process so that he can proceed. The procedure section includes a description of the first actions of the trainer. For example: The trainer points to the first part; if the learner does not reach out and take the part, the trainer takes the learner's left hand and places it on the part. The section obviously cannot detail the entire training situation, but it can indicate how the feedback procedures will be used with the content of the task so that the trainer will understand how to implement the task analysis.

Two other aspects of task analysis need to be mentioned in this brief description. One is criterion; the other is data collection. *Criterion* is defined as an arbitrary predetermined point at which it is assumed learning has taken place. Criterion for any piece of learning should be repeated observation of the behavior under the conditions where it is ultimately expected to occur. Criterion should be based on characteristics of the task and the conditions under which the learned behavior is to be demonstrated. Criterion for brushing teeth, for example, should be x consecutive correct trials, at home or wherever the learner brushes his teeth, independent of prompts or assistance. Until the learner meets this second criterion, meaningful learning cannot be assumed.

Data collection should be an integral part of any training session. The data collection form used in our research consists of rows and columns. Each row represents one trial (one completed cycle of all the steps of the task). The columns represent the steps into which the task has been divided; that is, each column corresponds to one step in the content task analysis.

The data collection form should also include the name of the individual being trained and additional columns for the date of each session and anecdotal information which might be of interest and which would not otherwise be shown on the data collection form. Time is also very useful information. For the tasks used in our research, plus (+) and minus (–) signs are used to describe learner performance on each step. Decisions are made in advance of training regarding what will be accepted as a plus for any particular step of the task. Inspection of the data forms provides a clear picture of the learner's activities. Examination of the rows shows how the learner is doing at any point on the entire task. Examination of the columns indicates which particular steps the learner is having difficulty with and shows progress for particular steps of the task.

Phase 4.

When Phases 1 through 3 are completed, training is begun. What happens when a task analysis has been done, people have been trained, and some of them have not learned the task? Table 1 shows the seven-phase sequence developed to maximize the probability that all learners will reach criterion.

Phase 5.

The decision to move to Phase 5 (or 6 or 7) is based on the judgment of the trainer. The decision is that for a particular learner or group of learners, the initial task analysis has insufficient power for criterion to be reached. A decision to go to Phase 5 generates the following questions: (a) Should a different format be tried? (If the original task analysis calls for the use of a total task format, for example, changing to a backward or forward chaining format might facilitate learning.) (b) What are some other kinds of feedback that might be used? (If visual discriminations were being taught by using only the expression "Try another way," other verbal cues such as "Try another way," or "The flat part goes up" might be tried.) Phase 5 should result in an increased number of individuals who reach criterion.

Table 1
The Seven-Phase Sequence for a Complete Task Analysis

Phase 1.	Decide on method.
Phase 2.	Do a content task analysis.
Phase 3.	Do a process task analysis.
Phase 4.	Begin training.
	When a decision has been made that the task analysis needs revision, go to Phase 5.
Phase 5.	Re-do the process task analysis.
	If more is needed, go to Phase 6.
Phase 6.	Re-do the content task analysis.
	If more is needed, go to Phase 7.
Phase 7.	Re-do the method.

Phase 6.

A decision to move to Phase 6 generates the following question: How can those steps which are not being learned be further subdivided into teachable components? If one step of the task is "Pick up the sock," this might be subdivided into "Point to the end of the sock that has the hole," "Insert thumb into hole," "Grasp sock by bringing forefinger down on outside of sock," "Lift sock." Phase 6 should result in a further increase in the number of individuals who reach criterion.

Phase 7.

A decision to move to Phase 7 generates the following question: Is there a different way to do the task or that particular part of the task with which the learners are having difficulty? In making a bed, for example, one can unfold the top sheet, then thrust it across the bed. An alternative method might include placing systematically prefolded top sheets at the foot of the bed, at one corner, with the folds of the sheet being in a specific orientation so that the sheet unfolds into its proper position on the bed. Phase 7 requires a return to Phase 2 (content task analysis) and might require changes in feedback (Phase 3). It should be noted that for any given task many methods are probably available and for each method the extent of the possible content task analysis is considerable; that is, almost any step can be further subdivided.

The 7-phase sequence can provide a training situation where failure is the most difficult task of all. The data presented in the next section of this article are intended to provide some initial validation of this system.

METHOD

Subjects

Subjects were 22 moderately, severely, and profoundly retarded blind and deaf-blind individuals living in a cottage at a large institution. Table 2 presents descriptive data for the population.

Materials

The training apparatus was a 15-inch by 45-inch tray containing 14 compartments, 1 for each part of the task. The dividers between each compartment were 1 inch high. A 1/2-inch divider ran parallel to the front of the tray, 3 inches back. The purpose of this divider was to separate the parts that were being used for a trial from the parts to be used in subsequent trials. The production apparatus was a Sempco #1424 Bench Frame, which contained sufficient bins to house quantities of each part. The unit was typical of those found in factories where bench assembly work is done. In addition to the bins, boards with 25 7/16-inch holes were used to hold the assembled units. The task was a 14-part Bendix, Model 70, coaster brake.

Table 2
Description, Acquisition, and Production Data

Subject Number	IQ	Disability[a]	Sex	Age	Length of Institutionalization	Trials	Production/Hour	Total Production Errors	Percentage of Errors
1	33	t	M	22	7	34(22)	17.2	1	6
2	32	t	M	43	38	23	15.7	6	3.8
3	42	t	M	31	14	28	15.4	3	1.9
4	40	t	M	29	23	9	16.6	0	0
5	14	ld	M	37	34	22(13)	12.4	10	8.1
6	33	t	F	27	21	23	13.3	22	16.5
7	41	t	M	45	13	17	14.5	4	2.8
8	28	ldp	M	22	16	20	13.7	0	0
9	31	l	M	27	14	94(42)	13.2	4	3.0
10	45	tp	F	22	9	69(31)	10.8	4	3.7
11	52	t	M	22	9	111(27)	9.7	0	0
12	32	t	F	33	28	49(15)	11.6	3	2.8
13	38	tp	M	27	22	194(75)	10.6	3	6.1
14	48	t	M	43	36	26	4.9	3	1.0
15	23	td	M	20	11	57(39)	9.7	1	5.7
16	17	t	F	29	12	191	12.3	7	5.6
17	47	t	F	72	53	105(63)	7.1	4	4.6
18	20	t	F	15	9	42	15.2	7	2.3
19	25	t	F	38	31	32	17.4	4	8.0
20	14	l	M	24	10	38	12.8	1	2.3
21	22	t	M	56	42	63	8.6	2	7.2
22	27	t	M	42	26	72	9.7	7	7.2
Mean	32			33	21.73	59.95	12.38	4.23	4.15

[a]The codes for the disabilities are as follows: t = totally blind, l = legally blind, d = deaf, and p = physically handicapped.

Trainers

One trainer worked throughout the study. A second trainer left the project after several weeks and was replaced by a third trainer. All three were first-line service personnel in the cottage. They received 2 days of training at the Institute for Child Behavior and Development. The project director spent 2 days per month at the project site providing further training, supervision, and assistance as problems developed. Frequent telephone communication was also used. The initial task analysis was done by the project director. Phases 5, 6, and 7 were done by the trainers with assistance from the project director.

General Procedure

Each subject was seated at a table on which the tray was placed, with four disassembled units in the compartments. The experimenter was seated to the left of the subject. No demonstration procedure was used, as was the case in previous studies with sighted individuals (Gold, 1972). The subject's left hand was placed on the first part and moved forward to the front of the tray. Then each subsequent part was picked up and moved to the front of the tray so that one complete set of 14 parts was at the front of the tray prior to beginning assembly. As each subsequent part was moved forward, the trainer provided less manual assistance than the time before, but enough so that the part was placed properly, until the subject set up the tray independently. In some cases this required several trials. One complete assembly of the brake constituted a trial. Errors made during the setup were corrected with direct manual assistance and were not recorded. For assembly, discrimination errors (putting a part on upside down) were corrected by using the expression "Try another way." Subjects who did not respond appropriately to this feedback were then given simultaneous manual assistance, which was faded until the verbal feedback alone facilitated the correct response. For the deaf subjects (deaf-blind) a gentle squeeze of the left wrist was used in place of the verbal feedback. When the error was corrected, the expression "Good" was used for hearing subjects. For deaf (deaf-blind) subjects no feedback was used following a correction. Manipulation errors (not fitting a part correctly) were corrected by manipulating the subject's hands into the proper position. No other feedback was used following such a correction. At the end of each trial the trainer said "Good" to the hearing subjects and touched the shoulder of the deaf-blind subjects.

The procedures followed for correcting persistent errors were developed in Phases 5, 6, and 7 of the 7-phase sequence. These procedures will be described in the results section because of the complex interaction in this study between procedures and results.

Criterion was six correct out of eight consecutive trials. Following criterion each subject produced 1 hour per day for 10 days using the production bins. Production differed from acquisition in several ways. There was no direct supervision during production. Subjects worked independently for the hour.

Errors during acquisition consisted of any incorrect part or placement. For production, an error consisted of an inappropriately assembled brake. Prior to the start of production, subjects were brought to a criterion of two consecutive correct assemblies on the production bins. No feedback on productivity was provided. The only external reinforcement was a "Thank you" or pat on the shoulder at the end of each session. Following each production period the trainer counted the completed assemblies. Errors were counted and recorded as the trainer diassembled the brakes, which was done in the absence of subjects so as to avoid motivational problems which might result from individuals' being aware that their work was undone.

RESULTS

Acquisition

Acquisition data are shown in Table 2. Training procedures were modified throughout the study. Consequently, performance will be described relevant to each of these modifications. Subjects were numbered according to their entrance into the study. Subject numbers also represent the descending relative capabilities of the subjects, as subjectively determined by cottage staff. The trainers were instructed to begin with the most capable individuals in the cottage and to work toward the more difficult to train as the study progressed. As seen in Table 2, IQ apparently was not the variable used to make these decisions.

The first three subjects, those perceived as the most capable prior to training, began their training using the procedures developed by Gold (1972). All three subjects had difficulty seating (correctly positioning) one particular piece, the arm, a part of the task that required increasing amounts of trainer attention as the study progressed. Subjects also had considerable difficulty with the series of steps involved in installing and seating the two shoes in the hub. Several verbal cues were developed to provide additional feedback for discrimination errors (Phase 5). For example, the trainer said, "Feel this and this," touching the subject's finger to the two surfaces that needed to be joined. There was also some further subdivision of some of the steps (Phase 6). For example, what had been one step became a series of steps. Each of the three subjects benefited from these modifications and reached criterion.

Prior to training Subject 4, a decision was made to change the method for inserting the shoes (Phase 7). A content task analysis was done on the new method for assembling these parts. With these changes made, Subjects 4 through 12 were trained. Subjects 4 through 8 reached criterion in 9, 22, 23, 17, and 20 trials, respectively. Subjects 9 through 12, however, took many more trials to reach criterion. The numbers presented in parentheses (Table 2) for these subjects reflect what their trials to criterion would have been had they not had difficulty seating the arm. As can be seen, this problem accounted for a considerable amount of training time. A decision was made to redo the content task analysis for seating the arm while Subjects 11 and 12 were still in training. Subject 12 was given the new procedure, starting at

Trial 43. From that point, Subject 12 made no further errors and went to criterion. Subject 11 was shown the new procedure at Trial 34 but took 111 trials to reach criterion. Examination of the data collection form for this subject revealed two points of interest. First, there were days when the subject refused to work, and consequently there were several lengthy periods during which time the subject did not receive training. Second, following Trial 49, seating of the arm was the only problem keeping the subject from criterion. For this subject, redoing the content task analysis for seating the arm obviously did not facilitate learning.

At the time Subject 13 began his training, the content task analysis consisted of 34 steps, the method for inserting the shoes had been changed, and it was clear that subjects were continuing to have difficulty seating the arm, even though that part of the task had received further analysis.

Subject 13 presented many problems during training. His hands were very stiff to work with; he cried a great deal; during the 17th session, he became very upset, and he once tried to overturn the table on which the tray was placed. After 75 trials, the only mistakes involved seating of the arm. While Subject 13 continued training, alternative methods were being explored to solve this problem. A new method was developed, a content task analysis was done on the new method, and Subject 13 was given the new procedure beginning with Trial 133. Subject 13 made two more seating errors using the new method. No more errors were made on that part of the task. However, discrimination errors on other parts of the task began to recur. Subject 13 reached criterion at 194 trials.

The data collection form for Subject 14 had numerous inconsistencies, suggesting interpretation problems not related to the performance of the learner, who did reach criterion. The data are reported for Subject 14, but because of their probable invalidity, they are not included in the group analyses. After 39 trials, Subject 15 was making errors only on steps of the task related to seating the arm. Criterion was reached on Trial 57.

Subject 16 required 191 trials to reach criterion. She was introduced to the new method of seating the arm on Trial 45. Although very few errors were made on this part of the task, following Trial 45, she continued to have numerous problems on all parts of the task. Examination of the data collection form for this subject shows very slow continuous growth throughout the training period.

Subject 17 was trained using the old method of seating the arm. This was an oversight since the new method was available. Table 2 shows that she reached criterion in 105 trials, but following Trial 63, errors were made only on those parts of the task involved with seating the arm.

Subjects 18, 19, and 20 began training using the new method for seating the arm. The content task analysis at this point consisted of 37 steps. These subjects had no problem seating the arm and reached criterion in 42, 32, and 38 trials, respectively.

Subject 21 was extremely difficult to train. The trainer had to rely almost exclusively on verbal assistance at the beginning of training because the subject did not like to be touched and would severely bite anyone who touched him. For the first seven sessions, when it was necessary for the trainer to touch the subject, she had to immediately jump away to avoid being severely bitten. The situation was further complicated in that when the subject could not bite the person who touched him, he would bite himself. During Session 8 this behavior ceased, and from that point normal training procedures could be used. Following Trial 46 this subject went home for a 1-month vacation. Training began upon his return, and criterion was reached in 63 trials.

Subject 22 reached criterion in 72 trials. His pattern of errors indicated no problems with any particular part of the task. The only modification in procedure for this subject was the dispensing of a cigar following each training session.

Production

Production data are shown in Table 2. Mean individual hourly production rate was 12.38 brakes per hour (range = 7.1 to 17.4 brakes per hour). Four subjects made no errors during production. Mean percent error rate was 4.15% with a range of 0 to 16.5%. Subjects 16 and 20 required some supervision during production because of occasionally reaching for the wrong part and then being confused. This problem was not resolved during the 10 hours of production for these two subjects. Hourly rate data for Subject 21 are extrapolated from half-hour sessions.

DISCUSSION

All three hypotheses were supported, and the following generalizations were drawn from these data.

1. *The more difficult it is for a person to acquire a task, the more the trainer must know about the task.* Examination of the data, both within and between subjects, clearly shows performance to be highly affected by the training procedures. When subjects had difficulty acquiring certain parts of the task, further inspection of the task, rather than the subject, provided solutions. Diagnostic and evaluative information regarding the subjects were irrelevant. Information about each subject, directly related to performance on the task, was obtained during training rather than prior to training (Gold, 1975b).

This assumption was tested using some of the subjects from the present study. In March, 1974, people in the United States found it difficult to obtain gasoline. A company which manufactured locking gas caps received orders for very large quantities of its product. The management recruited assistance from local sheltered workshops in producing the gas caps. At one workshop several mildly retarded sighted individuals received 2 full days of training but could not complete the task. Two of the trainers who participated in the present study task analyzed the locking gas caps and trained two blind subjects who had reached criterion on the bicycle brake (Subjects 3 and 4) to criterion on the caps. Time to criterion for each was less than 2 hours.

Using the task analysis developed by the two trainers, the workshop staff were able to bring to criterion the two individuals who had previously not been able to learn the task, and other individuals in the workshop. Attention to the *task* provided the key to the locking gas caps. In addition, all the individuals who at that time had participated in the present study were trained and they produced, for remuneration, the locking gas caps.

2. *The more the task analyst knows about the task, the fewer prerequisites are needed by the learner.* This study began training the most capable individuals. Their capabilities might be described in terms of (untested) prerequisites such as verbal skills, social interaction skills, coordination, and other assets which the trainers believed would make them the easiest subjects to train and which would require the least amount of power from the trainer.

Adherence to the zero-reject model necessitated the development of increasingly powerful training procedures in the absence of subject failure as an available alternative. This approach was successfully applied to the locking gas cap contract, to mobility training, and to dressing and bedmaking. There is no attempt here to suggest that all things can be taught to all people. A commitment to the zero-reject model, however, should significantly increase the willingness of staff to train the severely handicapped to do things not previously attempted, especially since success and failure from this perspective reflect trainer competencies rather than subject competencies. This strategy is also seen as increasing the probability that staff will avail themselves of more instructional technology.

3. *The decision to teach or not teach any task to the severely and profoundly handicapped must be based on whether or not that task can be analyzed into teachable components, rather than on some general feeling about the difficulty of the task.* There are no systems in existence for measuring in an absolute way the difficulty of a task (Cronbach, 1957). The most notable attempts to devise a system for assessing task difficulty can be found in the *Human Factors* literature (e.g., Fitts, 1951; Nickerson, 1965). Nickerson makes it clear that a measurement for task difficulty is yet to be developed.

In the absence of a system for measuring task difficulty the present data must be described subjectively in terms of their relevance to other tasks. What they suggest is that many tasks previously thought to be beyond the capabilities of the severely handicapped can probably be taught by using our task analysis system. Before this study was done, the cottage employed a full-time person to handle clothing for the residents. Since that time the position has been eliminated, closets have been installed for each resident, and residents are now responsible for taking care of their own clothing. Until this project began, all subjects went from place to place within the institution only under the supervision and leadership of a staff member. Mobility procedures were developed by using the task analysis system described, and presently more than half of the residents move independently from place to place within the institution. According to the cottage staff, demonstration of competence to assemble the bicycle brakes and locking gas caps provided a modification in staff expectancy which was necessary before training on these other behaviors was attempted. Successful performance on the bicycle brakes facilitated a positive change in the abilities of the residents, as perceived by staff, providing the motivation to attempt training the residents on tasks that had previously been perceived as too difficult (Gold, 1975a).

Changes in Data
Collection Procedures

This study, in addition to the assumptions generated, produced several meaningful changes in our data collection procedures. Early in the study it became evident that the data collection procedures used previously were inadequate. The more difficult it is to train someone, the less likely it is that the trainer's hands are available to record data. A procedure was instituted which required one trainer to train and a second person to record data. Recently this system was replaced by the use of a video recording system. With individuals who are difficult to train, some of the most meaningful data are not easily recorded using a conventional data collection form. Changes in self-destructive behavior and vocalizations, for example, are difficult to record simultaneously with changes in performance related directly to the task. It is also of considerable use to have visual documentation of progress and nonprogress when reanalysis through Phases 5, 6, and 7 is necessary.

In the present study *trials to criterion* was the only dependent measure for acquisition. Previous studies also used errors to criterion and, in some cases, time to criterion. The difficulty of data collection in the present study made reliable measures for time and errors difficult to obtain during the early stages of each subject's training. With the use of the video system, however, reliable measures for errors and time can be taken throughout training and consequently will be more systematically analyzed in future studies.

Interaction between Subject
Performance and Procedures

Perhaps the most interesting aspect of this study is the interaction which developed over the course of the study between subject performance and procedures. The study began with the most capable subjects and proceeded through to the least capable subjects. Subjects 1 through 8, viewed as a group, show rather homogeneous performance. Subjects 9 through 13 show homogeneity and, collectively, required considerably more training than the first group. Subjects 18 through 21, initially perceived as the most limited individuals in the study, learned the task in a manner not dissimilar from those subjects initially perceived as the most capable subjects. This obviously reflects significant increases in the power of the training procedures as the study progressed. If this finding generalizes to other tasks and other learners, it calls for a reconceptualization of the severely handicapped as individuals who require powerful training procedures in order to learn, rather than the present conceptualization which considers them as individuals who can learn very little.

Procedures used for production by the present subjects were not changed from the procedures used previously with sighted subjects (Gold, 1973). Mean hourly productivity for 1-hour production in that study was 24.90 brakes. For the present study the mean was almost exactly half that rate, 12.38 brakes per hour. Error rate in the previous study, for 1-hour production, was 6.30%, as compared to 4.15% for the present study. While there were numerous differences between the two subject populations, observation of production by the subjects in the present study suggests that their lower productivity resulted from problems of searching for parts in the production bins. For the present subjects, the conditions where the behavior was ultimately expected to occur (production) apparently presented problems not resolved by training to criterion in acquisition. Some analysis of the use of the production bins might significantly increase productivity. These data emphasize the importance of the second part of the definition of criterion mentioned earlier. This distinction between the learning environment and the doing environment probably takes on increasing importance as the difficulties of the learner in acquiring the task increase.

CONCLUSIONS

The basic structure of a system of analyzing tasks has been described. The many alternatives for each decision point within that structure were suggested but were not described in detail. Data were presented which demonstrated that people who have always been considered extremely difficult to train reached criterion on and produced a complex assembly task.

The results were presented as continuous, systematic interaction between performance and procedures. It is this interaction that distinguishes this system from most others currently utilized to train the severely handicapped. The results provide considerable motivation for this system to be applied, validated, and used with other tasks and other individuals and populations, and by other personnel.*

POSTSTATEMENT

I do not remember exactly when our group first used the expression *task analysis* to describe our own particular system of developing a training plan. The expression was used in a more general sense throughout the previous

---

*This project was supported in part by NICHHD Program Project Grant No. HD-05951 to Institute for Child Behavior and Development, University of Illinois at Urbana-Champaign and SRS Grant No. 54-P-71084/5 to Dixon State School (Dixon Developmental Center).

Appreciation is expressed to Anna Jeanblanc and Joanne Tornow, trainers, and to Roger C. Hoffman, Director, Unit X, Dixon Developmental Center, Dixon, Illinois.

articles in this book. Sometime after the film *Try Another Way** came out, we began to refer to the entire philosophical and technical package as the Try Another Way System, with task analysis being the term applied to the technical portion of it.

The term *zero-reject model* was used in this publication. The term generally means that a school setting has established a policy of accepting into its program any child, regardless of the severity of handicap. In this article the term was used to mean a commitment that once a subject had entered training, that training would not stop until the learner had reached criterion on the task. Because of the nature of the population used in this study, this was a significant commitment. As mentioned in the article, this proved to be a strong point. A prime reason for every subject in the study reaching criterion on the task was the commitment on the part of the trainer not to stop training, under any conditions, until criterion had been reached.

As of January, 1980, the technical part of the Try Another Way System was revised. A few concepts and strategies presented in this article have changed. The *method* is no longer considered a major component of the system but is considered a subdivision of the *content task analysis*. What we had for years called *feedback* was replaced by the term *trainer action*. The term feedback had always been confusing. The procedure section of the task analysis, originally a description of the proposed training plan, was replaced by presenting the content task analysis on the left side of the page and the trainer action on the right side. Therefore, the proposed training plan is specified within that split-page approach.

The general procedure section mentions that the bicycle brakes were disassembled at the end of each session. Remember that this was research rather than production. Rarely would the circumstance justify people in sheltered workshops or work activity centers being kept busy by one group assembling something and another group taking it apart. In most instances this is a distasteful practice.

This study very much helped to crystalize the task analysis part of the Try Another Way System. Having experimentally validated the system with people having severe and profound handicapping conditions, we then had the confidence to use the system in less controlled circumstances and to collect data in a much wider array of circumstances with a wider variety of people. The system has since continued to develop in terms of the technical components and in terms of validation. This carefully controlled experimental circumstance provided a strong base for proceeding with confidence.

---

*Glenn Roberts (Producer). *Try Another Way*. Indianapolis: Film Productions of Indianapolis, 1975.

CHAPTER 22

Task Analysis for Teaching 8 Practical Signs to Deaf-Blind Individuals

Marc W. Gold and Robert K. Rittenhouse

PRESTATEMENT

Bob Rittenhouse is a long-time professional in the area of services to the deaf-blind. He interrupted his service career to obtain a doctorate at the University of Illinois and as part of this was a student in the course that I taught on task analysis. This article began as his required work for that class. We reworked it, adding a beginning and an ending, and with the help of some of his friends, included illustrations.

There are approximately 6,000 deaf-blind children and young adults in the United States today (Dantona, 1976). Until recently, few of these individuals had been served in any meaningful way. Now, with the rapid increase in attention and commitment being given this population, programs are rapidly developing throughout the country. One significant contribution to this movement was the development by the Bureau of Education for the Handicapped of 10 regional centers to create and improve services for deaf-blind children. Public schools, private nonprofit agencies, and institutions across the country, in cooperation with these regional centers, are beginning to respond.

The quality of these emerging programs will depend, in part, on the development of an instructional technology that can be used to educate and train this population. Such technology should ultimately lead to meaningful participation in society by the deaf-blind individual. In the absence of such a technology the present movement will be yet another example of "progressive status-quoism" (Farber & Lewis, 1972). Considerable resources will be expended in an attempt to show that a problem is being tackled, yet the problem will remain unsolved.

Recent research with the deaf-blind has shown them to be capable of

Reprinted from *Teaching Exceptional Children* by Marc W. Gold and Robert K. Rittenhouse by permission of The Council for Exceptional Children. Copyright 1978 by The Council for Exceptional Children, 1920 Association Drive, Reston, Virginia 22091.

doing complex assembly work (Gold, 1976). The same instructional technology used to teach assembly work is being used successfully to teach mobility skills to severely and profoundly retarded blind and deaf-blind individuals (Gold, unpublished). This technology is presented here as it applies to the teaching of signs. (We suggest reading Gold, 1976, as background information for a more thorough understanding of this article.)

The lessons described here can be taught by people with no knowledge of sign language and little formal training. Since it is this type of person who often works with deaf-blind individuals, this form of task analysis seems to have considerable application.

CONTENT OF THE LESSONS

The content of these lessons consists of the following eight signs: *toilet, enough, more, sit, stand, eat, drink,* and *stay.* These signs provide a vocabulary that will assist in the communication of the basic needs that emerge in day to day activities. The purpose of each lesson is for the learner to be able to associate and use the particular sign with the behavior.

These eight signs, and all subsequent signs that one might teach using this general format, should be taught in the normal setting where association will be directly related to the learner's interaction with his environment. This is important. For the individuals learning this kind of task, creating an artificial environment for the purpose of training will only serve to postpone the more important goal of generalizability of the learned sign to the relevant situations. Implicit in this statement is a careful scrutiny of the learner's daily activities so that at each opportune time the appropriate sign can be given by the trainer or expected from the learner. In each instance the sign is communicated from the trainer to the learner in a tactual manner. The trainer should initially have the learner feel the formation of the sign and then help the individual to make the sign.

CRITERION

Criterion will be reached when the learner responds correctly to the appropriate sign on six successive occasions without error or assistance. Correct responses are those instances when the learner displays the behavior associated with the sign that was given in the natural setting. *Learner/expressive-trainer/ receptive* signs are those that require spontaneous, noncued communication on the part of the deaf-blind individual. *Trainer/expressive-learner/receptive* signs are those that require appropriate response by the learner to the sign given by the trainer.

Trainer/expressive-learner/receptive signs will, in general, be learned more quickly than learner/expressive-trainer/receptive signs. Appropriate use of learner/expressive-trainer/receptive signs is sometimes difficult to measure. Frequently, the trainer must look for other cues which, in combination with the expressed sign, indicate that the learner has made the appropriate association.

FORMAT OF THE LESSONS

A total task format is used for the lessons. The format calls for the learner to go through the entire task every time, as opposed to a forward chaining procedure where the learner learns just the first part of the task and then the next part, or a backward chaining format where the learner learns the last part of the task first and then the next to last part, and so on. This format is appropriate because the various movements of the hand and their close association with the behavior cannot be simply subdivided into pieces that can be learned independently.

FEEDBACK

Feedback refers to how the trainer indicates to the learner how he is doing and what is expected of him. Information regarding errors of sign formation are presented by the trainer through direct manipulation of the learner's fingers. Out of sequence errors are corrected by starting the sign over. Exceptions are noted in the lessons. Reinforcement, a sub-category of feedback, is described in each individual lesson.

PROCEDURES

The signs for *enough* and *more* and the signs for *sit* and *stand* should be taught in sequence and *stay* should be taught last. The sign for *toilet* can be taught independently of the other signs.

Lesson 1: Toilet
(Trainer/expressive-learner/receptive)

Content (See Figure 1)

1. Lay the learner's preferred hand flat on a table or other surface, palm down.
2. Tuck his/her fingers into the palm of his/her hand, making a fist.
3. Place the learner's thumb between his index finger and middle finger and extend his thumb above the tucked fingers.
4. Shake the learner's hand back and forth in a horizontal plane several times.

Procedure

This sign should be taught in connection with toileting. An attempt should be made by the trainer to work on this sign immediately after meals, before bed, first thing in the morning, and at other appropriate times. At the beginning of training, an attempt should be made to manipulate the learner's hand in order to bring about the sign immediately prior to toileting. This might mean, initially, that the trip to the bathroom has already begun or that the learner is in the bathroom about to toilet. Later on in training, the sign should be given closer and closer to the time of initiating the move toward the toilet or the bathroom. Assistance in making the sign or initiating the sign should diminish over trials.

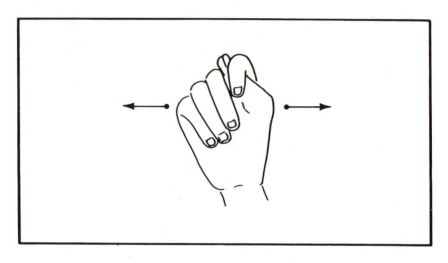

Figure 1. Toilet.

Lesson 2: Sit
(Trainer/expressive-learner/receptive)

Content (See Figure 2)

1. Lay both of the learner's hands flat on the surface, thumbs extended toward each other.
2. Tuck the thumb, little finger, and ring finger of each of his hands under so that the index finger and middle finger remain extended.
3. For each hand, the index finger and middle finger should be together.
4. Raise the learner's hands about 6 inches and point the two extended fingers to a 2 o'clock position.
5. Place the two extended fingers of the learner's right hand on top of the two extended fingers of his left hand at mid-knuckle and point them at approximately a 10 o'clock position.
6. Bend the learner's index finger and the middle finger of his right hand down.

Procedure

The sign *sit* should be taught where and when sitting is the logical thing to do. It is possible that the learner may not sit down when the trainer manipulates his hands through sign. If this occurs for what the trainer believes to be a legitimate reason, this should not be considered an error for purposes of determining criterion. During the early stages of teaching the sign, the trainer might assist the learner in sitting so he will connect the action to the sign. Care should be taken to make the assistance gentle and positive without arousing any negative feelings about the *sit* sign in particular or the use of signs in general.

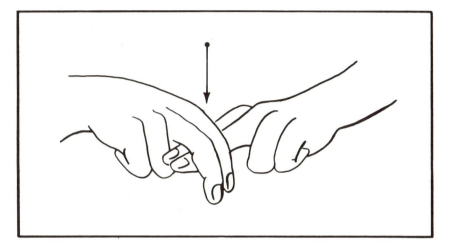

Figure 2. Sit.

Lesson 3: Stand
(Trainer/expressive-learner/receptive)

Content (See Figure 3)

1. Place the learner's nonpreferred hand on the table, palm up, fingers together, and thumb extended.

2. Raise the nonpreferred hand approximately 6 inches.

3. With the preferred hand next to the nonpreferred hand, palm down, make a V sign with the middle and forefinger of the learner's preferred hand, tucking the other three fingers into the palm.

4. Place the V into the palm of the learner's nonpreferred hand.

5. Raise the V so that it is standing, fingertips down, in the palm of the learner's nonpreferred hand.

Procedure

Follow the same procedure used for *sit*. The trainer should decide whether or not to teach the signs *sit* and *stand* in the same lesson at the same time. For some learners this would be helpful; for others it would get in the way of learning.

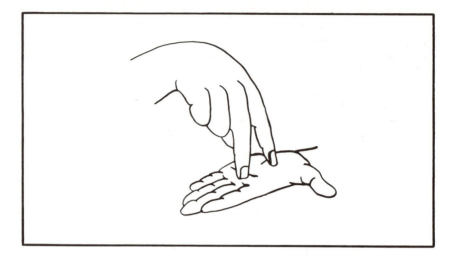

Figure 3. Stand.

Lesson 4: Eat
(Trainer/expressive-learner/receptive)

Content (See Figure 4)

1. Form a C with the learner's preferred hand. The C should be formed so that all four fingers are together forming the top of the C and the thumb forming the bottom.

2. Keeping his fingers together, touch the learner's thumb to his index finger.

3. Bring the learner's preferred hand to his mouth so that his fingertips touch his lips.

Procedure

This sign should be taught immediately prior to eating. The trainer may wish to use food as a reinforcer for the development of the sign. However, care should be taken not to fall into the habit of using strong reinforcements for teaching signs. Wherever possible, the power gained by the communication should serve as the reinforcement for learning the sign.

Lesson 5: Drink
(Trainer/expressive-individual/receptive)

Content (See Figure 5)

1. Form a C with the learner's preferred hand (same as for *eat*).

2. Place the C at waist or table top level, with the thumb-index finger side of the hand facing up.

3.   Raise the learner's hand to his mouth as if he were drinking from a glass.

Procedure

This sign can be taught around mealtime and throughout the day. Because drinking is an activity that takes place at various times, there is considerable latitude regarding appropriate times to teach this sign. The use of a drinking

Figure 4. Eat.

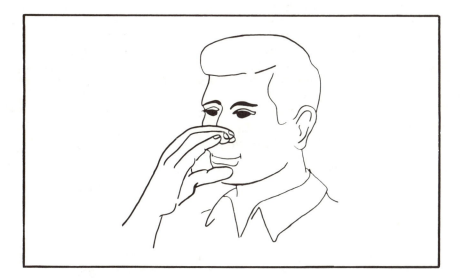

Figure 5. Drink.

fountain, a glass with various kinds of liquid, and other situations will help to teach the sign in a way that generalizes it to all drinking situations rather than to just one kind of drinking (i.e., out of a glass) and to various kinds of liquids rather than just one. The drink itself, in most cases, should be the only reinforcement necessary to provide motivation for learning the sign.

Lesson 6: More

This sign should be taught initially as a trainer/expressive-learner/receptive sign. After it has been learned it can also be used as a trainer/expressive-individual/receptive sign.

Content (See Figure 6)

1. Form a C with the learner's preferred hand (same as for *eat* and *drink*).

2. Keeping the fingers together, touch the learner's thumb to his index finger.

3. Form a C with the learner's nonpreferred hand, as in step 1.

4. Keeping the fingers together, touch the learner's thumb and index finger together as in step 2.

5. Bring both of the learner's hands together so that thumb/thumb, index finger/index finger, and middle finger/middle finger are touching.

Procedure

If these lessons are taught in the sequence suggested here, the learner has already acquired the skill of forming the C with the preferred hand. If this is the case it may be efficient to work on the formation of the C with the nonpreferred hand before putting the entire sign together. The trainer should record, initially, those instances during the day when the learner has the opportunity to use the sign *more* frequently. These opportunities might include finishing his meal, brushing his teeth, and other daily living activities and should also include tasks where the learner will find it very advantageous to learn the expression *more*, for example, for desserts or opportunities to use toys or at other relevant times.

Lesson 7: Enough
(Trainer/expressive-learner/receptive)

Content (See Figure 7)

1. Make a fist with the learner's nonpreferred hand, thumb overlapping the middle finger.

2. Lay the preferred hand on the surface, palm down with thumb extended, fingers together.

3. Place the learner's preferred hand on his nonpreferred hand which is positioned so that the thumb and index fingers are facing up.

4. Push the learner's preferred hand forward and off the nonpreferred hand.

Procedure

Same as for *more*.

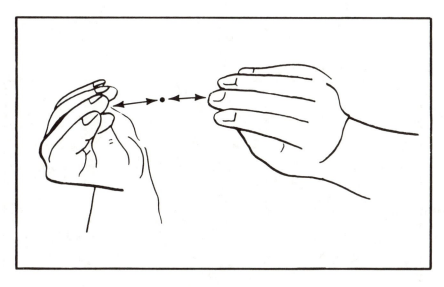

Figure 6. More.

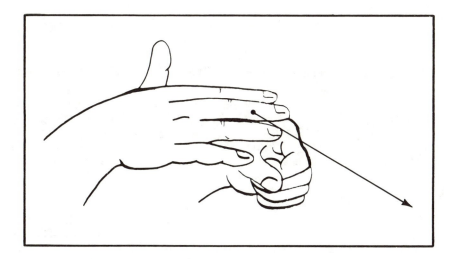

Figure 7. Enough.

Lesson 8: Stay
(Trainer/expressive-individual/receptive)

Content

1. Raise the learner's right hand as if he were taking an oath.

2. Place the palm of his hand against the learner's chest.

Procedure

Same as for *more*.

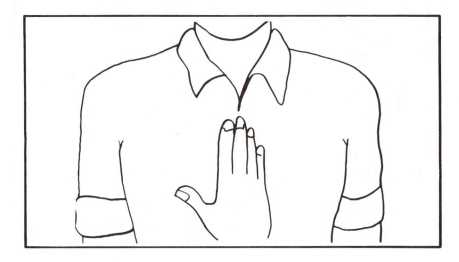

Figure 8. Stay.

DISCUSSION

This initial effort is designed for people who work with deaf-blind individuals and who have a limited amount of experience with sign language. Quite likely such people will also have limited knowledge of language acquisition and development theory. For this reason, two points stated in this article need to be emphasized. First, receptive language precedes expressive language according to current language acquisition theory and, second, the likelihood that an individual will generalize and express particular language behaviors is dependent, in part, on the ability to perceive environmental similarities.

Trainers who use this task analysis should understand that, initially, communication will be in one direction, trainer to learner. Over time, the learner should begin to express himself using the acquired signs. It is for this reason that we emphasize the importance of teaching signs in the learner's natural environment. By doing this, environmental dissimilarities are reduced and the likelihood that the learner will begin using expressive language is increased. When the learner repeatedly uses the signs spontaneously in a variety of situations (other than training situations) the ultimate criterion of this set of lessons will have been met.*

POSTSTATEMENT

Though it is not mentioned in this article, we were also interested in mobility skills training during this period of our research. The mobility skills task analyses, however, have never been sufficiently validated to publish. We thought of making them a part of this book but felt that they still were not in a form appropriate for dissemination.

There is a slightly unusual aspect of the content task analyses in this article. The content task analysis describes doing things with the learner's hands. Normally a content task analysis does not mention the learner at all. It usually describes how the task is properly performed but does not specify the interaction of the learner and trainer. For these particular task analyses, however, we felt that the majority of the actions required would involve both the trainer's and learner's hands. Thus, we made an exception describing the content task analysis in terms of the manual interaction between the trainer and the learner.

These task analyses have never been validated. They were published as suggestions. If any of the readers of this book have used them, we would appreciate hearing whether or not they worked. As mentioned earlier, we did not publish the mobility task analyses because we did not have sufficient data. Since the mobility task analyses are potentially dangerous if not appropriately validated, it is extremely important that they not yet be distributed. The analyses presented here have no potential for hurting anyone regardless of whether they are effective. We therefore felt much more comfortable about having them in print without their having been validated. The task analyses in this article do not appear in the task analysis bank of Marc Gold & Associates, Inc. because we include only analyses that have validation data.

---

*This work was supported in part by NICHHD Program Project Grant No. HD-05951 and the State of Illinois Department of Mental Health Grant 726-12 to the Institute for Child Behavior and Development, University of Illinois at Urbana-Champaign.

Appreciation is expressed to Will Gray Costello, Dixon Developmental Center, Dixon, Illinois, for use of his illustrations; and to Jeanne Jones, MacMurry College, Jacksonville, Illinois, and James J. Myers, Hope School for the Blind, Springfield, Illinois, for their assistance.

CHAPTER 23

Meeting the Needs of the Handicapped

Marc W. Gold

PRESTATEMENT

In October, 1976, the National and State Advisory Councils on Vocational Education sponsored the National Bicentennial Conference on Vocational Education. Attendance was by invitation. Included were leaders from business, industry, labor, and legislative and governmental agencies, as well as vocational educators and members of the National and State Advisory Councils on Vocational Education. I was invited to write and present a paper related to special needs (minorities, disadvantaged, handicapped, and women). I chose, with their approval, to focus on the area I was qualified to address, the handicapped and disadvantaged. Because this was a conference involving people in influential positions in a field that was just beginning to participate in the delivery of services to people labeled handicapped, I was very excited. It was additionally exciting because of the mandate from the committee that "all presentations should be developed to broaden the horizons of the participants in their examination of the future role of Vocational Education."

There is an interesting bit of trivia related to this paper and to the conference. The presentation was 1 hour long. The honorarium for that presentation was $1,000. The week before I had made a 1-hour presentation entitled, "Productivity and the Handicapped: A Therblig of a Different Color," to the Methods-Time Measurement Association. In appreciation they presented the speakers with a set of three bicentennial coins: a quarter, a half-dollar, and a dollar. I made $1.75 per hour 1 week and $1,000 per hour the next.

This paper includes a number of interesting issues, only a few of which have been covered in other chapters of this book. It includes the competence/deviance hypothesis (a repeat), which is amplified by my concept of intact systems with malfunctioning subsystems versus malfunctioning systems. The paper also includes some thoughts on mainstreaming, right to education, the issue of quality versus quantity of services, training strategies, and a list of eight optimistic predictions of what the future might hold.

This paper originally appeared in the Proceedings of the National Bicentennial Conference on Vocational Education, Minneapolis, Minnesota, October 1976. Reprinted by permission of the publisher.

INTRODUCTION

When the National Advisory Council provided the title for this presentation, they left an almost limitless range of possible topics. What is handicapped? Does that include individuals who are blind and deaf or who have behaviors that give them labels such as profoundly retarded, autistic, custodial and chronically mentally ill? What are needs? Does this include full acceptance by society? By some small segment of the society? Economic viability? If, indeed, there must always be a surplus population in a capitalistic society, are the handicapped prime candidates for permanent inclusion in this pool? And if so, then what are their needs? Since vocational education and education in general have only recently begun to consider their responsibility as including those individuals who find it most difficult to learn, then perhaps we had better begin by examining the concept of handicapped by distinguishing it from not handicapped or normal.

How does one get to be normal? It is not by adding a collection of things together so that one "fills up enough of his cup" to make it into normalcy. It is, instead, a complex interaction between a person's competence and his deviance, that is perceived by those around him as resulting in a net positive balance. Each of us remains in his various roles as members of communities, spouses, employees, friends, etc., only so long as the significant parties to those various roles continue to perceive us as having more things about us that are wanted, needed and not readily available (competence) than those things about us that bring negative attention and must be tolerated (deviance). According to the Competence/Deviance Hypothesis: The more competence an individual has, the more deviance will be tolerated in him by others (Gold, 1975). Using job performance as an example, if one performs successfully at a task which is essential to the business, and which no one else can perform without considerable training, that individual would have to display considerable deviance for dismissal to be considered. From this perspective, a meaningful definition of "normal" or "handicapped" requires recognition of this complex interaction between competence and deviance.

The phrase, "Hire the handicapped," for example, is a self-defeating marketing strategy. No one in business or industry wishes to expend resources to carry someone on the payroll. And no one wants to be hired because of his deviance. A more facilitative slogan would be, "Hire the competent . . . and know what competence means." Meeting the needs of people who have been labeled handicapped really means to fulfill the needs of society, the needs of business and industry and everyone else, except those whose need is to always have someone who needs them. To begin to meet these needs, we need only revise two of the basic assumptions which obviously underly current efforts. First, we must move away from a strategy that focuses almost exclusively on the elimination of deviance and towards a strategy that focuses almost exclusively on the development of competence. Second, we must recognize the inherent futility of benevolence as the energy source for meeting the needs of individuals who have been labeled handicapped. Give me dignity, give me respect, but give your benevolence to someone else.

The position taken here is that virtually all of the current attitudes, assumptions, and practices in the fields of education and rehabilitation preclude genuine and full participation of severely handicapped individuals in society (Gold, 1973). Those individuals with sensory handicaps, speech defects, minor emotional difficulties, and mild physical disabilities are seen as basically intact systems with malfunctioning subsystems, that is, "They're just like us but their eyes don't work, or their legs don't work." Our responsibility to these people is one which we have recently come to accept as providing the resources to give them sufficient competence to maintain a positive balance and therefore to be accepted as equally participating members of society. Since we see them as intact systems, we have no trouble justifying the expenditure of resources because of the predicted favorable cost/benefit ratio.

For those individuals with developmental disabilities, as they are currently described, individuals with moderate, severe and profound mental retardation, autism, severe physical and multiple disability, and the severely disturbed, we have a much different problem. We, as a society and profession, view these individuals as malfunctioning systems and, as such, incapable of achieving full participation in society. We have a long standing tradition dictating how we deal with intact systems which contain malfunctioning subsystems. Take the automobile as an example. You step out of your home one morning, get into the car, attempt to start it and find that nothing happens. The local garage sends a man who says the battery is dead and needs replacing; the alternator is broken and some of the wiring needs to be replaced. The car will not move but it is clear that it is an intact system and that the repair of the three malfunctioning subsystems will result in successful operation of the system. The decision is simple, fix it. Some of you may have had a different car, one that sat in the backyard, was without wheels, without a windshield or upholstery, and missing the carburetor, the radiator and the hood. Do you remember telling friends that the transmission was perfect? That the car had a new set of brake shoes? That the car had had a tuneup just 1500 miles ago? Of course not! This car is obviously a malfunctioning system and as such, intact subsystems, except to the junkman, are of no interest. Like the first car, the decision is simple. But, in this case, forget it, it is junk. One does not put resources into a malfunctioning system; one replaces it. There is one other car to discuss, the borderline car. It needs tires, a battery, a valve job, a new radiator and a paint job. What should you do? The only really difficult decision is deciding if it is a malfunctioning system or an intact system with a number of malfunctioning subsystems. Once this decision has been made, nothing else is difficult. Once we have decided whether or not something is an intact system or a malfunctioning system, that decision provides the basis for justifying either the use of resources to repair subsystems or the replacement of the system. This society has implicitly conceptualized some of its citizens as malfunctioning systems. Having done so, the best it hopes to do for those citizens is to take them out of the big old wrecking yards and put them into pretty little ones. The current movement to deinstitutionalize many of these persons has, in most cases, done only this. Some of our citizens with severe retardation are now watching colored television with two other people instead of black and white television with a hundred others. They are being taken care of better, living in nicer places, but they are still in the wrecking yard. Very few of them are "on the highway." For this to happen each of them must be re-perceived as an intact system with, in many cases, severely malfunctioning subsystems. To do this, we must take one subsystem and show it to be thoroughly functioning and competent. When this happens, we will then have to acknowledge that an intact subsystem cannot be observed functioning unless it is existing within a basically functioning system. Vocational skill performance is just such a subsystem. When we did an experiment to train individuals with severe and profound retardation, who are also blind, to assemble a complex industrial task (Gold, 1976), the ward staff who brought them to the research room, upon seeing them successfully assembling the task, asked why, if these individuals could do this, did they have to be dressed, fed and transported all of the time? Since then, all of these skills have been taught to these individuals. Once competence is demonstrated, one cannot help but look for more competence.

Meeting the needs of the handicapped requires, then, identifying relevant societal values, priorities and resources. Strategies must be developed with a strong awareness of the context in which individuals with handicapping conditions will exist. The following section attempts to provide some description of the current context.

CURRENT TRENDS AND THEIR IMPLICATIONS

The field of education has long suffered the bruises of jumping on and falling off bandwagons. Many of these bandwagons have a reasonable, conceptual and empirical foundation. The unit approach to teaching social studies (e.g., Ingram, 1953), the phonics method of teaching reading (e.g., Chall, 1967), and open classrooms (e.g., Featherstone, 1971) all might be so described. The problem with these becoming bandwagons has been that school systems have jumped on without learning how the wagon was constructed or where it was going. The results have been unfortunate.

The current movement to "mainstream" individuals who have been labeled handicapped is an interesting example (e.g., Birch, 1974). The basic notion is that pupils who have been served in special classes should be served in regular classes along with pupils who have not been so labeled. Support for this movement has included more than a dozen efficacy studies which failed to show significant advantages of special class placement for children labeled educable mentally retarded (see Kirk, 1964), litigation questioning the constitutionality of selected procedures for special classes (e.g., Bailey, 1972; Rosen & Soloyanis, 1974) and budgetary considerations. Observations of most attempts to provide vocational education for handicapped individuals shows a lack of awareness of this literature. Most of these attempts still segregate individuals with special needs into classes that are just for them and, in some cases, schools that are just for them. Attempts to meet the requirements of legislation calling for the expenditure of ten percent of federal funds to meeting the needs of individuals with handicapping conditions have also tended to be either segregated programs or outright misuse of the funds. The position taken here is that programs for normal individuals show a lack of systematic training strategy. Pupils are exposed to machinery, procedures and techniques and, with little assistance and carefully planned instructional technology, acquire enough information to satisfy those evaluating such programs. This may be fine for normal students, but under these circumstances, it is no wonder that individuals with special needs have been viewed as unsuccessful when integrated into these programs. For individuals with mild handicapping conditions, a shift by vocational educators to a more structured and carefully designed instructional environment for all students would allow individuals with special needs to enjoy success in an integrated circumstance and would probably yield significant increases in the skill capabilities of normal students in such classes.

For students with more severe handicapping conditions, the issue is more complicated. Under what organizational structure should these students be taught? The tendency, as with so many of the other movements, is to oversimplify, in this case, the distinction between mainstreaming and special class placement, as a simple dichotomy. Also, as with many of the other movements, the basic issue of what is best for the student has obviously been a low priority consideration. Decisions on where to teach should be based on the specific pieces of learning, information or skills with which a community wishes the student to leave school. Then, for each of these, decide where and how they are best taught. This will result in an organizational structure where the individual who has difficulty learning will acquire some skills along with individuals who do not have such difficulties, will acquire other skills with individuals who have problems similar to his, and will acquire yet other skills through individualized instruction. One need only listen to the compelling arguments on both sides of this issue to realize the need for a continuum of options. The development of these options by vocational educators might be one step in their pursuit of a leadership role in education.

Right to education is another current bandwagon in education. This movement got its start in Pennsylvania, where the courts mandated that the educational system of the state serve all school age pupils (PARC, 1971). One by one, most states are now legislating such action so that, on an increasing basis, schools will be required to provide services and programs for all school aged individuals including those who are most difficult to train. While there seems to be a general consensus that such individuals have a right to education, there is considerably less of a consensus as to whether or not the public school should be the service entity providing this education. In any case, children categorized using the educational jargon "trainable" and "subtrainable" will eventually be an integral part of our public school systems. Will we meet the letter of the law by simply having them there or will we develop viable programs for doing something with them? Vocational education, again, has the opportunity to provide important leadership in the development of programs which can have more of an impact on the lives of the individuals to be served than any program has ever had, the difference between societal existence or custodial care.

Another current trend which can contribute to both mainstreaming and Right to Education activities is the developing cooperative relationship between vocational education and special education. This trend, which began originally between vocational rehabilitation and special education, through the efforts of Charles Eskridge in Texas more than a decade ago (Eskridge & Partridge, 1963) seems to finally be a part of many public school and university efforts involving vocational programs for individuals with mild and moderate developmental disabilities. A current example is the series of National Workshops on Special Needs Vocational Teacher Education developed by Rupert Evans at the University of Illinois. The first workshop, held in 1975, received applications from over 70 institutions throughout the country, a strong indication of interest in this area. Another aspect of these conferences, of particular interest here, is that the impetus for this activity came from the vocational education sector rather than from special education, as has tended to be the case. The tendency, in fact, throughout this movement has been to pawn off the responsibility to special educators. To successfully address this problem, it is going to require full utilization of all of the resources and knowledge of both of these disciplines and probably some others, too.

From the special education side of this coalition individuals such as Gary Clark (e.g., Clark, 1974), Donn Brolin (Brolin, 1976), William Younie (e.g., Younie & Clark, 1969), Charles Kokaska (Kokaska, 1974) and others have begun to increase the communication between these two disciplines and establish priorities and goals out of which some programs have begun to emerge. With the exception of programs for the deaf, the overwhelming majority of the work that has been done as a cooperative effort has been limited to service to individuals with mild handicapping conditions. Although there are now more students receiving better service, expectancies for the vocational capabilities of individuals emerging from such programs have remained not much different than they were prior to cooperative programs being established. At present, then, there is a good base from which to build programs giving individuals with mild, moderate and severe handicapping conditions a better crack at the world of work than they have ever had before.

Another trend in the delivery of services to persons with handicapping conditions is the overwhelming emphasis on quantity at the expense of quality. Limited resources, a legitimate interest in serving all of those individuals who need service, the need to focus initially on the acquisition of basic resources such as space, staff, equipment and funds, have all mitigated against the development of quality services. It seems that each time a program finally has the resources to move into quality programming, a decision is made to drain resources away to expand the program quantitatively. The result has been, for the most part, that many more individuals in many more places are receiving services but the services they are receiving are usually no better than what a fewer number of people received in the past. This strategy should be changed. We should be improving services, not just giving them to more people. The demonstration of major significant performance by individuals who have been labeled handicapped, especially severely handicapped, is a more viable strategy for increasing available resources than showing little or no growth in many individuals (Gold, 1973). This strategy is not made easier by the other trends mentioned which have called for access to available resources by all individuals concerned. The long range goal of high quality service to all individuals in need of such service, however, is more attainable if we focus on quality first and quantity second.

The last trend discussed here relates to vocational training strategies. Almost all of the "strategies" found in programs are actually organizational structures rather than strategies, for example, on-campus work experience programs, on-the-job training, classroom instruction and real or simulated workshop experience. The focus of attention has been on these organizational structures rather than on the actual instructional technology to be used in those settings. The result has been that most learning which has occurred resulted from exposure in these settings rather than from systematic and carefully designed manipulations of these various environments. It is to our advantage to have a wide range of organizational structures available within which to provide training; however, none of these structures will carry us very far in the absence of well developed instructional technologies.

These trends simultaneously point up the tremendous growth we have undergone in the last twenty years and the urgent need for significant and major changes in what we are doing: We've come a long way, baby, but we've got a long way to go!

THE FUTURE: WHAT MIGHT IT BE LIKE?

The list below reflects a firmly entrenched optimism. For those who do not share this optimism a different list would have to be developed.

1. The proportions of unskilled, semi-skilled, skilled and professional jobs in this country will remain basically unchanged; however, specific jobs within each of these categories will come and go (Nixon, 1970). Decisions regarding the training of any individual, no matter how handicapped he is perceived to be, will rest on a carefully arrived at decision as to whether or not a job can be subdivided into teachable components rather than on some general feeling about the complexity of the particular job, as is now the case (Gold, 1976). The result of this will be that individuals with all kinds and severities of disabilities will be found in a tremendously wider variety of positions than is now the case.

2. Vocational training programs for persons who have been labeled handicapped will contribute individuals to the labor pool who are so clearly competent at a wide range of specific functions that those things which would previously have kept them from opportunities in the world of work will do so no longer. Business and industry will come to recognize the advantage of revising their recruitment, hiring, training and supervisory practices so as to gain access to this valuable new labor source.

3. The Protestant Ethic will continue to lose ground but a person will continue to be known by what that person does for a living (Parker, 1971). For those individuals whose observable deviance is minimal or non-existent, acceptance by members of society and community will continue to be enhanced but not determined by their vocational contributions. Individuals with observable deviance, especially those with severe disabilities, will come to be seen as thoroughly participating members of society and of communities, peers in virtually every respect, first through their contributions to the economy, and second, through the same mechanisms as the rest of us, once society has reason to look beyond those things that have distracted us.

4. The proportion of life skills that individuals acquire outside the school will increase. For some kinds of learning this means that schools will continue to develop activities outside of the school building and be involved in the use of those activities. It will also mean that schools, as entities, will contribute less and less to the educational process. Other viable teaching entities will include community groups, private enterprise, television, private individuals, and a wide range of individual and group auto-instructional activities. Following some adjustment problems, schools will take the opportunity to significantly increase the quality of instruction in those areas that continue to remain responsibilities of the schools to teach.

5. Sheltered workshops will continue to be a significant part of the vocational lives of individuals with severe handicapping conditions. They will undergo major changes in their operational philosophies and practices or go out of existence because of poor business practices and a lack of public support. As sheltered workshops begin to show their capabilities to provide genuinely meaningful training and work to individuals with severe handicapping conditions, they will become defined as special places where normal work is done instead of places where substandard work is done. Vocational education and special education will utilize sheltered workshops; however, the use of sheltered workshops as a convenient dumping ground for individuals with mild handicaps will cease.

6. Post-high school education will be utilized more and more to obtain information not specifically related to vocational goals. Self-help skills, crafts, recreation and other aspects of adult life will be pursued in adult education programs, colleges and universities. Public schools will begin to focus more on providing the groundwork for this kind of adult and continuing education. Vocational educators might expect to be held increasingly accountable for providing all individuals with a broader set of basic skills such as tool usage, home and auto repair, practical measurement skills and, perhaps, an even wider range of specific practical skills. The development of effective, efficient programs to meet these needs should include the teaching of these skills to all individuals with special needs served by public schools.

7. The whole issue of accountability is one that will have to be increasingly addressed by vocational educators. As advocacy continues to increase in popularity in this country, we can expect communities to become more and more demanding of benefits resulting from vocational education programs. If vocational educators maintain a leadership role in recognizing changing societal value structures and in addressing them, then they can maintain control over their own destiny. If societal needs are not addressed, however, vocational educators will find their options constrained by mandates. The mandates to spend ten percent of all federal vocational education funds on the handicapped and another fifteen percent on the disadvantaged are clear examples. If vocational educators had initiated strong, visible programs for such individuals, these mandates would have never come about. Passive leadership at this time in our development will probably result in more and more constraint on the options open to vocational education programs.

8. Pluralism will continue but the rules of the game will improve. Most of us in vocational education, special education and other disciplines and professions have spent all or most of our careers existing in a booming economy. Rapid program development has been the rule rather than the exception, and only recently has there been strong demand for cost-benefit justification. It seems reasonable to assume a stable but not rapidly growing economy, and that this set of circumstances will remain for a long period of time. If this happens, all of us special interest groups will be competing more than ever for available resources. The combination of the advocacy movement, limited resources, increased political accountability and public awareness in general should result in funds being distributed on the basis of demonstrated effectiveness in meeting current societal needs. If vocational educators are able to demonstrate major gains in the quality and quantity of skills in the people they serve, utilizing the resources they already have, they should expect a front row seat at the trough. Those disciplines that continue to demand more and more support in the absence of clear-cut effective utilization of existing resources will probably die.

CONCLUSION

We are an enlightened, capitalist society. We believe in the profit motive and in private enterprise to a point beyond which we become offended. We continue to have faith in the democratic process, but our minorities are becoming increasingly important to us. Each of us has special interests, as has always been the case, but each probably has more special interests than people have ever had before, allowing us, as a society, to broaden our acceptance of divergent points of view.

The boundary conditions of normalcy continue to undergo major expansion. In almost every aspect of our existence we have modified what we believe normal to be. For each of these, what is normal now? marital status?

sexual preference? hours worked per week? years of schooling? longevity at your present job? How many friends does the average person have that have things about them that might cause them to be labeled handicapped? What is normally thought when someone gives birth to a child with a major problem? Which political party is right?

In our lifetime people who are very different from people most of us have ever really known, lovely people, will be moving into our communities, living next door to us, growing up in our families, marrying our children and interacting with us in every conceivable way. Doesn't it make sense that they should have everything we have in the way of the opportunity to make it? Vocational educators could provide these citizens with many of the critical skills needed for full successful participation in society. For many of these skills vocational educators are the only logical and competent source.

POSTSTATEMENT

I like the way this paper is written and what it has to say. By now, you should be able to tell that I have some problems with writing and also some feelings of inadequacy about it. This paper is encouraging. I had not read it since it was written and presented. It really was fun. It was interesting to read the paragraph on right to education. This paper was written before October, 1976, and P.L. 94-142 went into effect in October, 1977. Therefore, this paper preceded the federal legislation and, in a sense, predicted it. It also pointed out the possibility, which has become a reality, that we would establish law and then simply do what was necessary to meet the letter of the law rather than creating really viable programs that derive their legitimacy from the law. The paragraph on quality versus quantity education is certainly as relevant today as it was in 1976. With resources becoming even tighter than they were then, the problem of lack of quality is increasing. This need not be the case. The emphasis should be on quality regardless of the amount of resources available.

In reading through the section on the future, I was looking to see if anything had happened since 1976 relevant to the eight predictions. Number 1 seemed to be true; Number 2 is beginning to become true; Number 3 was already happening and seems to be still continuing; Number 4 I do not know about. But it gives me an opportunity to slip in a point made by Lou Brown, associate professor at the University of Wisconsin-Madison. He says that as the age of a student increases, the amount of time that person spends in school should decrease, and the amount of time that person spends learning out in the community, possibly with assistance from school personnel, should increase. I agree completely. Number 5 is beginning to happen. Some sheltered workshops closed because of lack of public support. The rest of it has not changed much. No comment on Number 6 and Number 7. Number 8 is either true or too conservative. At this time (1980) the economy has not only stopped booming, but it has recessed considerably. And this has had considerable impact on programs throughout the country.

I still believe that people with severe handicapping conditions will become an integral part of everyone's everyday life but feel, as I did when the paper was written, that this situation will develop slowly and is a long way from becoming a reality.

Removing Some of the Limitations of Mentally Retarded Workers by Improving Job Design

Michael G. Wade and Marc W. Gold

PRESTATEMENT

Mike Wade is a professor at the Institute for Child Behavior and Development at the University of Illinois. While I was also a professor in that organization, we spent time together discussing our work. On one such occasion I made the point that accuracy should be taught first and then speed. Horrified, he looked at me and said, "I can't believe that you would say such a thing. I thought you were well read, and the literature clearly shows that speed should be taught first, then accuracy." I answered that I couldn't believe he would say that because the literature clearly showed my position was correct. When we finally began to settle down, we gradually realized that we had been brought up, professionally, in two completely different literatures. He was familiar with the sports research literature; I had been exposed to the industrial literature. We were both right. As a matter of fact, it makes sense. In sports most of the skills are ballistic and simply cannot be broken down into stop and start motions. For example, it is very difficult to describe a definable sequence of specific motions of a tennis serve because they all flow together. With such movement it does seem appropriate to get the overall flow of the series of motions going (speed) and then to refine that flow into increasingly more accurate motions (accuracy). On the other hand, operating most machines can be defined as a lengthy series of clearly identifiable motions which have logical beginnings and endings. Under this circumstance it is understandable that one develops accuracy of motions first and then, following cycle constancy, increases the rate of that established set of accurate motions until achieving an appropriate speed.

While that particular topic is not reflected in this article, those discussions did lead us to discuss collaborating on something. The invitation from Ray Nickerson to write an article for a special issue of *Human Factors* dealing with issues related to people labeled handicapped seemed like a good opportunity to collaborate. What then occurred was a long series of arguments and

This article originally appeared in *Human Factors*, 1978, *20* (3), 339-348. Reprinted by permission of the publisher.

discussions which eventually resulted in this article. It is not particularly obvious from reading the article, but on many of the points Mike and I had to compromise. The difference in our positions already described was one of many, but we found the exercise very rewarding. The article suffered somewhat in the sense that it was a fairly weak statement, but it represented the best compromise we could reach, considering our respective positions.

THE PROBLEM

Traditionally people with retardation have been regarded as among society's misfits and as such are viewed as essentially a non-productive element in the industrial milieu. In a capitalistic society where a surplus labor force is almost always present, it is no wonder that this has been of little concern to industry. Who needs a new source of labor when unemployment abounds (Farber, 1968)? Industry does. This is evidenced by the lack of fit between jobs needing people and people needing jobs, even during periods of high unemployment. Many production lines in industry have high employee turnover rates. One possible reason is a lack of fit between task characteristics and worker characteristics. This paper discusses this issue from the perspective of viewing the retarded person as a unique and needed labor source. Where such people have been placed in work-related situations, the employment has been considered therapeutic, and the tasks utilized have been minimal. Workers have swept floors or assembled the weekly Sunday newspaper supplements. Such tasks are relatively trivial and make very little financial impact on the worker involved or profit for the industry providing the contract.

This state of affairs has come about for three reasons. First, evaluating procedures for the selection of industrial personnel successfully screen out those individuals who do not make normal progress when exposed to traditional training methods. The screening procedures used by industry successfully avoid confrontation with training problems. Second, industry by and large has not considered the integration of these workers into its production line system based in part on the traditional misconception that persons with mental retardation are "insane" or otherwise sufficiently deviant to preclude consideration of them as viable members of the labor force. Both management and labor have done very little to further the use of this population in industry. Third, retarded persons have always been thought incapable of anything but the lowest level of work tasks, both in terms of quality and productivity.

To alleviate this problem, industry (both management and labor) must be convinced that the majority of retarded citizens, although possessing intellectual deficits and some behavioral idiosyncracies, are capable of reaching an acceptable level of job performance. The most viable strategy would be to produce data regarding the performance capabilities of these workers when involved in more realistic production line situations. If management and labor can be convinced that they are capable of producing within acceptable cost-profit margins, the traditional misconception of "retarded" being always synonymous with incompetent will hopefully diminish. Some of these data are already available (Gold, 1973).

Retarded Literature

To exploit to the full the capabilities of both people and machines in the system, the human factors engineer must satisfactorily solve the problem of allocation of function (AF). The guidelines for assigning responsibilities to both people and machines in the system are no less important when the human operator is retarded. The role of AF in system design is not new (Fitts, 1951; Swain & Wohl, 1961) but is relatively uncharted when applied to these workers. Bartlett (1962) and Jordan (1963) both commented on the critical importance of advances in machine capability and the need for regarding people and machines as complementary rather than comparable. Whitfield (1967) has pictured AF as the positioning of the interface or boundary between the human operators and the hardware of the system "in terms of the relative amounts of information processing to be performed by each part." To maximize the human-machine interface, a clear understanding of the task is required for the human operator's role, and the functional specifications are required to maximize machine capability. The problem is to attain the optimal trade-off, bearing in mind that an array of consequences from different AF schemes must be compared (Whitfield, 1967).

It can be readily appreciated that AF considerations are not simple when the operator is a retarded person. An important question that must be considered is the information processing capability of the worker with retardation and its role in job performance in the industrial setting. People with mental retardation are less able to process information when it is presented in certain contextual settings. An inability to transfer from the specific to the general case in learning (Campione and Brown, 1976) mirrors similar contexts requiring execution of skilled movement activity. The ever-changing road display and accompanying traffic conditions in driving, for example, cause problems for retarded persons that mitigate against safe driving. The ability to process information depends a great deal on the context and conditions extant when the task is being learned or performed. There is some evidence (reviewed below) to suggest that retarded persons possess a limited information processing (IP) capacity compared with their normal peers, and such a limitation will produce a constraint in skill acquisition in a variety of vocational settings. This IP limitation must be considered from both the viewpoint of task analysis and AF decisions.

The literature focusing on manual tasks and industrial assembly tasks involving retarded persons does not deal with the problem of limited IP capacity. The paucity of research in this area stems from the dominant clinical opinion in the 1950's of essential futility when considering the abilities of persons with retardation. Little research has been reported on the performance of retarded persons on motor tasks of one kind or another, and few studies have used IP capacity as a possible indicator of ability level. Recently, a renewed interest in vocational skill training has emerged (Gold, 1973).

The available research and its first appearance in print reflect the attitude toward the industrial work potential of retarded persons during the 1950's. Tizard and Loos (1954) tested six adults (IQ's 20-49) on a complex spatial relations task and reported rapid improvement in performance, and considerable transfer of training when tested on a similar task. A retest of the original task one month later showed performance level higher than at the beginning of the experiment. Tizard and Loos (1954) concluded that initial performance scores were a poor indicator of performance after practice. In a further study (Loos & Tizard, 1955) six subjects were required to assemble cardboard boxes. The task involved nine different bi-manual movements in a specific order. Within two weeks subjects with practice were performing more efficiently than counterparts 40 IQ points higher with equal practice. Clarke and Hermelin (1955) using the same subjects as Tizard and Loos (1954) collected performance data on four different assembly tasks. Task 1 required subjects to cut insulated wire in 25.5-cm lengths. The task required both dexterity and coordination to cut the wire to within 0.6 cm of the required length. Initial performance was poor ($\overline{X} = 27$ pieces), but after the second hour of practice the mean output was 49 pieces of wire per 5-min period. Task 2 required subjects to solder four colored wires to the correct terminals of an 8 pin TV tube. The task required both manual dexterity and discrimination of color and spatial relationships. Subjects had to place the tube into a wooden frame such that it was in a particular configuration and, having achieved the correct alignment of the tube in the frame, solder each of the four colored wires to the appropriate terminal. Over a 34-trial practice session, wiring time decreased from 8 min per tube to 2.5 min per tube. Task 3 was the assembly of a bicycle pump that involved nine discrete operations in a specified order. Initial assembly time scores ranged from 4-10 min with assistance from the experimenter. After 13 trials, times were between 54s and 110s without assistance. Task 4 required the subjects to learn in sequence the first three designs of the Wechsler Block Design Test. The task required the subject to copy a geometric design from a picture using multicolored blocks. With practice the subjects were able to copy successfully each of the three designs but were unable to learn the three designs as a sequence. The data provide evidence that initial performance scores are poor indicators of how well persons with retardation can perform after practice, and also that those individuals might usefully engage in a variety of industrial assembly tasks at acceptable work rates.

Comparing the IP capacity of the operator with the information load (IL) of the task was first considered by Fitts (1954). Fitts demonstrated that, with a range of tasks, rate of gain of information was consistent for normal subjects. Annett (1961) reported an experiment that investigated the relationship between IP capacity of the operator (three groups of retarded subjects) and the IL of the task. A peg assembly task involving four motion elements, "reach," "grasp," "carry," and "assemble," was used. The "reach" element was varied with respect to IL, by four levels of choice, one in two, one in four, and one in eight. The task required 0, 1, 2, and 3 bits of information, respectively, to resolve the uncertainty in the task. The subjects in

Annett's study formed three groups (IQ's $> 60; > 40; < 59; < 40$). Annett's (1961) data showed that the lowest IQ group (IQ < 40) performed poorly in terms of IP capacity and the high group (IQ > 60) performed in a normal fashion. Annett suggested that IP capacity was a correlate of what he referred to as "cortical integrity" and noted that information theory provided a means of assessing both the properties of the task (IL) and the capacity of the operator (IP). This is precisely the objective of AF in optimizing the human-machine interface. The possible relationship between IP capacity and cortical integrity has been expressed well by Crossman's (1960) reference to the modern-day industrial operator as a "mental craftsman" who plies his modern-day trade of "control skill."

The "cortical integrity" issue raised by Annett (1961) was investigated by Olsen (1971). He hypothesized that channel capacity was a sensitive index of degree of mental retardation, using visual apprehension tasks varying in information content from 1 to 8 bits. Subjects were young normal, educable, and trainable mentally retarded persons. Olsen's data suggested that by limiting the number of choices to four alternatives (2 bits), subjects with retardation (EMR and TMR) were able to approach the performance level of normal children (MA = 5 yr). Although speculative and recognized as such by Olsen (1971), an IP limitation of 2 bits was suggested as a not unreasonable level for these persons. Olsen's data are similar to those of Smith and Kaufman (1972). Using identification tasks, they reported that:

> . . . intellectual level plays a role in the ability to transmit information. . . This retardate deficit is further emphasized by the interactions of intellectual level with increasing information load (# of alternatives) and with increasing delays between presentation of the situations and presentation of the response matrix. (p. 324)

LIMITATIONS OF EXISTING
RESEARCH FINDINGS

The studies by Annett (1961), Olsen (1971), and Smith and Kaufman (1972) all share several shortcomings. First, the performance of subjects with retardation was measured under conditions of exposure rather than training. Training is used here to mean systematic manipulation designed to facilitate acquisition of the task. Exposure refers to presentation of the stimuli or task to the subject until something happens, i.e., practice in the absence of systematically administered external feedback. Considerable data are available (e.g., Gold, 1972; Gold & Barclay, 1973) that document the wide discrepancy in the performance of retarded persons between conditions of exposure and conditions of training. The studies by Annett (1961), Olsen (1971), and Smith and Kaufman (1972) did not utilize specific strategies for facilitating acquisition.

A second problem is related to whether or not the studies yield information warranting an interpretation that the IP limits of retarded persons have been established. Annett's findings were limited to performance on the first trial. The effect decreased with practice. Olsen pointed out that his two-bit limit was only an estimate and then acknowledged the speculative nature of his conclusions. Smith and Kaufman suggested that the notion of channel capacity deficit was inappropriate for persons with retardation. Their data support neither an acceptance nor a rejection for such a notion. They do not reflect the IP limits of these individuals; moreover, with practice these subjects showed significant gains in information transmitted, albeit the gains were significantly less than those shown by normal persons. Smith and Kaufman also mention that differences between normal individuals and those with retardation increased as delay between stimulus presentation and response matrix presentation increased. While this difference was significant, normal individuals also showed significant decrement in performance related to delay. They interpret the data to suggest that, as greater demands are put upon the subject, deficits increase in the performance of learners with retardation. Under exposure conditions this seems a tenable position, but when sophisticated training procedures are utilized, task demands may be subject to modification.

The third problem is the nature of the tasks used. None consisted of sequences of steps as was the case with the tasks used by Clarke and Hermelin (1955) and Gold (1972). When a task consists of several discrete operations, the level of information content (number of "bits") may be applied to each operation of the task, rather than to the task as a whole. A decision to teach or not to teach any task to individuals with retardation must be based on whether or not the task can be analyzed into teachable (2-bit?) components rather than on some general notion regarding the difficulty or complexity of the overall task (Gold, 1976).

A PROPOSED APPROACH TO TRAINING

The studies reviewed above, which span the twenty or so years between 1954 and the present, all proposed an information theory approach to analyzing performance of persons with retardation, but not all of the studies actually analyzed task variables in terms of information content. An examination of the assembly tasks employed by Loos and Tizard (1955) and Clarke and Hermelin (1955) reveals that the IL required for each discrete operation in the assembly task was never greater than three bits. Data from the studies reviewed suggest that if the IL of any one operation in an assembly-type task is greater than three bits, a performance limitation may be evident for the operator with retardation because of an IP limitation. In addition, a study by Gold (1972) was the only one which utilized systematic training procedures. The others relied on "a little help," "practice," "trial and error," and other forms of exposure.

Where retarded persons are involved with assembly tasks that require varying levels of information processing capacity and varying levels of manual dexterity and control, it would seem that for the operator to perform successfully, the information contained in the task must be reduced and an appropriate response generated. The evidence cited above, although not totally compelling, does suggest that there is a limit to the understanding of the abstract relationship involved in some industrial tasks. It is the aim of the task analyst to reduce industrial tasks into teachable components which stay within the information processing limits of the operator.

Modern production line procedures have utilized various forms of task analysis such as Methods Time Measurement, to subdivide seemingly difficult operations into a series of relatively uncomplicated actions (Maynard, Stegemerten, & Schwab, 1948). Division of labor and the subsequent development of "mass production" has resulted in an increased production, more jobs, and a diminution of the traditional skilled trades. In fact, the pendulum has swung so far today that industrial psychologists have warned about "oversimplification" of the production process because of the loss of interest of workers performing highly specific assembly line tasks (e.g., Hulin & Blood, 1968; Scott, 1973). Drilling holes for eight hours per day might pay well but produces attention deficits that endanger quality control, stemming from the low level of IP required on the part of the operator.

The evidence on learning by retarded persons suggests a lack of ability to transfer rules of procedure (strategies) acquired in one context to similar contextual settings. These individuals sometimes appear unable to form generalizable rules or strategies which they can successfully apply to a variety of similar tasks. Campione (1973) reported no real evidence of transfer in young normal children when the task format changes. Does a change in task format cause a shift in the IP of the task? It would seem that a change in task format would influence the information content and thus change the complexity dimension of the task. The human factors considerations would seem to involve task analysis and a breakdown of the task such that the information content for each discrete operation remains within acceptable IP limits. For retarded persons task analysis that maintains acceptable IP demands on the worker will not necessarily produce acceptable performance levels because understanding what the requirements of the task might be does not guarantee successful performance.

Task Analysis

From the human factors viewpoint, the application of efficient task analysis is paramount. Gold (1976) subdivides task analysis into three phrases: method, content, and process. Method refers to the procedural aspects of the task assembly; content refers to the subdivision of the task into teachable components that are within the abilities of the operator; process refers to the strategies to be developed that will enable the training program to be effective. The total task analysis view involves subdivision of the task and development of a training program. There are obviously constraints placed both upon the subdivision of the task into components and upon training methods. Regarding constraints on task analysis, Meister and Rabideau (1965) have noted: "The task analyst asks what the operator must perceive, discriminate, decide, and manipulate in order to accomplish the function" (p. 71). When the operator is a retarded person, a major consideration here is the IP limit of the operator to process stimulus information and generate the appropriate response. The task analysis most likely to be employed is, therefore, a step-wise task analysis, as opposed to a time-line task analysis. The latter would be inappropriate as variation in the temporal relationships between the step-wise components of the task is a potential source of information overload. Selection of tasks for these workers should attempt to minimize operator overload caused by time-sharing considerations. Considerations of individual differences and state variables of the operator, already well documented shortcomings of most task analysis techniques, are further complicated when the operator is a mentally retarded individual.

When one develops a task analysis for an industrial task or some other unfamiliar task, there is no existing method to bias decisions. Each component of the task is inspected step by step, with the intent being for the task analyst to become intimate with the components. What results from this process of careful inspection is the content task analysis, or the listing of steps into which the task has been arbitrarily divided. Hopefully, those steps represent teachable components. The notion that a component is teachable is really an hypothesis. It is operationalized during the training process when steps are, in fact, being acquired or not being acquired. The size of the divisions (i.e., how many steps) depends on preconceived notions regarding the capabilities of the learner. The same task can be divided into any number of components. For example, to teach an individual to add the numbers 2 + 3, the learner might be given a single instruction such as "Take two objects; put them together with three more; then count the new total." Such an instruction represents a very weak training strategy involving a content task analysis of three steps. To use this strategy, the trainer must assume that the learner has a well developed repertoire of entering behaviors. Alternatively, one could teach the 2 + 3 addition by including steps for the concepts of the numbers two and three, the concept of "putting things together," how to count, etc. Anybody with experience in teaching knows that some "clinical judgment" or sensitivity to the needs of individual students is important. Perhaps these terms can be understood, at least partially, as the ability to make subtle discriminations regarding the number of component steps needed for each learner. Such discriminations are indeed important. If a task is divided into an unnecessarily large number of components, efficiency is lost and, even more seriously, the task can become tedious and aversive to the learner. If each component is too large (e.g., too few steps), the learner will not acquire the skill. The ability to make these subtle discriminations can be developed by (1) preparing many content task analyses and implementing the training that they generate; (2) knowing the intended learner population; and (3) revising the content task analysis when necessary (Gold, 1976).

Behavioral assessment can be helpful in certain situations to determine priorities about what to teach. If such assessment is to be genuinely facilitative to the trainer, however, it must focus on the specific behaviors prerequisite to the target task. Assessments of general behavioral constructs are not seen as facilitative, and these general types of assessment usually result in limiting a trainer's expectations and willingness to train relatively complex skills. Further, little specific information is provided on whether or not the learner is ready or has the capacity to acquire a particular task. The focus, then, should be on task-specific assessment. In order to conduct such assessment, intimacy with the task is necessary because the trainer must know enough to be able to identify the specific behaviors which are needed to begin training on the target task.

Identifying necessary prerequisite skills for a particular task is another important reason for content task analysis. It forces the task analyst to identify what is expected of the learner upon entering the situation. It is interesting to note that the more the task analyst knows about the task, the less prerequisites are needed by the learner. As the task analyst learns the intricacies of the task, the behaviors which are needed by the learner become more and more apparent. It is common to conclude from the development of a content task analysis that there are skills and lessons that need to be completed prior to a learner entering the content task analysis being planned. When writing a content task analysis for time telling, for example, it becomes obvious that recognition of numerals from one to twelve is a necessary prerequisite. It is also clear that the clock is not the best place for teaching numeral recognition. The content task analysis would signal the trainer to assess whether or not the intended learners recognize their numerals from one to twelve and, if not, to have lessons on this (and other prerequisites) prior to entering the time-telling lesson. The logical extension of a content task analysis leads to a long sequence of lessons in those cases where many prerequisites are identified. In other cases content can be acquired without other skills in advance of the particular one being taught. In this sense the content analysis has an almost diagnostic function of signaling what the trainer must look for in terms of prerequisite skills.

There is another diagnostic aspect to content task analysis. Most training begins with some opportunity for the learner to demonstrate what he already knows about the task. Either the task is presented for him to do, the task is done once by the trainer, or something else happens that allows the learner to show what he knows. When the learner knows nothing about the task, it is obvious. When the learner can perform the task perfectly, that is obvious, too. Most learners, however, know something about most tasks. Observing such a learner proceed through a task, after having done a content task analysis, allows the trainer to identify clearly which components of a task the learner does and does not know. This is very helpful in focusing in on what needs to be taught and being able to evaluate how training is proceeding.

Regarding constraints on training programs, Welford (1975) has best summarized the problem by posing the question, "What can be trained?" Just as a step-wise task analysis requires recognition of the functional capacities of the operator, so training focuses on the development of optimal programming for the use of those capacities.

Research and application data from this laboratory considerably expand some of the previously held assumptions regarding the limits on tasks attainable by the retarded, especially the severely retarded. For example, Gold (1972) trained 64 moderately and severely retarded individuals enrolled in four sheltered workshops to assemble a 15-piece bicycle brake and then a 24-

piece bicycle brake. Training procedures utilized information obtained from the basic psychological research on discrimination learning. All subjects learned the training task. All but one subject reached criterion on the transfer task. Mean trials to criterion was 26. The performance of these subjects far exceeded expectancies of the field related to the abilities of this population.

Subsequent studies using those same tasks have yielded similar results to train severely retarded blind, profoundly retarded blind, and deaf blind persons. With modification in the training procedures, acquisition rates, in terms of trials to criterion, have remained essentially the same, even though the characteristics of the population would yield a prediction of considerably slower acquisition rates.

Other studies in this research program have utilized electronic printed circuit boards as tasks. In the studies by Merwin (1973, 1974) two boards of equal difficulty were used in each study, each board containing 12 components placed differently than the other board and different components. In the first study, which utilized 45 adult residents with a mean IQ of 55 and a range of 23 to 92, 39 of the subjects, 88.6%, learned to assemble both the training and the transfer boards each to a criterion of five consecutive correctly assembled boards (60 consecutive correct insertions). The mean number of trials (boards) to criterion across both boards was 16.5, and the mean total time for pre-training, training, and transfer was 170 min. The second study utilized 60 adults with a mean IQ of 40 and a range of 18 to 77. The boards and procedures were similar to those in the first study. Forty-eight out of the 60 subjects, 80%, reached criterion on both boards. Mean time to criterion on pre-training, training, and transfer for all subjects was 246 min.

Those tasks which can be analyzed into teachable units, where teachable is defined and tested operationally, should be open to consideration for all individuals. Lawler's (1969) concept of horizontal job enlargement provides a conceptual base already existing in the industrial literature for the form of increase in job function described as increases in difficulty. By horizontal job enlargement he refers to increasing the number and variety of operations that a worker performs. Enlarging a job vertically increases the degree to which the individual controls the planning and execution of his job.

Recently this research program established a policy of accepting for training any individual in participating agencies, and not concluding training until criterion has been reached. Work with the blind retarded is being conducted at a state institution in a cottage which contains 32 individuals described as severely and profoundly retarded, blind, and deaf blind, and many of them with additional handicaps. This cottage represents one of the more limited groups of individuals in the institution. Work has been completed with 24 of the individuals in this cottage, working on the bicycle brake and using a criterion of six consecutive correct assemblies of the task without assistance; all 24 individuals reached criterion (Gold, 1972). In order to train less and less capable individuals, more and more had to be known about the task, both in terms of its divisible units and in terms of the feedback mechanisms needed to teach the task. Of particular note here is the observation that, once there was a firm commitment to a zero reject model, the instructional procedures necessary to accomplish that goal were developed. In the past, when an individual was difficult to train, using existing procedures, it was rationalized that what this person needed was outside of the scope of the research, and he was eliminated from training. This is analogous to what industry has done. While no argument is made against the efficiency of such a tack, such a position has generated gross misconceptions regarding the attainable competencies of the retarded, especially the more severely retarded.

Recently the instructional technology from this research has been implemented in service programs and industry. Examples of tasks on which severely retarded workers are now working include battery tester assembly, printed circuit boards assembly, insertion of helicoils into fuel cells for jet helicopters (Galloway, 1977), and turn signal assembly and installation (Levy, 1977).

Another observation which is of note here is related to testing, and to prerequisite behaviors. The more sophisticated the training procedures become, the less prerequisite behaviors are required on the part of the learner. Some subjects at the beginning of training do not spontaneously close their hand when something is placed against their palm. With current procedures, even this behavior is not a prerequisite and can be taught during training. When training procedures include virtually everything that will be needed to perform the task, then testing, in the formal sense, becomes superfluous. The capabilities of any individual who is being trained to perform a particular task will be evidenced during that training; that is, if he knows some, most, or all of the behaviors necessary, this will show up immediately within the training process.

The boundary conditions of what a retarded person can learn, in terms of industrial tasks, may be determined more by the competencies of those doing the task analysis and job design than by the characteristics of the worker. AF considerations, in this light, shift to decisions regarding the efficiency and effectiveness with which resources are utilized. The data presented indicate that individuals who are considered high risks to train can learn tasks in rather brief periods of time which industry has always perceived as reasonably difficult, through procedures that are no more expensive than the cost of the training labor involved. Given reliable, consistent, and long-lived productivity following acquisition, such training of retarded individuals might show the best cost-benefit ratio of all possible alternatives. When this is shown to be the case, this previously untapped labor source should achieve considerable popularity.*

POSTSTATEMENT

There are a few good points in the article, but it obviously is not one of my favorites and not one that I recommend very often. The discussion of content

*This research was supported by NICHHD Program Project Grant No. HD05951 to the Institute for Child Behavior and Development, University of Illinois at Urbana-Champaign.

task analysis is comprehensive and helpful. This article also includes a distinction that should have been made in Levy, Pomerantz, and Gold (1977)* in Chapter 17 of this book. It is the distinction, made by Lawler, between horizontal and vertical job enlargement. The distinction is an interesting and useful one for the field.

---

*Sidney M. Levy, David J. Pomerantz, & Marc W. Gold. Work skill development. In N. G. Haring & L. Brown (Eds.), *Teaching the Severely Handicapped: A Yearly Publication of the American Association on Education of the Severely/Profoundly Handicapped* (Vol. 2). New York: Grune & Stratton, 1977.

CHAPTER 25

Mealtime

Marc and Ronna Gold

PRESTATEMENT

In early 1975 Robert Perske began working on the book *Mealtimes for Severely and Profoundly Handicapped Persons.* He called regularly during that time to bounce ideas off my wife Ronna and me. We played the role of friendly critic during quite a bit of that period. At one point he asked us to commit to paper the feelings that we had been expressing to him about people with significant handicapping conditions and, particularly, about their mealtime experiences. We said yes. And time passed. I kept a note in my briefcase telling me to do it, but kept putting it off. Then one day while sitting on an airplane I came up with the idea of trying to do it in poetic form and proceeded to do so. When I got home, I gave it to Ronna. She did a major overhaul, rebuilding, cutting and pasting, and adding other original material. Thus, the poem "Mealtime" was created.

The poem means a great deal to me. One of the important parts of the philosophy of Try Another Way relates to the importance of creating a balanced relationship between a trainer and a learner. I find it very difficult to thoroughly convey to the people we train just what we mean by that balanced relationship and how one goes about establishing and maintaining it. This poem addresses that balance. There are people in the field, especially in the more academic circumstances, that find esthetic forms of expression to be corny or inappropriate in professional communication. I obviously do not share that opinion. I feel a responsibility to use any communication strategy to get across the messages. And this is one of them.

How nice, it's time to eat.
Why do I say how nice?
Because now I won't be hungry?
Not really. Mealtime is so much more than that for me.

This poem originally appeared in Robert Perske, Andrew Clifton, Barbara M. McLean, and Jean Ishler Stein (Eds.), *Mealtimes for severely and profoundly handicapped persons: New concepts and attitudes* (Baltimore: University Park Press, 1977). Reprinted by permission of the publisher.

Mealtime is a spacer.
It's such a nice way to travel between each of the other moments in life.
It's a breath between getting from and going to,
And at the same time, it's somewhere to be.

It's food. The food part of a meal doesn't always have to be nice.
Just almost always.
I like cold things really cold.
There is only one way I really like eggs.
I like meat I can chew, but not when it chews back.
And bell peppers? Boooo!

You see, I don't ask much from my food.
I just want to like it almost always.
How do you feel about food?
I've never been able to ask if you hate bell peppers, too.

If food was all there was to meals,
I don't know what I'd do.
I'd just as well eat pills.
Or I could clank my spoon.
Meals are so much more.

People are at mealtime what seasoning is on food.
Meals are for US.
US means more to me than food.
When you have as much time for me as I have for you,
Mealtime is a great time for US.
Then I don't even remember what I eat.

At other times of the day it seems that only I need you.
At those times, could I also be important for you?
Those have been times of benevolence.
Benevolence—a badly paved one-way street.
Mealtimes are not benevolent times.
Mealtimes are balanced times
    for US.

I hate to remember before there was US.
I'll call that WE.
That's just you and me.
Not really together—not at all US.

WE didn't balance.
WE were just for the food.
I had no respect for you, and you none for me.

I wondered: can't meals be more than food?
And dribblechin, and hurryup,
And then, and again,
You don't look at me and I won't look at you.

Then something happened—the beginning of US.
You were teaching me to use a spoon.
WE had been working on that for weeks.
I didn't know why, and you didn't either.

That day, I put a spoonful of applesauce in my ear, and you laughed.
You laughed so hard, I began to laugh, too.
I still don't know why you stopped laughing when you saw me laugh
  with you.

Things have been so different ever since.
I think what happened was respect.
It comes out in so many ways.

Do you know that you stopped those awful smiles you used to give me?
I knew they were awful because you never gave them to your friends.
Your voice changed, too.
It used to be squeaky, now it's you.

You didn't think I could learn anything, did you?
Since the laugh, you have come up with so many new things for US.
And I know you think of me more.
I think more of you, too.
That's one of the nicest things about US.
I want to learn exactly as much as you want to teach.

Did you notice that I almost cried yesterday?
I couldn't tell if you did or not.
WE are together a lot of the day.
But until yesterday, mealtime was the only time for US.

Yesterday you asked me to help you make my bed.
My God, I thought, could the bedroom be for US, too?
The way you touched me.
The way you looked at me.

I don't understand the bed yet, but I'll do anything for US.
With those awful smiles, the squeaky voice, and your all-day-long
  bits of food,
WE never got anywhere.

BUT LOOK OUT FOR US.

POSTSTATEMENT

The poem describes benevolence as "a badly paved one-way street." Most
people working with the handicapped think benevolence is a positive concept
until they realize that it is not bidirectional. Also important is the fact that

when someone is observing a person labeled handicapped performing something complex, especially something that the observer is incapable of doing,
the feeling of benevolence is likely to be superceded by a feeling of respect.

Another point in the poem is the statement that the handicapped person
realized the smiles the trainer was giving were awful because "you never
gave them to your friends." That point stands on its own, yet it seems worth
emphasizing.

The last point relates to the subtle sexual implication near the end of
the poem. Frankly, the implication was not intentional. I did not realize
it was there until someone mentioned it to me. But, sure enough, the statement "My God, I thought, could the bedroom be for US, too?" certainly
does allow for a possible sexual interpretation, though it was unintentional
and is inappropriate since the poem addresses the trainer-learner relationship.
It does, however, bring up the important point of sexuality. I find it fascinating
that many people feel sexual activity between or with individuals having
significant handicapping conditions is repulsive. But do the handicapped not
have the same rights as others? Is is not likely that there will be honorable,
legitimate, close, personal, and possibly sexual, interactions between people
labeled normal and people labeled handicapped? My only reason for bringing
this up is that we claim to want them to be fully participating members of
society. If we really mean that, then this is one of the areas we should examine more closely. I hasten to add that any resolution of this issue is clearly a
long way off. But until we start thinking about it, it will continue to be far
in the future.

CHAPTER 26

Issues in Prevocational Training

Marc W. Gold and David J. Pomerantz

PRESTATEMENT

The writing of this chapter was a most agonizing experience. And I am not
even sure why. David Pomerantz and I were extremely busy at the time.
While we thought it would not be difficult, we found it almost impossible
to set aside chunks of time to collaborate, write, and rework this chapter.
We were also driving Marty Snell, the editor, crazy. She was patient and
lovely throughout, and fortunately we all ended the experience friends. This
chapter reflects a nice combination of those issues important to David and
those important to me. It includes the concept of vocational and prevocational
training, guidelines for vocational education strategies, and a fairly detailed
discussion of content task analysis, along with cycle constancy, information,
and judgment.

The provision of vocational and prevocational training to all individuals,
regardless of handicapping conditions, is a challenge for the fields of special
education and rehabilitation. Vocational training presents unusually difficult
programmatic questions because the content of relevant curricula is not
easily determined. No areas of instruction are purely vocational or purely
nonvocational. Furthermore, the world of work is so diverse that no standardized objectives fit all cases and no curriculum is universally appropriate. In
this chapter, we address the issue of defining vocational tasks in the hope
of stimulating the planning of vocational curricula and programs. Several
general strategies for vocational programming are suggested.

DEFINING VOCATIONAL SKILLS AND VOCATIONAL EDUCATION

How can a behavior be defined as a "vocational behavior" or "skill"? Are
certain skills, such as those concerned with technical matters (e.g., handling
machinery), "vocational" as compared with skills which are "social," "acade-

---

This chapter originally appeared in M. Snell (Ed.), *Systematic instruction of the moderately and severely handicapped.* (Columbus, Ohio: Charles E. Merrill, 1978). Reprinted
by permission of the publisher.

mic," "daily living," etc.? Such a definitional scheme does not hold up to close scrutiny (Parker, 1971). Many people have technical skills but use them as a hobby rather than a vocation (e.g., the weekend mechanic). Others are unskilled in technical matters but are vocationally successful. Obviously, any work setting involves communication skills, daily living and self-help skills, transportation skills, etc., as well as the specific tasks peculiar to a particular job. All socially appropriate behaviors are needed in the work world and are just as much "vocational" as they are any other arbitrary classification. There can be no topographical definition of a vocational task.

In order to understand vocational activity, it may be more fruitful to look at the effects of work in our society. Some major consequences of working are (1) financial support, (2) opportunities for social interaction, (3) opportunity to gain the respect of others, (4) opportunities to enhance skills in chosen areas, and (5) personal satisfaction (Terkel, 1974).

As a general statement, most working behavior is controlled by at least some, and possibly all, of these outcomes. The executive who hates the pressures of his job but enjoys the salary would probably leave if his salary were drastically reduced. The musician who is committed to writing and performing new materials is likely to leave the world of music altogether if forced to write and play only background music.

Although different jobs may require completely different skills to be performed in different kinds of settings, the functional relationships involved in working behavior have some degree of uniformity within the society. By emphasizing these functional relationships, vocational educators are most likely to meet the needs of handicapped students. Parker (1971) suggested that vocational education is training for gainful employment. This appears to be a straightforward and useful outlook, particularly if the term *gainful* is considered in a broad sense, encompassing the outcomes of work listed above. The first outcome of working (i.e., financial support) might, however, be weighted more heavily than the others because it may lead directly to the other outcomes (Ryan, 1971). Thus, for the purposes of this chapter, let us define *vocational skills* as those which enable an individual to earn a living and other normative reinforcers associated with working.

PROBLEMS CONCERNING VOCATIONAL OPPORTUNITY

At present, most individuals labeled as moderately, severely, or profoundly retarded work in sheltered employment if they work at all. The tasks performed in sheltered workshops and work activity centers are generally extremely simple, unimportant in industry, and nonremunerative (Gold, 1973; Greenleigh Associates, Note 1; Pomerantz & Marholin, 1977). In fact, many of these tasks are so low level that training is rarely needed nor particularly useful (Levy, Pomerantz, & Gold, 1977). Commonly, vocational and pre-vocational training programs use the same kinds of tasks as models and introduce sheltered workshoplike activity as the core of the curriculum. But is this vocational education? According to the definition used in this chapter, it is not. The performance of low-level tasks as the end product of a training program provides no access to financial independence. These tasks are not useful in competitive employment (Greenleigh Associates, Note 1) and generally pay considerably below the minimum wage rate in sheltered employment. Furthermore, it is difficult to see how the performance of such tasks could produce continuing skill development in any area, gain the respect of others, or lead to a sense of personal satisfaction. The disturbing conclusion which must be reached is that few moderately, severely, or profoundly retarded persons are currently engaged in vocational activity. School and rehabilitation programs which rely on the nonvocational tasks currently performed by handicapped workers are implicitly accepting and maintaining the status quo.

Opening opportunities: An orientation for vocational education

The educator who is involved in vocational programming must gear his or her efforts toward the upgrading and expanding of the retarded individual's opportunities in the world of work. Otherwise there is no purpose to prevocational or vocational programming. Training must be used as a strategy for increasing opportunity. For example, placement in competitive industry might be established as the objective for a prevocational program. With such a concrete target, training could be provided in situations that are actually relevant and important for reaching that target. Skills which are tied to specific opportunities (e.g., getting along with a particular supervisor, performing certain job skills) would be taught. Little time would be wasted in training ill-defined hypothetical constructs which may not even exist and are not likely to enhance usable skills (e.g., "eye-hand coordination," "figure-ground").

A second goal of prevocational programming to broaden vocational opportunities includes major changes in the sheltered workshop. Training can be used to demonstrate to those in charge of habilitation programs and to people in industry that the students can perform higher level, more remunerative work if such work is available. In both cases, a social change activity (obtaining jobs or better workshop contracts) is paired with effective training to meet a predetermined educational objective.

Guidelines for vocational education strategies

The following are general considerations in devising strategies to open vocational opportunities; each of the issues mentioned should be examined specifically, taking into consideration the particular resources and problems of the home community.

1. *Do skills which are taught have current utility and at the same time represent a future-oriented change strategy?* Part of the utility of the concept of vocational skill is that it causes teachers and curriculum planners to view students' activities as related to some life goal or activity that will be performed in adulthood. This perspective leads to the development of long sequences of lessons, in some cases years long. If we are to have severely

and profoundly handicapped individuals, for example, operating farm implements, we must task analyze the operation of this equipment and the skills which are prerequisite to such operation. The result would, it is to be hoped, be the identification of specific skills which may eventually be elaborated into machinery operation skills and which might even be taught to 4-year-olds. Caution must be taken, however, to ensure that the skills which are taught contribute to the successful existence of the student at the present time. If we fail to consider the long-range outcomes of our programs, too much time is spent teaching behaviors that have their only relevance in the school setting or during childhood. Conversely, ignoring current utility of skills leads to an inappropriate allocation of training time to information which can be used only in conjunction with a great deal of other information; and students end up with a great deal of unusable information.

If the future-oriented change strategy is well designed, there should be little problem identifying curriculum content which is both consistent with the goal of the strategy and currently useful to students. School programs should be designed (1) to create the need to train vocational skills in students by stimulating work opportunities in communities and (2) to follow through by providing the skills necessary to take advantage of these newly opened opportunities. The strategy should be kept specific (e.g., secure 10 jobs in the food-processing factories in town within 1 year). Similarly, the curriculum derived from the strategy should be a sequence of specific, clearly defined skills rather than vague constructs. For example, particular machine operation and factory maintenance skills which correspond to existing jobs in the target factories would be defined and analyzed into component skills.

In the context of a change strategy, training is most likely to meet students' current needs if target behaviors include some "competencies" rather than an exclusive focus on supposedly "normal" characteristics (Gold, 1975). "Competence" refers to a set of skills which is valued by society and not freely available. Competencies do not develop in nonhandicapped or handicapped individuals without training. Once they have been developed, however, an individual has something to offer society (i.e., the work world, for the purposes of this discussion) and is in a position of strength when he applies for a job. If a program turns out competent students, it can engineer change by demonstrating the students' ability to successfully engage in vocational activity. A young adult trained to operate one type of duplicating machine is obviously not skilled in operating all such machines. However, if the competence is demonstrated to a potential employer who needs an operator of duplicating machinery, the feasibility of training the student on other machines should be evident. Rather than asking for employment "handouts," the vocational programmer is selling competent labor.

A similar strategy is to obtain verbal commitments from businesspersons to consider for employment any individual who demonstrates specified skills. Training could then be directed in these skill areas, and a follow-up visit to the potential employers would be arranged when the skills are mastered. Such a procedure (1) gets "your foot in the door," always an important part of getting a job, (2) indicates that you can be trusted to fulfill commitments, and (3) demonstrates the students' work potential and receptivity to training.

Finally, the educator interested in vocational programming should attempt an analysis of employers' needs in the local community. By reading management literature and classified ads, talking to businesspersons, and any other means available, the educator must identify skills or worker characteristics that are truly needed and valued. Significant increases in vocational opportunity for handicapped individuals will occur when they are prepared to meet some real employment needs.

A first step might be to identify the types of industries operating in the community. What kinds of jobs exist within these industries? More specifically, what kinds of skilled, semiskilled, and unskilled jobs are common within an industry and are found in all factories or warehouses related to that industry? It is not uncommon for certain jobs to be characterized by high turnover rates over extended periods of time. Such jobs are ideal targets for job placement programs. If certain industrial settings are more receptive than others to the prospect of hiring trained handicapped workers, these settings should be analyzed in more detail. After several successful placements, the supervisors and workers might be willing to share their positive experiences with more hesitant employers.

Analysis of industry in a community is by no means limited to factories and production settings. What special features of the community contribute to the economy? In tourist areas, for example, the vocational educator could approach hotels and motels which might employ maids and related maintenance staffs. If students are appropriately trained, perhaps they will be hired during peak tourist seasons when the need for labor is highest. Once the students demonstrate that they are competent and reliable, it is possible that they will be retained on a year-round basis. Similarly, students trained in farm-related jobs might begin with a temporary placement during the spring or fall. Quality labor is always appreciated, and further opportunities should open once it is demonstrated that the handicapped worker is an asset.

2. *Does the change strategy operate within the values of the business world as well as the values of the helping professions?* Traditionally, appeals on behalf of the handicapped have asked for kindness and charity for "those who are less fortunate." The slogan "hire the handicapped," for example, implies that employers should change their hiring criteria, moving away from the workers who best meet their needs to those who need special help and favors. It is unreasonable and short-sighted to expect business interests to behave in a manner incompatible with the patterns that developed and maintain their current position in society. Rather, change efforts should purposefully arrange consequences to match business interests, which would make business more likely to extend opportunities to handicapped persons. Potential employers should be made aware of the assets of handicapped workers as well as aversive consequences for not integrating a labor force. Examples of positive and aversive consequences to business include worker reliability (cost savings from reduced turnover) and potential loss of govern-

ment contracts resulting from the potential legal action taken if handicapped persons are systematically excluded from a labor force (*Federal Register,* 1976). In placement activities, a vocational program should demonstrate to employers an understanding of the business world and make sensible arguments in business terms (Kelly & Simon, 1969). Those who implement a strategy for integrating and changing sheltered workshops must understand industry and know how to establish efficient production systems before they can expect to secure better contracts (Gold, 1973; Stroud, 1970; also refer to Chapter 12).

A teacher can enhance the chances of placing students into competitive jobs by keeping data bearing on the reliability and competence of students. Attendance records, acquisition data for vocational skills which have been taught, and records of time needed to train the more difficult skills should be organized into a "package presentation" for potential employers. A concise and clear presentation indicates to the employer that he is talking with people who know their business and can deliver on the promises being made. A data-based presentation may be especially effective because it speaks in terms used in the business world, not in the generalities and subjective labels which have traditionally dominated education and the social services.

3. *Does the program capitalize on existing community resources?* Unfortunately, some of the educators responsible for vocational programming know very little about the world of work. In the past, there has been little effort to obtain occupational information because low expectations prevented consideration of most kinds of jobs for students with special needs. This suggests that the fields of vocational education and special education must begin to work together (Gold, Note 2; Phelps, 1977). There is evidence that such an alliance is beginning to form (Chaffin & Clark, Note 3). For the present, however, programmers must make a concerted effort to familiarize themselves with a broad range of occupations. When target occupations have been selected (i.e., those job areas at which change strategies will be aimed), it is the programmer's responsibility to become knowledgeable about these jobs. Educators must move out from the confines of the school building and open lines of communication with those who recruit, employ, and train workers. The people who know the content of target jobs (i.e., requisite skills) have the information and materials to make great contributions to developing vocational curricula. Those of us whose expertise is in the teaching process (i.e., how, rather than what, to teach) must go to them for help.

4. *Are program criteria explicit?* The ambiguously stated objectives of current prevocational and vocational programs are not conducive to the achievement of any meaningful outcome. The intended result of a training program must be clearly delineated. Not only must target behaviors and skills be clearly defined, but the conditions in which these skills are to be performed should also be stated. For example, rather than simply specifying the operation of a buffing machine as the training goal, the programmer should indicate criteria for quality and quantity of performance; the locations where work will occur; the people likely to be around the worker; and the quality of supervision that can be expected. The problem which arises is

that complex criteria based on natural environmental conditions present an almost insurmountable challenge to the trainer. It is difficult enough to teach complex skills without worrying about the intricacies of the situations in which the skills must be performed. For this reason, we suggest two criteria be established prior to the initiation of training. Criterion I is an arbitrary point at which it can be assumed that the student has learned the skill. Criterion II is defined as demonstration of the skill in the situation where it is ultimately expected to occur (Gold, 1976).

Using these two criteria, the programmer can separate two equally vital tasks: establishing control over behavior and ensuring that control is exercised by the natural environment. There are some situations in which it is desirable to combine both tasks by teaching directly in the Criterion II situation or by training natural reinforcement agents (e.g., parents) to work with the student. With such a direct approach, there is little reliance on generalization. Teaching students to use public transportation provides a good example of a circumstance in which direct training in the Criterion II situation is advisable. The trainer cannot accurately simulate the buses and street corners that comprise Criterion II in this case, and generalization is most unlikely (Emshoff, Redd, & Davidson, 1976). Therefore, the trainer should "take to the streets" and slowly proceed through the sequence of skills needed by an individual who wishes to use the bus system.

Similarly, the operation of expensive machinery peculiar to one factory would be trained directly in the factory. It is not feasible for the school program to purchase similar machinery because of the cost and the existence of only one or two jobs related to the machinery. Rather than teaching the use of other machines and hoping for generalization, instruction would occur after the job is secured in the Criterion II setting. In this case, however, the teacher could establish a Criterion I and shift to Criterion II after the machine operation skills are acquired. For example, he could train during the least busy work shift, thereby reducing distraction and competition from activity around the machinery. When the task is reliably performed under these conditions, the student would be introduced into the shift that he will actually work.

When it is extremely difficult to establish control in the Criterion II setting, or it is impractical to use the Criterion II setting for training, the programmer must design an instructional situation which (1) is conducive to training or establishment of behavioral control and (2) is no more discrepant from Criterion II than is absolutely necessary. Under the artificial conditions that are established, skills are taught until the student demonstrates reliable performance. At this point, Criterion I has been achieved. For example, in handling money, when the student can make change without error 5 consecutive times, the trainer can reasonably assume that the basic skill is intact. At this point, generalization to Criterion II conditions must be actively programmed (Pomerantz & Redd, Note 4). In this example, the student's handling of money might be monitored in a crowded store and additional training implemented if the target skills are not exhibited in the appropriate form or at the appropriate times.

Programming generalization to Criterion II has been accomplished by varying irrelevant aspects of the instructional environment or by gradually fading to Criterion II conditions after the target behavior has been established. If only a single trainer has conducted the program, newly acquired skills may be restricted to the presence of that trainer (Reiss & Redd, Note 5). Similarly, instruction in a single setting (Wahler, 1969), with a specific series of prompts (Rincover & Koegel, 1975), or with a single set of instructional materials (Redd, 1972) may inhibit generalization to Criterion II. Using more than one trainer (Reiss & Redd, Note 5) or multiple settings and materials (Emshoff et al., 1976) may enhance performance in Criterion II. For example, several supervisors might be asked to participate in teaching janitorial skills within a work setting. In this way, the student is more likely to respond appropriately to instructions from all people to whom he is responsible than if one supervisor or teacher conducts all training. Alternatively, a program similar to the one employed by Pomerantz and Redd (Note 4) could be initiated. In such a program, critical differences between the training and Criterion II settings are identified. Artificial aspects of training are then gradually eliminated and natural Criterion II characteristics are introduced into the instructional setting. An extremely difficult assembly task might be color-coded in order to facilitate acquisition. The color cues would be removed eventually, however, because the actual materials on the job do not contain reliable color cues.

OPENING OPPORTUNITY THROUGH TRAINING

All of the programmatic questions which have been raised are important. All vocational education strategies, however, rest on the assumption that useful work skills can be taught to handicapped students. From our perspective, such an assumption is reasonable if the teacher is able to carefully analyze the skills and tasks needed for vocational activity.

Content Task Analysis

Content task analysis is a term used in our instructional system to mean breaking a task into teachable components (Gold, 1976). "Teachable" is determined by the skills of the teacher and the skills of the learner. There are a variety of reasons for a content task analysis. Perhaps the most important is that the trainer or teacher must develop intimacy with the task. One principal reason why many handicapped individuals learn so little is that their teachers have failed to recognize the distinction between being able to do something and being "intimately familiar" with that same thing. Take as an example a rather trivial task found in both work and nonwork settings, the dropping of one's pants to go to the bathroom. The task is one that everyone performs. How much do we really know about this task? Where are the feet positioned in relationship to the toilet before beginning the process? Is it done the same every time? When the pants are first touched, which hand is used and exactly where is it placed? Is a palmer grasp used, or the thumb and forefinger? Are the pants touched in any place or does the thumb go to the exact place every time? If the pants have a zipper, are they first unzipped or unbuttoned? Are the outer garment and undergarment lowered simultaneously, or one at a time? How far are the garments dropped, above the knees or down to the ankles? Few individuals could answer these questions about a task that they have performed thousands of times. Furthermore, task intimacy is not necessarily indicated even for somebody who can answer all of these questions. What are the possible alternative ways of performing each of these functions? Are there methods of performing this task that are different from the one that you use for yourself, that are more efficient and effective for the people you are responsible for training? Most tasks, of course, are not so familiar.

When we develop a task analysis for an industrial task or some other task that we have never seen before, we have no already existing method of our own to bias our decisions. We proceed step by step through each component of the task and, being unfamiliar with it, inspect and become intimate with the components. What results from this process of careful inspection is the content task analysis, or the listing of the steps into which the task has been arbitrarily divided. It is to be hoped that these steps represent teachable components. The notion that a component is teachable is really a hypothesis. It is proven during the training process when we find out which steps are, in fact, being acquired and which are not. The size of the divisions (i.e., how many steps) depends on preconceived notions regarding the capabilities of the learner. The same task can be divided into any number of components. For example, to teach a person to add the numbers 2 and 3, we might give a single instruction such as "Take 2 objects; put them together with 3 more; then count the new total." Such an instruction represents a very weak training strategy involving a content task analysis of 3 steps. To use this strategy the teacher must assume that the learner has a well-developed repertoire of entering behaviors. Alternatively, one could teach 2 + 3 by including steps for the concepts of the numbers 2 and 3, the concept of "putting things together," how to count, etc. Anybody with experience in teaching knows that some "clinical judgment" or sensitivity to the needs of individual students is important. Perhaps these terms can be understood, at least partly, as the ability to make subtle discriminations regarding the number of component steps needed for each student. Such discriminations are indeed important. If we divide a task into an unnecessarily large number of components, efficiency is lost, and even more seriously, the task can become tedious and aversive to the student. If each component is too large (i.e., too few steps), the student will not acquire the skill. The ability to make these subtle discriminations can be developed by (1) preparing many content task analyses and implementing the training that they generate, (2) knowing the intended student population, and (3) revising the content task analysis when necessary (Gold, 1976).

Assessment. Since the above statements indicate the need to know student characteristics, some discussion of the issue of assessment is in order. Behavioral assessment can be helpful in certain situations to determine priorities about what to teach. If such assessment is to be genuinely useful to the trainer, however, it must focus on the specific behaviors prerequisite to the target task. Assessment of general behavioral constructs is not seen as particularly useful. These general types of assessment usually result in limiting a teacher's expectations and willingness to teach relatively difficult skills. They provide little specific information on whether a learner is ready to acquire a particular task. The focus, then, should be on task-specific assessment. In order to conduct such assessment, intimacy with the task is necessary because the trainer must know enough to be able to identify the specific behaviors needed to begin lessons on the target task.

Identifying necessary prerequisite skills for a particular task is another important reason for a content task analysis. It forces the task analyst to identify what is expected of the learner upon entering the situation. It is interesting to note that the more the task analyst knows about the task, the fewer prerequisites are needed by the learner. As the task analyst learns the intricacies of the task, the behaviors needed by the learner become more and more apparent. It is common to conclude from the development of a content task analysis that there are skills and lessons that need to be completed before a learner may enter the planned situation. When writing a content task analysis for time telling, for example, it becomes obvious that recognition of numerals 1 to 12 is a necessary prerequisite. It is also clear that the clock is not the best place for teaching numeral recognition. The content task analysis signals the trainer to assess whether the intended learners recognize numbers from 1 to 12 and, if not, to have lessons on this (and other prerequisites) before entering the time-telling lesson. The logical extension of a content task analysis leads to a long sequence of lessons in those cases where many prerequisites are identified. In other cases, content can be acquired without mastering other skills in advance of the particular one being taught. In this sense the content task analysis has an almost diagnostic function of signaling what the trainer must look for in terms of prerequisite skills.

There is another diagnostic aspect to content task analysis. Most training begins with some opportunity for the learner to demonstrate what he already knows about the task. Either the task is presented for him to do, it is demonstrated once for the learner to copy, or something else happens that allows the learner to show what he knows. When the learner can perform the task perfectly, that is obvious also. Most learners know something about most of the tasks that we teach them. Watching such a learner proceed through a task, after a content task analysis has been done, allows the trainer to clearly identify which components of the task the learner does and does not know. This is very helpful in focusing on what needs to be taught and evaluating how training is proceeding.

The data collection system which has been used in our research on skill training relies on the content task analysis. As illustrated below, each step in the analysis is written across the top of a data sheet. Positioned vertically are the training trials. During each cycle (i.e., trial) the trainer marks a symbol for correct, error, or correct with assist. Thus, in reviewing a data sheet the trainer knows the precise components of the skills that have been mastered or are causing problems. Errors should decrease with each additional trial. In some cases, however, they do not and revisions in the content task analysis (i.e., smaller steps) must be made.

Cycle constancy. Another important reason for doing a content task analysis relates to the concept of cycle constancy. *Cycle constancy* is a term used in industry to describe a production situation in which the worker's series of motions are consistent each time he does whatever he does. Without a content task analysis it is almost impossible to clearly evaluate whether or not a series of motions is consistent each time an individual performs the task. Cycle constancy is a critical variable for training individuals who have been labeled severely or profoundly retarded. Establishing an invariant set of operations as the initial condition for training makes sense with this population. We have found in our research that moving from a cycle constant circumstance to a more generalized set of circumstances is more efficient than trying to teach the generalized set in the initial stages of training. Similarly, in manual tasks, the content task analysis allows the trainer to demand consistent use of the left and right hands, thereby making constant the movement cycle of the task. Random switching of hands makes acquisition of complex skills less efficient.

Example of content task analysis. One sample content task analysis is shown below to clarify the procedure. Purposes, materials, prerequisites, and how to teach the content are covered separately in this system.

Task: Winding bobbin of sewing machine

1. Release thread for spool
2. Place spool of thread on spool pin
3. Pull thread with left hand to thread guide hook
4. Wrap thread around hook (from back to front, 3/4 revolution) and drop thread
5. Pick up bobbin with right hand (holes on top)
6. Put thread through one of the holes in bobbin (from under side)
7. Hold thread with right thumb on top of bobbin
8. Hand wrap thread around bobbin axle (2 full revolutions)
9. Place bobbin on winder spindle with holes up
10. Push bobbin to right to engage winder
11. Release coupling wheel (turn top to bottom, counterclockwise)
12. Step on foot control—lift foot when bobbin is full (machine will stop automatically when bobbin is full)
13. Push bobbin to left (disengage winder)
14. Retighten coupling wheel (turn clockwise)

The complexities of various tasks become evident when a content task analysis has been done. We have found two general qualities of tasks that, when identified, add considerably to our ability to design powerful training procedures. We refer to these as "information" and "judgment."

Information and Judgment

In the past, decisions about which tasks could and could not be taught to retarded individuals were based on estimates of the individuals' potential to learn (see Wolfensberger, 1967; Gold, 1973). This practice was plagued by inappropriately low expectation levels of training personnel (Gold, 1975). One contribution of a systematic task analysis approach is that it provides criteria for making such decisions on the basis of task characteristics and available training methods. That is, there are parameters which signal the trainer about the "teachability" of various tasks. An important example is the distinction between what we call *information* and *judgment*. This distinction has proven especially valuable in planning instructional methods for tasks that do not have cycle constancy (e.g., social skills). "Information" is discrete, dichotomous, and absolute. "Information" refers to situations in which a set of correct responses can be clearly specified. "Judgment" is not discrete. "Judgment" is used in circumstances in which there is a range of correct responses without discrete boundaries.

The distinction between information and judgment is sufficiently important to warrant a few examples. Take the task of putting 1-inch wooden cubes into a box. If you take one cube at a time and place it in the box, exactly 300 will fill the box. That is information. If there are 301, then one sticks up; 299, there is a 1-inch hole. That is information. If a supervisor says to a worker, "Hey, man, I'm not going to pay you to put one cube at a time in that box, just put all that stuff in there," the task changes. It turns out that, depending on how the cubes lie when thrown in, anywhere from 260 to 285 cubes fill the box. There is no exact number or even an exact appearance that says too few or too many cubes have been put in. It is a range of correctness without discrete, definable boundaries and as such comprises a judgmental task.

The difference between information and judgment is critical for several reasons. The first is that instructional technology is quite sophisticated for teaching information but provides little help for teaching judgment. In fact, the most common, systematic way to teach judgment is to restrict the range of acceptable performance. The learner is then given feedback which restricts his performance within these close boundaries, thus increasing the probability that subsequent performance will fall within the broader true range.

The second reason for distinguishing between information and judgment concerns job selection. For individuals with moderate, severe, and profound mental retardation, how can we "meaningfully" assess which jobs and which workers might go together? Looking at the information and judgmental aspects of tasks and jobs is quite revealing. For example, what is the simplest job in a gas station?: pump jockey, the person hired for $2 an hour to take care of the pumps. Let us look at this job from the perspective of hiring and training a person who is labeled severely retarded. Informational aspects of this job include squeezing the handle until certain numbers show on the pump, taking the handle and putting it back on the pump, walking over to the window, collecting the money from the customer, and returning proper change according to the amount of money listed on the pump. Judgmental aspects of this job include cleaning the windshield, conversing with the driver, giving directions, and cleaning the pump area. The job of pump jockey includes several critical tasks which are judgmental and very difficult to teach to someone who finds it difficult to learn.

Now let us look at the job of mechanic, which pays more than four times that of pump jockey. We estimate that a mechanic spends approximately 40% of his time in disassembly, 20% on diagnosis and evaluation, and about 40% on reassembly, correcting all of the problems. Disassembly for most things done by a mechanic is a semiskilled operation. Let us take a brake job as an example. The first two operations are judgmental, putting a car up on jacks and taking off the hubcaps. Now come the informational parts of this job: placing a small stool at the left front wheel; getting an air hose; taking an impact wrench off the wall and connecting the hose up to it; setting it for removal; putting it to each lug nut and removing each of the nuts; pulling the wheel off and setting it down; removing the dust cap on a front wheel bearing; removing the cotter pin, nut and bearing; and pulling the drum off. To continue the job, the mechanic removes the springs, removes the shoes, takes the 7/16-inch wrench and removes the brake line, takes the same wrench and removes 4 bolts and the wheel cylinder, putting all these parts into a bucket. All of these steps are informational and, with readily available instructional procedures, we can teach them to individuals with severe and profound mental retardation. In the meantime the $14-an-hour mechanic has gone ahead and spent that 40% of his time putting other brake jobs together.

The information-judgment aspect of content task analysis indicates that jobs which have always been considered simple may present complex training problems. Other jobs which are seemingly more difficult involve many informational steps that can be readily taught. As Gold (1976) emphasized, the decision to teach or not teach any task to the severely/profoundly handicapped must be based on whether or not that task can be analyzed into teachable components rather than on some general feeling about the difficulty of the task. The concepts of information and judgment help the trainer to arrive at this decision.

CONCLUSION

Analyses of the world of work and vocational needs of the handicapped indicate the necessity for improvement in vocational education programs. The curriculum content must be designed to give students functional skills and the opportunities to use these skills in meaningful jobs. Once a curriculum is established, content analyses of specific tasks can be performed. Decisions regarding the particular skills to be emphasized in training and the instructional methods to be used should be made on the basis of what is learned from content task analyses.*

*Preparation of this chapter was supported by NICHHD Program Project Grant No. HD05951 to Institute for Child Behavior and Development, University of Illinois at Urbana-Champaign.

POSTSTATEMENT

The first part of this chapter is powerful. The definitions of vocational skills make sense. The critique of existing programs based on those definitions makes a great deal of sense also. The conceptual framework provided should be valuable for people trying to design prevocational and vocational programs.

In the discussion of Guideline 1 a statement suggests that high turnover jobs would make ideal job placement targets. That statement needs to be qualified. If the reasons for high turnover relate to poor working conditions, then they would not be good target jobs. If the high turnover is due to job dissatisfaction because of the characteristics of the people that were hired, and if the placement of people with significant handicapping conditions into those jobs results in considerable job satisfaction for both the handicapped and the employer, then the statement is true.

At the end of Guideline 4 we suggest that some difficult tasks might sometimes be color coded. For clarification, you are referred to the discussions about color coding in Chapter 11 of this book.

You may have noticed considerable redundancy between the last section of this article and some points in Chapter 24. No apologies. The majority who read one of these articles never saw the other. The point was needed with both readerships, and so the repetition was necessary. The fact that both of these would someday show up in the same book was never anticipated.

CHAPTER 27

Behind the Wheel Training and Individuals Labeled Moderately Retarded

Steven J. Zider and Marc W. Gold

PRESTATEMENT

This was the last experiment to be conducted in our research program prior to my leaving the University of Illinois. It seems like a very appropriate piece of work to "cap off" 10 years of research activity. Steve Zider, the person who did this experiment as his PhD dissertation, had been involved with the research program for many years, both as an undergraduate and as a graduate student. Having a very thorough knowledge of the system, he wished to use his dissertation as an opportunity to further test the limits of the Try Another Way System. This experiment did just that.

Individuals labeled mentally retarded often are difficult to train. Difficulty in training, until a few decades ago, resulted uniformly in severe skill deficits for individuals labeled moderately, severely, and profoundly mentally retarded. Recent interests and efforts concerning the needs of individuals who are difficult to train have led to the research and development of several training technologies (e.g., Brown, Scheuerman, Cartwright, & York, 1973; Bellamy, Peterson, & Close, 1975; Gold, 1976). These technologies have enabled teachers to effectively train people labeled moderately, severely, and profoundly retarded in areas previously perceived as not feasible, e.g., complex vocational assembly, mobility skills, daily living skills, and language.

One of the technologies responsible for increased skill manifestation by individuals labeled handicapped is a system of task analysis developed by Marc Gold. An important assumption by Gold (1976) serves as the impetus for this research:

> The decision to teach or not teach any task to the severely/profoundly handicapped must be based on whether or not that task can be analyzed into teachable components rather than some general feelings about the difficulty of the task. (p. 81)

Reprinted from *Exceptional Children* by Steven J. Zider and Marc W. Gold, by permission of The Council for Exceptional Children. Copyright 1981 by The Council for Exceptional Children, 1920 Association Drive, Reston, Virginia 22091.

Systems for determining task difficulty have been attempted (Fitts, 1951; Nickerson, 1965) but never achieved (Cronbach, 1957). Furthermore, perceptions concerning the capabilities of individuals labeled mentally retarded have been far from accurate. An individual's potential for learning is not determined by capabilities claimed to be associated with a particular IQ and/or classification. Limitations exist, rather, in the extent of resources and quality of available technology to teach (Gold, 1975).

Driver education for individuals labeled moderately retarded is in an embryonic stage. There are, however, studies which suggest that individuals with that label are capable of learning to operate an automobile safely (Gutshall, Harper, & Burke, 1968; Bologna, Kellering, Mullen, & Stickler, 1971). Studies done in several states, e.g., Illinois, Michigan, Pennsylvania, Maine, and New York, led Budig and Carter (1975) to conclude that individuals labeled mentally retarded are capable of driving. Of the studies cited, research and special driver education programs have focused only on individuals labeled as educable mentally handicapped (EMH). Teaching individuals labeled moderately mentally retarded to drive has not been previously approached. To move in the direction of developing procedures for training them is a logical extension and progression of the current status and trends in this area.

An initial attempt to develop procedures for training individuals with moderate and severe mental retardation to drive was piloted by Zider (1977). Four individuals labeled moderately and severely mentally retarded were trained on the following predriving skills: assuming a position in the simulator, buckling the seat belt, starting the simulator, engaging the gears of the simulator, maintaining a constant speedometer reading of 30 mph, and braking under various hazardous circumstances. The main question of interest was whether or not these skills could be broken down into teachable components and taught to these individuals. The mean response time for the individuals with mental retardation in the simulated hazardous situation was .77 seconds. The mean response time of normal individuals tested in a hazardous situation is .75 seconds. While direct comparisons are not possible, the similarity of response times in Zider's experiment was encouraging.

The present experiment had three working hypotheses: (a) All skills learned in the simulator would be transferred, with assistance, to the training vehicle. (b) Individuals labeled moderately mentally retarded could be trained to competently perform skills found in driver education curricula. (c) The resultant data would be sufficiently convincing to continue developing procedures for the driver training of individuals labeled moderately mentally retarded.

METHOD

Subjects

Two subjects were selected from those who had participated in the initial study by Zider (1977). The decision to select these two subjects was based on subject interest and present employment status. If a subject was currently working in competitive employment or attempting to seek competitive employment, driving might be important in the future. IQ scores ranged between 48 and 42 on a standard WAIS IQ test. This falls in the range of the moderately mentally retarded (Grossman, 1973). Such data had no direct bearing on this study for two reasons: (a) A particular IQ score was not a criterion for subject selection. (b) There is little relationship between a person's ability to perform complex skills and IQ (Gold, 1972, 1976; Bellamy, Peterson, & Close, 1975; Zider, 1977). Procedures in the present study did not restrict participation to individuals with language skills. Only subjects with language skills participated in this experiment, however, to insure that they understood they were *not* to attempt to drive, whether or not they used skills learned in the study.[1] Four normal subjects also participated in this study. Two of these four individuals were nondrivers; the other two were experienced drivers.

Equipment

The Link-Singer simulator[2] was used for the simulation training. A driver education training car provided by the University of Illinois Department of Health and Safety Education was used for the range training. This car was equipped with a dual-control brake which, when engaged, overrode the driver's brake. The trainer completed the certification course required for anyone using a driver training vehicle for instruction. Four 3-ft. pylons were used for measurement purposes. A standard stop sign was also used to indicate the target point for the braking segment of range training. Eighteen 6-in. pylons were used to indicate three different traffic lanes for the passing segment. Two 60-second stop watches were also used. The in-car phases of this experiment were conducted in a large, closed-off parking area.

Procedure

As implied by the description of equipment, training was divided into two major phases: simulation training and driving range training.

During simulator training, two subjects were taken to the simulator facility each day. Each subject sat in the back of the room while the other was being trained. The data collector was positioned to the left of the subject. Skills trained in the simulator were initially trained without the use of the simulation film. Following attainment of criterion on skills without the film, each subject was trained to perform the skill in the context of the simulation film. The audio portion of the film was deleted so that the language would not interfere with the training.

---

[1] Both subjects labeled mentally retarded did not have enough language capabilities to be able to pass the required multiple choice test for receiving a driver's license or even a learner's permit.

[2] 1970 Link Driving Simulator System made by the Link Division of the Singer Company, Binghamton, New York.

After simulator training, subjects were given the opportunity to transfer the skills learned there to the driving range. Four task groups were covered in both the simulation training phase and driving range phase. Those task groups and their specific skills are shown in Table 1.

Criterion

Criterion I conditions, that is, "a predetermined point at which you assume learning has taken place" (Gold, 1976), were, for simulator training:

1. Driver preparation—Four consecutive trials without errors or assistance.

2. Starting and engaging into drive—Six consecutive trials without errors or assistance.

3. Speed maintenance and braking—Four consecutive trials without errors or assistance, with and without simulation films.

4. Turning and passing—Four consecutive trials without errors or assistance, with and without simulation films. Since the films consisted of several instances of these maneuvers, a subject was required to complete at least two film segments without error or assistance, i.e., 22 different instances, which can be considered as 22 different trials when compared to skill training without the films. There were three parts to the entire film. Part 1 had 6 different instances of turning right. Part 2 had 6 different instances of turning left, and Part 3 had 10 different instances of turning right and left.

The decision concerning criterion levels was based on Zider's (1977) previous experiment, which had been arbitrary but which was also supported by Gold's (1976) research which states that attainment of Criterion I is an arbitrary decision.

Table 1
Skills Trained in Simulator and Driver Training Vehicle

1. Driver preparation (correct positioning of self and equipment)
2. Starting and engaging into drive
3. Speed maintenance braking
    a. Moving forward (starting); attaining a constant speed; holding speed constant; stopping
4. Turning and passing
    a. Moving forward; attaining a constant speed; holding speed constant; stopping; turning *left*; stopping
    b. Repeating (a), turning *right*
    c. Repeating (a) (turning *left*) at a contrived intersection under traffic conditions, i.e., one car traveling in opposite direction, at appropriate time
    d. Repeating (c), turning *right*
    e. Moving forward; attaining constant speed; holding speed constant; accelerating 5 mph; changing lane, *left*; decelerating to constant speed; stopping
    f. Repeating (e) changing lane, *right*
    g. Repeating (e) with slow moving vehicle in *left* lane moving in the same direction
    h. Repeating (f) with slow moving vehicle in *right* lane moving in the same direction

The Criterion II environment for this experiment was the driving range. Criterion II calls for "repeated demonstrations of the behavior under the conditions where it is ultimately expected to occur" (Gold, 1976, p. 79). For the 4 task groups and their skills, Criterion II required 4 consecutive trials without error or assistance per training session across 3 consecutive days.

Formats

1. Simulation Training—For the first component skill, a total task format was employed, i.e., each step of the content task analysis was performed in sequence every trial with assistance from the trainer. After each subject reached criterion on Skill 1, a forward chaining format was used to link and train the preceding component skill to the next one; i.e., each step taught previously was repeated before moving to the next step.

2. Driving Range Training—All component skills were trained using the total task format. After subjects were given the opportunity to transfer the driver preparation skills and four trials without error or assistance were completed, a short "assimilation" period occurred. This assimilation period consisted of each subject's taking his or her foot off the brake, letting the car move forward, pressing down on the accelerator very slightly, and braking to a stop. Once the trainer was convinced that each subject understood and could control the effects of the car, training of driving manuevers began.

Modifications

Overall training procedures remained constant throughout the experiment. Component steps within some of the component skills, however, were modified in accordance with entering levels of behavior manifested; i.e., one subject naturally combined movements that the other subject did not.

Nondrivers labeled mentally retarded received all treatments in the experiment: simulator training, in-car turning and passing, and in-car speed maintenance. Drivers labeled normal and nondrivers labeled normal received the third treatment: in-car speed maintenance and braking.

Design

A single-subject design was employed. Dependent measures were number of trials, number of errors and time to criterion, and description of the modifications of the training procedures which facilitated criterion performance for each subject. During the in-car speed maintenance and braking, two other criterion measures were employed. The first measure was the amount of time spent traveling a designated 200-ft. interval while cruising at 20 mph. Subjects were required to maintain speed for 6.0 to 6.8 sec. for the 200-ft. interval. (This range was permitted because of experimenter error and subject variability.) The second measure was the subjects' ability to brake accurately 83 ft. after the end of the 200-ft. interval. Subjects were required to stop within 3 ft. on either side of a designated target.

RESULTS

Both subjects labeled mentally retarded reached criterion on all skills in simulator training. Data on acquisition during this phase are presented in Table 2.

Both subjects labeled mentally retarded also reached criterion on all skills in the in-car turning and passing phase of the experiment. Acquisition data for those skills are presented in Table 3.

All subjects reached criterion on the skills in the in-car speed maintenance and braking skills of the experiment. Drivers labeled normal had the skills prior to the onset of training. The data obtained from their performance, therefore, were criterion data rather than acquisition data. Nondrivers labeled normal required less time and fewer trials, and made fewer errors than nondrivers labeled mentally retarded. Means and standard deviations obtained on subjects' performance on holding a constant speed and braking during this phase are reported in Tables 4 and 5, respectively.

In summary, all subjects learned all of the skills under the criterion conditions stated in the method section. A total of 442 min., roughly 7 1/2 hours, was required in order for Subject 1 (the first of the two labeled mentally retarded) to learn all skills in the simulator and automobile. A total of 312 min., roughly 5 1/4 hrs., was required for Subject 2 (the second nondriver labeled mentally retarded) to learn all skills in the simulator and automobile.

Table 2

Simulator Training: Total Trials, Errors, and Time Required for Skill Acquisition

Subject	Skill	Trials	Errors	Time (in min.)
1	(1) Simulator retraining[a]	14	11	27
	(2) Turn left (TL)	28	58	13
	TL with film	8	20	44
	(3) Turn right (TR)	23	44	16
	TR with film	3	1	16.5
	(4) Change lane left	5	1	5
	(5) Change lane right	9	2	8
	(6) Film test; TR/TL	5	8	32
2	(1) Simulator retraining	7	3	10.5
	(2) Turn left (TL)	27	22	16
	TL with film	4	3	22
	(3) Turn right (TR)	10	10	8
	TR with film	2	0	11
	(4) Change lane left	7	3	6
	(5) Change lane right	4	0	2
	(6) Film test; TR/TL	2	0	16

[a]Simulator retraining consisted of: fastening seat belt, placing foot on brake pedal, starting simulator, engaging into drive, accelerating to 20 mph, maintaining 20 mph, braking, disengaging into park, and turning off ignition.

Table 3
In-Car Turning and Passing: Total Trials, Errors,
and Time Required for Skill Acquisition

Subject	Skill [a]	Trials	Errors	Time (in min.)
1	1&2 Driver preparation, starting, and engaging into drive	12	0	2
	4 Turning and passing			
	a. Turn left (TL)	12	0	16
	b. Turn right (TR)	12	0	15
	c. TL intersection	13	1	20.5
	d. TR intersection	12	0	25
	e. Change lane left (CLL)	15	4	16
	f. Change lane right (CLR)	16	6	19
	g. CLL pass car	12	0	16
	h. CLR pass car	12	0	14
2	1&2 Driver preparation, starting, and engaging into drive	12	0	2
	4 Turning and passing			
	a. Turn left (TL)	16	4	24
	b. Turn right (TR)	12	0	17
	c. TL intersection	13	1	17
	d. TR intersection	12	0	17
	e. Change lane left (CLL)	14	2	16
	f. Change lane right (CLR)	12	0	12
	g. CLL pass car	12	0	12.5
	h. CLR pass car	12	0	14

[a]The driving skill numbers and letters correspond to those in Table 1.

DISCUSSION

All nondriver subjects with mental retardation learned the entire skill sequence in the simulator and in the automobile under the driving range condition. Prior to training, the expectation was that both subjects would be able to acquire all skills in the simulator and transfer all skills into the automobile. There was, however, considerable apprehension regarding the extent to which some of these skills could be trained under the driving range condition.

The interaction between a trainer's expectation and task difficulty was an important part of the rationale for this study. It was assumed that the decision to teach tasks to individuals with severe/profound mental retardation should be based on the trainer's ability to break the task into teachable components (Gold, 1976). Without this assumption training would not have been attempted in either the first piece of research (Zider, 1977) or this one.

The trainer's confidence regarding ability to teach all the skills in the simulator was based on previous experience and success in the simulator and on the trainer's ability to break judgmental behaviors into discrete behaviors. The extent to which a trainer's expectancy and perceptions of self-competency actually determine success in a particular area is, to say the least, an

Table 4
Time Spent Driving Standard Distance at Constant Speed:
Means and Standard Deviations

Subject		Criterion Trials					
		Mean[a]			Standard Deviation		
		T_T (in sec.)	T_1 (in sec.)	T_2 (in sec.)	T_T (in sec.)	T_1 (in sec.)	T_2 (in sec.)
Nondrivers labeled	1	6.51	3.21	3.29	.197	.188	.138
mentally retarded	2	6.23	2.97	3.25	.186	.137	.162
Nondrivers labeled	5	6.48	3.05	3.43	.186	.144	.142
normal	6	6.26	2.99	3.30	.123	.067	.159
Drivers labeled	3	6.32	2.99	3.33	.150	.010	.097
normal	4	6.56	3.13	3.43	.178	.121	.098
		Acquisition Trials					
		Mean			Standard Deviation		
Nondrivers labeled	1	6.88	3.39	3.39	.634	.313	.138
mentally retarded	2	6.42	3.07	3.30	.721	.300	..433
Nondrivers labeled	5	6.61	3.09	3.47	.431	.264	.268
normal	6	5.91	2.89	3.03	.164	.104	.136

Note: Trials were defined as criterion trials if (a) the time spent driving 200 ft. (T_T) was between 6.0 and 6.8 seconds and the time for covering either half of the distance (T_1 or T_2) was between 3.0 and 3.6 seconds and (b) the trial was one of four successive trials where the times fell within permissible limits.

[a]All subjects received 12 criterion trials. All trials not defined as criterion trials were included in the data labeled Acquisition Trials.

Table 5
Amount of Error in Braking: Means and Standard Deviation Scores

Subject		Criterion Trials	Acquisition Trials	
		Mean	Mean	Standard Deviation
Nondrivers labeled	1	0	−.44[a]	1.48
mentally retarded	2	0	−.23	1.38
Nondrivers labeled	5	0	+.45	.69
normal	6	0	+.63	.52
Drivers labeled	3	0		
normal	4	+.25		

Note: Criterion trials are those in which nondriver subjects stopped on target for four consecutive trials across 3 days. All subjects received 12 criterion trials. Acquisition trials are all trials that are not included in criterion trials.

[a]Each unit represents a 6-ft. interval. The range of measurement was:

Undershoot				Overshoot		
-3	-2	-1	0	+1	+2	+3
18 ft.	12 ft.	6 ft.	On target	6 ft.	12 ft.	18 fr.

intriguing issue that will be argued empirically and intuitively for many decades to come.

The specific skills of most concern, under driving range conditions, were braking, in immediate and nonimmediate situations, and variable accelerations. The trainer's anxiety regarding his ability to teach these skills was further exacerbated during the first week of training the experimental subjects. While training the skills of accelerating and braking, the trainer was subjected to several instances of hard jolts and his own nausea from the rapid changes in speed. There were and are not, as far as the trainer can determine, any insights or anecdotes that will help prevent these natural consequences experienced by the trainer. If one can tolerate such disequilibrium while in the midst of it, time, training expertise, and a commitment to the learner will eventually transform this imbalance into a balanced and exciting accomplishment for both the trainer and the learner.

Simulator Training

After 18 months of not having an opportunity to practice the skills they acquired in the first experiment (Zider, 1977), both nondrivers labeled mentally retarded retained the entire skill sequence from the first experiment. It has long been argued in the field of learning, with regard to individuals labeled mentally retarded, that they do not retain information as do individuals with normalcy (Belmont, 1966). These data suggest that a retention problem did not exist for individuals in this study on these tasks. The limitations of this study, however, preclude making any generalizations regarding retention.

In the first experiment (Zider, 1977) the only skill that really required subjects to make quick decisions followed by an appropriate response—and thus the potential for discrimination errors—was in the reaction time test. Subjects were required to make emergency stops when a pedestrian entered their lane of traffic (simulator training). During the reaction time test the most common error, for all subjects, was the discrimination error; that is, subjects were required to brake when a pedestrian entered their lane of traffic, but they did not. These errors occurred with high frequency. In this experiment all of the new skills trained additionally required subjects to make decisions about which skill was required at a specific time; in that, several alternatives were available. The particular part of the simulator training that required continuous decisions and, therefore, continuous opportunity for frequent discrimination errors, was in the film training. Subjects were exposed to at least 22 different film sequences where combinations of skills, differing from situation to situation, were required. On the first trial Subject 1 was exposed to six different filmstrips. Only one discrimination error was made. Subject 1 was exposed to, in total, 116 driving circumstances, or filmstrips where at least two discrimination errors could have been made per driving circumstance. In total Subject 1 made five discrimination errors. Subject 2 made two discrimination errors on her first trial on film training. In total, three discrimination errors were made.

The virtual absence of discrimination errors manifested by subjects in this experiment, as compared to the first experiment, has at least two plausible and important implications: (a) Generalization of skills to new and different circumstances can be achieved by individuals labeled moderately mentally retarded, given appropriate training, time, and a systematic progression of circumstances with contextual and environmental similarity. Transfer of skills or knowledge to new situations appears related to the degree of contextual similarity and training between material or circumstances (Campione & Beaton, 1972; Pomerantz, 1976, 1978; Zider, 1977). (b) Individuals labeled moderately mentally retarded can make decisions.

Prior to the onset of training a decision was made that if, in the trainer's opinion, the subjects acquired the skills in the simulator with not too much difficulty, an attempt would be made to train the subjects to perform the acquired skills upon verbal command, e.g., "Turn right, turn left, speed up, slow down, soft left, soft right, brake and stop." The relative ease with which subjects acquired the skills, therefore, led the trainer to include this aspect in the simulation training phase, even though it was not originally intended to be included in this experiment.

In-Car Turning and Passing

During the training of passing a car, both subjects labeled mentally retarded exhibited use of their judgment. During the passing training, the driver of the other vehicle would vary the speed from trial to trial. The subjects passing that vehicle were, therefore, required to judge that there was enough clearance so that they could change lanes. This is significant since the issue of subjects' ability to make ongoing decisions is central to this research.

Second, as training progressed it seemed obvious to the trainer and data collector that each subject displayed significant changes in affective behavior. At the onset of training Subject 1 would vigorously laugh following a rough braking response. This vigorous laughing stopped. Subject 1 would tell the trainer, on the way to training each day, to stop at stop signs and stop lights. Subject 1's mother commented on several occasions that she "hadn't seen her son so elated in ages." During the in-car training, Subject 2 encountered some medical difficulties. Her parents exclaimed that it was difficult to keep her calm at home because she was so excited about what she was learning. At the onset of training, Subjects 1 and 2 did not interact when together. By the end of range training they were interacting a great deal.

In-Car Speed Maintenance and Braking

A descriptive comparison of dependent measures during speed maintenance acquisition trials between nondrivers labeled normal and nondrivers labeled mentally retarded is interesting. Nondrivers labeled mentally retarded during acquisition more closely approximated the 6.66 second level on their T_T. Means were: nondrivers labeled mentally retarded, $\overline{X}_{T_T}$ = 6.65; drivers labeled normal, $\overline{X}_{T_T}$ = 6.26. Means and standard deviations for individual subjects are reported in Table 4. During acquisition trials the same pattern holds true between these individuals on T_1 and T_2. There are, however, no real differences between these individuals on these measures. The range is only .39 seconds. It is also important to note that the means reported previously have very unequal n's: n_1 = 70; n_2 = 20. Conclusions, furthermore, should be drawn only from the criterion data, if at all, considering the experimental design and small sample size employed.

The most interesting aspect of the data obtained in in-car speed maintenance and braking is subject performance on the criterion measures T_T, T_1, and T_2. Visual inspection of the data obtained during criterion trials leads to the obvious conclusion that no difference exists among subjects on all the criterion measures. The means for T_T are: nondrivers labeled mentally retarded $\overline{X}_T$ = 6.37; drivers labeled normal = 6.44; nondrivers labeled normal = 6.37. Similar means are also present for T_1 and T_2. Inspection of the standard deviations also shows homogeneity. For T_T the average standard deviations are: nondrivers labeled mentally retarded = .198; drivers labeled normal = .170; and nondrivers labeled normal = .152.

Data similar to those obtained in the measurement of subjects' ability to hold 20 mph constant across a designated 200-ft. interval were obtained during the braking accuracy training. Once again the drivers labeled normal had the skill prior to the onset of training. Subject 4 did make three overshoots of 6 ft. each on the second day. These errors, however, were interpreted as being due to carelessness rather than task complexity. This interpretation is reasonable since those were the only errors made by either of these subjects and the errors were not clearcut; i.e., Subject 4 stopped the car approximately halfway between the designated target and the first error marker.

Also, as in the 20 mph segment braking accuracy, the nondrivers labeled normal required significantly less time and assistance and made fewer errors than the nondrivers labeled mentally retarded. All subjects met the criterion of stopping smoothly at the target four consecutive times, without errors or assistance, across 3 consecutive days. Once both categories of subjects acquired the skill of braking to a smooth stop 83 ft. after they were told to decelerate from 20 mph, no difference existed among individuals.

SUMMARY AND CONCLUSION

As an attempt to further investigate a strategy to teach individuals labeled moderately mentally retarded to perform skills required for driving an automobile, this research strongly suggests that these individuals, indeed, can perform competently skills found in a curriculum which serves to train future drivers. All expected outcomes did result. These outcomes were: (a) All skills learned in the simulator were transferred, with assistance, to the training vehicle. (b) Individuals labeled moderately mentally retarded were trained to perform competently some of the skills found in driver education curricula. (c) The resultant data are sufficiently convincing to suggest the feasibility of continuing the development of procedures for the driver training of individuals labeled moderately mentally retarded.

With all the expectations of this research now an empirical reality, needs for future research include: (a) a further analysis of the simulator and classroom curricula of existing driver education and training based on that analysis; (b) analysis and training of more sophisticated driving skills via simulation training with films; (c) further controlled driving situations including higher speeds combined with emergency maneuvers; (d) transference and refinement of new skills under dynamic driving conditions in the community; and (e) investigation into the possibility of modifying existing regulations which prevent individuals without language skills from obtaining a driver's permit.

Research must continue to explore the ability of individuals labeled mentally retarded to be trained to drive under conditions where driving skills naturally occur. Then and only then will there be an answer to the question of whether or not individuals labeled mentally retarded can be taught to drive an automobile. The importance of mobility in this society provides a strong impetus for the continuation of this research. The issue of language's being a prerequisite to driving can no longer be placed on the back burner.

At the conclusion of this experiment the trainer felt very strongly that individuals being trained could have driven under light or moderate traffic conditions in the community and under clear-weather, daylight conditions.

The data obtained from this study support the claim that individuals labeled moderately mentally retarded are capable of performing complex behaviors. These data do not show that individuals labeled moderately mentally retarded can drive an automobile, especially under continuously changing driving conditions; nor do they suggest that individuals labeled moderately mentally retarded cannot be taught to drive a car in the future.*

POSTSTATEMENT

The masters thesis that preceded this experiment has a principal goal of looking at reaction time and movement time of persons labeled moderately mentally retarded. That thesis was somewhat inconclusive in that there were some methodological questions raised by people with interest in motor performance. The study presented here in a sense bypassed the issues of reaction time and movement time, except as they related practically to actual behind-the-wheel performance, making this study clearly a piece of applied research rather than basic laboratory research.

The data, from our perspective, were quite conclusive about the capabilities of the two experimental subjects regarding their ability to perform the

*This study was supported in part by the University of Illinois Research Board, University of Illinois at Urbana-Champaign and NICHHD Program Project Grant No. HDO-5951 to Institute for Child Behavior and Development, University of Illinois at Urbana-Champaign.

Appreciation is expressed to Susan Kasch for her assistance in data collection.

operations trained within normal boundaries of performance. Whether or not they could perform these behaviors under varying normal road conditions is a question that has not yet been answered. This last piece of formal research in our research program provides a provocative set of questions yet to be answered while, at the same time, it answers very clearly the question of whether or not further study is warranted. I am pleased that this was the final piece of research in that program and hope that we will be able to continue this research under other than university-based circumstances.

References

CHAPTER 5

Belmont, J. M. Long-term memory in mental retardates. In N. R. Ellis (Ed.), *International review of research in mental retardation* (Vol. 1). New York: Academic Press, 1966.

Berlyne, D. *Conflict, arousal, and curiosity.* New York: McGraw-Hill, 1960.

Bousfield, W. A. The occurrence of clustering in the recall of randomly arranged associates. *Journal of General Psychology*, 1953, *49*, 229–240.

Brown, A. L. Subject and experimental variables in the oddity learning of normal and retarded children. *American Journal of Mental Deficiency*, 1970, *75*, 142–151.

Gold, M. W. Preworkshop skills for the trainable: A sequential technique. *Education and Training of the Mentally Retarded*, 1968, *3*(1), 31–37.

Gold, M. W. The acquisition of a complex assembly task by retarded adolescents. Final Report, Project No. 8-8060, University of Illinois, Urbana-Champaign, May 1969.

Heal, L. W., & Bransky, M. L. The comparison of matching-to-sample with discrimination learning in retardates. *American Journal of Mental Deficiency*, 1966, *71*, 481–485.

House, B. J., & Zeaman, D. Transfer of a discrimination from objects to patterns. *Journal of Experimental Psychology*, 1960, *59*, 298–302.

Moore, R., & Goldiamond, I. Errorless establishment of visual discrimination using fading procedures. *Journal of the Experimental Analysis of Behavior*, 1964, *7*(3), 269–272.

Scott, K. G. Engineering attention: Some rules for the classroom. *Education and Training of the Mentally Retarded*, 1966, *1*, 125–129.

Scott, K. G. Learning theory, intelligence, and mental development. *American Journal of Mental Deficiency*, 1978, *82* (4), 325–336.

Shepp, B., & Zeaman, D. Discrimination learning of size and brightness by retardates. *Journal of Comparative and Physiological Psychology*, 1966, *62*, 55–59.

Terrace, H. S. Stimulus control. In W. K. Honig (Ed.), *Operant behavior: Areas of research and application.* New York: Appleton-Century-Crofts, 1966.

Wolff, J. L. Concept shift and discrimination-reversal learning in humans. *Psychological Bulletin*, 1967, *68* (6), 369–408.

Zeaman, D. Learning processes of the mentally retarded. In S. Osler, & R. Cooke (Eds.), *The biosocial basis of mental retardation.* Baltimore: The Johns Hopkins Press, 1965.

Zeaman, D. *The law of redundancy.* Paper presented at Gatlinburg Conference on Research and Theory in Mental Retardation, Gatlinburg, Tenn., March 1968.

Zeaman, D., & House, B. J. The role of attention in retardate discrimination learning. In N. R. Ellis (Ed.), *Handbook of mental deficiency.* New York: McGraw-Hill, 1963.

CHAPTER 6

Acker, M., & Thompson, D. A. Development of the prevocational unit: Stanford Rehabilitation Service. *Archives of Physical Medicine and Rehabilitation*, 1960, *41*, 195–198.

Belmont, J. M. Long-term memory in mental retardates. In N. R. Ellis (Ed.), *International review of research in mental retardation* (Vol. 1). New York: Academic Press, 1966.

Blank, M. The effects of training and verbalization on reversal and extradimensional learning. *Journal of Experimental Child Psychology*, 1966, *4*, 50–57.

Brown, L., & Pearce, E. Increasing the production rates of trainable retarded students in a public school simulated workshop. *Education and Training of the Mentally Retarded*, 1970, *5*, 15–22.

Burdett, A. D. An examination of selected pre-vocational techniques utilized in programs for the mentally retarded. *Mental Retardation*, 1963, *1*, 230–237.

Campione, J., Hyman, L., & Zeaman, D. Dimensional shifts and reversals in retardate discrimination learning. *Journal of Experimental Child Psychology*, 1965, *2*, 255–263.

Cowan, L., & Goldman, M. The selection of the mentally deficient for vocational training, and the effect of this training on vocational success. *Journal of Consulting Psychology*, 1959, *23*, 78–84.

Crosson, J. E. A technique for programming sheltered workshop environments for training severely retarded workers. *American Journal of Mental Deficiency*, 1969, *73* (5), 814–818.

Evans, G. W., & Spradlin, J. E. Incentives and instructions as controlling variables of productivity. *American Journal of Mental Deficiency*, 1966, *71* (1), 129–132.

Furth, H. G., & Youniss, J. Effect of overtraining on three discrimination shifts in children. *Journal of Comparative and Physiological Psychology*, 1964, *57*, 290–293.

Heal, L. W. The role of cue value, cue novelty, and overtraining in the discrimination shift performance of retardates and normal children of comparable discrimination ability. *Journal of Experimental Child Psychology*, 1966, *4*, 126–142.

Hermelin, B. Memory in the severely subnormal. In R. I. Brown (Ed.), *The assessment and education of slow-learning children*. London: University of London Press, 1967.

House, B. J., & Zeaman, D. Transfer of a discrimination from objects to patterns. *Journal of Experimental Psychology*, 1960, *59*, 298–302.

Huddle, D. D. Work performance of trainable adults as influenced by competition, cooperation, and monetary reward. *American Journal of Mental Deficiency*, 1967, *72* (2), 198–211.

Hunt, J. G., & Zimmerman, J. Stimulating productivity in a simulated sheltered workshop setting. *American Journal of Mental Deficiency*, 1969, *74* (1), 43–49.

Kolstoe, O. P. The employment evaluation and training program. *American Journal of Mental Deficiency*, 1960, *65*, 17–31.

Ladas, P. G. Work sample learning rates of the mentally retarded trainee as indicators of production in a work-training center. *Personnel and Guidance Journal*, 1961, *39*, 396–402.

Marsh, G. Effect of overtraining on reversal and nonreversal shifts in nursery school children. *Child Development*, 1964, *35*, 1367–1372.

Meadow, L., & Greenspan, E. Employability of lower level retardates. *American Journal of Mental Deficiency*, 1961, *65*, 623–628.

Ohlrich, E. S., & Ross, L. E. Reversal and nonreversal shift learning in retardates as a function of overtraining. *Journal of Experimental Psychology*, 1966, *72*, 622–624.

Shepp, B. E., & Turrisi, F. D. Effects of overtraining on the acquisition of intradimensional and extradimensional shifts. *Journal of Experimental Psychology*, 1969, *82*, 46–51.

Tighe, L. S., & Tighe, T. J. Overtraining and discrimination shift behavior in children. *Psychonomic Science*, 1965, *2*, 365–366.

Tobias, J. Evaluation of vocational potential of mentally retarded young adults. *Training School Bulletin*, 1960, *56*, 122–135.

Uhl, N. P. Intradimensional and extradimensional shifts as a function of amount of training and similarity between training and shift stimuli. *Journal of Experimental Psychology*, 1966, *72*, 429–433.

Wagner, E. E., & Hawver, D. A. Correlations between psychological tests and sheltered workshop performance for severely retarded adults. *American Journal of Mental Deficiency*, 1965, *69*, 685–691.

White, B., & Redkey, H. *The pre-vocational unit in a rehabilitation center.* Office of Vocational Rehabilitation, U. S. Department of Health, Education, & Welfare, Washington, D. C., 1956.

Youniss, J., & Furth, H. G. Discrimination shifts as a function of degree of training in children. *Journal of Experimental Psychology,* 1965, *70,* 424–427.

Zeaman, D., & House, B. J. The role of attention in retardate discrimination learning. In N. R. Ellis (Ed.), *Handbook of mental deficiency.* New York: McGraw-Hill, 1963.

Zimmerman, J., Overpeck, C., Eisenberg, G., & Garlick, B. Operant conditioning in sheltered workshops. *Rehabilitation Literature,* 1969, *30,* 326–334.

Zimmerman, J., Stuckey, T., Garlick, B., & Miller, M. Effects of token reinforcement on productivity in multiply handicapped clients in a sheltered workshop. *Rehabilitation Literature,* 1969, *30,* 34–41.

CHAPTER 7

Ackerman, L. Training programs: Goals, means, and evaluation. *Personnel Journal,* 1968, *47,* 725–727.

Ackerman, L. Let's put motivation where it belongs—within the individual. *Personnel Journal,* 1970, *49,* 559–562.

Affleck, P. A. Research and demonstration project on task training methods for the severely mentally retarded. Final Report, Goodwill Industries, Inc., Springfield, Mass. Research Grant RD2125-P, U. S. Department of Health, Education, & Welfare, December 1967.

Appell, M. J., Williams, C. M., & Fishell, K. N. Significant factors in placing mental retardates from a workshop situation. *Personnel and Guidance Journal,* 1962, *41,* 260–265.

Ayers, G. E. (Ed.). Innovations in vocational rehabilitation and mental retardation. Proceedings of the Vocational Rehabilitation Subdivision Meetings held at the American Association on Mental Deficiency Conference, San Francisco, May 12–17, 1969.

Babbage, C. *On the economy of machinery and manufactures.* Philadelphia: Carez & Lea, 1832.

Bae, A. Y. Factors influencing vocational efficiency of institutionalized retardates in different training programs. *American Journal of Mental Deficiency,* 1968, *72,* 871–874.

Bailey, J. O. The work trial method of vocational evaluation. *Journal of Rehabilitation,* 1958, *24* (1), 12–14.

Bitter, J. A., & Bolanovich, O. J. Job training of retardates using 8 mm film loops. *Audiovisual Instruction,* 1966, *11,* 731–732.

Blackman, L. S., & Siperstein, G. N. Employment of the mentally retarded in a competitive industrial setting. Final Report, Human Resources Center, Albertson, Long Island, N.Y., February 1967.

Blackman, L. S., & Siperstein, G. N. Job analysis and the vocational evaluation of the mentally retarded. *Rehabilitation Literature,* 1968, *29,* 103–106.

Brethower, O. M., & Rummler, G. A. For improved work performance: Accentuate the positive. *Personnel,* 1966, *43* (5), 40–49.

Brewser, P. When it pays to contract out. *Industrial Engineering,* 1969, *1* (2), 37–39.

Broadwell, M. M. Training the trainers. *Personnel,* 1966, *43* (5), 50–54.

Brolin, D., & Thomas, B. Preparing teachers of secondary level educable mentally retarded: Proposal for a new model. Project Report No. 1, Department of Rehabilitation and Manpower Services, School of Education, Stout State University, Menomonee Wis., April 1971.

Brown, L., Bellamy, T., Perlmutter, L., Sackowitz, P., & Sontag, E. The development of quality, quantity, and durability in the work performance of retarded students in a public school prevocational workshop. *Training School Bulletin,* 1972, *69* (2), 58–69.

Brown, L., Johnson, S., Gadberry, E., & Fenrick, N. Increasing individual and assembly line production rates of retarded students. *Training School Bulletin*, 1971, *67*, 206–212.

Brown, L., & Pearce, E. Increasing the production rates of trainable retarded students in a public school simulated workshop. *Education and Training of the Mentally Retarded*, 1970, *5*, 15–22.

Brown, L., Van Deventer, P., Perlmutter, L., Jones, S. E., & Sontag, E. Effects of consequences on production rates of trainable retarded and severely emotionally disturbed students in a public school workshop. *Education and Training of the Mentally Retarded*, 1972, *7* (2), 74–81.

Bucklow, M. Research into the nature of work and job design. *Personnel Practice Bulletin*, 1967, *23*, 27–38.

Budde, J. F. *The utilization of a systems approach for a prevocational experience program for low-moderate and severely retarded trainees*. Paper presented in part at the 93rd Annual Convention of the American Association on Mental Deficiency, San Francisco, May 1969.

Burke, R. O. The science of rehabilitation—does it exist? *Journal of Rehabilitation*, 1971, *37* (2), 2.

Campbell, N. Techniques of behavior modification. *Journal of Rehabilitation*, 1971, *37* (4), 28–31.

Carrington, J. A. The personnel executive and social responsibility. *Personnel Journal*, 1970, *49*, 504–507.

Carrol, N. F., & Pati G. C. Organized labor and social responsibility. *Personnel Journal*, 1970, *49*, 810–815.

Cegelka, W. J. A review of the development of work-study programs for the mentally retarded. *Training School Bulletin*, 1970, *67*, 87–118.

Chaffin, J. O. Production rate as a variable in the job success or failure of educable mentally retarded adolescents. *Exceptional Children*, 1969, *35*, 533–538.

Chin-Quan, A., & Eastaugh, H. The use of training aids—a survey. *Personnel Practice Bulletin*, 1969, *25*, 135–143.

Chione, J., & Snyder, W. J. MTM methods helping a community. *Journal of Methods—Time Measurement*, 1968, *13*(3), 6–8.

Clark, G. M. A state-wide school work program for the mentally retarded. *Mental Retardation*, 1967, *5*(6), 7–10.

Cohen, J. S., & Williams, C. E. A five phase vocational training program in a residential school. *American Journal of Mental Deficiency*, 1961, *66*, 230–237.

Conant, E. H., & Kilbridge, M. D. An interdisciplinary analysis of job enlargement: Technology, costs, and behavioral implications. *Industrial and Labor Relations Review*, 1965, *18*, 377–395.

Cronbach, L. J. The two disciplines of scientific psychology. *American Psychologist*, 1957, *12*, 671–684.

Crosson, J. E. A technique for programming sheltered workshop environments for training severely retarded workers. *American Journal of Mental Deficiency*, 1969, *73* (5), 814–818.

Crosson, J. E., & deJung, J. E. The experimental analysis of vocational behavior in severely retarded males. Final Report, University of Oregon, Eugene, 1967.

Crosson, J. E., Youngberg, C. D., & White, O. R. Transenvironmental programming: An experimental approach to the rehabilitation of the retarded. In H. J. Prehm (Ed.), *Rehabilitation research in mental retardation*. Monograph No. 2. Eugene, Oreg.: Rehabilitation Research and Training Center in Mental Retardation, University of Oregon, 1970.

Davis, K. Understanding the social responsibility puzzle. *Business Horizons*, 1967, *10*(4), 45–50.

Davis, K., & Blomstrom, R. L. *Business and its environment*. New York: McGraw-Hill, 1966.

Davis, L. E. Job design and productivity: A new approach. *Personnel*, 1957, *33*, 418–430.

Davis, L. E. The design of jobs. *Industrial Relations*, 1966, *6*(1): 21–45.

Davis, L. E., & Canter, R. R. Job design research. *Journal of Industrial Engineering*, 1956, *2*(6), 275-282.

Delp, H. A. Criteria for vocational training of the mentally retarded: A revised concept of the necessary mental level. *Training School Bulletin*, 1957, *54*, 14-20.

Deno, E. The school-work approach to rehabilitation. In H. J. Prehm (Ed.), *Rehabilitation research in mental retardation.* Monograph No. 2. Eugene, Oreg.: Rehabilitation Research and Training Center in Mental Retardation, University of Oregon, 1970.

Denova, C. C. Is this any way to evaluate a training activity? You bet it is! *Personnel Journal*, 1968, *47*, 488-493.

DiMichael, S. G. Vocational diagnosis and counseling of the retarded in sheltered workshops. *American Journal of Mental Deficiency*, 1960, *64*, 652-657.

DiMichael, S. G. The current scene. In D. Malikin & H. Rusalem (Eds.), *Vocational rehabilitation of the disabled: An overview.* New York: New York University Press, 1969.

Distefano, M. K., Ellis, N. R., & Sloan, W. Motor proficiency in mental defectives. *Perceptual and Motor Skills*, 1958, *8*, 231-234.

Doleshal, L. L., Jr., & Jackson, J. S. Evaluation and follow-up study of the Texas Cooperative School Program, *Rehabilitation Literature*, 1970, *31*, 268-269.

Dolnick, M. M. *Contract procurement practices of sheltered workshops.* Chicago: National Society for Crippled Children and Adults, 1963.

Dolnick, M. M. Contractor opinions of sheltered workshops. *Journal of Rehabilitation*, 1964, *30*(2), 23-25.

Dolnick, M. M. Sheltered workshop programs in The Netherlands. *Rehabilitation Record*, 1971, *12*(2), 35-38.

Dubrow, M. Work procurement and job production. *American Journal of Mental Deficiency*, 1958, *63*, 355-359.

Dybwad, G. Rehabilitation for the adult retardates. *American Journal of Public Health*, 1961, *51*, 998-1004.

Eldred, D. M. Use of P.I. at Vermont State Hospital. *Programmed Instruction*, 1965, *5* (2), 9-11.

Elkin, L. Predicting productivity of trainable retardates on experimental workshop tasks. *American Journal of Mental Deficiency*, 1967, *71*, 576-580.

Eskridge, C. S. An approach through special education and vocational rehabilitation in preparing educable retarded youth for work. In F. E. Lord, J. Stubbins, & H. V. Wall (Chm.), *Institutes on work education for educable retarded youth.* Los Angeles: California State College at Los Angeles, 1964.

Etienne, J., & Morlock, D. A. A pre-vocational program for institutionalized mental retardates. *Training School Bulletin*, 1971, *67*, 228-234.

Evans, G. W., & Spradlin, J. E. Incentives and instructions as controlling variables of productivity. *American Journal of Mental Deficiency*, 1966, *71*(1), 129-132.

Farber, B. *Mental retardation: Its social context and social consequences.* Boston: Houghton Mifflin, 1968.

Ferguson, R. G. Evaluating vocational aptitudes and characteristics of mentally retarded young adults in an industrial-agricultural workshop. *American Journal of Mental Deficiency*, 1958, *62*, 787-791.

Firth, W. G. Employment of mentally handicapped workers. *Personnel Practice Bulletin*, 1965, *21* (5), 24-25.

Fleishman, E. A. The prediction of total task performance from prior practice on task components. *Human Factors*, 1965, *7*, 18-27.

Fleishman, E. A., & Hempel, W. E., Jr. A factor analysis of dexterity tests. *Personnel Psychology*, 1954, *7*, 15-32.

Franks, V., & Franks, C. M. Classical conditioning procedures as an index of vocational adjustment among mental defectives. *Perceptual and Motor Skills*, 1962, *14*, 241-242.

Fry, M. A predictive measure of work success for high grade mental defectives. *American Journal of Mental Deficiency*, 1956, *61*, 402-408.

Gassler, L. S. How companies are helping the undereducated worker. *Personnel*, 1967, *44* (4), 47-55.

Gilbreth, F. B. *Motion study*. New York: Van Nostrand, 1911.

Gilbreth, F. B., & Gilbreth, L. M. *Applied motion study*. New York: Sturgis & Walton, 1917.

Gilbreth, F. B., & Gilbreth, L. M. Motion study for the handicapped. In W. R. Spreigel & C. E. Myers (Eds.), *The writings of the Gilbreths*. Homewood, Ill.: Richard O. Irwin, 1953.

Gold, M. W. Preworkshop skills for the trainable: A sequential technique. *Education and Training of the Mentally Retarded*, 1968, *3*, 31–37.

Gold, M. W. The acquisition of a complex assembly task by retarded adolescents. Final Report, Project No. 8-8060, University of Illinois, Urbana-Champaign, May 1969.

Gold, M. W. Middle road research: A statement and an example. Paper presented at the Gatlinburg Conference on Research and Theory in Mental Retardation, Gatlinburg, Tenn., March 1970.

Gold, M. W. Stimulus factors in skill training of retarded adolescents on a complex assembly task: Acquisition, transfer, and retention. *American Journal of Mental Deficiency*, 1972, *76*, 517–526.

Gold, M. W., & Scott, K. G. Discrimination learning. In W. B. Stephens (Ed.), *Training the developmentally young*. New York: John Day, 1971.

Greenstein, M., & Fangman, T. J. Vocational training for the mentally retarded in a metropolitan setting. *Focus on Exceptional Children*, 1969, *1* (5), 1–6.

Groff, G. K. Worker productivity: An integrated view. *Business Horizons*, 1971, *15* (2), 78–86.

Guest, R. H. Job enlargement—A revolution in job design. *Personnel Administration*, 1957, *20* (2), 9–16.

Hamerlynck, L. A., & Espeseth, V. K. Dual specialist: Vocational rehabilitation counselor and teacher of the mentally retarded. *Mental Retardation*, 1969, *7* (3), 49–50.

Heiny, R. W. History of special education. In L. C. Deighton (Ed.), *Encyclopedia of education* (Vol. 8). New York: Macmillan, 1971.

Hennessey, D. E. Getting results from programmed instruction. *Personnel*, 1967, *44* (5), 69–73.

Henze, R., & Meissner, A. Cooperative school-rehabilitation centers. Final Report, Project RD-1810-G interdistrict school. Rehabilitation program for less able retarded adolescents. Educational Research and Development Council of the Twin Cities Metropolitan Area, Minneapolis, July 1970.

Herzberg, F. One more time: How do you motivate employees? *Harvard Business Review*, 1968, *46* (1), 53–62.

Holmes, W. G. *Applied time and motion study*. New York: Ronald Press, 1945.

Honeycutt, J. M., Jr. *The basic motions of MTM*. Pittsburgh: Maynard Foundation, 1963.

Howe, M. A. Employment of the handicapped. *Personnel Practice Bulletin*, 1965, *21* (5), 7–13.

Huddle, D. D. Work performance of trainable adults as influenced by competition, cooperation, and monetary reward. *American Journal of Mental Deficiency*, 1967, *72* (2), 198–211.

Hulin, C. L., & Blood, M. R. Job enlargement, individual differences, and worker responses. *Psychological Bulletin*, 1968, *69* (1), 41–55.

Hunt, J. G., & Zimmerman, J. Stimulating productivity in a simulated sheltered workshop setting. *American Journal of Mental Deficiency*, 1969, *74* (1), 43–49.

Jones, M. B. Individual differences. In E. A. Bilodeau (Ed.), *Acquisition of skill*. New York: Academic Press, 1966.

Katz, E. (Ed.). Second Progress Report, unpublished report on URA Project No. RD-205, Aid Retarded Children, San Francisco, 1959.

Kazdin, A. Toward a client administered token reinforcement program. *Education and Training of the Mentally Retarded*, 1971, *6*, 52–55.

Kelly, J. M., & Simon, A. J. The mentally handicapped as workers—a survey of company experience. *Personnel*, 1969, *46* (5), 58–64.

Kennedy, R. J. R. A Connecticut community revisited. Report on Project No. 655, Office of Vocational Rehabilitation, U. S. Department of Health, Education, and Welfare, Washington, D. C., January 1966.

Kirk, S. A., Karnes, M. B., & Kirk, W. B. *You and your retarded child.* New York: Macmillan, 1955.

Kokaska, C. J. *The vocational preparation of the educable mentally retarded.* Ypsilanti, Mich.: University Printing, Eastern Michigan University, 1968.

Kolstoe, O. P. The employment evaluation and training program. *American Journal of Mental Deficiency,* 1960, *65,* 17–31.

Kolstoe, O. P. An examination of some characteristics which discriminate between employed and not employed mentally retarded males. *American Journal of Mental Deficiency*, 1961, *66,* 472–482.

Kugel, R., & Wolfensberger, W. *Changing patterns in residential services for the mentally retarded.* Washington, D.C.: President's Committee on Mental Retardation, 1969.

Kylen, N.G., Sommarstrom, I., & Akesson, A. Work adjustment and developmental levels in mental retardation. Unpublished report, Institution of Applied Psychology, University of Stockholm, 1971.

Ladas, P. G. Work sample learning rates of the mentally retarded trainee as indicators of production in a work-training center. *Personnel and Guidance Journal,* 1961, *39,* 396–402.

Levine, A. S. Job training programs for the disadvantaged: How can they become more effective? *Welfare in Review,* 1970, *8*(1), 1–7.

Levine, M. J. Subcontracting—rights and restrictions. *Personnel,* 1967, *44*(3), 42–53.

Loban, L. N. The problem of imposed handicap. *Personnel Journal,* 1968, *47,* 323–327.

Logan, O. L., Kinsinger, J., Shelton, G., & Brown, J. M. The use of multiple reinforcers in a rehabilitation setting. *Mental Retardation,* 1971, *9*(3), 3–6.

Lowry, S. M., Maynard, H. B., & Stegemerten, G. J. *Time and motion study.* New York: McGraw-Hill, 1940.

Lupton, T. Wage and salary payment for higher productivity. *Work Study & Management Services,* 1971, *15,* 272–281.

Mackay, F. A. M. Training of semi-skilled workers at Fibremakers Ltd. *Personnel Practice Bulletin,* 1966, *22*(3), 17–26.

Marangell, F. The new language of skills. *Personnel Journal,* 1971, *50,* 280–287.

Mathews, M. G. One hundred institutionally trained male defectives in the community under supervision. *Mental Hygiene,* 1919, *6,* 332–342.

Maynard, H. B., Stegemerten, G. J., & Schwab, J. L. *Methods–time measurement.* New York: McGraw-Hill, 1948.

McGehee, W., & Thayer, P. W. *Training in business and industry.* New York: Wiley, 1961.

McIntosch, W. J. Follow-up study of one thousand non-academic boys. *Exceptional Children,* 1949, *15,* 166–170, 191.

Meadow, L., & Greenspan, E. Employability of lower level mental retardates. *American Journal of Mental Deficiency,* 1961, *65,* 623–628.

Miller, L. E. A follow-through high school program for the mentally handicapped. *American Journal of Mental Deficiency,* 1954, *58,* 553–556.

Mocek, E., Lerner, J. S., Rothstein, J. H., & Umbenhaur, G. W. Report of special on-the-job training demonstration project for mentally retarded youth and adults. Children's Home for Mentally Retarded Children and Adults, San Mateo, Calif., 1965.

Monge, J. P. Untapped labor force. *Personnel,* 1969, *46*(5), 1.

Morrow, R. L. *Time study and motion economy.* New York: Ronald Press, 1946.

Muller, V., & Lewis, M. A work program for the mentally retarded students. *Journal of Secondary Education,* 1966, *41*(2), 75–80.

Nelson, N. *Workshops for the handicapped in the United States.* Springfield, Ill.: Thomas, 1971.

Nixon, R. A. Impact of automation and technological change on employability of the mentally retarded. *American Journal of Mental Deficiency,* 1970, *75,* 152–155.

O'Neil, L. P. Evaluation of relative work potential: A measure of self-concept development. *American Journal of Mental Deficiency,* 1968, *72,* 614–619.

Overs, R. P. *Evaluation for work by job sample tasks* (Prelim. ed.), Vocational Guidance and Rehabilitation Services, Cleveland, 1964.

Overs, R. P., Koechert, G. A., & Bergman, R. H. Obtaining and using actual job samples in a work evaluation program. Final Report Project No. RD-412 VRA, Vocational Guidance and Rehabilitation Services, Cleveland, 1964.

Parker, J. F., & Fleishman, S. A. Use of analytical information concerning task requirements to increase the effectiveness of skill training. *Journal of Applied Psychology,* 1961, *45,* 295–302.

Patterson, C. H. Methods of assessing the vocational adjustment potential of the mentally handicapped. *Training School Bulletin,* 1964, *61,* 129–152.

Patterson, O. G., & Rundquist, E. The occupational background of feeblemindedness. *American Journal of Psychology,* 1933, *45,* 118–124.

Pauling, T. P. Job enlargement—an experience at Philips Telecommunication of Australia Ltd. *Personnel Practice Bulletin,* 1968, *24,* 194–196.

Petit, T. A. *The moral crisis in management.* New York: McGraw-Hill, 1967.

Platt, H., Cifelli, J., & Knaus, W. Automation in vocational training of the mentally retarded. Final Report, Devereux Foundation, Devon, Pa., Research Grant 993-P-63, VRA, U.S. Department of Health, Education, & Welfare, Washington, D.C., undated.

Porteus, S. D. *The Maze Test and clinical psychology.* Palo Alto, Calif.: Pacific Books, 1959.

Prehm, H. J. (Ed.). *Rehabilitation research in mental retardation.* Monograph No. 2 Eugene, Oreg.: Rehabilitation Research and Training Center in Mental Retardation, University of Oregon, 1970.

Prieve, E. A., & Wentorf, O. A. Training objectives—philosophy or practice? *Personnel Journal,* 1970, *49,* 235–240.

Redkey, H. Undergraduate curriculum: A success. *Journal of Rehabilitation,* 1971, *37* (6), 15–17.

Rehabilitation Institute for the Crippled and Disabled. TOWER: Testing orientation and work evaluation. New York: Author, 1967.

Riessman, F. New careers: A workable approach to hard-core unemployment. *Personnel,* 1968, *45*(5), 37–41.

Rohmert, W. Predetermined motion-time systems. *Work Study & Management Services,* 1971, *15*(1), 16–28.

Rusalem, H. The research role. In O. Malikin & H. Rusalem (Eds.), *Vocational rehabilitation of the disabled: An overview.* New York: New York University Press, 1969.

Screven, C. C., Straka, J. A., & Lafond, R. Applied behavioral technology in a vocational rehabilitation setting. In W. I. Gardner (Ed.), *Behavior modification in mental retardation: The education and rehabilitation of the mentally retarded adolescent and adult.* Chicago: Aldine-Atherton, 1971.

Sengstock, W. Planning an in-school work experience program for educable mentally retarded boys and girls. *High School Journal,* 1964, *48,* 179–184.

Sinick, D. Client evaluation: Work task approach. *Rehabilitation Record,* 1962, *3*(2), 6–8.

Sloan, S. Evaluating training programs for the disadvantaged. *Personnel Administrator,* 1970, *15*(6), 15–21.

Smith, P. Operator training for productivity gains. *Personnel Practice Bulletin,* 1968, *24,* 100–109.

Speiser, S., & Cohen, M. The current status of evaluation and prevocational training programs in the United States. Unpublished report, Richmond Professional Institute, School of Rehabilitation Counselling, Richmond, Va., Contract No. 66-21, VRA, Department of Health, Education, & Welfare, Washington, D. C., 1966.

Steinman, W. M. The effects of reinforcement on a vocational rehabilitation task. Unpublished report, Children's Research Center, University of Illinois, Urbana-Champaign, 1971.

Stewart, P. A. Job enlargement. Center for Labor and Management, College of Business Administration, No. 3, University of Iowa, Iowa City, 1967.

Stroud, R. R. Work measurement in rehabilitation workshops: time study and predetermined motion time systems (Monograph No. 2). College Park: Regional Rehabilitation Research Institute, University of Maryland, 1970.

Taylor, F. W. A piece rate system. *Transactions of the American Society of Mechanical Engineers,* Paper No. 647, June, 1895.

Taylor, F. W. Shop management. *Transactions of the American Society of Mechanical Engineers,* Paper No. 1003, June 1903.

Taylor, F. W. *The principles of scientific management.* New York: Harper, 1911.

Thomas, H. P. The employment history of auxiliary pupils between 16 and 21 years of age in Springfield, Massachusetts. *Proceedings and Addresses of the American Association for the Study of the Feebleminded,* 1928, *33,* 132–148.

Tobias, J. Evaluation of vocational potential of mentally retarded young adults. *Training School Bulletin,* 1960, *56,* 122–135.

Tobias, J., & Gorelick, J. The effectiveness of the Purdue Pegboard in evaluating work potential of retarded adults. *Training School Bulletin,* 1960, *57,* 94–104. (a)

Tobias, J., & Gorelick, J. An investigation of "orderliness" as a characteristic of mentally retarded adults. *American Journal of Mental Deficiency,* 1960, *64,* 761–764. (b)

Tobias, J., & Gorelick, J. The utility of the Goodenough Scale in the appraisal of retarded adults. *American Journal of Mental Deficiency,* 1960, *65,* 64–68. (c)

Tobias, J., & Gorelick, J. The Porteus Maze Test and the appraisal of retarded adults. *American Journal of Mental Deficiency,* 1962, *66,* 600–606.

Tredgold, A. F. *A text-book of mental deficiency (amentia).* London: Bailliére, 1908.

Tuggle, G. Job enlargement: An assault on assembly line inefficiencies. *Industrial Engineering,* 1969, *1*(2), 26–31.

Turrentine, J. L. A corporate program for urban action. *Personnel,* 1968, *45*(4), 15–20.

Usdane, W. M. Vocational counseling with the severely handicapped. *Archives of Physiological Medicine and Rehabilitation,* 1953, *34,* 607–616.

Wagner, E. E., & Hawver, D. A. Correlations between psychological tests and sheltered workshop performance for severely retarded adults. *American Journal of Mental Deficiency,* 1965, *69,* 685–691.

Weir, K. C. Hard core training and employment. *Personnel Journal,* 1971, *50,* 364–366.

White, G. R. New audio-visual approach cuts employee training time. *Personnel Journal,* 1968, *47,* 509–510.

Whitesell, W. E., & Pietrus, J. T. Training and the learning process. *Personnel,* 1965, *42,* 45–50.

Williams, P. Industrial training and remunerative employment of the profoundly retarded. *Journal of Mental Subnormality,* 1967, *13,* 14–23.

Wolfensberger, W. Vocational preparation and occupation. In A. A. Baumeister (Ed.), *Mental retardation: Appraisal, education, and rehabilitation.* Chicago: Aldine, 1967.

Younie, W. J. Increasing cooperation between school programs for the retarded and rehabilitation services: An experimental teaching approach. *Mental Retardation,* 1966, *4*(3), 9–14.

Younie, W. J. Developing instructional materials for vocational education of the retarded. In G. E. Ayers (Ed.), *New directions in habilitating the mentally retarded.* Vocational Rehabilitation Subsection, American Association on Mental Deficiency Conference, Denver, May 1967.

Younie, W. J., & Clark, G. M. Personnel training needs for cooperative secondary school programs for mentally retarded youth. *Education and Training of the Mentally Retarded,* 1969, *4,* 186–194.

Zeaman, D., & House, B. J. The role of attention in retardate discrimination learning. In N. R. Ellis (Ed.)., *Handbook of mental deficiency.* New York: McGraw-Hill, 1963.

Zimmerman, J., Overpeck, C., Eisenberg, G., & Garlick, B. Operant conditioning in sheltered workshops. *Rehabilitation Literature,* 1969, *30,* 326–334.

Zimmerman, J., Stuckey, T., Garlick, B., & Miller, M. Effects of token reinforcement on productivity in multiply handicapped clients in a sheltered workshop. *Rehabilitation Literature,* 1969, *30,* 34–41.

CHAPTER 9

Brown, L., & Foshee, J. G. Comparative techniques for increasing attending behavior of retarded students. *Education and Training of the Mentally Retarded,* 1971, *6,* 4–11.

Gold, M. W. Preworkshop skills for the trainable: A sequential technique. *Education and Training of the Mentally Retarded,* 1968, *3,* 31–37.

Gold, M. W. Research on the vocational habilitation of the retarded: The present, the future. In N. R. Ellis (Ed.), *International review of research in mental retardation* (Vol. 6). New York: Academic Press, 1973.

Gold, M. W., & Scott, K. G. Discrimination learning. In W. B. Stephens (Ed.), *Training the developmentally young.* New York: John Day, 1971.

House, B. J., & Zeaman, D. Transfer of a discrimination from objects to patterns. *Journal of Experimental Psychology,* 1960, *59,* 298–302.

Maynard, H. B., Stegemerten, G. J., & Schwab, J. L. *Methods-time measurement.* New York: McGraw-Hill, 1948.

Shepp, B., & Zeaman, D. Discrimination learning of size and brightness by retardates. *Journal of Comparative and Physiological Psychology,* 1966, *62,* 55–59.

Touchette, P. E. The effects of graduated stimulus change on the acquisition of a simple discrimination in severely retarded boys. *Journal of Experimental Analysis of Behavior,* 1968, *11,* 39–48.

Touchette, P. E. Tilted lines as complex stimuli. *Journal of Experimental Analysis of Behavior,* 1969, *12,* 211–214.

Zeaman, D., & House, B. J. The role of attention in retardate discrimination learning. In N. R. Ellis (Ed.), *Handbook of mental deficiency.* New York: McGraw-Hill, 1963.

CHAPTER 10

Belmont, J. M. Long-term memory in mental retardates. In N. R. Ellis (Ed.), *International Review of Research in Mental Retardation* (Vol. 1). New York: Academic Press, 1966.

Gold, M. W. Stimulus factors in skill training of retarded adolescents on a complex assembly task: Acquisition, transfer, and retention. *American Journal of Mental Deficiency,* 1972, *76,* 517–526.

Harter, S. Discrimination learning set in children as a function of IQ and MA. *Journal of Experimental Child Psychology,* 1965, *2,* 31–43.

Shepp, B. E., & Turrisi, F. D. Learning and transfer of mediating responses in discriminative learning. In N. R. Ellis (Ed.), *International Review of Research in Mental Retardation* (Vol. 2). New York: Academic Press, 1966.

Zigler, E., & Balla, D. Lauria's verbal deficiency theory of mental retardation and performance on sameness, symmetry, and opposition tasks: A critique. *American Journal of Mental Deficiency,* 1971, *75,* 400–413.

CHAPTER 11

Brown, L., Johnson, S., Gadberry, E., & Fenrick, N. Increasing individual and assembly line production rates of retarded students. *Training School Bulletin,* 1971, *67,* 206–212.

Crosson, J. E. A technique for programming sheltered workshop environments for training severely retarded workers. *American Journal of Mental Deficiency,* 1969, *73*(5), 814–818.

Dolnick, M. M. Sheltered workshop programs in The Netherlands. *Rehabilitation Record,* 1971, *12*(2), 35–38.

Evans, G. W., & Spradlin, J. E. Incentives and instructions as controlling variables of productivity. *American Journal of Mental Deficiency,* 1966, *71*(1), 129–132.

Farber, B. *Mental retardation: Its social context and social consequences.* Boston: Houghton Mifflin, 1968.

Gold, M. W. Stimulus factors in skill training of retarded adolescents on a complex assembly task: Acquisition, transfer, and retention. *American Journal of Mental Deficiency,* 1972, *76,* 517–526.

Gold, M. W. Research on the vocational habilitation of the retarded: The present, the future. In N. R. Ellis (Ed.), *International review of research in mental retardation* (Vol. 6). New York: Academic Press, 1973.

Heiny, R. W. History of special education. In L. C. Deighton (Ed.), *Encyclopedia of education* (Vol. 8). New York: Macmillan, 1971.

Huddle, D. D. Work performance of trainable adults as influenced by competition, cooperation, and monetary reward. *American Journal of Mental Deficiency,* 1967, *72*(2), 198–211.

Hunt, J. G., & Zimmerman, J. Stimulating productivity in a simulated sheltered workshop setting. *American Journal of Mental Deficiency,* 1969, *74*(1), 43–49.

Rehabilitation Institute for the Crippled and Disabled. TOWER: Testing orientation and work evaluation. New York: Author, 1967.

Schroeder, S. R. A program for research and training of complex rehabilitative performance skills among the retarded. *Psychological Record,* 1972, *22,* 63–70.

Screven, C. G., Straka, J. A., & Lafond, R. Applied behavioral technology in a vocational rehabilitation setting. In W. I. Gardner (Ed.), *Behavior modification in mental retardation: The education and rehabilitation of the mentally retarded adolescent and adult.* Chicago: Aldine-Atherton, 1971.

Tate, B. G., & Baroff, G. S. Training the mentally retarded in the production of a complex product: A demonstration of work potential. *Exceptional Children,* 1967, *33,* 405–408.

U. S. Department of Labor. Philadelphia system work samples: Signposts on the road to occupational choice. Final Report, Experimental & Demonstration Project No. 82-40-67-40, Manpower Administration, JEVS, Philadelphia, September 1968.

Zimmerman, J., Stuckey, T., Garlick, B., & Miller, M. Effects of token reinforcement on productivity in multiply handicapped clients in a sheltered workshop. *Rehabilitation Literature,* 1969, *30,* 34–41.

CHAPTER 12

Gold, M. W. Stimulus factors in skill training of retarded adolescents on a complex assembly task: Acquisition, transfer, and retention. *American Journal of Mental Deficiency,* 1972, *76,* 517–526.

Gold, M. W. Research on the vocational habilitation of the retarded: The present, the future. In N. R. Ellis (Ed.), *International review of research in mental retardation* (Vol. 6). New York: Academic Press, 1973.

Gold, M. W., & Scott, K. G. Discrimination learning. In W. B. Stephens (Ed.), *Training the developmentally young.* New York: John Day, 1971.

Zeaman, D., & House, B. J. The role of attention in retardate discrimination learning. In N. R. Ellis (Ed.), *Handbook of mental deficiency.* New York: McGraw-Hill, 1963.

CHAPTER 14

Grossman, H. J. (Ed.). *Manual on terminology and classification in mental retardation* (Rev. ed.). Washington, D.C.: American Association on Mental Deficiency, 1977.

CHAPTER 15

Brown, L., & Pearce, E. Increasing the production rates of trainable retarded students in a public school simulated workshop. *Education and Training of the Mentally Retarded,* 1970, *5,* 15–22.

Evans, G. W., & Spradlin, J. E. Incentives and instructions as controlling variables of productivity. *American Journal of Mental Deficiency,* 1966, *71*(1), 129–132.

Gold, M. W. Stimulus factors in skill training of retarded adolescents on a complex assembly task: Acquisition, transfer, and retention. *American Journal of Mental Deficiency,* 1972, *76,* 517–526.

Gold, M. W. Factors affecting production by the retarded: Base rate. *Mental Retardation,* 1973, *11* (6), 41–45.(a)

Gold, M. W. Research on the vocational habilitation of the retarded: The present, the future. In N. R. Ellis (Ed.), *International review of research in mental retardation* (Vol. 6). New York: Academic Press, 1973.(b)

Gold, M. W. Redundant cue removal in skill training for the mildly and moderately retarded. *Education and Training of the Mentally Retarded,* 1974, *9,* 5–8.

Gold, M. W., & Barclay, C. R. The effects of verbal labels on the acquisition and retention of a complex assembly task. *Training School Bulletin,* 1973, *70*(1), 38–42. (a)

Gold, M. W., & Barclay, C. R. The learning of difficult visual discriminations by the moderately and severely retarded. *Mental Retardation,* 1973, *11*(2), 9–11. (b)

Merwin, M. R. The use of match-to-sample technique to train retarded adolescents and adults to assemble electronic circuit boards. Unpublished master's thesis, University of Illinois, Urbana-Champaign, 1973.

Rein, R. PRI: Will its time ever come? *Foundation News,* 1973, November/December, 13–24.

Schroeder, S. R. Rate vs. variability as a measure of behavioral adequacy among the retarded. *North Carolina Journal of Mental Health,* 1971, *4,* 3–9.

Wolfensberger, W. Vocational preparation and occupation. In A. A. Baumeister (Ed.), *Mental retardation: Appraisal, education, and rehabilitation.* Chicago: Aldine, 1967.

CHAPTER 16

Bailey, R. C. Due process overdue for the mentally retarded. *The Barrister,* 1972, *30,* 44–45.

Bijou, S. W. Studies in the experimental development of left-right concepts in retarded children using fading techniques. In N. R. Ellis (Ed.), *International review of research in mental retardation* (Vol. 3). New York: Academic Press, 1968.

Binet, A., & Simon, T. Upon the necessity of establishing a scientific diagnosis of inferior states of intelligence. In W. Dennis (Ed.), *Readings in the history of psychology.* New York: Appleton-Century-Crofts, 1948.

Bishop, R. C., & Hill, J. W. Effects of job enlargement and job change on contiguous but nonmanipulated jobs as a function of workers' status. *Journal of Applied Psychology,* 1971, *55,* 175–181.

Boggs, E. M. Federal legislation. In J. Wortis (Ed.), *Mental retardation: an annual review* (Vol. 4). New York: Grune & Stratton, 1972.

Bousfield, W. A. The occurrence of clustering in the recall of randomly arranged associates. *Journal of General Psychology,* 1953, *49,* 229–240.

Brolin, D. Value of rehabilitation services and correlates of vocational success with the mentally retarded. *American Journal of Mental Deficiency,* 1972, *76,* 644–651.

Brown, A. L. Subject and experimental variables in the oddity learning of normal and retarded children. *American Journal of Mental Deficiency,* 1970, *75,* 142–151.

Brown, L., Bellamy, T., & Sontag, E. The development and implementation of a public school prevocational training program for trainable level retarded and severely emotionally disturbed students. Part I. Madison, Wis.: Madison Public Schools, 1971.

Brown, L., Scheuerman, N., Cartwright, S., & York, R. The design and implementation of an empirically based instructional program for severely handicapped students: Toward the rejection of the exclusion principle. Part III. Madison, Wis.: Madison Public Schools, 1973.

Brown, L., & Sontag, E. Toward the development and implementation of an empirically based public school program for trainable mentally retarded and severely emotionally disturbed students. Part II. Madison, Wis.: Madison Public Schools, 1972.

Brown, L., Williams, W., & Crowner, T. A collection of papers and programs related to public school services for severely handicapped students. Part IV. Madison, Wis.: Madison Public Schools, 1974.

Carpenter, M. S. A study of the occupations of 207 subnormal girls after leaving school. University of Michigan, Department of Vocational Education. Special Studies, No. 2, 1921.

Close, D. W. The use of token reinforcement with trainable mentally retarded in a work activity setting. *Vocational Evaluation and Work Adjustment Bulletin,* 1973, *6,* 6–14.

Cronback, L. J. The two disciplines of scientific psychology. *American Psychologist,* 1957, *12,* 671–684.

Diamond, M. Sexuality and the handicapped. *Rehabilitation Literature,* 1974, *35,* 34–40.

Elkin, L. Predicting productivity of trainable retardates on experimental workshop tasks. *American Journal of Mental Deficiency,* 1967, *71,* 576–580.

Fairbanks, R. E. The subnormal child—seventeen years after. *Mental Hygiene,* 1933, *17,* 177–208.

Farber, B. *Mental retardation: Its social context and social consequences.* Boston: Houghton Mifflin, 1968.

Fisher, M. A., & Zeaman, D. An attention-retention theory of retardate discrimination learning. In N. R. Ellis (Ed.), *International review of research in mental retardation* (Vol. 6). New York: Academic Press, 1973.

Fleishman, E. A. On the relationship between abilities, learning, and human performance. *American Psychologist,* 1972, *27,* 1017–1032.

Foxx, R. M., & Azrin, N. H. *Toilet training the retarded: A rapid program for day and nighttime independent toileting.* Champaign, Ill.: Research Press, 1973.

Gallagher, J. J. Organization and special education. *Exceptional Children,* 1968, *34,* 485–491.

Gardner, W. I. *Behavior modification in mental retardation: The education and rehabilitation of the mentally retarded adult.* Chicago: Aldine-Atherton, 1971.

Gibson, D., & Fields, D. L. Habilitation forecast in mental retardation: The configural search strategy. *American Journal of Mental Deficiency,* 1970, *74,* 558–562.

Gold, M. W. Stimulus factors in skill training of retarded adolescents on a complex assembly task: Acquisition, transfer, and retention. *American Journal of Mental Deficiency,* 1972, *76,* 517–526.

Gold, M. W. Factors affecting production by the retarded: Base rate. *Mental Retardation,* 1973, *11*(6), 41–45. (a)

Gold, M. W. Research on the vocational habilitation of the retarded: The present, the future. In N. R. Ellis (Ed.), *International review of research in mental retardation* (Vol. 6). New York: Academic Press, 1973. (b)

Gold, M. W., & Barclay, C. R. The learning of difficult visual discriminations by the moderately and severely retarded. *Mental Retardation,* 1973, *11*(2), 9–11.

Gold, M. W., & Scott, K. G. Discrimination learning. In W. B. Stephens (Ed.), *Training the developmentally young.* New York: John Day, 1971.

Goldberg, I. I. Toward a systematic approach to educational planning for the TMR. *Education and Training of the Mentally Retarded,* 1971, *6,* 148–155.

Hulin, C. L., & Blood, M. R. Job enlargement, individual differences, and worker responses. *Psychological Bulletin,* 1968, *69*(1), 41–55.

Itard, J. M. G. *De l'education d'un homme sauvage.* Paris: Goujonfils, 1801.

Jones, R. J., & Azrin, N. H. An experimental application of a social reinforcement approach to the problems of job finding. *Journal of Applied Behavioral Analysis,* 1973, *6,* 345–353.

Kazdin, A. E. Methodological and assessment considerations in evaluating reinforcement programs in applied settings. *Journal of Applied Behavioral Analysis,* 1973, *6,* 517–531.

Keys, N., & Nathan, J. M. Occupations for the mentally handicapped. *Journal of Applied Psychology,* 1932, *16,* 497–511.

Kirk, S. A. *Educating exceptional children* (2nd ed.). Boston: Houghton Mifflin, 1972.

Korman, A. K. Toward an hypothesis of work behavior. *Journal of Applied Psychology,* 1970, *54,* 31–41.

Laski, F. Civil rights victories for the handicapped. *Social Rehabilitation Record,* 1974, *1,* 15–20.

Menolascino, F. J. Developmental attainments in Down's Syndrome. *Mental Retardation,* 1974, *12,* 13–17.

Merwin, M. R. The effect of pretraining on the training and transfer of circuit board assembly skills of retarded adults. Unpublished doctoral dissertation, University of Illinois, Urbana-Champaign, 1974.

Merwin, M. R. The use of match-to-sample technique to train retarded adolescents and adults to assemble electronic circuit boards. Unpublished master's thesis, University of Illinois, Urbana-Champaign, 1973.

Micek, L. A., & Bitter, J. A. Service delivery approaches for difficult rehabilitation clients. *Rehabilitation Literature, 1974, 35,* 258–263, 271.

Olshansky, S., & Beach, D. A five-year follow-up of mentally retarded clients. *Rehabilitation Literature, 1974, 35,* 48–49.

Palmer, R. *Prediction of work performance and work adjustment in mentally retarded adults.* Uppsala, Sweden: Scandinavian University Books, 1974.

Panda, K. C., & Lynch, W. W. Effects of social reinforcement on the retarded child: A review and interpretation for classroom instruction. *Education and Training of the Mentally Retarded, 1972, 7,* 115–123.

Parker, S. *The future of work and leisure.* London: MacGibbon & Kee, 1971.

Patterson, C. H. Methods of assessing the vocational adjustment potential of the mentally handicapped. *Training School Bulletin, 1964, 61,* 129–152.

Rosen, M., Floor, L., & Baxter, D. Prediction of community adjustment: A failure at cross-validation. *American Journal of Mental Deficiency, 1972, 77,* 111–112.

Rosen, M., Kivitz, M. S., Clark, G. R., & Floor, L. Prediction of post-institutional adjustment of mentally retarded adults. *American Journal of Mental Deficiency, 1970, 74,* 726–734.

Rosen, D., & Soloyanis, G. *American Association on Mental Deficiency Special Convention Publication, Social and Legislative Issues.* 98th Annual Meeting of the American Association on Mental Deficiency, Toronto, Canada, June 1974.

Rowan, B. The retarded offender. *The Barrister, 1972, 30,* 30–35.

Schroeder, S. R. Automated transduction of sheltered workshop behaviors: Technical note. *Journal of Applied Behavioral Analysis, 1972, 5,* 523–525. (a)

Schroeder, S. R. Parametric effects of reinforcement frequency, amount of reinforcement, and required response force on sheltered workshop behavior. *Journal of Applied Behavioral Analysis, 1972, 5,* 431–441. (b)

Schroeder, S. R. A program for research and training of complex rehabilitative performance skills among the retarded. *Psychological Record, 1972, 22,* 63–70. (c)

Scott, R. D. Job enlargement—The key to increasing job satisfaction? *Personnel Journal, 1973, 52,* 313–317.

Screven, C. G., Straka, J. A., & Lafond, R. Applied behavioral technology in a vocational rehabilitation setting. In W. I. Gardner (Ed.), *Behavior modification in mental retardation: The education and rehabilitation of the mentally retarded adolescent and adult.* Chicago: Aldine-Atherton, 1971.

Stabler, E. M. Follow-up study of retarded clients from a training workshop. *Mental Retardation, 1974, 12*(3), 7–9.

Tobias, J., & Gorelick, J. The effectiveness of the Purdue Pegboard in evaluating work potential of retarded adults. *Training School Bulletin, 1960, 57,* 94–104.

Touchette, P. E. The effects of graduated stimulus change on the acquisition of a simple discrimination in severely retarded boys. *Journal of Experimental Analysis of Behavior, 1968, 11,* 39–48.

U. S. Department of Health, Education, and Welfare, Office of Coordination. Mental Retardation Rehabilitation Act of 1973. *Program for the Handicapped.* Washington, D. C.: November 1973.

Wagner, E. E., & Hawver, D. A. Correlations between psychological tests and sheltered workshop performance for severely retarded adults. *American Journal of Mental Deficiency, 1965, 69,* 685–691.

Whelan, E. Developing work skills: A systematic approach. In P. Mittler (Ed.), *Assessment for learning in the mentally handicapped.* Edinburgh and London: Churchill Livingstone, 1973.

Whitten, E. B. The Rehabilitation Act of 1973 and the severely disabled. *Journal of Rehabilitation, 1974, 40,* 2.

Wolfensberger, W. Vocational preparation and occupation. In A. A. Baumeister (Ed.), *Mental retardation: Appraisal, education, and rehabilitation.* Chicago: Aldine, 1967.

Zeaman, D. Learning processes of the mentally retarded. In S. Osler, & R. Cooke (Eds.), *The biosocial basis of mental retardation.* Baltimore: The Johns Hopkins Press, 1965.

Zisfein, L., & Rosen, M. Self-concept and mental retardation: Theory, measurement and clinical utility. *Mental Retardation,* 1974, *12,* 15–19.

CHAPTER 17

Argyris, C. The individual organization: An empirical test. *Administrative Science Quarterly,* 1959, *4*(2), 145–167.

Argyris, C. *Integrating the individual in the organization.* New York: Wiley, 1964.

Baldamus, W. *Efficiency and effort.* London: Travistock, 1961.

Baroff, G. S. *Mental retardation: Nature, cause, and management.* Washington, D. C.: Hemisphere, 1974.

Biganne, J. F., & Stewart, P. A. Job enlargement: A case study. Research Series No. 25, State University of Iowa, Bureau of Labor and Management, 1963.

Bishop, R. C., & Hill, J. W. Effects of job enlargement and job change on contiguous but nonmanipulated jobs as a function of workers' status. *Journal of Applied Psychology,* 1971, *55,* 175–181.

Brown, L., & York, R. Developing programs for severely handicapped students: Teacher training and classroom instruction. *Focus on Exceptional Children,* 1974, *6,* 1–11.

Cairns, R. The information properties of verbal and non-verbal events. *Journal of Personality and Social Psychology,* 1967, *5,* 353.

Cairns, R. Meaning and attention as determinants of social reinforcer effectiveness. *Child Development,* 1970, *41,* 1067.

Conant, E. H., & Kilbridge, M. D. An interdisciplinary analysis of job enlargement: Technology, costs, and behavioral implications. *Industrial and Labor Relations Review,* 1965, *18,* 377–385.

Davis, L. E. Job design and productivity: A new approach. *Personnel,* 1957, *33,* 418–430.

Davis, L. E., & Werling, R. Job design factors. *Occupational Psychology,* 1960, *34,* 109–132.

Farber, B. *Mental retardation: Its social context and social consequences.* Boston: Houghton Mifflin, 1968.

Ford, R. N. *Motivation through the work itself.* New York: American Management Association, 1969.

Gilhool, T. K. Education: "An inalienable right." *Exceptional Children,* 1973, *39,* 547–604.

Gold, M. W. The acquisition of a complex assembly task by retarded adolescents. Final Report, Project No. 8-8060, University of Illinois, Urbana-Champaign, May 1969.

Gold, M. W. Stimulus factors in skill training of retarded adolescents on a complex assembly task: Acquisition, transfer, and retention. *American Journal of Mental Deficiency,* 1972, *76,* 517–526.

Gold, M. W. Factors affecting production by the retarded: Base rate. *Mental Retardation,* 1973, *11*(6), 41–45. (a)

Gold, M. W. Research on the vocational habilitation of the retarded: The present, the future. In N. R. Ellis (Ed.), *International review of research in mental retardation* (Vol. 6). New York: Academic Press, 1973. (b)

Gold, M. W. Vocational training. In J. Wortis (Ed.), *Mental retardation and developmental disabilities: An annual review* (Vol. 7). New York: Brunner/Mazel, 1975.

Guest, R. H. Men and machines. *Personnel,* 1955, *18,* 496–503.

Guest, R. H. Job enlargement—A revolution in job design. *Personnel Administration,* 1957, *20*(2), 9–16.

Herzberg, F. *Work and the nature of man.* Cleveland: World, 1966.

Hill, K. T., Emmerich, H. R., Gelber, E. R., Lazar, M. A., & Schickedanz, D. Children's interpretation of adult non-reaction: A trial-by-trial self report assessment and evidence for contrast effects in an observational context. *Journal of Experimental Child Psychology,* 1974, *17,* 482–494.

Hulin, C. L., & Blood, M. R. Job enlargement, individual differences, and worker responses. *Psychological Bulletin,* 1968, *69*(1), 41–55.

Kilbridge, M. D. Do workers prefer larger jobs? *Personnel,* 1960, *37,* 45–48.

Kornhauser, A. W. *Mental health of the industrial worker: A Detroit study.* New York: Wiley, 1965.

Kunin, T. The construction of a new type of attitude measure. *Personnel Psychology,* 1955, *8,* 65–77.

Lawler, E. E. Job design and employee motivation. *Personnel Psychology,* 1969, *22,* 426–434.

MacKinney, A. C., Wernimont, P. F., & Galitz, W. O. Has specialization reduced job satisfaction? *Personnel,* 1962, *39,* 8–17.

Maslow, A. H. A theory of human motivation. *Psychological Review,* 1943, *50,* 370–396.

Merwin, M. R. The use of match-to-sample techniques to train retarded adolescents and adults to assemble electronic circuit boards. Unpublished master's thesis, University of Illinois, Urbana-Champaign, 1973.

Merwin, M. R. The effect of pretraining on the training and transfer of circuit board assembly skills of retarded adults. Unpublished doctoral dissertation, University of Illinois, Urbana-Champaign, 1974.

Paris, S. G., & Cairns, R. B. An experimental and ethological analysis of social reinforcement with retarded children. *Child Development,* 1972, *43,* 717–729.

Pelissier, R. F. Successful experience with job design. *Personnel Administration,* 1965, *28*(2), 12–16.

Scott, K. G. A multiple-choice audio-visual discrimination apparatus with quick interchange display and response panels. *Journal of Experimental Child Psychology,* 1970, *9,* 43–50.

Scott, R. D. Job enlargement—The key to increasing job satisfaction? *Personnel Journal,* 1973, *52,* 313–317.

Scott, W. E., Jr. Activation theory and task design. *Organizational Behavior and Human Performance,* 1966, *1,* 3–30.

Shepard, J. M. *Organizational issues in industrial society.* Englewood Cliffs, N. J.: Prentice-Hall, 1972.

Smith, P. C. The prediction of individual differences in susceptibility to industrial monotony. *Journal of Applied Psychology,* 1955, *39,* 322–329.

Smith, P. C., & Lem, C. Positive aspects of motivation in repetitive work: Effects of lot size upon spacing of voluntary rest periods. *Journal of Applied Psychology,* 1955, *39,* 330–333.

Spence, J. T. Verbal-discrimination performance as a function of instructions and verbal-reinforcement combination in normal and retarded children. *Child Development,* 1966, *37,* 269–281.

Stevenson, H. W. Social reinforcement of children's behavior. In L. P. Lipsitt & C. C. Spiker (Eds.), *Advances in child development and behavior* (Vol. 2). New York: Academic Press, 1965.

Susman, G. I. Job enlargement: Effects of culture on workers' responses. *Industrial Relations: A Journal of Economy & Society,* 1973, *12,* 1–15.

Taylor, F. W. A piece rate system. *Transactions of the American Society of Mechanical Engineers,* Paper No. 647, June 1895.

Taylor, F. W. Shop management. Transactions of the American Society of Mechanical Engineers, Paper No. 1003, June 1903.

Taylor, F. W. *The principles of scientific management.* New York: Harper, 1911.

Turner, A. N., & Lawrence, P. R. *Industrial jobs and the worker: An investigation of response to task attributes.* Boston: Harvard University, Graduate School of Business Administration, 1955.

Turner, A. N., & Miclette, A. L. Sources of satisfaction in repetitive work. *Occupational Psychology,* 1962, *36,* 215–231.

Walker, C. R. The problem of the repetitive job. *Harvard Business Review,* 1950, *28*(3), 54–59.

Walker, C. R., & Guest, R. H. *The man on the assembly line.* Cambridge, Mass.: Harvard University Press, 1952.

Walker, C. R., & Marriot, R. A study of some attitudes to factory work. *Occupational Psychology*, 1951, *25*, 181–191.

Zeaman, D., & House, B. J. The role of attention in retardate discrimination learning. In N. R. Ellis (Ed.), *Handbook of mental deficiency*. New York: McGraw-Hill, 1963.

Zigler, E. Personality structure in the retardate. In N. R. Ellis (Ed.), *International review of research in mental retardation* (Vol. 1). New York: Academic Press, 1966.

CHAPTER 19

Badad, E. V. Pygmalion in reverse. *Journal of Special Education*, 1977, *11*, 81–90.

Bailer, I. Conceptualization of success and failure in mentally retarded and normal children. *Journal of Personality*, 1961, *29*, 303–320.

Baller, W. R., Charles, D. C., & Miller, E. L. Mid-life attainment of the mentally retarded: A longitudinal study. *Genetic Psychology Monographs*, 1967, *75*, 235–329.

Beez, W. V. Influence of biased psychological reports on teacher behavior and pupil performance. Unpublished doctoral dissertation, Department of Educational Psychology, Indiana University, 1968.

Begab, M. J. The mentally retarded and society: Trends and issues. In M. J. Begab & S. A. Richardson (Eds.), *The mentally retarded and society: A social science perspective*. Baltimore: University Park Press, 1975.

Braginsky, D. D., & Braginsky, B. M. *Hansels and Gretels: Studies of children in institutions*. New York: Holt, Rinehart & Winston, 1971.

Budoff, M., & Gottlieb, J. Special class EMR children mainstreamed: A study of aptitude (learning potential) x treatment interaction. *American Journal of Mental Deficiency*, 1976, *81*, 1–11.

Cromwell, R. L. A social learning approach to mental retardation. In N. R. Ellis (Ed.), *Handbook of mental deficiency*. New York: McGraw-Hill, 1963.

Dentler, R. A., & Mackler, B. Ability and sociometric status among normal and retarded children: A review of the literature. *Psychological Bulletin*, 1962, *59*, 273–283.

Dweck, C. S. The role of expectations and attributions in the alleviation of learned helplessness. *Journal of Personality and Social Psychology*, 1975, *31*, 674–685.

Edgerton, R. B. *The cloak of competence: Stigma in the lives of the mentally retarded*. Berkeley: University of California Press, 1967.

Farber, B. *Mental retardation: Its social context and social consequences*. Boston: Houghton Mifflin, 1968.

Farina, A., Thaw, J., Felner, R. D., & Hust, B. E. Some interpersonal consequences of being mentally ill or mentally retarded. *American Journal of Mental Deficiency*, 1976, *80*, 414–422.

Festinger, L. A theory of social comparison processes. *Human Relations*, 1954, 7, 117–140.

Foster, G., & Ysseldyke, J. Expectancy and halo effects as a result of artificially induced teacher bias. *Contemporary Educational Psychology*, 1976, *1*, 37–45.

Gold, M. W. Stimulus factors in skill training of retarded adolescents on a complex assembly task: Acquisition, transfer, and retention. *American Journal of Mental Deficiency*, 1972, *76*, 517–526.

Gold, M. W. Vocational training. In J. Wortis (Ed.), *Mental retardation and developmental disabilities: An annual review* (Vol. 7). New York: Brunner/Mazel, 1975.

Gold, M. W., & Close, D. W. Five year retention of an assembly task by the severely retarded. Unpublished paper, University of Illinois, Urbana-Champaign, 1975.

Gold, M. W., & Pomerantz, D. J. Issues in prevocational training. In M. Snell (Ed.), *Teaching the moderately, severely, and profoundly retarded*. Columbus, Ohio: Merrill, 1978.

Gottlieb, J. Public, peer, and professional attitudes toward mentally retarded persons. In J. J. Begab & S. A. Richardson (Eds.), *The mentally retarded and society: A social sciences perspective*. Baltimore: University Park Press, 1975.

Gozali, J., & Meyen, E. L. The influence of the teacher expectancy phenomenon on the academic performances of educable mentally retarded pupils in special classes. *Journal of Special Education*, 1970, *4*, 417–424.

Guskin, S. L. Social psychologies of mental deficiencies. In N. R. Ellis (Ed.), *Handbook of mental deficiency*. New York: McGraw-Hill, 1963.

Guskin, S. L. & Spicker, H. H. Educational research in mental retardation. In N. R. Ellis (Ed.), *International review of research in mental retardation* (Vol 3). New York: Academic Press, 1968.

Hayes, C. S., & Prinz, R. J. Affective reactions of retarded and nonretarded children to success and failure. *American Journal of Mental Deficiency, 1976, 81,* 100–102.

Heider, F. *The psychology of interpersonal relations.* New York: Wiley, 1958.

Hoffman, J., & Weiner, B. Effects of attributions for success and failure on the performance of retarded adults. *American Journal of Mental Deficiency, 1978, 82,* 449–452.

Hollander, E. P. Conformity, status, and idiosyncracy credit. *Psychological Review, 1958, 65,* 117–127.

Hollander, E. P. Competence and conformity in the acceptance of influence. *Journal of Abnormal and Social Psychology, 1960, 61,* 365–369.

Horai, J., & Guarnaccia, V. J. Performance and attributions to ability, effort, task, and luck of retarded adults after success or failure feedback. *American Journal of Mental Deficiency, 1975, 79,* 690–694.

Jones, R. L. Research on the special education teacher and special education teaching. *Exceptional Children, 1966, 33,* 251–257.

Kelley, H. H. Attribution theory in social psychology. In D. Levine (Ed.), *Nebraska Symposium on Motivation* (Vol. 15). Lincoln: University of Nebraska Press, 1967.

Kelley, H. H. The processes of causal attribution. *American Psychologist, 1973, 23,* 107–128.

Keogh, B. K., Cahill, C. W., & MacMillan, D. L. Perception of interruption by educationally handicapped children. *American Journal of Mental Deficiency, 1972, 77,* 107–108.

Kurtz, P. D., Harrison, M., Neisworth, J. T., & Jones, R. T. Influence of "mentally retarded" label on teachers' nonverbal behavior toward preschool children. *American Journal of Mental Deficiency, 1977, 82,* 204–206.

Latimer, R. Current attitudes toward mental retardation. *Mental Retardation, 1970, 8,* 30–32.

Lee, D.V., Syrnyk, R., & Hallschmid, C. Self-perception of intrinsic and extrinsic motivation: Effects on institutionalized mentally retarded adolescents. *American Journal of Mental Deficiency, 1976, 81,* 331–337.

MacMillan, D. L. Motivational differences: Cultural-familial retardates versus normal subjects on expectancy for failure. *American Journal of Mental Deficiency, 1969, 74,* 254–258.

MacMillan, D. L. Effect of experimental success and failure on the situational expectancy of EMR and nonretarded children. *American Journal of Mental Deficiency, 1975, 80,* 90–95.

MacMillan, D. L., Jones, R. L., & Aloia, G. F. The mentally retarded label: A theoretical analysis and review of the research. *American Journal of Mental Deficiency, 1974, 79,* 241–261.

MacMillan, D. L., & Keogh, B. K. Normal and retarded children's expectancy for failure. *Developmental Psychology, 1971, 4,* 343–348.

McMahan, I. D. Relationships between causal attributions and expectancy of success. *Journal of Personality and Social Psychology, 1973, 28,* 108–114.

Mercer, J. R. *Labelling the mentally retarded.* Berkeley: University of California Press, 1973.

Panda, K. C., & Lynch, W. W. Effects of race and sex on attribution of intellectual achievement: Responsibility for success and failure situations among educable mentally retarded children. *Indian Journal of Mental Retardation, 1974, 7,* 72–80.

Revi, J., & Illyes, S. Success expectancy and achievement expectancy in trainable mentally retarded and in nonretarded children. *Studia Psychologica, 1976, 18,* 222–228.

Rosenbaum, R. M. A dimensional analysis of the perceived causes of success and failure. Unpublished doctoral dissertation, Department of Psychology, University of California, Los Angeles, 1972.

Rosenthal, R., & Jacobson, L. F. *Pygmalion in the classroom: Teacher expectations and pupils' intellectual development.* New York: Holt, Rinehart & Winston, 1968. (a)

Rosenthal, R., & Jacobson, L. F. Teacher expectations for the disadvantaged. *Scientific American*, 1968, *218*, 19–23. (b)

Schuster, S. O., & Gruen, G. E. Success and failure as determinants of the performance predictions of mentally retarded and nonretarded children. *American Journal of Mental Deficiency*, 1971, *76*, 190–196.

Schwartz, R. H., & Cook, J. J. Teacher expectancy as it relates to the academic achievement of EMR students. *Journal of Educational Research*, 1972, *65*, 393–396.

Severance, L. J., & Gasstrom, L. L. Effects of the label "mentally retarded" on causal explanation for success and failure outcomes. *American Journal of Mental Deficiency*, 1977, *81*, 547–555.

Shipe, D. The relationship among locus of control and some measures of persistence in mentally retarded and normal subjects. *Abstracts of Peabody Studies in Mental Retardation*, 1960, *1*, 58.

Solomon, S., & Saxe, L. What is intelligent, as well as attractive, is good. *Personality and Social Psychology Bulletin*, 1977, *3*, 670–673.

Soule, D. Teacher bias effects with severely retarded children. *American Journal of Mental Deficiency*, 1972, *77*, 208–211.

Sperry, L. Effects of expectation, social class, and experience on in-service teacher behavior in small groups. *Journal of Applied Psychology*, 1974, *59*, 244–246.

Strang, L., Smith, M. D., & Rogers, C. M. Social comparison, multiple reference groups, and the self-concepts of academically handicapped children before and after mainstreaming. *Journal of Educational Psychology*, 1978, *70*(1), 487–497.

Tymchuk, A. J. Personality and sociocultural retardation. *Exceptional Children*, 1972, *38*, 721–728.

Valle, V. A., & Frieze, I. H. The stability of causal attributions as a mediator in changing expectations for success. *Journal of Personality and Social Psychology*, 1976, *33*, 579–587.

Weiner, B. (Ed.). *Achievement motivation and attribution theory.* Morristown, N.J.: General Learning Press, 1974.

Weiner, B., Frieze, I., Kukla, A., Reed, L., Rest, S., & Rosenbaum, R. M. Perceiving the causes of success and failure. In E. E. Jones and others (Eds.), *Attribution: Perceiving the causes of behavior.* Morristown, N. J.: General Learning Press, 1972.

Wooster, A. D. Acceptance of responsibility for school work by educationally subnormal boys. *British Journal of Mental Subnormality*, 1974, *20*, 23–27.

CHAPTER 20

Gold, M. W. Stimulus factors in skill training of retarded adolescents on a complex assembly task: Acquisition, transfer, and retention. *American Journal of Mental Deficiency*, 1972, *76*, 517–526.

Gold, M. W. Factors affecting production by the retarded: Base rate. *Mental Retardation*, 1973, *11*(6), 41–45.

Gold, M. W. Redundant cue removal in skill training for the mildly and moderately retarded. *Education and Training of the Mentally Retarded*, 1974, *9*, 5–8.

Zeaman, D., & House, B. J. The role of attention in retardate discrimination learning. In N. R. Ellis (Ed.), *Handbook of mental deficiency.* New York: McGraw-Hill, 1963.

CHAPTER 21

Cronbach, L. J. The two disciplines of scientific psychology. *American Psychologist*, 1957, *12*, 671–684.

Dweck, C. S. The role of expectations and attributions in the alleviation of learned helplessness. *Journal of Personality and Social Psychology*, 1975, *31*, 674–685.

Fitts, P. M. Engineering psychology and equipment design. In S. S. Stevens (Ed.), *Handbook of experimental psychology.* New York: Wiley, 1951.

Gardner, W. I. *Behavior modification in mental retardation: The education and rehabilitation of the mentally retarded adult.* Chicago: Aldine-Atherton, 1971.

Gold, M. W. Stimulus factors in skill training of retarded adolescents on a complex assembly task: Acquisition, transfer, and retention. *American Journal of Mental Deficiency,* 1972, *76,* 517–526.

Gold, M. W. Factors affecting production by the retarded: Base rate. *Mental Retardation,* 1973, *11*(6), 41–45.

Gold, M. W. Redundant cue removal in skill training for the mildly and moderately retarded. *Education and Training of the Mentally Retarded,* 1974, *9,* 5–8.

Gold, M. W. *Symposium on applying attribution theory to social problems: Vocational skill functioning of the severely retarded.* Paper presented at the American Psychological Association, Chicago, September 1975. (a)

Gold, M. W. Vocational training. In J. Wortis (Ed.), *Mental retardation and developmental disabilities: An annual review* (Vol. 7). New York: Brunner/Mazel, 1975. (b)

Gold, M. W., & Barclay, C. R. The learning of difficult visual discriminations by the moderately and severely retarded. *Mental Retardation,* 1973, *11*(2), 9–11.

Gold, M. W., & Scott, K. G. Discrimination learning. In W. B. Stephens (Ed.), *Training the developmentally young.* New York: John Day, 1971.

Holding, D. H. Knowledge of results. In O. Legge (Ed.), *Skills.* Baltimore: Penguin Books, 1965.

Kazdin, A. E. Methodological and assessment considerations in evaluating reinforcement programs in applied settings. *Journal of Applied Behavioral Analysis,* 1973, *6,* 517–531.

Levy, S. M., Pomerantz, D. J., & Gold, M. W. Work skill development. In N. G. Haring and L. J. Brown (Eds.), *Teaching the severely handicapped* (Vol. 2). New York: Grune & Stratton, 1977.

Merwin, M. R. The use of match-to-sample technique to train retarded adolescents and adults to assemble electronic circuit boards. Unpublished master's thesis, University of Illinois, Urbana-Champaign, 1973.

Merwin, M. R. The effect of pretraining on the training and transfer of circuit board assembly skills of retarded adults. Unpublished doctoral dissertation, University of Illinois, Urbana-Champaign, 1974.

Nickerson, R. S. Short-term memory for complex meaningful visual configurations: A demonstration of capacity. *Canadian Journal of Psychology,* 1965, *19,* 155–160.

Steinman, W. M. The social role of generalized imitation. *Journal of Applied Behavioral Analysis,* 1970, *3,* 159–167.

Zeaman, D. Learning processes of the mentally retarded. In S. Osler & R. Cooke (Eds.), *The biosocial basis of mental retardation.* Baltimore: The Johns Hopkins Press, 1965.

CHAPTER 22

Dantona, R. *Status report on services for deaf-blind children.* Paper presented at the conference on Personnel Preparation, Boston, July 1976.

Farber, B., & Lewis, M. Compensatory education and social justice. *Peabody Journal of Education,* 1972, *49,* 85–96.

Gold, M. W. Task analysis of a complex assembly task by the retarded blind. *Exceptional Children,* 1976, *43,* 78–84.

CHAPTER 23

Bailey, R. C. Due process overdue for the mentally retarded. *The Barrister,* 1972, *30,* 44–45.

Birch, J. W. *Mainstreaming: Educable mentally retarded children in regular classes.* Reston, Va.: Council for Exceptional Children, 1974.

Brolin, D. E. *Vocational preparation of retarded citizens.* Columbus, Ohio: Charles E. Merrill, 1976.

Chall, J. S. *Learning to read: The great debate.* San Francisco: McGraw-Hill, 1967.

Clark, G. M. Career education for the mildly handicapped. *Focus on Exceptional Children,* 1974, *5*(9), 1–10.

Eskridge, C. S., & Partridge, D. L. Vocational rehabilitation for exceptional children through special education. *Exceptional Children*, 1963, *29*, 452–458.

Featherstone, J. *Schools where children learn.* New York: Liveright, 1971.

Gold, M. W. Research on the vocational habilitation of the retarded: The present, the future. In N. R. Ellis (Ed.), *International review of research in mental retardation* (Vol. 6). New York: Academic Press, 1973.

Gold, M. W. Vocational training. In J. Wortis (Ed.), *Mental retardation and developmental disabilities: An annual review* (Vol. 7). New York: Brunner/Mazel, 1975.

Gold, M. W. Task analysis of a complex assembly task by the retarded blind. *Exceptional Children*, 1976, *43*, 78–84.

Ingram, C. P. *Education of the slow learning child.* New York: Ronald Press, 1953.

Kirk, S. A. Research in education. In H. A. Stevens & R. Heber (Eds.), *Mental retardation: A review of research.* Chicago: University of Chicago Press, 1964.

Kokaska, C. The declassified retarded: Implications of the 1973 definition. *Training School Bulletin*, 1974, *71*(1), 5–8.

Nixon, R. A. Impact of automation and technological change on employability of the mentally retarded. *American Journal of Mental Deficiency*, 1970, *75*, 152–155.

Parker, S. *The future of work and leisure.* London: MacGibbon & Kee, 1971.

Pennsylvania Association for Retarded Children v. Commonwealth of Pennsylvania (PARC), 334 F. Supp. 1257 (E.D. pa. 1971).

Rosen, D., & Soloyanis, G. *American Association on Mental Deficiency Special Convention Publication, Social and Legislative Issues.* 98th Annual Meeting of the American Association on Mental Deficiency, Toronto, Canada, June 1974.

Younie, W. J., & Clark, G. M. Personnel training needs for cooperative secondary school programs for mentally retarded youth. *Education and Training of the Mentally Retarded*, 1969, *4*, 186–194.

CHAPTER 24

Annett, J. The information capacity of young mental defectives in an assembly task. In J. Jancar (Ed.), *Stoke Park Studies–Mental Subnormality.* Bristol, England: J. Wright & Son, 1961.

Bartlett, F. C. The future of ergonomics. *Ergonomics,* 1962, *4,* 505–612.

Campione, J. C. The generality of transfer: Effects of age and similarity of training and transfer tasks. *Journal of Experimental Child Psychology*, 1973, *15*, 407–418.

Campione, J. C., & Brown, A. L. Memory and metamemory development in educable retarded children. In R. V. Kail & J. W. Hagan (Eds.), *Perspectives on the development of memory and cognition.* Hillsdale, N. J.: Lawrence Erlbaum, 1976.

Clarke, A. D. B., & Hermelin, B. F. Adult imbeciles: Their abilities and trainability. *Lancet*, 1955, *2*, 337–339.

Crossman, E. R. F. W. Information processes in human skill. *British Medical Bulletin*, 1960, *20*(1), 32–37.

Farber, B. *Mental retardation: Its social context and social consequences.* Boston: Houghton Mifflin, 1968.

Fitts, P. M. (Ed.). *Human engineering for an effective air navigation and traffic control system.* Washington, D. C.: National Research Council, 1951.

Fitts, P. M. The information capacity of the human motor system in controlling the amplitude of movement. *Journal of Experimental Psychology*, 1954, *47*, 381–391.

Galloway, C. H. *Fourth quarterly report of the California project.* Urbana, Ill.: Marc Gold & Associates, Inc., 1977.

Gold, M. W. Stimulus factors in skill training of retarded adolescents on a complex assembly task: Acquisition, transfer, and retention. *American Journal of Mental Deficiency*, 1972, *76*, 517–526.

Gold, M. W. Research on the vocational habilitation of the retarded: The present, the future. In N. R. Ellis (Ed.), *International review of research in mental retardation* (Vol. 6). New York: Academic Press, 1973.

Gold, M. W. Vocational training. In J. Wortis (Ed.), *Mental retardation and developmental disabilities: An annual review* (Vol. 7). New York: Brunner/Mazel, 1975.

Gold, M. W. Task analysis of a complex assembly task by the retarded blind. *Exceptional Children*, 1976, *43,* 78–84.

Gold, M. W., & Barclay, C. R. The learning of difficult visual discriminations by the moderately and severely retarded. *Mental Retardation,* 1973, *11*(2), 9–11.

Hulin, C. L., & Blood, M. R. Job enlargement, individual differences, and worker responses. *Psychological Bulletin,* 1968, *69*(1), 41–55.

Jordan, N. Allocation of functions between man and machine in automated systems. *Journal of Applied Psychology,* 1963, *47,* 161–165.

Lawler, E. E. Job design and employee motivation. *Personnel Psychology,* 1969, *22,* 426–434.

Levy, S. M. The measurement of retarded and normal workers' job performances through the use of naturalistic observation in sheltered and industrial work environments. Unpublished doctoral dissertation. University of Illinois, Urbana-Champaign, 1977.

Loos, F. M., & Tizard, J. The employment of adult imbeciles in a hospital workshop. *American Journal of Mental Deficiency,* 1955, *59,* 395–403.

Maynard, H. B., Stegemerten, G. J., & Schwab, J. L. *Methods-time measurement.* New York: McGraw-Hill, 1948.

Meister, D., & Rabideau, G. F. *Human factors evaluation in system development.* New York: Wiley, 1965.

Merwin, M. R. The use of match-to-sample technique to train retarded adolescents and adults to assemble electronic circuit boards. Unpublished master's thesis, University of Illinois, Urbana-Champaign, 1973.

Merwin, M. R. The effect of pretraining on the training and transfer of circuit board assembly skills of retarded adults. Unpublished doctoral dissertation, University of Illinois, Urbana-Champaign, 1974.

Olsen, D. R. Information processing limitations of mentally retarded children. *American Journal of Mental Deficiency,* 1971, *75,* 478–486.

Scott, R. D. Job enlargement—The key to increasing job satisfaction? *Personnel Journal,* 1973, *52,* 313–317.

Smith, J., & Kaufman, H. Identification capacities of retarded and normal children. *Psychonomic Science,* 1972, *28,* 321–325.

Swain, A. D., & Wohl, J. G. *Factors affecting degree of automation in test and checkout equipment.* Stanford, Conn.: Dunlap, 1961.

Tizard, J., & Loos, F. M. The learning of a spacial relations test by adult imbeciles. *American Journal of Mental Deficiency,* 1954, *59,* 95–100.

Welford, A. T. What can be trained? Paper presented at the 18th International Congress of Applied Psychology, Montreal, Canada, August 1975.

Whitfield, D. Human skill as a determinant of allocation of function. *Ergonomics,* 1967, *10,* 154–160.

CHAPTER 26

Emshoff, J. G., Redd, W. H., & Davidson, W. S. Generalization training and the transfer of treatment effects with delinquent adolescents. *Journal of Behavior Therapy and Experimental Psychiatry,* 1976, *7,* 141–144.

Federal Register, April 16, 1976, *41*(75), 16147–16155.

Gold, M. W. Research on the vocational habilitation of the retarded: The present, the future. In N. R. Ellis (Ed.), *International review of research in mental retardation* (Vol. 6). New York: Academic Press, 1973.

Gold, M. W. Vocational training. In J. Wortis (Ed.), *Mental retardation and developmental disabilities: An annual review* (Vol. 7). New York: Brunner/Mazel, 1975.

Gold, M. W. Task analysis of a complex assembly task by the retarded blind. *Exceptional Children,* 1976, *43,* 78–84.

Kelly, J. M., & Simon, A. J. The mentally handicapped as workers—a survey of company experience. *Personnel,* 1969, *46*(5), 58–64.

Levy, S. M., Pomerantz, D. J., & Gold, M. W. Work skill development. In N. G. Haring & L. J. Brown (Eds.), *Teaching the severely handicapped* (Vol. 2). New York: Grune & Stratton, 1977.

Parker, S. *The future of work and leisure.* London: MacGibbon & Kee, 1971.

Phelps, L. A. *Instructional development for special needs.* Urbana, Ill.: University of Illinois, Department of Vocational and Technical Education, 1977.

Pomerantz, D. J., & Marholin, D. Vocational habilitation: A time for change in existing service delivery systems. In E. Sontag, N. Certo, & J. Smith (Eds.), *Educational programming for the severely handicapped.* Reston, Va.: Council for Exceptional Children, Division of Mental Retardation, 1977.

Redd, W. H. Attention span and generalization of task-related stimulus control: Effects of reinforcement contingencies. *Journal of Experimental Child Psychology,* 1972, *13*(3), 527–539.

Rincover, A., & Koegel, R. L. Setting generality and stimulus control in autistic children. *Journal of Applied Behavior Analysis,* 1975, *8,* 235–246.

Ryan, W. *Blaming the victim.* New York: Viking Press, 1971.

Stroud, R. R. *Work measurement in rehabilitation workshops: Time study and predetermined motion time systems* (Monograph No. 2). College Park: Regional Rehabilitation Research Institute, University of Maryland, 1970.

Terkel, S. *Working: People talk about what they do all day and how they feel about what they do.* New York: Pantheon, 1974.

Wahler, R. G. Setting generality: Some specific and general effects of child behavior therapy. *Journal of Applied Behavior Analysis,* 1969, *2,* 239–246.

Wolfensberger, W. Vocational preparation and occupation. In A. A. Baumeister (Ed.), *Mental retardation: Appraisal, education and rehabilitation.* Chicago: Aldine, 1967.

Notes

1. Greenleigh Associates. *The role of the sheltered workshop in the rehabilitation of the severely handicapped.* Report to the U. S. Department of Health, Education, and Welfare, Rehabilitation Services Administration, 1975.

2. Gold, M. W. *Meeting the needs of the handicapped.* Paper presented to the National Bicentennial Conference on Vocational Education, Minneapolis, Minn., October 11, 1976.

3. Chaffin, J. D., & Clark, G. M. *Proceedings of organizing for cooperation: A multi-agency conference.* Sponsored by Rehabilitation Services Administration, Kansas City, Mo., July, 1973.

4. Pomerantz, D. J., & Redd, W. H. *Programming generalization through stimulus fading in one-to-one instruction with retarded children.* Unpublished manuscript, University of Illinois, Urbana-Champaign, 1977.

5. Reiss, S., & Redd., W. H. Suppression of screaming behavior in an emotionally disturbed, retarded child. *Proceedings of the American Psychological Association,* 1971, 741–742.

CHAPTER 27

Bellamy, T., Peterson, L., & Close, D. Habilitation of the severely and profoundly retarded: Illustration of competence. *Education and Training of the Mentally Retarded,* 1975, *10,* 174–186.

Belmont, J. M. Long-term memory in mental retardates. In N. R. Ellis (Ed.), *International review of research in mental retardation* (Vol. 1). New York: Academic Press, 1966.

Bologna, J., Kellering, W., Mullen, R. C., & Stickler, D. J. The measurement and comparison of variables related to driver and highway safety between educable mentally retarded and normal high school age students in Pennsylvania. Department of Special Education, Millersville State College, Pennsylvania, February, 1971.

Brown, L., Scheuerman, N., Cartwright, S., & York, R. *The design and implementation of an empirically based instructional program for severely handicapped students: Toward the rejection of the exclusion principle.* Part III. Madison, Wis.: Madison Public Schools, 1973.

Budig, R. L., & Carter H. *Teaching the exceptional student to drive: An analytical approach for the teacher.* Normal, Ill.: Illinois State University, 1975.

Campione, J. C., & Beaton, V. L. Transfer of training: Some boundary conditions and initial theory. *Journal of Experimental Child Psychology,* 1972, *13,* 94–114.

Cronbach, L. J. The two disciplines of scientific psychology. *American Psychologist,* 1957, *12,* 671–684.

Fitts, P. M. Engineering psychology and equipment design. In S. S. Stevens (Ed.), *Handbook for experimental psychology.* New York: Wiley, 1951.

Gold, M. W. Stimulus factors in skill training of retarded adolescents on a complex assembly task: Acquisition, transfer, and retention. *American Journal of Mental Deficiency,* 1972, *76,* 517–526.

Gold, M. W. Vocational training. In J. Wortis (Ed.), *Mental retardation and developmental disabilities: An annual review* (Vol. 7). New York: Brunner/Mazel, 1975.

Gold, M. W. Task analysis of a complex assembly task by the retarded blind. *Exceptional Children,* 1976, *43,* 78–84.

Grossman, H. J. (Ed.). *Manual on terminology and classification in mental retardation.* Baltimore: Garamond/Pridemark Press, 1973.

Gutshall, R. W., Harper, C., & Burke, D. An exploratory study of the inter-relationship among driving ability, driving exposure, and socioeconomic status of low, average and high intelligence males. *Exceptional Children,* 1968, *35,* 43–50.

Nickerson, R. S. Short-term memory for complex meaningful visual configurations: A demonstration of capacity. *Canadian Journal of Psychology,* 1965, *19,* 155–160.

Pomerantz, D. J. Generalization training. Unpublished master's thesis, University of Illinois, Urbana-Champaign, 1976.

Pomerantz, D. J. A situational analysis of the transfer of children's academic gain from one-to-one to unsupervised instructional settings. Unpublished doctoral dissertation, University of Illinois, Urbana-Champaign, 1978.

Zider, S. J. Driver's training of individuals with moderate and severe mental retardation. Unpublished master's thesis, University of Illinois, Urbana-Champaign, 1977.

Index

A

Ability, manifest and potential, 223
Accountability, in vocational education, 88, 267
Accuracy, need for, in assembly tasks, 10–11
Acquisition, definition of, 127
Activation theory, 186–187
Adaptive behavior, 105–110, 149
Adaptive Behavior Scales, 105
Advocacy, role of, in vocational education, 267
Allocation of function, in system design, 273
American Association for the Education of the Severely/Profoundly Handicapped, 175
American Association on Mental Deficiency, 15, 105, 208
  definition of, on mental retardation, 146, 147, 149
"An End to the Concept of Mental Retardation: Oh, What a Beautiful Mourning," 144
Anxiety Differential Test, 188
Artificial informing, 141
Assembly tasks
  effects of verbal labels on, 117–123
  retention of skills in, 54–55, 56, 60 120–121, 122–123, 225–230
  use of attention theory in teaching, 38–42, 84
  use of sequential technique in teaching, 5–13
  use of stimulus factors in skill training of retarded on, 45–60
Association for the Help of Retarded Children, 69
Association for the Severely Handicapped, 175
Attention
  and clustering, 34
  and criterion performance, 34–35
  definition of, 28
  dimensions of, 31–32
  and discrimination, 28–29
  and fading, 34, 44
  and failure sets, 35–36
  and generalization, 28–29
  general principles of, 28–32
  and irrelevant cues, 33–34
  and novelty, 36
  and overlearning, 35
  and redundancy, 32–33
  and sequencing, 35
  shifts in, 31–32
Attention-retention theory, 169
Attention span, need for, in teaching self-direction skills, 11
Attention theory, 27, 28, 29–30, 38–42, 45, 46, 84–85, 112, 137, 141, 189
Attribution-expectancy cycle, 210–211, 218–219, 220, 222.
  See also Expectancy cycle
Attribution theory, 207, 223
Audio-visual machines, use of, in teaching the handicapped, 94
Autism, 195, 196–197, 205–206
Autoinstructional techniques, use of, in vocational habilitation, 81–82, 91
Automation, effect of, on vocational training, 68, 102

B

Backward chaining, 233, 235
Balanced relationship, importance of, between trainer and learner, 3, 283
Base-rate production level, 80, 125–136, 218
Behavior
  causality of, 211
  definition of entering, 6
  definition of terminal, 6
  facilitation of new, 81–85, 91

About the
Author

Marc Gold first began working with students labeled retarded as a teacher in the Los Angeles City School system. His interest led him to pursue a doctorate in experimental child psychology and special education, which he received from the University of Illinois in 1969. He then joined the faculty of the University of Illinois as a research professor working at the Institute for Child Behavior and Development. While at the Institute, Dr. Gold conducted research focusing on the application of information from stimulus control research to the development of a vocational training technology for persons labeled moderately and severely retarded.

As an outgrowth of this research, Dr. Gold developed the "Try Another Way" system of philosophy and technology for those who find it difficult to learn. He created and now heads an organization, Marc Gold & Associates, Inc., which disseminates information about the system and trains people in its use. The system is usable with many different populations, for example, persons labeled retarded, autistic, deaf/blind, and multihandicapped, and many kinds of tasks, for example, self-help, mobility, vocational, and social tasks.

Throughout his career, Dr. Gold has participated in several organizations. He served as President of the Workshop Division of the Illinois Rehabilitation Association in 1972, as a member of the Executive Board of the American Association for the Education of the Severely/Profoundly Handicapped in 1975–1977, and as Vice-President of the Vocational Rehabilitation Division of the American Association on Mental Deficiency in 1976–1978. He also has been a consulting editor or a member of the editorial board for the *American Journal of Mental Deficiency, Mental Retardation,* and *Education and Treatment of Children.*